Not For Tourists™ Guide to **SAN FRANCISCO**

Not For Tourists Inc New York

2004

Published and designed by:

Not For Tourists, Inc
NFT™—Not For Tourists™ Guide to SAN FRANCISCO 2004

www.notfortourists.com

Concept by
Jane Pirone

Information Design
Jane Pirone
Rob Tallia
Scot Covey
Diana Pizzari

Editor
Jane Pirone

Managing Editors
Rob Tallia
Diana Pizzari

City Editors
Jim Bahan
Jim Nawrocki

Writing and Editing
Jane Pirone
Diana Pizzari
Rob Tallia
Jim Bahan
Jim Nawrocki
Lisa Levine
Annie Holt
Sherry Wasserman
Sharyn Jackson

Database Design
Scot Covey

**Graphic Design /
  Production**
Scot Covey
Matt Knutzen
Nick Trotter
James Martinez
Ana Albu
Rob Tallia
Sherry Wasserman
Sharyn Jackson
Hyoun-Jong Kim

Research / Data Entry
Diana Pizzari
Lisa Levine
Annie Holt
Sherry Wasserman
Anne-Cecile Bourget
Sharyn Jackson
Alli Hirschman

Proofing
Jack Schieffer

Contributors
Kim Bowen
Scott Corbin
Tracy Corbin
Victoria Smith
Adam Holt

Scale for maps ;
34, 35, 39, 40

Scale for maps 10, 12, 13,
15-18, 20-24, 28-33, 37, 38

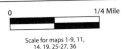

Scale for maps 1-9, 11,
14, 19, 25-27, 36

Printed in China
ISBN# 0-9740131-3-7 $14.95

Dear NFT User:

We are happy to present our Not For Tourists guide to San Francisco. We hope this guide helps you deal with a new neighborhood and discover its unique style and personality, or better yet, find something new in an old favorite. We've provided easy-to-use maps to help you find what you need, when you need it. In each map we've plotted the information that we hope will make your life easier and get you through your day (with as few headaches as possible).

We've also chosen a smattering of our favorite places, from cheap to expensive, nice to grungy, mellow to happening (bottom line – if it's in the book, it's worth your time). We've left out most of the big chains because, as a local, you already know where those are—and, typically, they're the least interesting! The back of the book has more specific information on the larger cultural, sporting, and recreational places in the area. NFT is reprinted yearly, so if we've left something out or made a mistake, we want to hear about it—email us at www.notfortourists.com.

Did we say we're excited to have a San Francisco book? We are. Do we love San Francisco? We do. Is it one of the few other cities in the country where we could justify moving NFT's world headquarters to someday? It is. Food, fog, and Ferlighetti—ah, the city by the bay. We're jealous.

Here's hoping you find what you need,

Jim & **Jim, Jane** & **Rob**

Central

Map 1 • Marina / Cow Hollow (West) 6
Map 2 • Marina / Cow Hollow (East) 10
Map 3 • Russian Hill / Fisherman's Wharf 14
Map 4 • North Beach (East) / Telegraph Hill .18
Map 5 • Pacific Heights / Western Addition . .22
Map 6 • Pacific Heights / Japantown 26
Map 7 • Nob Hill / Chinatown / SOMA 30
Map 8 • Union Square / Embarcadero /
    South Beach 34
Map 9 • Haight Ashbury / Cole Valley 38
Map 10 • Castro / Lower Haight 42
Map 11 • Hayes Valley / The Mission 46
Map 12 • SOMA / Potrero Hill (North) 50
Map 13 • SOMA East 54
Map 14 • Noe Valley 58
Map 15 • Mission (Outer) 62

Map 16 • Potrero Hill (Southwest) 66
Map 17 • Potrero Hill (Southeast) 70

Richmond

Map 18 • Outer Richmond (West) /
    Ocean Beach 74
Map 19 • Outer Richmond (East) / Seacliff . .78
Map 20 • Richmond 82
Map 21 • Inner Richmond 86
Map 22 • Presidio Heights/Laurel Heights . .90

Sunset

Map 23 • Outer Sunset .94
Map 24 • Sunset 98
Map 25 • Inner Sunset/Golden Gate Heights . .102
Map 26 • Parkside (Outer) 106
Map 27 • Parkside (Inner) 110
Map 28 • SFSU / Park Merced 114

Table of Contents

Upper Market and Beyond

Map 29 • Twin Peaks 118
Map 30 • West Portal 122
Map 31 • Mt. Davidson 126
Map 32 • Diamond Heights / Glen Park 130
Map 33 • Ingleside 134
Map 34 • Oceanview 138

Bernal Heights, Bay View and Beyond

Map 35 • Bernal Heights 142
Map 36 • Bay View / Silver Terrace 146
Map 37 • Indian Basin / Hunter's Point 150
Map 38 • Excelsior / Crocker Amazon 154
Map 39 • Visitacion Valley 158
Map 40 • Bay View / Candlestick Point 162

Parks & Places

Golden Gate Park 166
The Presidio 168
Muir Woods 170
Lincoln Park 171
Ghirardelli Square 172
Exploratorium 173
Mt Tamalpais 174
Moscone Center 175
Cow Palace 176
Yerba Buena Center 177
Fisherman's Wharf / Pier 39 178
San Francisco State University 180
University of California, San Francisco 182
University of California, Berkeley 184
Berkeley 186
Sausalito 188
Ferry Building & Plaza 190

Beaches and Marinas

Stinson Beach 191
Crissy Field 192
Ocean Beach 194
Baker Beach 195
Black Sands Beach 196
China Beach / Mile Rock Beach 197
San Francisco Marina & Marina Green 198
Pier 39 Marina 199

Sports

Candlestick Park (3Com Park) 200
Pacific Bell Park 201
Network Associates Coliseum 202
The Arena in Oakland 204
HP Pavilion at San Jose 205

Golf 206
Swimming & Bowling 207
Tennis 208
Hiking 209
Biking & Skating 210

Transit

San Francisco International Airport 211
Oakland International Airport 214
San Jose International Airport 216
Airlines 218
Airport Shuttles 218
San Francisco Ferries 219
Bay Area Bridges 220
Driving in San Francisco 222
Parking in San Francisco 223
San Francisco Buses 224
Bay Area Rapid Transit (BART) 226
Muni Metro 228
Caltrain 230

General Information

Calendar of Events 231
Practical Information 232
Zip Codes 234
Post Offices 235
Police 235
FedEx Locations 236
Hospitals 238
Libraries 238
Landmarks 239
Gay & Lesbian 244
Hotels 246
24-Hour Services 252
Dog Runs 254

Arts & Entertainment

SFMOMA 255
Art Galleries 256
Museums 257
Bookstores 258
Bars 262
Clubs & Cabarets 266
Movie Theaters 267
Restaurants 268
Shopping 275
Theaters 280

Street Index 281

Driving Map & Bay Area Map
foldout, last page

Map 1 · **Marina / Cow Hollow (West)**

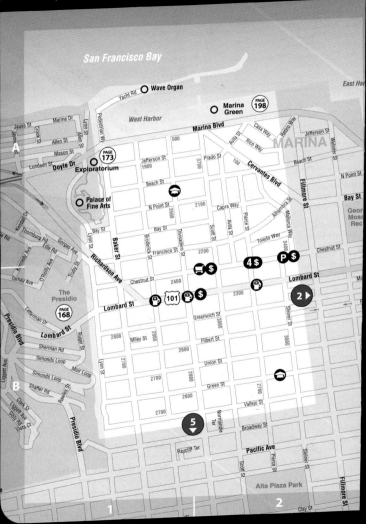

San Francisco Bay

Wave Organ

Marina Green

PAGE 198

Yacht Rd

West Harbor

Marina Blvd

East Har

MARINA

Jauss St · Crook St

Marine Dr

Lyon St

Pierce St

Casa Way

Retiro Way

Jefferson St

Webster St

Allen St · Allen St

Mason St

Avila St

Rico Way

Beach St

N Point St

Lundeen St

Doyle Dr

PAGE 173
Exploratorium

Jefferson St
1900

500

3700

Prado St

100

Cervantes Blvd

Filmore St

Bay St

Geor
Moso
Rec

Beach St

N Point St

2100

Capra Way

Palace of
Fine Arts

3500

Alhambra Way

Mallorca Way

Chestnut St

Kendall Dr

Thornburg Rd

Gorgas Ave

Edie Rd

Bay St

Bay St

Avila St

Pierce St

Toledo Way

3400

Kreiling Cir

O'Reilly Ave

Clay St

Lyon St

Richardson Ave

Baker St

Broderick St

Divisadero St

Francisco St

2200

Scott St

Lombard St

Torney Ave

Chestnut St

2400

🖥️💲

4💲

P💲

Leffersontown Dr

The
Presidio

PAGE 168

Lombard St

101

💲

2300

💊

2▶

Steiner St

Presidio Blvd

Lombard St

Greenwich St
3000

Sherman Rd

2800

Miley St

2900

Filbert St

Simonds Loop

2600

Union St

3000

Simonds Loop

Muir Loop

2700

2800

Green St

2700

Shafter Rd

Lyon St

Normandie Ter

Vallejo St

2700

Clark St

Lippert Ave

Liggett Ave

5
▼

Broadway St

Raycliff Ter

Pacific Ave

Scott St

Pierce St

Steiner St

Filmore St

Alta Plaza Park

Clay St

1

2

Young and healthy professionals gravitate here; they use the nearby Presidio and Chrissy Field as their playgrounds. If you're looking for ethnic variety, you won't find it here. Chestnut Street is the commercial center of the 'hood.

$ Banks

- **Bank of America** · 2200 Chestnut St
- **Bank of America** · 2460 Lombard St
- **Bank of America** · 3601 Lyon St
- **California Federal Bank** · 2198 Chestnut St
- **Citibank** · 2197 Chestnut St
- **Washington Mutual** · 2166 Chestnut St
- **Wells Fargo** · 2055 Chestnut St
- **World Savings & Loan Assn** · 2298 Chestnut St

Gas Stations

- **76** · 2498 Lombard St
- **Chevron** · 2301 Lombard St
- **Valero** · 2601 Lombard St

O Landmarks

- **Exploratorium** · 3601 Lyon St
- **Marina Green** · Marina Blvd (between Scott and Webster)
- **Palace of Fine Arts** · Marina Blvd & Lyon St
- **Wave Organ** · At the end of the jetty on Yacht Rd (St Francis Yacht Club)

P Parking

Schools

- **Claire B Lilienthal Alt Elementary School** · 3630 Divisadero St
- **St Vincent De Paul School** · 2350 Green St

Supermarkets

- **Marina Super** · 2323 Chestnut St

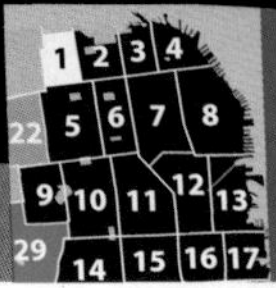

Sundries / Entertainment

Map 1

1 2 3 4
22 5 6 7 8
9 10 11 12 13
29 14 15 16 17

With the exception of a few well-known chain stores and necessities, this part of the Marina is better known for its food than its shopping. Steiner Street has most of the noteworthy restaurants, packed into the block between Lombard and Chestnut.

Coffee

- **Coffee Roastery** · 2331 Chestnut St
- **Peet's** · 2156 Chestnut St
- **Starbucks** · 2132 Chestnut St
- **The Grove** · 2250 Chestnut St

Copy Shops

- **Pip Printing** · 2459 Lombard St

Gyms

- **Body Kinetics** · 2399 Greenwich St
- **Gorilla Sports** · 2324 Chestnut St

Liquor Stores

- **California Wine Merchant** · 3237 Pierce St
- **Marina Delicatessen & Liquors** · 2299 Chestnut St
- **United Liquor & Deli** · 2401 Chestnut St

Movie Theaters

- **Century Presidio** · 2340 Chestnut St

Pet Shops

- **Animal Connection II** · 2419 Chestnut St
- **Catnip & Bones** · 2220 Chestnut St

Restaurants

- **Ace Wasabi's** · 3339 Steiner St
- **Andale Taqueria** · 2150 Chestnut St
- **Baker Street Bistro** · 2953 Baker St
- **Bistro Aix** · 3340 Steiner St
- **Café Marimba** · 2317 Chestnut St
- **Cozmo's Corner Grill** · 2100 Chestnut St
- **Dragon Well** · 2142 Chestnut St
- **Isa** · 3324 Steiner St
- **Izzy's Steak and Chops** · 3345 Steiner St
- **Liverpool Lil's** · 2942 Lyon St
- **Marinette** · 3352 Steiner St
- **Meze's** · 2372 Chestnut St
- **Parma** · 3314 Steiner St
- **Rose's Café** · 2298 Union St
- **The Grove** · 2250 Chestnut St
- **Zao Noodle Bar** · 2406 California St

Shopping

- **Benefit** · 2219 Chestnut St
- **Body Options** · 2108 Chestnut St
- **Books Inc** · 2251 Chestnut St
- **Chadwick's of London** · 2068 Chestnut St
- **City Optix** · 2154 Chestnut St
- **Fiori** · 2314 Chestnut St
- **Fleet Feet** · 2076 Chestnut St
- **House of Magic** · 2025 Chestnut St
- **Lucca Delicatessen** · 2120 Chestnut St
- **Lucky Brand** · 2301 Chestnut St
- **Pure Beauty** · 2085 Chestnut St
- **Smash** · 2030 Chestnut St

Video Rental

- **Blockbuster Video** · 2460 Lombard St

Map 2 • **Marina / Cow Hollow (East)**

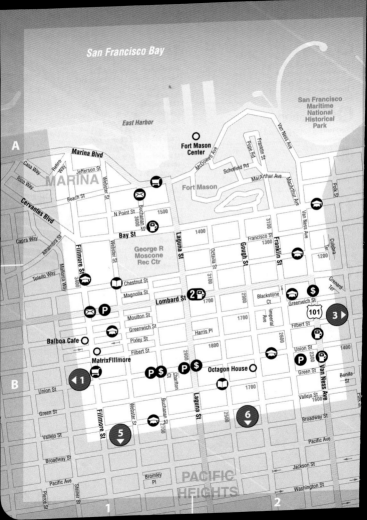

San Francisco Bay

San Francisco Maritime National Historical Park

East Harbor

Fort Mason Center

Fort Mason

A

Marina Blvd

MARINA

Casa Way

Retro Way

Rico Way

Jefferson St

Beach St

Webster St

N Point St

Buchanan St

1500

3600

Cervantes Blvd

Capra Way

Alhambra St

Mallorca Way

Bay St

1400

George R Moscone Rec Ctr

Laguna St

McDowell Ave

Pope Rd

Franklin St

Schofield Rd

MacArthur Ave

MacArthur Ave

Van Ness Ave

Polk St

3100

Francisco St

1300

Gough St

Octavia St

3100

Franklin St

Van Ness Ave

Culebra Ter

1200

Toledo Way

Fillmore St

3400

Chestnut St

Magnolia St

Lombard St

2

1700

2900

Blackstone Ct

Greenwich St

$

Grenard Ter

101

3

Moulton St

Greenwich St

Pixley St

Filbert St

1700

Harris Pl

1800

Imperial Ave

Filbert St

2600

Union St

1400

Balboa Cafe

MatrixFillmore

2600

Charlton Ct

Octagon House

2300

Green St

P

Bonita St

B

Union St

1

P **$**

P **$**

1700

Vallejo St

1600

Green St

Webster St

Buchanan St

Laguna St

2500

6

Broadway St

Vallejo St

5

Broadway St

Pacific Ave

Bromley Pl

PACIFIC HEIGHTS

Jackson St

Washington St

Pierce St

Steiner St

1

2

The Marina Green is a great place to take advantage of the waterfront and to check out the boats, windsurfers, and kites. Fort Mason is a unique cultural destination for small galleries, museums, and theaters.

$ Banks

- **Bank of America** · 1995 Union St
- **Washington Mutual** · 2750 Van Ness Ave
- **Wells Fargo** · 1900 Union St

Gas Stations

- **Chevron** · 1598 Bay St
- **Chevron** · 1790 Lombard St
- **Chevron** · 2465 Van Ness Ave
- **Gawfco Enterprises** · 2559 Van Ness Ave
- **Shell** · 1800 Lombard St

O Landmarks

- **Balboa Café** · 3199 Fillmore St
- **Fort Mason Center** · Buchanan & Marina Blvd
- **MatrixFillmore** · 3138 Fillmore St
- **Octagon House** · 2645 Gough St

Libraries

- **Golden Gate Valley Library** · 1801 Green St
- **Marina Branch Library** · 1890 Chestnut St

P Parking

Post Offices

- 3749 Buchanan St
- 2055 Lombard St

Schools

- **Galileo High School** · 1055 Bay St
- **Hamlin School** · 2129 Vallejo St
- **Hergl School** · 1570 Greenwich St
- **Marina Middle School** · 3500 Fillmore St
- **San Francisco School-Massage** · 1327 Chestnut St
- **Sherman Elementary** · 1651 Union St
- **Tule Elk Park** · 2110 Greenwich St

Supermarkets

- **Real Food Company** · 3060 Fillmore St
- **Safeway** · 15 Marina Blvd

Map 2

Galleries / Entertainment

Union Street is the chic main drag in Cow Hollow, with great boutique shopping and restaurants—a great place to while away the afternoon. Hit Fillmore Street for cocktails; it has all of the bars and the infamous "Triangle" at Fillmore and Greenwich (formed by Balboa Café, Matrix Fillmore, and City Tavern). This is a happening part of town and it can get a little crazy on the weekends.

Bars

- **Blue Light Café** · 1979 Union St
- **Bus Stop** · 1901 Union St
- **City Tavern** · 3200 Fillmore St
- **Mauna Loa** · 3009 Fillmore St

Coffee

- **Coffee Roastery** · 2191 Union St
- **Starbucks** · 1899 Union St
- **The Grove** · 2106 Union St

Copy Shops

- **Kinko's Copies** · 3225 Fillmore St

Gyms

- **24 Hour Fitness** · 3741 Buchanan St

Hardware Stores

- **Fredericksen Hardware** · 3029 Fillmore St

Liquor Stores

- **Albertino's** · 1897 Lombard St
- **Gold Mine Liquors** · 1600 Lombard St
- **Michaelis Wine & Spirits** · 2198 Union St
- **Silver Platter Delicatessean** · 2501 Van Ness Ave

Movie Theaters

- **UA Metro** · 2055 Union St

Pet Shops

- **Marina Pet Hospital** · 2024 Lombard St

Restaurants

- **Alegrias, Food From Spain** · 2018 Lombard St
- **Amici's East Coast Pizzeria** · 2033 Union St
- **Balboa Café** · 3199 Fillmore St
- **Betelnut Pejiu Wu** · 2030 Union St
- **Brazen Head** · 3166 Buchanan St
- **Charlie's** · 1838 Union St
- **Greens** · Fort Mason Center, Building A
- **La Canasta** · 3006 Buchanan St
- **Mas Sake** · 2030 Lombard St
- **Merenda** · 1809 Union St
- **Pasta Pomodoro** · 1875 Union St
- **PlumpJack Café** · 3127 Fillmore St
- **Zao Noodle Bar** · 2031 Chestnut St

Shopping

- **Ambassador Toys** · 1981 Union St
- **Ambiance** · 1864 Union St
- **Canyon Beachwear** · 1728 Union St
- **Jest Jewels** · 1869 Union St
- **Kozo Arts** · 1969A Union St
- **Krimsa** · 2190 Union St
- **MetroSport** · 2198 Filbert St
- **PlumpJack Wines** · 3201 Fillmore St
- **Uko** · 2070 Union St

Video Rental

- **Diamond Video** · 1410 Lombard St

Russian Hill has some of the steepest hills in town and is notoriously difficult to park in, so bring your patience if you bring the car and leave your high heels at home. Architecturally, Macondray Lane is probably the most charming little "street" in town and is definitely worth a visit.

9 10 11 12 13
29 14 15 16 17

Ma

Banks

- **Bank of America** · 2325 Polk St
- **Bank of America** · 757 A Beach St

Car Rental

- **Avis** · 500 Beach St · 415-441-4186
- **Hertz** · 500 Beach St · 415-674-8330

Gas Stations

- **76** · 490 Bay St

O Landmarks

- **Bimbo's 365 Club** · 1025 Columbus Ave
- **Fisherman's Wharf** · From Aquatic Park to Pier 39
- **Ghirardelli Square** · 900 North Point St
- **Lombard Street** · Between Hyde St & Leavenworth St
- **Macondray Lane** · Jones St between Green St & Union St
- **National Maritime Museum** · 900 Beach St
- **San Francisco Art Institute** · 800 Chestnut St

Parking

Schools

- **Chinatown-North Beach College** · 940 Filbert St
- **San Francisco Art Institute** · 800 Chestnut St
- **Yick Wo Alternative Elementary** · 2245 Jones St

Map 3 • **Russian Hill / Fisherman's Wharf**

For food on Russian Hill, La Folie on Polk is still nice and really good. Breakfast at Polker's should cure any hangover you've acquired from the previous night's adventures. Hyde Street is more quaint and feels totally "San Francisco" when the cable car rumbles by. The only reason you should ever go to Fisherman's Wharf is to grab a burger at In-N-Out.

Bars

- **2211 Club** · 2211 Polk St
- **Bacchus Wine & Sake Bar** · 1954 Hyde St
- **Bimbo's 365 Club** · 1025 Columbus Ave
- **Greens Sports Bar** · 2239 Polk St
- **Royal Oak** · 2201 Polk St

Coffee

- **Café Espresso** · 2800 Leavenworth St
- **Coffee Roastery** · 1207 Union St
- **Royal Ground Coffee** · 2216 Polk St
- **Starbucks** · 2165 Polk St
- **Starbucks** · 2801 Jones St
- **Tully's Coffee** · 2164 Polk St

Gyms

- **Gorilla Sports** · 2330 Polk St

Liquor Stores

- **Cannery** · 2801 Leavenworth St
- **Wharf Liquors & Deli** · 2730 Taylor St
- **Willie's Liquor** · 1018 Columbus Ave

Pet Shops

- **Russian Hill Dog Grooming** · 1929 Hyde St

Restaurants

- **Antica Trattoria** · 2400 Polk St
- **Baldoria** · 2162 Larkin St
- **Boulange de Polk** · 2310 Polk St
- **Frascati** · 1901 Hyde St
- **Gary Danko** · 800 North Point St
- **Gaylord India** · 900 North Point St
- **I Fratelli** · 1896 Hyde St
- **In-N-Out Burger** · 333 Jefferson St
- **La Folie** · 2316 Polk St
- **Le Petit Robert** · 2300 Polk St
- **Pesce** · 2227 Polk St
- **Rex Cafe** · 2323 Polk St
- **Spoon** · 2209 Polk St
- **Sushi Groove** · 1916 Hyde St
- **Yabbies Coastal Kitchen** · 2237 Polk St
- **Za Pizza** · 1919 Hyde St
- **Zarzuela** · 2000 Hyde St

Shopping

- **Andrew Rothstein Fine Foods** · 2238 Polk St
- **Atelier des Modistes** · 1903 Polk St
- **Brown Dirt Cowboy** · 2406 Polk St
- **Focus Gallery** · 2423 Polk St
- **Nest** · 2340 Polk St
- **Prize** · 1415 Green St
- **Smoke Signals** · 2223 Polk St
- **Swallowtail** · 2217 Polk St
- **Tower Records** · 2525 Jones St
- **William Cross Wine Merchants** · 2253 Polk St

Video Rental

- **Tower Records/Video/Books** · 2525 Jones St
- **United Video (Chinese, Japanese and English)** · 900 Filbert St

Map 4 • **North Beach (East) / Telegraph Hill**

North Beach is an Italian neighborhood and former home to the literary Beat movement of the '50s. Bohemians, writers, and artists still live here and, with City Lights Bookstore (Map 8) on Columbus, North Beach remains a literary hotspot. The neighborhood is a favorite of both locals and tourists, so it is nearly impossible to park on the street here. Simply a great neighborhood.

$ Banks

- **Bank of America** · 1455 Stockton St
- **Bank of America** · 330 Bay St
- **Bank of the West** · 480 Columbus Ave
- **Bay View Bank** · 1435 Stockton St
- **Citibank** · 580 Green St
- **Wells Fargo** · 1255 Battery St
- **Wells Fargo** · 350 Bay St
- **Wells Fargo** · 468 Columbus Ave

Car Rental

- **Budget** · 2500 Mason St · 415-837-1830
- **Enterprise** · 350 Beach St · 415-474-9600

Car Washes

- **City Carwash & Detail** · Pier 27 Embarcadero

Community Gardens

O Landmarks

- **Coit Tower** · 1 Telegraph Hill Blvd
- **Filbert Steps** · Filbert St, just past Sansome
- **Saints Peter and Paul Church** · 666 Filbert St

Libraries

- **North Beach Branch Library** · 2000 Mason St

P Parking

Police

- **Central Police Station** · 766 Vallejo St

Post Offices

- 2200 Powell St
- 1640 Stockton St

Schools

- **Francisco Middle School Health** · 2190 Powell St
- **Garfield Elementary** · 420 Filbert St
- **Sts Peter & Paul School** · 660 Filbert St

Supermarkets

- **Safeway** · 350 Bay St

Map 4 • **North Beach (East) / Telegraph Hill**

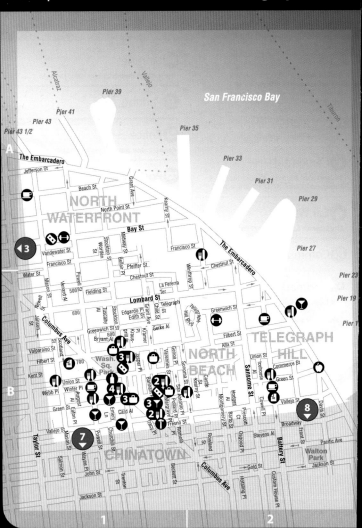

Sundries / Entertainment

Map 4

There is great local flavor and live music all over North Beach. For coffee, hit Café Grecco or Trieste. For old-school bars, hit Tosca. For breakfast, go to Mama's; for dinner, Moose's. Grant and Green and The Saloon are great for live blues. On the Telegraph Hill side, Pier 23 is great for a casual waterfront lunch or drinks, and Houston's is a favorite for fancy burgers.

Bars

- **Grant and Green** · 1371 Grant Ave
- **Hawaii West** · 729 Vallejo St
- **Lost and Found Saloon** · 1353 Grant Ave
- **North Star Café** · 1560 Powell St
- **O'Reilly's Irish Bar & Restaurant** · 622 Green St
- **Pier 23 Café** · Pier 23
- **Savoy Tivoli** · 1434 Grant Ave
- **Spec's 12 Adler Museum Café** · 12 Saroyan Pl

Coffee

- **Coffee Roastery** · 950 Battery St
- **Curly's Coffee Shop** · 1624 Powell St
- **Starbucks** · 1225 Battery St
- **Wharf Coffee Shop** · 358 Beach St

Copy Shops

- **Pip Printing** · 700 Filbert St
- **Speedway Copy Systerns** · 911 Battery St

Farmer's Markets

- **Ferry Plaza** · Sat: Green St & Embarcadero; Tu & Th: Justin Herman Plaza

Gyms

- **24 Hour Fitness** · 350 Bay St
- **Bay Club - The San Francisco** · 150 Greenwich St

Hardware Stores

- **Tower True Value Hardware** · 1300 Grant Ave

Liquor Stores

- **Coit Liquors** · 585 Columbus Ave

Restaurants

- **Café Jacqueline** · 1454 Grant Ave
- **Capp's Corner** · 1600 Powell St
- **L'Osteria del Forno** · 519 Columbus Ave
- **Golden Boy Pizza** · 542 Green St
- **Houston's** · 1800 Montgomery St
- **Mama's on Washington Square** · 1701 Stockton St
- **Mario's Bohemian Cigar Store Café** · 566 Columbus Ave
- **Michelangelo Restaurant Caffe** · 579 Columbus Ave
- **Mo's Grill** · 1322 Grant Ave
- **Moose's** · 1652 Stockton St
- **North Beach Pizza** · 1499 Grant Ave
- **North Beach Pizza** · 1310 Grant Ave
- **Pasta Pomodoro** · 655 Union St
- **Pier 23 Café** · Pier 23, The Embarcadero
- **Pipperade** · 1015 Battery Street
- **Rose Pistola** · 532 Columbus Ave
- **Trattoria Contadina** · 1800 Mason St
- **Washington Sqaure Bar & Grill** · 1707 Powell St

Shopping

- **101 Music** · 1414 Grant Ave
- **AB Fits** · 1519 Grant Ave
- **A Cavelli & Sons** · 1441 Stockton St
- **Eastwind Books & Trading Co** · 1435 Stockton St
- **Liguria** · 1700 Stockton St
- **Tilt** · 507 Columbus Ave

Video Rental

- **Borders Books & Music** · 350 Bay St
- **Film Yard Video** · 1610 Stockton St
- **North Beach Video** · 1398 Grant Ave

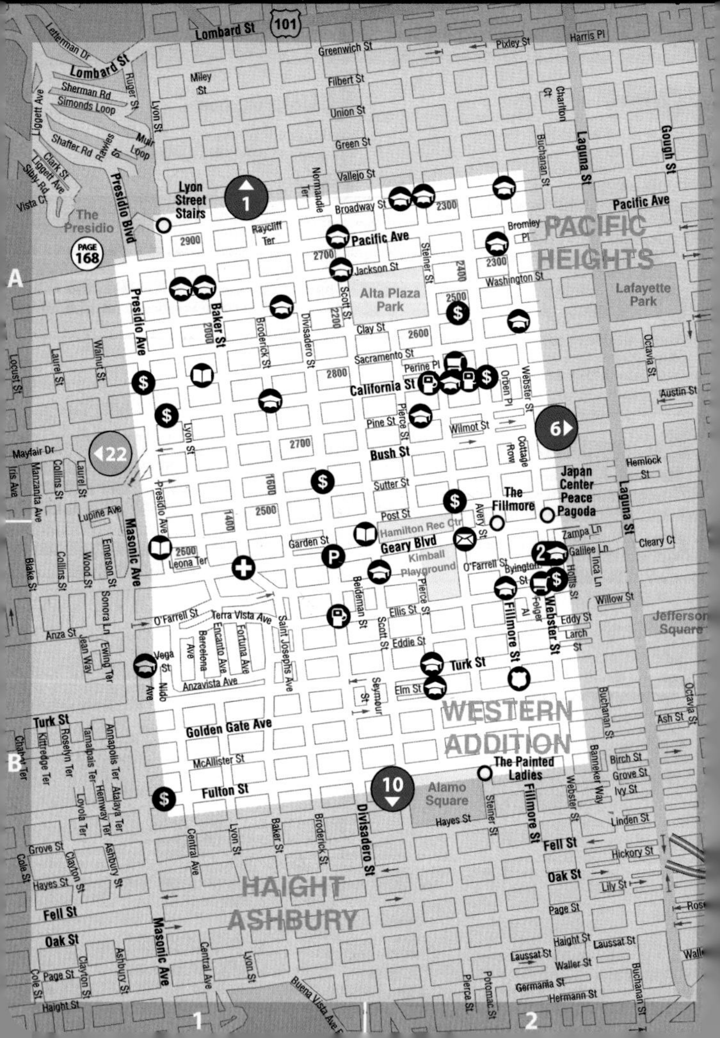

Map 3 • Pacific Heights / Western Addition

Lombard St
101
Greenwich St
Pixley St
Harris Pl
Letterman Dr
Miley St
Filbert St
Sherman Rd
Simonds Loop
Union St
Chariton Ct
Buchanan St
Laguna St
Gough St
Lyon St
Mall Loop
Shafter Rd
Green St
Lombard St
Ruger St
Normandie Ter
Vallejo St
Broadway
2300
Bromley Pl
Pacific Ave
PACIFIC HEIGHTS
Clark St
Tippett Rd
Shafter Rd
Vista Ct
Lyon Street Stairs
1
Raycliff Ter
2900
Pacific Ave
2700
Jackson St
Shefer St
2400
2300
Washington St
Lafayette Park
The Presidio
PAGE 168
A
Presidio Blvd
Baker St
Broderick St
Divisadero St
Scott St
Alta Plaza Park
2500
Clay St
2600
$
Locust St
Laurel St
Walnut St
2000
Lyon St
2200
Sacramento St
Perine Pl
California St
2800
Orben Pl
Webster St
Octavia St
Laguna St
Austin St
Mayfair Dr
Iris Ave
Manzanita Ave
Collins St
Lupine Ave
2700
Pine St
Pierce St
Bush St
Wilmot St
Cottage Row
6
Hemlock St
Masonic Ave
22
Sutter St
Post St
Alvey St
The Fillmore
Japan Center
Peace Pagoda
Zampa Ln
Galilee Ln
Emerson St
Wood St
Sonora Ln
2600
Leona Ter
2500
1600
Garden St
Geary Blvd
Hamilton Rec Ctr
Kimball Playground
O'Farrell St
2
Buchanan St
Byington St
Raycliff St
Cleary Ct
Willow St
B
Anza St
Blake St
Collins St
O'Farrell St
Terra Vista Ave
Fortuna Ave
Saint Joseph's Ave
Beideman St
Ellis St
Eddie St
Scott St
Pierce St
Webster St
Alger Al
Eddy St
Larch St
Jefferson Square
Vega St
Encanto Ave
Barcelona Ave
Anzavista Ave
Turk St
Elm St
Seymour St
WESTERN ADDITION
Octavia St
Ash St
Turk St
Roselyn Ter
Kittredge Ter
Annapolis Ter
Chabot Ter
Lloyd St
Ewing Ter
Golden Gate Ave
McAllister St
Broderick St
Baker St
Divisadero St
The Painted Ladies
Birch St
Grove St
Ivy St
Webster St
Banneker Way
B
$
Fulton St
10
Alamo Square
Hayes St
Fell St
Steiner St
Linden St
Central Ave
Grove St
Cole St
Hayes St
Masonic Ave
Lyon St
Divisadero St
Fell St
Oak St
Page St
Hickory St
Lily St
Rose
Fell St
Oak St
Page St
Cole St
Clayton St
HAIGHT ASHBURY
Haight St
Buena Vista Ave E
Germania St
Waller St
Lausatt St
Potomac St
Pierce St
Hermann St
Laussat St
Walle
1
2

Pacific Heights has some of the most beautiful (and expensive) homes in town. Go to the Lyon Street stairs for an amazing view of the bay. On the other hand, the nearby Western Addition is arguably the most ethnic and economically diverse neighborhood in town. Check out the Painted Ladies in Alamo Square for infamous examples of Victorian architecture. Japantown edges into this map as well, but we cover it on Map 6.

$ Banks

- **Bank of America** · 1700 Fillmore St
- **Bank of America** · 2310 Fillmore St
- **Citibank** · 3296 Sacramento St
- **Wells Fargo** · 3150 California St
- **Wells Fargo** · 1750 Fulton St
- **Wells Fargo** · 2100 Fillmore St
- **Wells Fargo** · 1750 Divisadero St
- **Wells Fargo** · 1335 Webster St

Gas Stations

- **76** · 1301 Divisadero St
- **Chevron** · 2500 California St
- **Shell** · 2501 California St

Hospitals

- **Kaiser Permanante Medical Center** · 2425 Geary Blvd

O Landmarks

- **Japan Center Peace Pagoda** · Geary Blvd & Webster St
- **Lyon Street Stairs** · Lyon St & Broadway
- **The Fillmore** · 1805 Geary Blvd
- **The Painted Ladies** · Steiner St between Grove St & Fulton St

Libraries

- **Municipal Railway Library** · 949 Presidio Ave
- **Presidio Branch Library** · 3150 Sacramento St
- **Western Addition Library** · 1550 Scott St

Parking

Police

- **Northern Police Station** · 1125 Fillmore St

Post Offices

- 1849 Geary Blvd

Schools

- **American College-Chinese Med** · 1426 Fillmore St
- **Benjamin Franklin Middle School** · 1430 Scott St
- **Convent of the Sacred Heart Elementary School** · 2200 Broadway
- **Convent of the Sacred Heart High School** · 2222 Broadway
- **Creative Arts Charter School** · 1512 Golden Gate Ave
- **Drew College Preparatory School** · 2901 California St
- **Golden Gate Elementary** · 1601 Turk St
- **Hillwood Academic Day School** · 2521 Scott St
- **Newcomer High School** · 2340 Jackson St
- **Raoul Wallenberg Alternative High** · 40 Vega St
- **San Francisco** · 3016 Jackson St
- **San Francisco University High School** · 3065 Jackson St
- **San Francisco Waldorf School** · 2938 Washington St
- **St Dominic's Elementary** · 2445 Pine St
- **Sterne School** · 2690 Jackson St
- **Stuart Hall for Boys School** · 2252 Broadway
- **Stuart Hall High School** · 2252 Broadway
- **Town School for Boys** · 2750 Jackson St
- **University of the Pacific** · 2155 Webster St
- **William L Cobb Elementary** · 2725 California St

Supermarkets

- **Mollie Stone's** · 2435 California St
- **Safeway** · 1335 Webster St

Map 5 • **Pacific Heights / Western Addition**

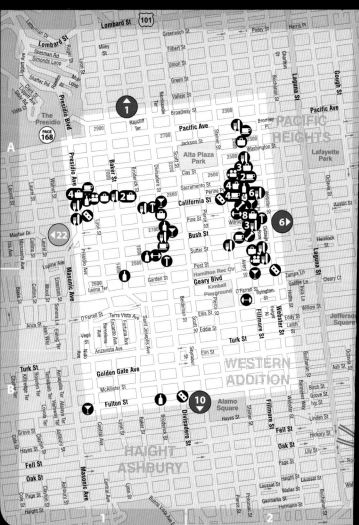

Fillmore Street in Pac Heights has all your chic and trendy shops and restaurants. Florio and Fillmore Grill are good bets for restaurants; for great cheese go to Artisan Cheese on California; and for an amazing French bakery go to Boulangerie Bay Bread on Pine. If you're on Divisadero in the Western Addition, you've got to stop for ribs at Brother-in-Laws BBQ. Bill Graham's Fillmore Auditorium is here too and still a totally excellent place to see a show.

Bars

- **Boom Boom Room** · 1601 Fillmore St
- **Frankie's Bohemian Café** · 1862 Divisadero St
- **Harry's on Fillmore** · 2020 Fillmore St
- **Lion's Den** · 2062 Divisadero St
- **Storyville** · 1751 Fulton St

Coffee

- **Coffee Bean & Tea Leaf** · 2201 Fillmore St
- **Peet's** · 2197 Filmore St
- **Starbucks** · 2435 California St
- **Starbucks** · 2222 Filmore St
- **Starbucks** · 1750 Divisadero St
- **Royal Grove Coffee** · 2060 Fillmore St
- **Royal Grove Coffee** · 3313 Sacramento St
- **The Grove** · 2016 Fillmore St
- **Tully's Coffee** · 2455 Fillmore St

Copy Shops

- **Copy Net** · 2404 California St

Gyms

- **Club One at Fillmore Center** · 1755 O'Farrell St
- **Gorilla Sports** · 2450 Sutter St
- **Pacific Heights Health Club** · 2356 Pine St

Hardware Stores

- **Divisadero Lock & Hardware** · 1649 Divisadero St
- **Fillmore Hardware** · 1930 Fillmore St
- **Pacific Heights True Value Hardware** ·
  2828 California St

Liquor Stores

- **A A Market** · 667 Broderick St
- **D & M Wine & Liquor** · 2200 Fillmore St
- **Royal Market** · 1401 Baker St
- **Stewart's Grocery** · 2498 Sutter St
- **WC Liquor** · 1836 Divisadero St
- **Wilking Wine & Liquor** · 3273 Sacramento St

Movie Theaters

- **AMC Kabuki 8** · 1881 Post St
- **Landmark Clay** · 2261 Filmore St
- **UA Vogue** · 3290 Sacramento St

Pet Shops

- **Barry For Pets** · 1840 Fillmore St
- **George** · 2411 California St

Restaurants

- **Café Kati** · 1963 Sutter St
- **Chez Nous** · 1911 Fillmore St
- **Dino's Pizzeria** · 2101 Fillmore St
- **Elite Café** · 2049 Fillmore St
- **Eliza's** · 2877 California St
- **Ella's** · 500 Presidio Ave
- **Fillmore Grill** · 2298 Fillmore St
- **Florio** · 1915 Fillmore St
- **Galette** · 2043 Fillmore St
- **Garibaldi's on Presidio** · 347 Presidio Ave
- **Godzilla Sushi** · 1800 Divisadero St
- **Jackson Fillmore Trattoria** · 2506 Fillmore St
- **Julia** · 2101 Sutter St
- **La Mediterranee** · 2210 Fillmore St
- **Pasta Pomodoro** · 1865 Post St
- **Vivande Porta Via** · 2125 Fillmore St
- **Zao Noodle Bar** · 2406 California St

Shopping

- **American Pie** · 3101 Sacramento St
- **Artisan Cheese** · 2413 California St
- **Benefit** · 2117 Fillmore St
- **Betsy Johnson** · 2033 Fillmore St
- **Boulangerie Bay Bread** · 2325 Pine St
- **Button Down** · 3145 Sacramento St
- **Crossroads** · 1901 Fillmore St
- **Departures from the Past** · 2028 Fillmore St
- **Fetish** · 344 Presidio Ave
- **Forrest Jones** · 3274 Sacramento St
- **Fresh Air Bicycles** · 1943 Divisadero St
- **George** · 2411 California St
- **Gimme Shoes** · 2358 Fillmore St
- **Kiehl's** · 2360 Fillmore St
- **Marcus Books** · 1712 Fillmore St
- **Margaret O'Leary** · 2400 Fillmore St
- **Mrs Dewson's Hats** · 2050 Fillmore St
- **Narumi** · 1902 Fillmore St
- **Nest** · 2300 Fillmore St
- **Paper Source** · 1925 Fillmore St
- **Quatrine** · 3235 Sacramento St
- **Shabby Chic** · 2185 Fillmore St
- **Sue Fisher King** · 3067 Sacramento St
- **The Bar** · 340 Presidio Ave
- **Zinc Details** · 1905 Fillmore St
- **Zonal** · 1942 Fillmore St

Video Rental

- **Blockbuster Video** · 1493 Webster St
- **Choi's Home Video** · 2410 California St
- **Four Star Videos** · 803 Divisadero St
- **Hollywood Video** · 3150 California St

This part of Pacific Heights is dominated by the tiered Lafayette Park and beautiful homes. Cathedral Hill is marked by the impressive Cathedral of St. Mary's, St. Mark's Lutheran, and big, modern apartment buildings. Japantown is also represented here with the Miyako Mall, Kintetsu Mall, and the Kinokuniya Building as its hub.

$ Banks

- **Bank of America** · 601 Van Ness Ave
- **Bank of America** · 1000 Van Ness Ave
- **Bank of America** · 1640 Van Ness Ave
- **Bay View Bank** · 540 Van Ness Ave
- **California Bank & Trust** · 1696 Post St
- **California Federal Bank** · 1801 Van Ness Ave
- **California Federal Bank** · 1399 Post St
- **First Republic Bank** · 2001 Van Ness Ave
- **San Francisco Federal CU** · 770 Golden Gate Ave
- **Sterling Bank & Trust** · 2045 Van Ness Ave
- **Union Bank** · 1675 Post St
- **United Commercial Bank** · 711 Van Ness Ave
- **Wells Fargo** · 1560 Van Ness Ave

Car Rental

- **Budget** · 1600 Van Ness Ave · 415-775-6607
- **Enterprise** · 1133 Van Ness Ave · 415-441-3369
- **Enterprise** · 901 Van Ness Ave · 415-351-5171
- **Hertz** · 1644 Pine St · 415-923-1119

Gas Stations

- **Chevron** · 1501 Van Ness Ave
- **Shell** · 800 Turk St
- **Shell** · 1898 Van Ness Ave

Hospitals

- **California Pacific Medical Center—
  Pacific Campus** · 2333 Buchanan St

O Landmarks

- **Hass-Lillienthal House** · 2007 Franklin St
- **Spreckel's Mansion** · 2080 Washington St
- **St John Coltrane African Orthodox Church** ·
  930 Gough St
- **St Mary's Cathedral** · 1111 Gough St

P Parking

Schools

- **Alemany College** · 750 Eddy St
- **Hamlin School** · 2120 Broadway
- **John Swett Alternative Elementary** ·
  727 Golden Gate Ave
- **La Mel** · 1801 Bush St
- **Raphael Weill Children's Center** ·
  1501 O'Farrell St
- **Rosa Parks Elementary** · 1501 O'Farrell St
- **Sacred Heart Cathedral Preparatory** · 1055 Ellis
  St
- **St Brigid School** · 2250 Franklin St
- **Trinity College of Hartford Ct** · 1735 Franklin St

Go for noodles at Mifune in Japantown. The Kinokuniya Bookshop and Maruwa Supermarket are also unique Japantown shops. Japantown also stretches into map 5, where you will find the Kabuki movie theater.

Coffee

- **May's Coffee Shop** · 1737 Post St
- **Starbucks** · 1401 Van Ness Ave
- **Starbucks** · 1560 Van Ness Ave
- **Tully's Coffee** · 1661 Pine St

Copy Shops

- **Copy Mill** · 780 Van Ness Ave
- **Express Print** · 1410 Franklin St
- **Kinko's Copies** · 1800 Van Ness Ave
- **Sir Speedy Printing Ctr** · 1111 Geary Blvd
- **Speedway Copy Systems** · 2055 Van Ness Ave
- **Staples** · 1700 Van Ness Ave

Gyms

- **24 Hour Fitness** · 1200 Van Ness Ave
- **Body Tonic** · 1300 Sutter St
- **Cathedral Hill Plaza Athletic** · 1333 Gough St
- **Crunch Fitness** · 1000 Van Ness Ave
- **Guarantee Fitness** · 1801 Bush St

Hardware Stores

- **Soko Hardware** · 1698 Post St

Liquor Stores

- **Sutter-Franklin Liquors** · 1400 Sutter St
- **Van Ness Food Co** · 1356 Van Ness Ave

Movie Theaters

- **AMC 1000 Van Ness** · 1000 Van Ness Ave
- **Landmark Opera Plaza Cinemas** · 601 Van Ness Ave
- **UA Galaxy 4** · 1285 Sutter St

Restaurants

- **Harris'** · 2100 Van Ness Ave
- **House of Prime Rib** · 1906 Van Ness Ave
- **Mifune** · Japan Ctr, 1737 Post St

Shopping

- **American Rag** · 1305 Van Ness Ave
- **Maruwa Food Co** · 1737 Post St
- **Whole Foods Market** · 1765 California St

Video Rental

- **Jus' Another Video Depot** · 1748 Buchanan St
- **Nihonmachi Video Rental (Japanese)** · 1832 Buchanan St
- **People Video Rental (Japanese)** · 1740 Buchanan St
- **Wherehouse Music** · 1303 Van Ness Ave

Remarkable apartment buildings and nice hotels define Nob Hill. The 450 Sutter Medical Building is an amazing example of Art Deco architecture. Davies Symphony Hall, the War Memorial Opera House, the new Main Library, the Asian Art Museum, and City Hall make the Civic Center a cultural focal point of the city.

$ Banks

- **Bank of America** · 1 Powell St
- **Bank of America** · 335 Powell St
- **Bank of America** · 445 Powell St
- **Bank of America** · 944 Stockton St
- **Bank of Canton** · 1301 Stockton St
- **Bank of the Orient** · 1023 Stockton St
- **California Savings & Loan** · 800 Market St
- **East West Bank** · 1241 Stockton St
- **First Republic Bank** · 1088 Stockton St
- **Oceanic Bank** · 447 Sutter St
- **San Francisco Federal CU** · 1 Dr Carlton Goodlett Pl
- **Sincere Federal Savings Bank** · 1226 Stockton St
- **United Commercial Bank** · 1318 Stockton St
- **Washington Mutual** · 1500 Polk St
- **Washington Mutual** · 1201 Market St
- **Wells Fargo** · 84 Ellis St
- **Wells Fargo** · 374 Golden Gate Ave
- **Wells Fargo** · 865 Market St
- **Wells Fargo** · 1266 Market St

Car Rental

- **A Continental Rent-A-Car** · 434 O'Farrell St
- **Ace Rent-A-Car** · 415 Taylor St
- **Alamo** · 750 Bush St
- **Avis** · 675 Post St
- **Budget** · 321 Mason St
- **Budget** · 333 O'Farrell St
- **City Car Share** · 410 Jessie St
- **City Rent-A-Car** · 1433 Bush St
- **Discount Rentals** · 349 Mason St
- **Dollar** · 364 O'Farrell St
- **Enterprise** · 222 Mason St
- **Enterprise** · 819 Ellis St
- **Hertz** · 335 Powell St
- **Hertz** · 433 Mason St
- **Hertz** · 950 Mason St
- **National** · 320 O'Farrell St
- **Reliable Rent-A-Car** · 349 Mason St
- **Thrifty** · 520 Mason St

Car Washes

- **Marina Auto Polishing** · 500 Post St
- **Woody and Sons' Auto Detailing** · 843 Polk St

Community Gardens

Gas Stations

- **Shell** · 300 5th St
- **Tom's BP** · 901 Pacific Ave

Hospitals

- **Chinese Hospital** · 845 Jackson St
- **St Francis Memorial Hospital** · 1150 Bush St

O Landmarks

- **450 Sutter Medical Building** · 450 Sutter St
- **Asian Art Museum** · 200 Larkin St
- **Cable Car Museum** · 1201 Mason St
- **Chambord Apartments** · 1298 Sacramento St
- **City Hall** · 1 Dr Carlton Goodlett Pl
- **Civic Center** · Franklin to Leavenworth, & Turk to Hayes
- **Defenestration** · 6th St & Howard St
- **Fleur de Lys** · 777 Sutter St
- **Glide Memorial Church** · 330 Ellis St
- **Grace Cathedral** · 1100 California St
- **Imperial Tea Court** · 1411 Powell St
- **Masonic Auditorium** · 1111 California St
- **Pacific Union Club** · 1000 California St
- **San Francisco Main Library** · 100 Larkin St
- **The Huntington Hotel** · 1075 California St

Libraries

- **Chinatown Branch Library** · 1135 Powell St
- **Main Library** · 100 Larkin St
- **San Francisco Law Library** · 400 McAllister St

P Parking

Police

- **Tenderloin Police Station** · 301 Eddy St

Post Offices

- 867 Stockton St
- 101 Hyde St
- 450 Golden Gate Ave
- 170 O'Farrell St
- 1400 Pine St

Schools

- **California Art Institute** · 1170 Market St
- **California Culinary Academy** · 625 Polk St
- **Cathedral School for Boys** · 1275 Sacramento St
- **Chinese Education Elementary** · 843 Stockton St
- **Commodore Stockton Pre-K School** · 950 Clay St
- **Cumberland Chinese School** · 865 Jackson St
- **Fashion Institute of Design** · 55 Stockton St
- **Gordon J Lau Elementary** · 950 Clay St
- **Great Western University** · 545 Sutter St
- **Hastings College of the Law** · 200 McAllister St
- **Jean Parker Elementary** · 840 Broadway
- **Redding Child Dev Center** · 1421 Pine St
- **San Francisco Renaissance** · 275 5th St
- **Spring Valley School** · 1451 Jackson St
- **St Mary's Chinese Day School** · 910 Broadway
- **Tenderloin Elementary School** · 627 Turk St
- **Youth Chance** · 220 Golden Gate Ave

Supermarkets

- **CalaFoods** · 1095 Hyde St

Have tea in Chinatown at Imperial Tea Court, cocktails at Bambuddah or the Redwood Room, blues at the Blue Lamp, cheap Indian at Shalimar, Italian at Venticello, and breakfast at Sears Fine Foods. Part of Union Square sneaks into this map so you can do some serious shopping too.

Bars

- **Bambuddah** • The Phoenix Hotel, 601 Eddy St
- **Blind Tiger** • 787 Broadway
- **Blue Lamp** • 561 Geary St
- **Bobby's Owl Tree** • 601 Post St
- **Club 181** • 181 Eddy St
- **Edinburgh Castle** • 950 Geary Blvd
- **Gold Dust Lounge** • 247 Powell St
- **Harry Denton's Starlight Room** • Sir Francis Drake Hotel, 21st fl, 450 Powell St
- **Julip** • 839 Geary St
- **Ruby Skye** • 420 Mason St
- **Shanghai Kelly's** • 2064 Polk St
- **The Cinch Saloon** • 1723 Polk St
- **The Red Room** • 827 Sutter St
- **The Redwood Room** • Clift Hotel, 495 Geary St
- **Tonga Room** • Fairmount Hotel, 950 Mason St

Coffee

- **Coffee Roastery** • 865 Market St
- **Cup a Joe Coffee House** • 896 Sutter St
- **Golden Coffee House** • 901 Sutter St
- **Lafayette Coffee Shop** • 250 Hyde St
- **Little Paris Coffee Shop** • 939 Stockton St
- **Muffin Coffee Shop** • 39 Taylor St
- **Peet's** • 2133C Polk St
- **Royal Grove Coffee** • 1605 Polk St
- **Starbucks** • 442 Geary St
- **Starbucks** • 1231 Market St
- **Starbucks** • 222 Mason St
- **Starbucks** • 201 Powell St
- **Starbucks** • 901 Market St
- **Starbucks** • 390 Stockton St
- **Taylor Street Coffee Shop** • 375 Taylor St

Copy Shops

- **Copy Action** • 29 Grove St
- **Copy Circle** • 1701 Polk St
- **Copy Pro** • 833 Market St
- **Cyber Copy** • 272 O'Farrell St
- **K K Copying & Printing** • 528 Larkin St
- **United Copy Svc** • 230 Hyde St

Farmer's Markets

- **Heart of the City** • Market St between 7th & 8th St

Gyms

- **Bert's Conditioning Clinic** • 450 Sutter St
- **Club One** • 535 Mason St
- **Club One at Federal Fitness Center** • 450 Golden Gate Ave
- **Club One at Nob Hill** • 950 California St
- **Gym Club at Hotel Nikko** • 222 Mason St
- **Personalized Athletic Care** • 620 Sutter St
- **YMCA** • 220 Golden Gate Ave

Hardware Stores

- **Ace Hardware** • 1333 Pacific Ave
- **Brownie's Ace Hardware** • 1563 Polk St
- **Double Eagle Hardware** • 530 O'Farrell St
- **Golden City Building Supply** • 1333 Pacific Ave
- **Haji's Hardware** • 1170 Sutter St
- **Peerless General Supply** • 156 Leavenworth St
- **Yee Cheong Building Supply** • 1319 Stockton St

Liquor Stores

- **Arsen's Liquors & Deli** • 1754 Polk St
- **Civic Center Market** • 1292 Market St
- **Empire Market** • 399 Eddy St
- **Fox Liquor & Delicatessen** • 570 Larkin St
- **Fred's Liquor & Groceries** • 151 6th St
- **Fred's Liquor Store** • 300 Mason St
- **G & H Liquors** • 201 Jones St
- **GNG Liquors** • 40 5th St
- **Grand Liquor Market** • 67 Taylor St
- **Haz Liquors** • 1401 Polk St
- **Hyde & Pacific Liquors** • 1600 Hyde St
- **Imperial Square Liquors** • 251 Ellis St
- **International Deli & Spirits** • 587 Post St
- **Jug Shop** • 1567 Pacific Ave
- **King Liquor & Deli** • 693 Post St
- **Liquor & Deli on Union Square** • 423 Stockton St
- **Maikin's Liquor & Groceries** • 199 6th St
- **Marine Club Liquor & Deli** • 615 Sutter St
- **Marty's Liquor & Gourmet** • 657 Sutter St
- **Mason Liquor & Deli** • 530 Mason St
- **Nob Hill Liquors** • 1000 Hyde St
- **O'Farrell Liquors** • 405 O'Farrell St
- **Polk Clay Liquor** • 1700 Polk St
- **Royal Liquors** • 65 6th St
- **Sonoma Liquor** • 65 6th St
- **Tenderloin Liquors** • 22 Turk St
- **Traveler's Liquors** • 22 7th St
- **Woerner's Liquors** • 901 Geary St
- **Zain's at the Hilton Spirits** • 333 O'Farrell St

Movie Theaters

- **Landmark Lumiere** • 1572 California St

Pet Shops

- **Catnip & Bones** • 1463 Broadway
- **Petco** • 1677 Washington St

Restaurants

- **Acquerello** • 1722 Sacramento St
- **Allegro** • 1701 Jones St
- **Big Four** • Huntington Hotel, 1075 California St
- **Crustacean** • 1475 Polk St
- **Farallon** • 450 Post St
- **Fleur de Lys** • 777 Sutter St
- **Hyde Street Bistro** • 1521 Hyde St
- **Millennium** • Abigail Hotel, 246 McAllister St
- **Nob Hill Café** • 1152 Taylor St
- **Pakwan** • 501 O'Farrell St
- **Sears Fine Food** • 439 Powell St
- **Shalimar** • 532 Jones St
- **Swan Oyster Depot** • 1517 Polk St
- **The Bagelry** • 2139 Polk St
- **Venticello** • 1257 Taylor St
- **Victoria Pastry Co** • 1362 Stockton St

Shopping

- **City Discount** • 1542 Polk St
- **European Book Co** • 925 Larkin St
- **General Bead** • 637 Minna St
- **Ghiradelli** • 44 Stockton St
- **Imperial Tea Court** • 1411 Powell St
- **Leonard's 2001** • 2001 Polk St
- **Plants on Polk** • 1475 Polk St
- **Rasputian's** • 69 Powell St
- **The Levi's Store** • 300 Post St
- **Zonal** • 2139 Polk St

Video Rental

- **Blockbuster Video** • 1094 Bush St
- **Borders Books & Music** • 400 Post St
- **Film Yard** • 1032 Market St
- **Golden Gate Video** • 1259 Polk St
- **Hollywood Video** • 1538 Polk St
- **JBC Rental Video** • 149 Turk St
- **Le Salon** • 626 Ellis St
- **Power Vision** • 1032 Market St
- **San Vanh Video (Thai)** • 651 Larkin St
- **Tak Tat (Chinese)** • 1341 Stockton St
- **Thong Video (Vietnamese)** • 666 Larkin St
- **Top Video** • 888 O'Farrell St
- **US Video Rental** • 720 Geary St
- **Video Tokyo (Japanese and English)** • 282 O'Farrell St
- **Video Wave** • 1651 Polk St
- **Video Zone** • 786 Bush St

Map 8 • Union Sq/Embarcadero/So. of Ma

Columbus Ave

Montgomery St

Sansome St

Battery St

Front St

Davis St

The Embarcadero

4

Walton Park

Broadway

City Lights Bookstore

Portsmouth Square

Pacific Ave

Osgood Pl

Gold St

Jackson St

Battery St

Hotaling

Cordova House

Washington St

200

200

Justin Herman Plaza

Ferry Building

FINANCIAL DISTRICT

Sentinel Building

Clay St

Sacramento St

Drumm St

Merchant St

Transamerica Pyramid

Merchant St

The Embarcadero Ctr

Leidesdorff St

Halleck St

Front St

Davis St

Commercial St

California St

Bank of America

Montgomery St

Pine St

Bush St

Spring St

Belden St

St George Alley

Sansome St

Market St

Embarcadero

Cupid's Span

Spear St

Steuart St

Main St

Sing Buildings

Kearny St

Grant Ave

Quincy St

Waverly Pl

Claude Ln

Hallidie Building

7

VC Morris Building

Lotta's Fountain

Post St

Geary St

O'Farrell St

Ellis St

Stockton St

Grant Ave

Kearny St

Maiden Ln

Agnello

New Montgomery St

Ecker

Stevenson St

Jessie St

Montgomery St

Fremont St

Natoma St

James Lick

Tehama St

Clementina St

Beale St

1st St

Folsom St

Harrison St

Guy Pl

Lansing St

Mission St

Yerba Buena Center

Minna St

Hunt St

SF MoMA

PAGE 255

PAGE 177

PAGE 175

Hawthorne St

2nd St

Essex St

Stillman St

Bryant St

Delancy St

Brannan St

City Hall

Powell St

Jessie St

Stevenson St

Sony Metreon

PAGE 600

3rd St

Moscone Center

Lapu Lapu St

Mabini St

Rizal St

Bonifacio St

80

4th St

Jack London Aly

Taber Pl

Varney Pl

400

Sea Change Sculpture

SOUTH OF MARKET

Geary St

Folsom St

Shipley St

Clara St

5th St

Howard St

600

2nd St

Welsh St

Clyde St

Freelon St

13

Tandang

Ritch St

2nd St

PAGE 201

King St

Pacific Bell Park

Townsend St

$ Banks

- **Bank of America** · 785 Market St
- **Bank of America** · 345 Montgomery St
- **Bank of America** · 33 New Montgomery St
- **Bank of America** · 345 3rd St
- **Bank of America** · 100 1st St
- **Bank of America** · 45 Spear St
- **Bank of America** · 163 Brannan St
- **Bank of America** · 701 Grant Ave
- **Bank of America** · 50 California St
- **Bank of America** · 500 Battery St
- **Bank of Canton** · 743 Washington St
- **Bank of Canton** · 555 Montgomery St
- **Bank of Guam** · 404 Montgomery St
- **Bank of the Orient** · 233 Sansome St
- **Bank of the West** · 505 Montgomery St
- **Bank of the West** · 1 Front St
- **Bank of the West** · 295 Bush St
- **Bank of the West** · 933 Grant Ave
- **Bay View Bank** · 201 Montgomery St
- **Bay View Bank** · 525 Market St
- **California Bank & Trust** · 465 California St
- **California Federal Bank** · 99 Post St
- **California Federal Bank** · 44 Montgomery St
- **California Federal Bank** · 700 Market St
- **California Federal Bank** · 100 Pine St
- **California Federal Bank** · 1000 California Ave
- **California Pacific Bank** · 601 Montgomery St
- **Cedars Bank** · 555 Montgomery St
- **Citibank** · 1 Embarcadero Ctr
- **Citibank** · 451 Montgomery St
- **Citibank** · 1 Sansome St
- **Citibank** · 245 Market St
- **Citibank** · 845 Grant Ave
- **Citibank** · 260 California St
- **City National Bank** · 150 California St
- **County Bank** · 130 Battery St
- **Far East National Bank** · 711 Sacramento St
- **Far East National Bank** · 500 Montgomery St
- **First Bank & Trust** · 735 Montgomery St
- **First Bank & Trust** · 550 Montgomery St
- **First Bank & Trust** · 1001 Grant Ave
- **First Republic Bank** · 44 Montgomery St
- **First Republic Bank** · 101 Pine St
- **Golden Gate Bank** · 225 Bush St
- **National American Bank** · 520 Montgomery St
- **Northern Trust Bank** · 580 California St
- **Oceanic Bank** · 130 Battery St
- **Sequoia National Bank** · 65 Post St
- **Sterling Bank & Trust** · 600 Montgomery St
- **Trans Pacific National Bank** · 46 2nd St
- **Union Bank** · 400 California St
- **Union Bank** · 160 Sutter St
- **United Commercial Bank** · 1066 Grant Ave
- **United Commercial Bank** · 900 Kearny St
- **Washington Mutual** · 401 California St
- **Washington Mutual** · 10 Kearny St
- **Washington Mutual** · 1040 Grant Ave
- **Wells Fargo** · 201 3rd St
- **Wells Fargo** · 425 Market St
- **Wells Fargo** · 760 Market St
- **Wells Fargo** · 120 Kearny St
- **Wells Fargo** · 439 Washington St
- **Wells Fargo** · 464 California St
- **Wells Fargo** · 1 Montgomery St
- **Wells Fargo** · 100 Spear St
- **Wells Fargo** · 525 Market St
- **Wells Fargo** · 2 Grant Ave
- **Wells Fargo** · 292 Battery St
- **Wells Fargo** · 1 California St
- **Wells Fargo** · 1160 Grant Ave
- **Wells Fargo** · 420 Montgomery St
- **Westamerica Bank** · 214 California St
- **World Savings & Loan Assn** · 75 1st St

🚗 Car Rental

- **Alamo** · 687 Folsom St
- **Avis** · 821 Howard St
- **Budget** · 5 Embarcadero Ctr
- **Enterprise** · 77 Folsom St
- **Hertz** · 55 4th St
- **National** · 687 Folsom St
- **Thrifty** · 8 Main St

🚗 Car Washes

- **Detail Factory** · 525 Harrison St

⛽ Gas Stations

- **76** · 390 1st St
- **76** · 800 Folsom St
- **Shell** · 551 3rd St
- **Shell** · 598 Bryant St

O Landmarks

- **Bank of America Building** · 555 California St
- **City Lights Bookstore** · 261 Columbus Ave
- **Cupid's Span** · Rincon Park
- **Embarcadero Center** · Sacramento, Clay, Drumm, and Battery Streets
- **Ferry Building** · Embarcadero & Market St
- **Hallidie Building** · 130-150 Sutter St
- **Justin Herman Plaza** · Market St @ Embarcadero
- **Lotta's Fountain** · Kearny/Geary @ Market St
- **Portsmouth Square** · Kearny St between Clay St & Washington St
- **Sea Change Sculpture** · Embarcadero at 2nd St & Townsend St
- **Sentinel Building** · 916 Kearny St
- **SFMoMA** · 151 3rd St
- **Sing Chong and Sing Fat Buildings** · Grant St & California St
- **Sony Metreon** · 101 4th St
- **Transamerica Pyramid** · 600 Montgomery St
- **VC Morris Building (Circle Gallery)** · 140 Maiden Ln
- **Yerba Buena Center for the Arts** · 701 Mission St

📖 Libraries

- **Foundation Center, San Francisco** · 312 Sutter St

P Parking

✉ Post Offices

- 460 Brannan St
- 226 Harrison St
- 180 Sutter St
- 150 Sutter St

🎓 Schools

- **Academy of Art College** · 79 New Montgomery St
- **Asia Pacific Intl University** · 250 4th St
- **Ben Gurion University of Negev** · 220 Bush St
- **Brandon College** · 25 Kearny St
- **Bryan College of San Francisco** · 731 Market St
- **Chinese Education Center** · 657 Merchant St
- **Cornell University** · 220 Montgomery St
- **Dharma Realm Buddhist Univ** · 800 Sacramento St
- **Downtown Campus of CCSF** · 800 Mission St
- **John Yehall Chin Elementary** · 350 Broadway
- **Notre Dame Des Victoires School** · 659 Pine St
- **San Francisco Institute of Architecture** · 555 Howard St
- **San Francisco State University** · 425 Market St
- **Sand Paths Academy** · 169 Stillman St
- **Saybrook Graduate School** · 450 Pacific Ave
- **UC Berkeley Extension Downtown** · 425 Market St
- **University of Judaism** · 703 Market St
- **Western Institute of Science and Health** · 78 1st St
- **Wharton School (West)** · 101 Howard St

🛒 Supermarkets

- **Bon Appetit** · 145 Jackson St

Map 8 • Union Sq/Embarcadero/South Beach

Columbus Ave

Montgomery St

Sansome St

Vallejo St

Broadway

Osgood Pl

Pacific Ave

Kearny St

Bickett St

Wentworth Pl

Gold St

Davis St

Walton Park

Jackson St

Front St

200

The Embarcadero

Battery St

Hotaling Pl

Washington St

200

Merchant St

Clay St

Justin Herman Plaza

Walter U Lum Pl

Grant Ave

Waverly Pl

Merchant St

The Embarcadero Ctr

FINANCIAL

Commercial St

Leidesdorff St

Sacramento St

DISTRICT

Spring St

Halleck St

Davis St

Kearny St

California St

Montgomery St

Market St

Quincy St

Pine St

Embarcadero

Claude Ln

St George Aly

Trinity Pl

Robert Kirk Ln

Bush St

Sansome St

Steuart St

Spear St

Main St

Lick Pl

Post St

Grant Ave

Harlan Pl

Maiden Ln

Geary St

New Montgomery St

Montgomery St

Sutter St

Beale St

Fremont St

Howard St

1st St

Folsom St

Harrison St

O'Farrell St

Stevenson St

Mirna St

Hunt St

Natoma St

Jessie St Lick

Shaw Aly

Tehama St

Ecker

Guy Pl

Lansing St

Essex St

Ellis St

Jessie St

Mission St

Yerba Buena Center

SF MoMA

PAGE 255

PAGE 177

3rd St

Hawthorne St

2nd St

Powell St

Howard St

PAGE 175

Moscone Center

600

Bryant St

Delancey St

Gallagher Ln

Mabini St

Lapu Lapu St

Bonifacio St

Rizal St

Stillman St

400

Taber Pl

Jack London Aly

S Park Ave

Varney Pl

Brannan St

Folsom St

Shipley St

Clara St

4th St

80

Ritch St

Zoe St

Wash St

5th St

Freelon St

Welsh St

Townsend St

PAGE 201

SOUTH OF MARKET

King St

Pacific Bell Park

13

1

2

Map 8

There is something for everyone here. Favorite Chinese? Hunan. Vietnamese? Slanted Door. Fancy Greek? Kokkari. Martini? Bix. Swing? Hi-Ball Lounge. Books? City Lights and William Stout. Movie? Embarcadero for arthouse films and the Metreon for the blockbusters.

Bars

- 7-11 Club • 711 Market St
- 850 Cigar Bar • 850 Montgomery St
- Bamboo Hut • 479 Broadway
- Bix • 56 Gold St
- Buddha Lounge • 901 Grant Ave
- Carnelian Room • Bank of America Bldg, 52nd fl, 555 California St
- Frankie's Bohemian Café • 443 Broadway
- Gordon Biersch • 2 Harrison St
- Harry Denton's • 161 Steuart St
- Hi-Ball Lounge • 473 Broadway
- Hotel Utah Saloon • 500 4th St
- House of Shields • 39 New Montgomery St
- Jazz at Pearl's • 256 Columbus Ave
- Kate O'Brien's • 579 Howard St
- Li Po Cocktail Lounge • 916 Grant Ave
- Royal Exchange • 301 Sacramento St
- San Francisco Brewing Company • 155 Columbus Ave
- South Beach Billiards • 270 Brannan St
- Spec's 12 Adler Museum Café • 12 Adler Way
- The Condor Sports Bar • 300 Columbus Ave
- The Irish Bank Bar & Restaurant • 10 Mark Ln
- The Saloon • 1232 Grant Ave
- The Sound Factory • 525 Harrison St
- The Thirsty Bear • 661 Howard St
- Tosca Café • 242 Columbus Ave
- Vesuvio Café • 255 Columbus Ave

Coffee

- Caffe Centro • 102 S Park St
- Coffee Roastery • 536 Davis St
- Coffee Roastery • 180 Howard St
- Java House • Pier 40
- Ming's Coffee Shop • 54 2nd St
- Starbucks:
  - 359 Grant Ave
  - 120 4th St
  - 201 3rd St
  - 730 Howard St
  - 555 California St
  - 15 Sutter St
  - 36 2nd St
  - 505 Sansome St
  - 200 Pine St
  - 398 Market St
  - 333 Market St
  - 50 Beale St
  - 199 Fremont St
  - 99 Jackson St
  - 123 Mission St
  - 1 Market Plz
  - 780 Market St
  - 101 4th St
  - 74 New Montgomery St
  - 369 Pine St
  - 44 Montgomery St
  - 264 Kearny St
  - 565 Clay St
  - 343 Sansome St
  - 123 Battery St
  - 455 Market St
  - 701 Battery St
  - 340 Mission St
  - 27 Drumm St
  - 52 California St
  - 201 Spear St
  - 2 Harrison St
- Peet's • 217 Montgomery St
- Peet's • 22 Battery St
- Peet's • 595 Mission St
- Peet's • Ferry Building
- Tully's Coffee • 100 California St
- Tully's Coffee • 225 Bush St
- Tully's Coffee • 275 Battery St
- Tully's Coffee • 303 2nd St
- Tully's Coffee • 425 Market St

Copy Shops

- ABC-San Francisco • 234 Bush St
- ABCCopy • 721 Commercial St
- American Legal Copy • 28 2nd St
- At Your Service • 247 3rd St
- Bestway Print & Copy • 9 Columbus Ave
- Better Choice • 654 Sacramento St
- BPS Reprographic Service • 149 2nd St
- Capitol Reprographics • 500 Sansome St
- Copi Solutions • 201 Sansome St

- Copy Central:
  - 9 Maritime Plz
  - 705 Market St
  - 425 California St
  - 110 Sutter St
  - 71 Stevenson St
  - 650 California St
  - 603 Battery St
  - 4 Embarcadero Ctr
- Copy Corps • 500 Sansome St
- Copy Edge • 354 Sansome St
- Copy Mat • 120 Howard St
- Copy Mat • 27 1st St
- Copy Service • 385 Bush St
- Copy Shoppe • 33 Stevenson St
- Copy Star Central • 120 Montgomery St
- Copy Station • 450 Sansome St
- Copy Station • 199 2nd St
- Direct Copy • 50 Post St
- Document Services Unlimited • 447 Battery St
- DTI • 123 2nd St
- International Minute Press • 90 New Montgomery St
- Kaizen Reprographics • 625 Market St
- Kinko's Copies:
  - 369 Pine St
  - 303 2nd St
  - 50 Fremont St
  - 201 Sacramento St
- Krishna Digital Imaging • 150 Columbus Ave
- Let Us Copy • 565 Commercial St
- Metro Copy • 225 Bush St
- Midnight Run Copy • 98 Battery St
- Minuteman Press • 529 Commercial St
- Panda Legal Copy • 23 Stevenson St
- Printing Etc • 260 Kearny St
- Pro Image Printing • 44 Montgomery St
- Professional Copy & Print • 603 Mission St
- Ready Copy • 633 Battery St
- San Francisco Legal Copy • 100 California St
- Speedway Copy Systems:
  - 201 Sansome St
  - 47 Belden Pl
  - 578 Market St
  - 121 Spear St
  - 610 3rd St
  - 524 Washington St
  - 227 Front St
- Speedway Typesetting & Design • 475 4th St
- Techno Reprographics • 465 California St
- Whitmont Legal Copying • 142 Minna St

Gyms

- 24 Hour Fitness • 100 California St
- 24 Hour Fitness • 303 2nd St
- Bally Total Fitness • 345 Spear St
- Bally Total Fitness • 61 New Montgomery St
- Bay Club - Bank of America Center • 555 California St
- Club One • 1 Sansome St
- Club One • 101 California St
- Club One • 350 3rd St
- Federal Fitness Center at 75 • 95 Hawthorne St
- Golden Gateway Fitness & Swim • 370 Drumm St
- Nautilus Health Club • 303 2nd St
- Pinnacle Fitness • 1 Post St
- Pinnacle Fitness • 345 Spear St
- Pinnacle Fitness • 61 New Montgomery St

Hardware Stores

- Cole Fox Hardware • 70 4th St
- EM Hurley Hardware • 617 Bryant St
- Front Ace Hardware • 195 Pine St
- Ginn Wall Hardware • 1016 Grant Ave
- New City Hardware • 809 Kearny St

Liquor Stores

- Broadway Cigars & Liquors • 550 Broadway
- Drumm Liquor & Deli • 15 Drumm St
- John Walker & Co • 175 Sutter St
- K & L Wines & Spirits • 766 Harrison St
- San Francisco Deli & Liquor • 810 Mission St
- Whiskey Shop • 76 Geary St

Movie Theaters

- Landmark Embarcadero • 1 Embarcadero Ctr
- Lowes Theater/IMAX at Metreon • 150 4th St

Pet Shops

- Hung Ming Aquarium • 660 Broadway

Restaurants

- Bacar • 448 Brannan St
- B44 • 44 Belden Pl
- Bix • 56 Gold St
- Boulevard • 1 Mission St
- Cafe Bastille • 22 Beldon Pl
- Caffe Centro • 12 S Park St
- Caffe Macaroni • 50 Columbus Ave
- Elisabeth Daniel Restaurant • 550 Washington St
- Enrico's Sidewalk Café • 504 Broadway
- Fifth Floor • Hotel Palomar, 12 4th St
- Globe • 290 Pacific Ave
- Harbor Village • 4 Embarcadero Ctr
- House of Nanking • 919 Kearny St
- Hunan • 110 Natoma St
- Hunan • 674 Sacramento St
- Hunan Home's Restaurant • 622 Jackson St
- Kokkari Estiatorio • 200 Jackson St
- Kyo-Ya • Palace Hotel, 2 New Montgomery St
- Le Central Bistro • 453 Bush St
- Maya • 303 2nd St
- MoMo's • 760 2nd St
- North Beach Pizza • 715 Harrison St
- One Market • 1 Market St
- Pakwan • 653 Clay St
- Plouf • 40 Belden Pl
- Rubicon • 558 Sacramento St
- Slanted Door • 100 Brannan St
- South Park Cafe • 108 S Park St
- Tadich Grill • 240 California St
- Tommaso's • 1042 Kearny St
- Tommy Toy's Cuisine Chinoise • 655 Montgomery St
- Yank Sing • Rincon Ctr, 101 Spear St
- Zare • 568 Sacramento St

Shopping

- Adolph Gasser • 181 2nd St
- AG Ferrari Fine Foods • 688 Mission St
- Califia Books • 20 Hawthorne St
- City Lights • 261 Columbus Ave
- Discount Cameras • 33 Kearny St
- Don Sherwood's Golf & Tennis World • 320 Grant Ave
- Gump's • 135 Post St
- Japonesque • 824 Montgomery St
- John Walker & Co • 175 Sutter St
- Margaret O'Leary • 1 Claude Ln
- Marina Morrison, Ltd Bridal Salon • 30 Maiden Ln
- Scharffen Berger • Ferry Building, The Embarcadero
- Stacey's Bookstore • 581 Market St
- Sur La Table • 77 Maiden Ln
- Sur La Table • Ferry Building, The Embarcadero
- William Stout Architectural Books • 804 Montgomery St
- Wings America • 262 Sutter St

Video Rental

- Kukjea Video (Korean) • 1030 Kearny St
- South Beach Video • 151 Brannan St
- Starsight Video Entertainment (Cantonese) • 766 Sacramento St

Map 9 • **Haight Ashbury / Cole Valley**

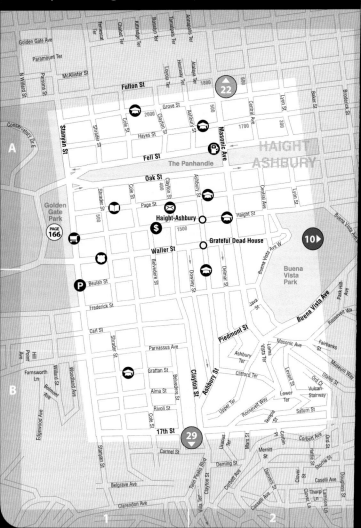

Nothing left to do but smile, smile, smile. It's a little grungy in the Haight, but filled with good ol' tie-dyed flavor. Beware of the pushy young panhandlers, and drugs remain a problem here. There are great examples of old Victorians all over the place. Cole Valley is a more subdued, family-oriented neighborhood. Parking is awful.

9 10 11 12 13
29 14 15 16 17

Ma

$ Banks

- **Wells Fargo** · 1653 Haight St

Gas Stations

- **Chevron** · 1698 Fell St

+ Hospitals

- **St Mary's Medical Center** · 450 Stanyan St

O Landmarks

- **Grateful Dead House** · 710 Ashbury St
- **Haight-Ashbury** · Haight St & Ashbury St

Libraries

- **Park Branch Library** · 1833 Page St

P Parking

Police

- **Park Police Station** · 1699 Waller St

Post Offices

- · 554 Clayton St

Schools

- **Grattan Elementary** · 165 Grattan St
- **John Adams Community College** · 1860 Hayes St
- **Lycee Francais** · 755 Ashbury St
- **New Traditions Alternative** · 2049 Grove St
- **Urban School of San Francisco** · 1563 Page St
- **William R De Avila Elementary School** · 1351 Haight St

Supermarkets

- **CalaFoods** · 690 Stanyan St

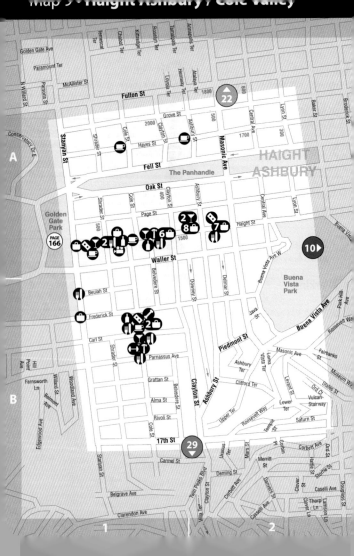

Aside from vestiges of the '60s hippie culture, shopping and nightlife are the main draws to the Upper Haight. Great vintage clothing, shoe stores, independent music, and tattoo and piercing shops abound. Cole Valley, on the other hand, has your mom-and-pop shops and quieter restaurants. There is outstanding cheese at Say Cheese.

Bars

- **Deluxe** · 1511 Haight St
- **Finnegan's Wake** · 937 Cole St
- **Martin Mack's** · 1568 Haight St
- **Murio's Trophy Room** · 1811 Haight St
- **Persian Aub Zam Zam** · 1633 Haight St

Coffee

- **Cantata Coffee Company** · 1708 Haight St
- **Cup a Joe** · 1901 Hayes St
- **Reverie Coffee Café** · 848 Cole St
- **Rockin' Java Coffee House** · 1821 Haight St
- **Sacred Grounds Coffee House** · 2095 Hayes St

Gyms

- **Cole Valley Fitness** · 957 Cole St

Hardware Stores

- **Cole Hardware** · 956 Cole St
- **Roberts Hardware** · 1629 Haight St

Liquor Stores

- **Haight & Cole Liquors** · 1699 Haight St
- **Sunshine Wine & Liquor** · 1754 Haight St
- **Van de Cole Liquors** · 906 Cole St

Movie Theaters

- **Red Vic** · 1727 Haight St

Pet Shops

- **Cole Valley Pets** · 910 Cole St

Restaurants

- **Boulange de Cole Valley** · 1000 Cole St
- **Cha Cha Cha** · 1801 Haight St
- **Eos Restaurant & Wine Bar** · 901 Cole St
- **Kan Zaman** · 1793 Haight St
- **North Beach Pizza** · 1649 Haight St
- **North Beach Pizza** · 800 Stanyan St
- **Pork Store Café** · 1451 Haight St
- **Zazie's** · 941 Cole St

Shopping

- **Ambiance** · 1458 Haight St
- **Amoeba Music** · 1855 Haight St
- **Anubis Warpus** · 1525 Haight St
- **Backseat Betty** · 1590 Haight St
- **Cal Surplus** · 1541 Haight St
- **Crossroads** · 1519 Haight St
- **Discount Fabrics** · 1432 Haight St
- **Haight Ashbury Music Center** · 1540 Haight St
- **Kweejibo** · 1612 Haight St
- **La Rosa Vintage** · 1711 Haight St
- **Luichiny** · 1529 Haight St
- **Mendel's Art Supplies** · 1556 Haight St
- **Occasions Boutique** · 858 Cole St
- **Off the Wall** · 1669 Haight St
- **Piedmont Boutique** · 1452 Haight St
- **Positively Haight** · 1400 Haight St
- **San Francisco Cyclery** · 494 Fredrick St
- **Say Cheese** · 856 Cole St
- **Shoe Biz** · 1446 Haight St
- **Shoe Biz II** · 1553 Haight St
- **Super Shoe Biz** · 1420 Haight St
- **The Booksmith** · 1644 Haight St
- **Villains** · 1672 Haight St
- **Villains Vault** · 1653 Haight St
- **Wasteland** · 1660 Haight St
- **X Generation** · 1401 Haight St

Video Rental

- **Blockbuster Video** · 1855 Haight St
- **Irish Imports (Irish)** · 1439 Haight St
- **Video Nook** · 842 Cole St

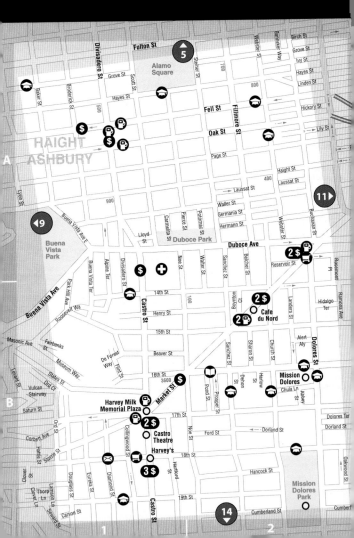

The Castro is the center of the gay community and proud of it. This is a vital neighborhood that always seems to be buzzing. The beautiful Castro Theater is one of San Francisco's last single-screen movie palaces. Nearby Lower Haight is a rougher and more diverse neighborhood. Not as touristy as the Upper Haight, it is full of grungy local flavor.

Banks

- **Bank of America** · 45 Castro St
- **Bank of America** · 501 Castro St
- **Bank of America** · 1275 Fell St
- **Bay View Bank** · 443 Castro St
- **California Federal Bank** · 444 Castro St
- **California Federal Bank** · 2099 Market St
- **Sterling Bank & Trust** · 2122 Market St
- **Wells Fargo** · 2020 Market St
- **Wells Fargo** · 2308 Market St
- **Wells Fargo** · 498 Castro St
- **Wells Fargo** · 557 Castro St
- **Wells Fargo** · 425 Divisadero St
- **Wells Fargo** · 2020 Market St

Gas Stations

- **76** · 1998 Market St
- **76** · 2175 Market St
- **76** · 443 Divisadero St
- **Arco** · 1175 Fell St
- **Arco** · 376 Castro St
- **Chevron** · 2399 Market St
- **Shell** · 1070 Oak St
- **Shell** · 2198 Market St

Hospitals

- **California Pacific Medical Center—Davies Campus** · Castro St & Duboce St

O Landmarks

- **Café du Nord** · 2170 Market St
- **Castro Theatre** · 429 Castro St
- **Harvey Milk Memorial Plaza** · 400 Castro St

- **Harvey's** · 500 Castro St
- **Mission Dolores** · 3321 16th St
- **Mission Dolores Park** · Church St & 18th St

Libraries

- **Eureka Valley / Harvey Milk Memorial Library** · 3555 16th St

Post Offices

- · 4304 18th St

Schools

- **Children's Day School** · 333 Dolores St
- **Everett Middle School** · 450 Church St
- **Harvey Milk Civil Rights Academy** · 4235 19th St
- **Ida B Wells High School** · 1099 Hayes St
- **John Muir Elementary** · 380 Webster St
- **McKinley Elementary** · 1025 14th St
- **Mission Dolores** · 3321 16th St
- **Mission High School** · 3750 18th St
- **Pacific Primary School** · 1500 Grove St
- **Sacred Heart Elementary** · 735 Fell St
- **Sanchez Elementary** · 325 Sanchez St

Supermarkets

- **CalaFoods** · 4201 18th St
- **Safeway** · 2020 Market St

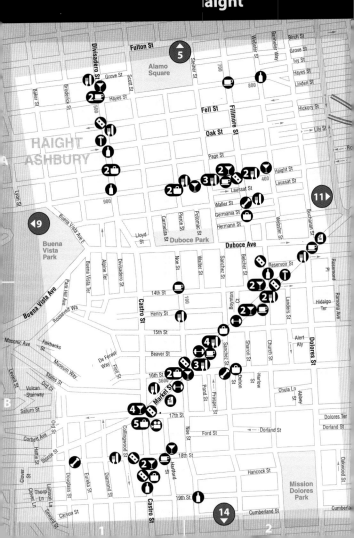

We love the soups and salad bar at Harvest Market. RNM is a great newcomer to the restaurant scene in the Lower Haight. There's a plethora of bars to support the vibrant nightlife in both of these neighborhoods. Check out Midnight Sun in the Castro. Toronado on Haight has an outstanding selection of beers. Cafe du Nord is an excellent venue for live music.

Bars

- **Café Du Nord** · 2170 Market St
- **Detour** · 2348 Market St
- **Harvey's** · 500 Castro St
- **Justice League** · 628 Divisadero St
- **Lucky 13** · 2140 Market St
- **Mad Dog in the Fog** · 530 Haight St
- **Midnight Sun** · 4067 18th St
- **Nickie's BBQ** · 460 Haight St
- **Noc Noc** · 557 Haight St
- **Pilsner Inn** · 225 Church St
- **The Badlands** · 4121 18th St
- **The Bar on Castro** · 456B Castro St
- **The Café** · 2367 Market St
- **The Metro Bar and Restaurant** · 3600 16th St
- **The Transfer** · 198 Church St
- **The Twin Peaks** · 401 Castro St
- **Toronado** · 647 Haight St

Coffee

- **Bean Bag Coffee House** · 601 Divisadero St
- **Fillmore Grind Coffee House** · 711 Fillmore St
- **Horse Shoe Coffee House** · 566 Haight St
- **Jumpin' Java Coffee House** · 139 Noe St
- **Muddy Waters Coffee House** · 262 Church St
- **Peet's** · 2257 Market St
- **Sawa Café** · 559 Divisadero St
- **Starbucks** · 2018 Market St
- **Starbucks** · 4094 18th St

Copy Shops

- **Copy Central** · 2336 Market St
- **Kinko's Copies** · 1967 Market St

Gyms

- **24 Hour Fitness** · 2145 Market St
- **Gold's Gym** · 2301 Market St
- **Muscle System** · 2275 Market St

Hardware Stores

- **Handy Handyman Hardware** · 2075 Market St
- **SF Hardware** · 512 Divisadero St

Liquor Stores

- **Friendly Spirits** · 572 Castro St
- **George's Market & Deli** · 702 14th St
- **H & W Liquors** · 801 Hayes St
- **Haight & Devisadero Liquor** · 250 Divisadero St
- **New Star Ell Liquors** · 501 Divisadero St
- **Noe Hill Market** · 4001 19th St

Movie Theaters

- **Castro Theater** · Castro St & Market St

Pet Shops

- **Best in Show** · 300 Sanchez St
- **Health Wize for Pets** · 157 Fillmore St
- **My Best Friend** · 4455 18th St

Restaurants

- **2223 Restaurant** · 2223 Market St
- **Brother-in-Law's Bar-B-Que** · 705 Divisadero St
- **Burger Joint** · 700 Haight St
- **Café Flore** · 2298 Market St
- **Chow** · 215 Church St
- **Harvest Market** · 2258 Market St
- **Home** · 2100 Market St
- **Indian Oven** · 233 Fillmore St
- **Kate's Kitchen** · 471 Haight St
- **La Mediterranee** · 288 Noe St
- **Ma Tante Sumi** · 4243 18th St
- **Mecca** · 2029 Market St
- **Pasta Pomodoro** · 598 Haight St
- **Pasta Pomodoro** · 2304 Market St
- **RNM** · 598 Haight St
- **Rosamunde Sausage Grill** · 545 Haight St
- **Thai House** · 2200 Market St
- **Thai House** · 151 Noe St
- **Thep Phanom Thai Cuisine** · 400 Waller St
- **Tin-Pan Asian Bistro** · 2251 Market St
- **Zao Noodle Bar** · 3583 16th St

Shopping

- **A Different Light** · 489 Castro St
- **AG Ferrari Fine Foods** · 468 Castro St
- **Best in Show** · 300 Sanchez St
- **Cookin'** · 339 Divisadero St
- **Costumes on Haight** · 735 Haight St
- **Crossroads** · 2231 Market St
- **Gamescape** · 333 Divisadero St
- **Groove Merchant** · 687 Haight St
- **H Starch** · 142 Fillmore St
- **Harvest Market** · 2285 Market St
- **Manasek** · 2344 Market St
- **Only on Castro** · 518A Castro St
- **Streetlight Records** · 2350 Market St
- **The Bead Store** · 417 Castro St
- **Tower Records** · 2280 Market St

Video Rental

- **Blockbuster Video** · 160 Church St
- **Castro Video** · 2358 Market St
- **Castro Video** · 525 Castro St
- **Lee's Divisadero Video** · 542 Divisadero St
- **Naked Eye News & Video** · 533 Haight St
- **Superstar Video** · 3989 17th St
- **Superstar Video 18th** · 4141 18th St
- **Tower Records/Video/Books** · 2280 Market St
- **Video Control** · 2095 Market St

Hayes Valley has really improved over the years and now it's a great offbeat little shopping district. South of Market street is a small, gritty, happening part of the larger Mission District. Valencia Street is really cool with unusual and one-of-a-kind boutiques, and Mission Street is the bustling center of Latino culture.

$ Banks

- **Bank of America** · 1525 Market St
- **Bank of America** · 10 S Van Ness Ave
- **Bank of America** · 2017 Mission St
- **California Savings & Loan** · 3000 16th St
- **Mission National Bank** · 3060 16th St
- **Wells Fargo** · 3027 16th St
- **Wells Fargo** · 2300 16th St

Car Rental

- **City Rent-A-Car** · 1748 Folsom St
- **Hertz** · 241 10th St
- **National** · 1600 Mission St
- **Specialty Car Rentals** · 1600 Mission St

Car Washes

- **Auto City Brushless Car Wash** · 505 S Van Ness Ave
- **California Detailing** · 340 Fell St
- **Tenth & Harrison Car Wash** · 1394 Harrison St

Gas Stations

- **Arco** · 1798 Mission St
- **Auto City Brushless Car Wash** · 505 S Van Ness Ave
- **Mission Self Service** · 599 S Van Ness Ave
- **Shell** · 400 Guerrero St
- **Shell** · 400 S Van Ness Ave
- **Shell** · 793 S Van Ness Ave

O Landmarks

- **Good Vibrations** · 601B Valencia St
- **Maestrapeace** · 18th St & Valencia St

Libraries

- **City and County Law Library** · 1390 Market St

P Parking

Police

- **Mission Police Station** · 630 Valencia St

Post Offices

- 1600 Bryant St
- 1390 Market St
- 1655 Bryant St

Schools

- **Alternative/Opportunity** · 135 Van Ness Ave
- **California Institute of Integral Studies** · 1453 Mission St
- **Chinese American Intl School** · 150 Oak St
- **County Community Day School** · 1950 Mission St
- **French-American Intl School** · 150 Oak St
- **John O'Connell Alternative High School** · 2355 Folsom St
- **Marshall Elementary** · 1575 15th St
- **Mission Language & Vocational** · 2929 19th St
- **New College of California** · 777 Valencia St
- **San Francisco Law School** · 20 Haight St
- **St Charles School** · 3250 18th St
- **The Walden School** · 214 Haight St
- **UC Berkeley Extension** · 55 Laguna St

Supermarkets

- **Costco** · 450 10th St

Map 11 · **Hayes Va**

Alabaster, for alabaster, is just one of the unique shops on Hayes; there are so many more. Suppenkuche is great for beer and German food. Flax on Market is excellent for art supplies. Subterranean Shoe Room on Valencia is your stop for cool, urban sneakers.

Bars

- **Beauty Bar** • 2299 Mission St
- **Dalva** • 3121 16th St
- **DNA Lounge** • 375 11th St
- **Doctor Bombay's** • 3192 16th St
- **Elbo Room** • 647 Valencia St
- **Este Noche** • 3079 16th St
- **Hayes & Vine** • 377 Hayes St
- **Kilowatt** • 3160 16th St
- **Lexington** • 3464 19th St
- **Liquid** • 2925 16th St
- **Martuni's** • 4 Valencia St
- **Paradise Lounge Transmission Theater** • 1501 Folsom St
- **Slim's** • 333 11th St
- **The Albion** • 3139 16th St
- **Twenty Tank Brewery** • 316 11th St

Coffee

- **Muddy Waters Coffee House** • 521 Valencia St
- **Peet's** • 2300 16th St
- **Starbucks** • 2300 16th St
- **Starbucks** • 2727 Mariposa St

Copy Shops

- **A Print 1** • 1540 Market St
- **Cyber Copy** • 3128 16th St
- **Preferred Legal Service** • 210 Fell St
- **Strategic Office Solutions** • 1540 Market St

Gyms

- **24 Hour Fitness** • 1645 Bryant St
- **Valencia St Muscle & Fitness** • 333 Valencia St

Hardware Stores

- **City Door & Hardware** • 165 13th St
- **Discount Builders Supply** • 1695 Mission St

Liquor Stores

- **Fred's Liquor & Delicatessen** • 200 Valencia St
- **Stagi Sixteenth St Liquors** • 3055 16th St
- **Victoria Liquors & Sandwiches** • 201 Gough St

Movie Theaters

- **Roxie** • 3117 16th St

Pet Shops

- **Amore Animal Supplies** • 696 Valencia St
- **Petco** • 1685 Bryant St

Restaurants

- **Absinthe** • 398 Hayes St
- **Andalu** • 3198 16th St
- **Blowfish, Sushi To Die For** • 2170 Bryant St
- **Burger Joint** • 807 Valencia St
- **Caffe Delle Stelle** • 395 Hayes St
- **Cha Cha Cha @ Original McCarthy's** • 2327 Mission St
- **Chez Spencer** • 82 14th St
- **Citizen Cake** • 399 Grove St
- **Delfina** • 3621 18th St
- **Hayes Street Grill** • 320 Hayes St
- **It's Tops Coffee Shop** • 1801 Market St
- **Jardiniare** • 300 Grove St
- **Manora's Thai Cuisine** • 1600 Folsom St
- **paul K** • 199 Gough St
- **Suppenkuche** • 601 Hayes St
- **Sushi Groove** • 1516 Folsom St
- **Taqueria Can-Cun** • 2211 Mission St
- **Tartine Bakery** • 600 Guerrero St
- **Ti Couz** • 3108 16th St
- **Timo's** • 842 Valencia St
- **Tokyo Go Go** • 3174 16th St
- **Universal Café** • 2814 19th St
- **Vicolo** • 201 Ivy St
- **Zuni Café** • 1658 Market St

Shopping

- **826 Valencia** • 826 Valencia St
- **AC Trading** • 2370 Mission St
- **Alabaster** • 597 Hayes St
- **Alternative Design Studio** • 3458 18th St
- **Anderson Harrison** • 552 Hayes St
- **Babies** • 235 Gough St
- **Bombay Ice Creamery** • 552 Valencia St
- **Borderlands** • 866 Valencia St
- **Buu** • 506 Hayes St
- **Champ de Mars** • 347 Hayes St
- **Dark Garden** • 321 Linden St
- **El Toro Taqueria** • 588 Valencia St
- **Evelyn's** • 381 Hayes St
- **Flax** • 1699 Market St
- **Flight 001** • 525 Hayes St
- **Get Lost** • 1825 Market St
- **Gimme Shoes** • 416 Hayes St
- **Good Vibrations** • 601B Valencia St
- **Howling Bull Syndicate** • 826 Valencia St
- **Limon** • 3316 17th St
- **M&W** • 2352 Mission St
- **Midori Mushi** • 465 Grove St
- **Pakwan** • 3180 16th St
- **Paxton's Gate** • 824 Valencia St
- **Pomp** • 516 Hayes St
- **Prop City** • 1645 Market St
- **Rainbow Grocery** • 1745 Folsom St
- **Subterranean Shoe Room** • 877 Valencia St
- **Taqueria Pancho Villa** • 3071 16th St
- **Trout Farm Retrospect Fine Furniture** • 1649 Market St

Video Rental

- **Blockbuster Video** • 2300 16th St
- **Into Video** • 552 Hayes St
- **Leather Tongue Video** • 714 Valencia St
- **Pyramid Video** • 299 Guerrero St

Map 12 • **SOMA / P**   **hill (North)**

Also known as the "wine country," the area around 6th street in this part of SOMA is pretty run-down. Most people drive through here only on their way to the freeway. Defenestration, the building at 6th & Howard with the furniture all over it, is a wonderful piece of urban art. Potrero Hill, south of Division, is where a lot of the city's interior designers work. And don't miss the Anchor Brewing Co. (you can take a tour).

$ Banks

- **Bank of America** · 680 8th St
- **Business Bank** · 640 Townsend St
- **First National Bank-Northern** · 640 Brannan St
- **San Francisco Federal CU** · 850 Bryant St

Car Rental

- **Enterprise** · 312 8th St · 415-703-9000
- **Thrifty** · 229 7th St · 415-788-8111

Car Washes

- **Apex Hand Car Washing and Detailing** · 301 6th St
- **Wo Wo Wash** · 1001 Harrison St

Gas Stations

- **76** · 401 Potrero Ave
- **Chevron** · 1000 Harrison St
- **Shell** · 1201 Harrison St
- **Shell** · 377 6th St
- **Shell** · 388 Potrero Ave

O Landmarks

- **Anchor Brewing Company** · 1705 Mariposa St
- **Flower Mart** · 640 Brannan St

P Parking

Police

- **Southern Police Station** · 850 Bryant St

Schools

- **Bessie Carmichael Elemantary** · 55 Sherman St
- **California College of Arts and Crafts** · 1111 8th St
- **Enola Maxwell Middle School** · 655 De Haro St
- **International Studies Academy** · 693 Vermont St
- **Life Learning Academy** · 651 8th St
- **Live Oak School** · 1555 Mariposa St

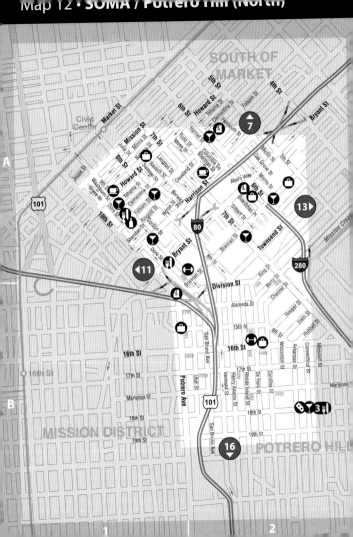

Map 12 • **SOMA / Potrero Hill (North)**

SOUTH OF
MARKET

Civic
Center

Market St

Mission St

5th St

Howard St

9th St

Tehama St

Clementina St

Folsom St

Clara St

4th St

Bryant St

7

Jessie St

Julia St

Minna St

7th St

8th St

Howard St

Natoma St

Langton St

Russ St

Moss St

Russ St

Rausch St

Columbia Sq

Cleveland St

Gordon St

Sumner St

Mission St

Harrison St

Merlin St

Oak Grove St

5th St

Morris St

Ahern Way

6th St

Bowman St

13▶

A

10th St

Washburn St

Dore St

Tehama St

Clementina St

Folsom St

Shipley St

Clara St

Sheridan St

Hallam St

Ringold St

Brush St

Harrison St

Hylton St

7th St

Gilbert St

Townsend St

Brannan St

8th St

Bryant St

Dore St

Brannan St

◀11

Division St

King St

Berry St

Channel St

Alameda St

Hooper St

Irwin St

Hubbell St

80

280

Mission Creek

2200

15th St

2000

16th St

16th St

101

San Bruno Ave

Potrero Ave

8th St

Wisconsin St

Arkansas St

Connecticut St

Missouri St

1400

Utah St

Vermont St

Henry Adams St

Rhode Island St

De Haro St

Carolina St

1500

Mariposa

16th St

17th St

2200

17th St

Mariposa St

18th St

101

18th St

3

B

MISSION DISTRICT

19th St

19th St

16
▼

POTRERO HILL

1

2

Lots of nightlife south of Market here. End Up never seems to close, so if you run out of places to go, head there for late-night dancing. The Flower Market really is the best place to buy flowers, but go early. This part of Potrero Hill has some great neighborhood restaurants—try Chez Papa for French, Thanya and Sallee for Thai, and Goat Hill Pizza for…pizza.

Bars

- **Asia SF** · 201 9th St
- **Cat Club** · 1190 Folsom St
- **Endup** · 401 6th St
- **Lingba Lounge** · 1469 18th St
- **Mars Café** · 798 Brannan St
- **Ten15 Folsom** · 1015 Folsom St
- **The Stud** · 399 9th St

Coffee

- **SF Coffee Company** · 12 Sherman St
- **Starbucks** · 1298 Howard St

Copy Shops

- **City Copy & Sign** · 960 Folsom St
- **Document Overflow Center** · 314 Harriet St
- **Lone Star Legal & Copy Service** · 340 Division St

Gyms

- **Gold's Gym** · 1001 Brannan St
- **World Gym Fitness Center** · 290 De Haro St

Liquor Stores

- **Diana** · 282 9th St

Restaurants

- **AsiaSF** · 201 9th St
- **Chez Papa** · 1401 18th St
- **Eliza's** · 1457 18th St
- **Goat Hill Pizza** · 300 Connecticut St
- **Hunan** · 1016 Bryant St

Shopping

- **Flower Mart** · 640 Brannan St
- **Joseph Schmidt Confections** · 1489 16th St
- **Podesta Baldocci** · 410 Harriet St
- **Stormy Leather** · 1158 Howard St
- **The Ribbonerie** · 191 Potrero Ave

Video Rental

- **Dr Video** · 1521 18th St

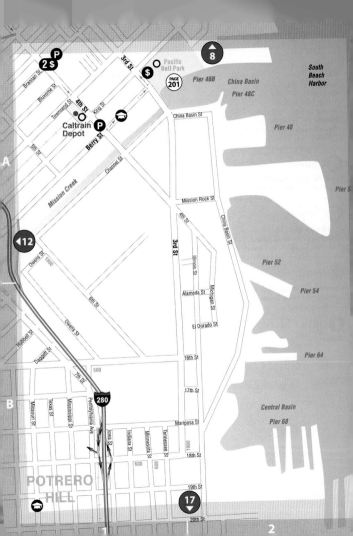

Pac Bell Park is here, so the place gets jammed when there's a Giants game. The city has cleaned up the area really well for the new ballpark, but there is still mainly an industrial aesthetic here. The CalTrain station is also here, so the area stays busy with commuters.

9 10 11 13
29 14 15 16 17

Ma

$ Banks

- **Bank of America** · 501 Brannan St
- **Wells Fargo** · 737 3rd St
- **Wells Fargo** · 490 Brannan St

O Landmarks

- **Caltrain Depot** · 4th St & King St
- **Pacific Bell Park** · 24 Willie Mays Plaza

P Parking

Schools

- **Daniel Webster Elementary** · 465 Missouri St
- **University of Phoenix Learning** · 185 Berry St

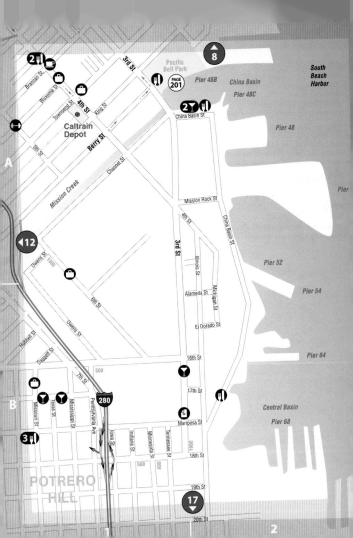

Brannan St
Bluxome St
4th St
3rd St
Townsend St
King St
Caltrain Depot
Berry St
5th St
Channel St
Mission Creek

Pacific Bell Park
PAGE 201
Pier 46B
China Basin
Pier 48C
China Basin St
China Basin St
Pier 48
Mission Rock St
4th St
3rd St
Illinois St
Pier 52
Alameda St
Michigan St
Pier 54
El Dorado St
Owens St
1000
6th St
Hubbell St
Daggett St
7th St
500
16th St
Pier 64
17th St
Missouri St
Texas St
Mississippi St
Pennsylvania Ave
280
Iowa St
Indiana St
Minnesota St
Tennessee St
Mariposa St
1000
900
18th St
600
19th St
POTRERO HILL
20th St

South Beach Harbor
Pier
Central Basin
Pier 68

8
12
17

K&L is the best place to buy wine in town, and Sports Basement is a big draw for warehouse-priced sporting goods. Go to Mission Bay Golf Center for a two-story urban driving range. Go to The Ramp to kick back, listen to live music, and have a drink on the water.

Bars

- **Bottom of the Hill** · 1233 17th St
- **Sno-Drift** · 1830 3rd St
- **The Ramp** · 855 China Basin St

Coffee

- **Starbucks** · 490 Brannan St

Copy Shops

- **Pip Printing** · 2001 3rd St

Gyms

- **San Francisco Tennis Club** · 645 5th St

Restaurants

- **Acme Chop House** · 24 Willie Mays Plaza
- **Aperto** · 1434 18th St
- **Bizou** · 598 4th St
- **Chez Papa Bistrot** · 1401 18th St
- **Fringale** · 570 4th St
- **Kelly's Mission Rock** · 817 China Basin St
- **The Ramp** · 855 Terry Francois Blvd
- **Thanya & Sales** · 1469 18th St

Shopping

- **Arch** · 99 Missouri St
- **K & L Wine Merchants** · 638 4th St
- **Limn** · 290 Townsend St
- **Sports Basement** · 1301 6th St

9 10 11 12 13
29 14 15 16 17

Ma

As they say, "The sun always shines in Noe Valley." Formerly known as a primarily lesbian neighborhood, Noe Valley continues to grow with more and more families moving in. The Victorians, the restaurants, and the assorted shops give this area an intimate neighborhood feel. Parking is manageable but never easy.

$ Banks

- **Bank of America** · 4098 24th St
- **Washington Mutual** · 3998 24th St
- **Wells Fargo** · 4023 24th St

✳ Community Gardens

📖 Libraries

- **Noe Valley Branch Library / Sally Brunn** ·
  451 Jersey St

🚌 Schools

- **Alvarado Elementary** · 625 Douglass St
- **Edison Charter Academy** · 3531 22nd St
- **Immaculate Conception Academy** · 3625 24th St
- **James Lick Middle School** · 1220 Noe St
- **St James School** · 321 Fair Oaks St
- **St Philip's School** · 665 Elizabeth St

The nightlife scene in Noe Valley is a bit mellow, but the restaurant scene makes up for it. Firefly is a neighborhood institution. The Noe Valley Bread Co. makes wonderful breads, and Plumpjack Wines has a great selection of good and lesser-known wines. Go to Miss Millie's for breakfast.

Bars

- **Noe's Bar** · 1199 Church St
- **Rat and Raven** · 4054 24th St
- **The Dubliner** · 3838 24th St

Coffee

- **Starbucks** · 3995 24th St

Copy Shops

- **Jensen's Mail & Copy** ·
  5214 Diamond Heights Blvd

Gyms

- **Purely Physical Fitness** · 1300 Church St

Hardware Stores

- **Tuggey's Hardware** · 3885 24th St

Liquor Stores

- **Graystone Wine & Liquors** · 4100 24th St
- **J & J Grocery & Liquor** · 3751 24th St
- **Mama's Market** · 3500 22nd St
- **Plumpjack Wines Noe Valley** · 4011 24th St
- **St Clair Liquors** · 3900 24th St

Pet Shops

- **Animal Company** · 4298 24th St
- **Noe Valley Pet Co** · 1451 Church St

Restaurants

- **Chloe's Café** · 1399 Church st
- **Eric's** · 1500 Church St
- **Firefly** · 4288 24th St
- **Lovejoy's Tea Room** · 1351 Church St
- **Miss Millie's** · 4123 24th St
- **Pasta Pomodoro** · 4000 24th St

Shopping

- **Ambiance** · 3985 24th St
- **Noe Valley Bread Co** · 4073 24th St
- **Plumpjack Wines** · 4011 24th St
- **See Jane Run** · 3870 24th St
- **Streetlight Records** · 3979 24th St

Video Rental

- **Noe Valley Video** · 3936 24th St
- **Video Wave of Noe Valley** · 1431 Castro St
- **West Coast Video** · 1201 Church St

Here you're in the thick of the Mission's largely Latino flavor. It's rough, grubby, and bustling with ethnic diversity—and there is a real sense of community. This is also one of the warmest neighborhoods in terms of weather.

$ Banks

- **Bank of America** · 2701 Mission St
- **Bank of America** · 2850 24th St
- **Bank of the West** · 2501 Mission St
- **Bay View Bank** · 2601 Mission St
- **Pan American Bank** · 2773 Mission St
- **Washington Mutual** · 2900 Mission St
- **Wells Fargo** · 2595 Mission St

✳ Community Gardens

⛽ Gas Stations

- **76** · 1298 Valencia St
- **76** · 2831 Cesar Chavez St
- **Abbas's Alliance Service** · 2901 Bryant St
- **Chevron** · 1198 Valencia St
- **Shell** · 899 Valencia St

📖 Libraries

- **Mission Branch Library** · 300 Bartlett St

✉ Post Offices

- 1198 S Van Ness Ave

🚍 Schools

- **Bryant Elementary** · 1050 York St
- **Cesar Chavez Elementary** · 825 Shotwell St
- **Downtown High School** · 110 Bartlett St
- **George R Moscone Elementary** · 2576 Harrison St
- **Horace Mann Middle School** · 3351 23rd St
- **Katherine Michiels School** · 1335 Guerrero St
- **Leonard Flynn Elementary** · 3125 Cesar Chavez St
- **Mission Campus of CCSF** · 106 Bartlett St
- **Synergy Elementary** · 1387 Valencia St

🛒 Supermarkets

- **CalaFoods** · 1245 S VanNess Ave

Map 15 · **Mission (Outer)**

Trendy restaurants next to authentic taquerias and hip bars define this area. La Taqueria hands down has the best tacos in town. If you need that old red booth supper club vibe, go to Bruno's. Herbivore has good, clean vegetarian options.

Bars

- **26 Mix** · 3024 Mission St
- **Latin American Club** · 3286 22nd St
- **Lone Palm** · 3394 22nd St
- **The Make-Out Room** · 3225 22nd St

Hardware Stores

- **House of Color** · 2862 24th St
- **U Save Plumbing & Hardware** · 1146 Valencia St
- **Workingman's Headquarters** · 2871 Mission St

Liquor Stores

- **ABC Market** · 2801 Bryant St
- **Cobo's Liquor Market** · 2681 21st St
- **Ed & Danny's Market & Liquor** ·
  999 S Van Ness Ave
- **Gateway Liquor & Deli Market** · 3101 24th St
- **Jessie's Market** · 3380 20th St
- **Mike's Liquors & Groceries** · 2499 Mission St
- **P & S Liquor Store** · 3100 24th St
- **Samy's Liquor and Groceries** · 2847 24th St
- **That's It Market** · 2699 Mission St
- **Tony's Market and Liquor** · 2751 24th St

Movie Theaters

- **Foreign Cinema** · 2534 Mission St

Pet Shops

- **Bernie's Pet Supply & Grooming** ·
  1367 Valencia St

Restaurants

- **Bruno's** · 2389 Mission St
- **Cha Cha Cha** · 2327 Mission St
- **Firecracker** · 1007 1/2 Valencia St
- **Foreign Cinema** · 2534 Mission St
- **Herbivore** · 983 Valencia St
- **Jay's Cheese Steak** · 3285 21st St
- **La Luna** · 3126 24th St
- **La Rondalla** · 901 Valencia St
- **La Taqueria** · 2889 Mission St
- **Roosevelt Tamale Parlor** · 2817 24th St
- **Watergate** · 1152 Valencia St

Shopping

- **Aquarius Records** · 1055 Valencia St
- **Retro Fit** · 910 Valencia St
- **The Freewheel** · 980 Valencia St
- **Valencia Cyclery** · 1077 Valencia St
- **X-21 Modern** · 896 Valencia St

Video Rental

- **Hollywood Video** · 1575 S Van Ness Ave
- **Lost Weekend Video** · 1034 Valencia St
- **Midnight Video** · 2999 Mission St
- **US Video** · 2969 Mission St
- **World Pioneer Video** · 2830 24th St

This part of Potrero Hill is predominately residential. The views of downtown are really good and the weather here is generally better than in the rest of San Francisco. The old Magdalene Grotto and San Francisco General are here, too.

Community Gardens

Hospitals
· **San Francisco General Hospital** ·
1001 Potrero Ave

Libraries
· **Potrero Library** · 1616 20th St

Schools
· **Buena Vista Alternative Elementary** ·
 2641 25th St
· **Daniel Webster Elementary School** ·
 456 Mission St
· **Meadows-Livingstone School** · 1499 Potrero Ave
· **Starr King Elementary** · 1215 Carolina St

The restaurant and bar scene here is generally nonexistent. If you want to go out or buy something, head to the northern part of Potrero Hill (Map 12).

 # Liquor Stores

• **L & L Liquors** • 2449 23rd St

 # Restaurants

• **Klein's Delicatessen** • 501 Connecticut St

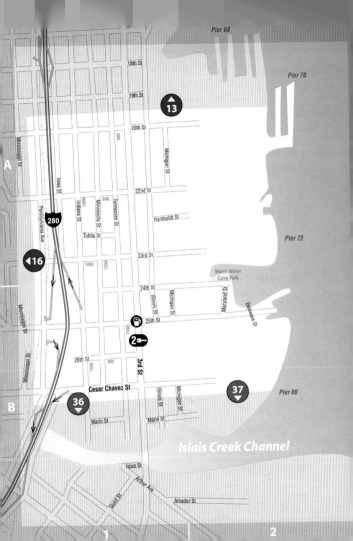

This edge of Potero Hill is totally industrial with warehouses and some loft spaces.

Car Rental

- **Priceless Rent-A-Car** · 2955 3rd St
- **Rent A Wreck** · 2955 3rd St

Gas Stations

- **Shell** · 2890 3rd St

Map 17 · **Potrero Hill (Southeast)**

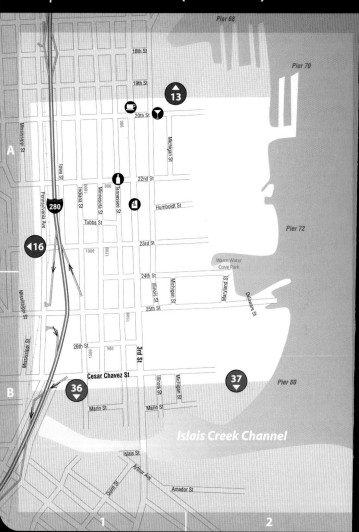

Bars
· **Sublounge** · 628 20th St

 Coffee
· **Tropicana Coffee Shop** · 2291 3rd St

Copy Shops
· **Copyworld** · 2565 3rd St

Liquor Stores
· **Reno's Liquor Store** · 728 22nd St

Map 18 • **Outer Richmond (West)/Ocean Beach**

Pacific Ocean

Lincoln Park

PAGE 171

El Camino Del Mar

Lincoln
Munic
Golf Co

A

POINT LOBOS

Veteran Affairs
Medical Center

Clement St

400

Seal Rock Dr

Alta Mar Way

Merrie Way

Point Lobos Ave

Point Lobos Ave

Geary Blvd

7900

500

Sutro
Heights
Park

48th Ave

47th Ave

46th Ave

45th Ave

44th Ave

43rd Ave

42nd Ave

41st Ave

40th Ave

39th Ave

500

500

Anza St

Seal
Rocks
State
Beach

5500

600

Sutro Heights Ave

19

Upper Great Hwy

Balboa St

La Playa St

700

4200

Cabrillo St

4600

32

B

Golden
Gate
National
Recreation
Area

Fulton St

Golden
Gate
Park

John F Kennedy Dr

Golden Gate
Municipal
Golf Course

North Lake

PAGE 166

Chain Of Lakes Dr W

John F Ken

Chain Of Lakes Dr E

Middle L

Great Hwy

1

2

This largely residential area is foggy more often than not. Skip the Cliff House and check out the ruins at the Sutro Baths. The Palace of the Legion of Honor is the most beautiful museum we have in the city. Four miles of Ocean Beach starts here, just south of the Cliff House.

$ Banks

- **Wells Fargo** · 850 La Playa St

✚ Hospitals

- **San Francisco VA Medical Center** · 4150 Clement St

O Landmarks

- **Cliff House** · 1090 Point Lobos Ave
- **Fort Miley** · El Camino Del Mar @ Clement St
- **Palace of the Legion of Honor** · 34th Ave & Clement St
- **Sutro Baths** · Just west of Cliff House on Point Lobos Ave

Schools

- **California Vocational College** · 3951 Balboa St
- **St Thomas The Apostle School** · 3801 Balboa St

🛒 Supermarkets

- **Safeway** · 850 La Playa St

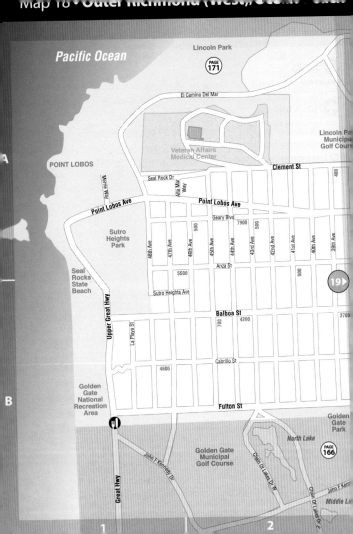

Map 18 • **Outer Richmond (West,** Ocean

Pacific Ocean

Lincoln Park

PAGE 171

El Camino Del Mar

Veteran Affairs
Medical Center

Lincoln Pa
Municipa
Golf Cours

Clement St

400

POINT LOBOS

Seal Rock Dr

Alta Mar Way

Point Lobos Ave

Point Lobos Ave

Merrie Way

Geary Blvd

7900

500

Sutro
Heights
Park

48th Ave

47th Ave

46th Ave

45th Ave

44th Ave

43rd Ave

42nd Ave

41st Ave

40th Ave

39th Ave

500

Anza St

5500

600

Seal
Rocks
State
Beach

Sutro Heights Ave

19▶

Upper Great Hwy

Balboa St

4200

3700

La Playa St

700

Cabrillo St

4600

Golden
Gate
National
Recreation
Area

Fulton St

Golden
Gate
Park

North Lake

PAGE 166

John F Kennedy Dr

Golden Gate
Municipal
Golf Course

Chain Of Lakes Dr W

Chain Of Lakes Dr E

John F Kenn

Middle La

Great Hwy

1

2

There's not a lot going on out here if you're not a surfer living in the city. If you're at the beach, stop by the Beach Chalet for a beer.

23 24 25 29

Ma

Restaurants

· **Beach Chalet Brewery** · 1000 Great Hwy

Map 19

Pacific Ocean

South Bay

China Beach
PAGE 197

Gibson Rd

25th Ave N

Sea Cliff Ave

Scenic Way

25th

El Camino Del Mar

W Clay St

Golden Gate National Recreation Area

McLaren Ave

28th Ave

Lake St

200

El Camino Del Mar

Lake St

2800

A

California St

300

Lincoln Park
Golf Course

Legion of Honor Dr

Sea View Ter

Marvel
Ct

32nd Ave

◄18

Clement St.

2700

400

20►

Shore View Ave

400

400

31st Ave

Geary Blvd

6500

30th Ave

29th Ave

28th Ave

27th Ave

26th Ave

25th Ave

24th Ave

23rd Ave

500

7000

500

39th Ave

38th Ave

37th Ave

36th Ave

35th Ave

34th Ave

33rd Ave

32nd Ave

4400

600

Anza St

3600

600

700

**George
Washington
Park**

31st Ave

700

Balboa St

2800

RICHMOND

B

3700

Cabrillo St

25th Ave

Fulton St

30th Ave

31st Ave

30th Ave

Spreckels Lake Dr

Spreckels Lake

Golden Gate Park

Marx Meadow Dr

PAGE 166

1

2

Exclusive Seacliff has some of the most beautiful homes and views in the city. Just inland is the bland but more affordable Richmond district. This is a largely residential area.

$ Banks

- **Bank of America** · 3701 Balboa St
- **California Federal Bank** · 6100 Geary Blvd
- **United Commercial Bank** · 6001 Geary Blvd
- **United Commercial Bank** · 3555 Balboa St

Community Gardens

Gas Stations

- **76** · 301 25th Ave
- **76** · 7355 Geary Blvd
- **Chevron** · 6000 Geary Blvd

O Landmarks

- **Lincoln Park Golf Course** · 300 34th Ave

Libraries

- **Anza Branch Library** · 550 37th Ave

Schools

- **Cabrillo Elementary** · 735 24th Ave
- **George Washington High School** · 600 32nd Ave
- **Katherine Delmar Burke School** · 7070 California St
- **Kittredge School** · 2355 Lake St
- **Lafayette Elementary** · 4545 Anza St
- **Mother Goose School** · 334 28th Ave
- **Presidio Middle School** · 450 30th Ave
- **St John of SF Orthodox Academy** · 6210 Geary Blvd
- **The Freeman School** · 862 28th Ave

Supermarkets

- **CalaFoods** · 6333 Geary Blvd

Map 19 Outer Richmond (East, South)

Pacific Ocean

South Bay

China Beach
PAGE 197

Golden Gate National Recreation Area

Gibson Rd

26th Ave N

Seal Cliff Ave

Scenic Way

25th Ave

El Camino Del Mar

W Clay St

El Camino Del Mar

28th Ave

McLaren Ave

Lake St

32nd Ave

Lake St

200

Sea View Ter

Lincoln Park
Golf Course

Legion of Honor Dr

◄18

2800

California St

300

Marvel
Ct

Clement St

2700

400

20►

400

400

Shore View Ave

31st Ave

Geary Blvd

6500

500

25th Ave

39th Ave

38th Ave

37th Ave

36th Ave

35th Ave

34th Ave

33rd Ave

32nd Ave

30th Ave

29th Ave

28th Ave

27th Ave

26th Ave

24th Ave

23rd Ave

7000

500

Anza St

3600

600

4400

600

George
Washington
Park

Balboa St

3700

700

31st Ave

2800

RICHMOND

700

Cabrillo St

25th Ave

Fulton St

PAGE 166

36th Ave

Spreckels Lake Dr

31st Ave

30th Ave

Golden Gate Park

Marx Meadow Dr

1

Spreckels Lake

2

Lincoln Park Golf Course is a great pubic course with beautiful views. We also like Trad'r Sam's—an unpretentious tikki bar out in the avenues.

23 24 25 29

Bars

- **Trad'r Sam's** · 6150 Geary Blvd

Coffee

- **Royal Grove Coffee** · 2348 Clement St
- **Joe's Coffee Shop** · 6134 Geary Blvd

Hardware Stores

- **Bay View Hardware** · 6114 Geary Blvd
- **Crown Lock** · 3615 Balboa St

Liquor Stores

- **Twenty-Five and Clement Liquors** · 2400 Clement St

Movie Theaters

- **Balboa Theater** · 3630 Balboa St

Video Rental

- **Poppa Opp's** · 3739 Balboa St

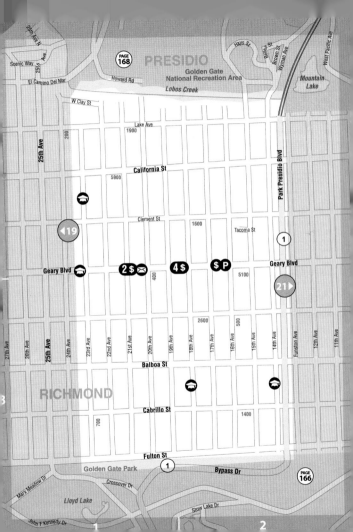

More of the bland and foggy Richmond district here, but it does start to become more ethnically diverse. You'll hear lots of Asian dialects, Russian, Spanish, and Italian spoken. Parking can be difficult, but the MUNI light rail does come all the way out here, providing another option.

Banks

- **Bank of America** · 5500 Geary Blvd
- **Bank of Canton** · 5501 Geary Blvd
- **California Bank & Trust** · 5255 Geary Blvd
- **First Republic Bank** · 5628 Geary Blvd
- **Sterling Bank & Trust** · 5498 Geary Blvd
- **Washington Mutual** · 5655 Geary Blvd
- **Wells Fargo** · 5455 Geary Blvd

Parking

✉ Post Offices

- 5654 Geary Blvd

🏫 Schools

- **Alamo Elementary** · 250 23rd Ave
- **Argonne Alternative Elementary** · 680 18th Ave
- **Hebrew Academy** · 645 14th Ave
- **St Monica's School** · 5920 Geary Blvd

Map 20 · **Richmond**

This is where the food starts to get interesting in the Richmond. Along Geary and Clement, you can find Russian, Italian, Mexican, and all kinds of Asian. Most people come to this part of town just to eat; go to Kabuto for sushi, Ton Kiang for authentic Chinese and dim sum, La Vie for Vietnamese, and Chapeau! for French. And, of course, Tommy's for margaritas.

23 24 25 29

Bars

· **Tommy's Mexican Restaurant** · 5929 Geary Blvd

Coffee

· **Royal Grove Coffee** · 5301 Geary Blvd

Gyms

· **YMCA** · 360 18th Ave

Hardware Stores

· **Creative Paint & Wallpaper** · 5435 Geary Blvd

Liquor Stores

· **J & J Wines & Spirits** · 5620 Geary Blvd
· **Martell's Liquors & Groceries** · 5615 Geary Blvd

Movie Theaters

· **Four Star** · 2200 Clement St
· **UA Alexandria** · 5400 Geary Blvd

Pet Shops

· **Pet Source** · 5221 Geary Blvd

Restaurants

· **Chapeau!** · 1408 Clement St
· **Hong King Flower Lounge** · 5322 Geary Blvd
· **Kabuto Sushi** · 5116 Geary Blvd
· **Khan Toke Thai House** · 5937 Geary Blvd
· **La Vie** · 5830 Geary Blvd
· **Tia Margarita** · 300 19th Ave
· **Ton Kiang** · 5821 Geary Blvd

Shopping

· **Hobby Company of San Francisco** ·
  5150 Geary Blvd
· **Purple Skunk** · 5820 Geary Blvd
· **San Francisco Brewcraft** · 1555 Clement St

Video Rental

· **Blockbuster Video** · 5240 Geary Blvd
· **Pheuan Thai Video (Thai)** · 2036 Balboa St
· **Video Cafe 24 Hours** · 5700 Geary Blvd

Presidio Golf Course

Park Blvd

Baker St

Brown St

Wyman Ave

Halts St

West Pacific Ave

Presidio Ter

West Pacific Ave

Mountain Lake

Mountain Lake Park

Arguello Blvd

Cherry St

PRESIDIO HEIGHTS

Lake St
500

100

Temple Emanu-El

A

California St

Cornwall St

California St

200

4900

200

Arguello Blvd

Euclid A

22

Palm Ave

Jordan Ave

Clement St

2 $

$

$

100

1

$

$

$

Park Presidio Blvd

15th Ave

14th Ave

Funston Ave

12th Ave

11th Ave

10th Ave

9th Ave

8th Ave

7th Ave

6th Ave

5th Ave

4th Ave

3900

3rd Ave

2nd Ave

Almaden Ct

Lorraine Ct

2

Geary Blvd

Geary Blvd

400

$

2 $

500

6th

400

Anza St

500

Edward St

500

1700

B

120

1000

Balboa St

100

Golden Gate Ave

Arguello Blvd

McAllister St

N Willard St

700

Cabrillo St

Fulton St

Golden Gate Park

John F Kennedy Dr

Tea Garden Dr

Conservatory Dr W

Conservatory

1

2

The ethnic diversity is wonderful in this modest neighborhood, where you'll find people from all walks of life. Also known as the "New Chinatown," the Inner Richmond on Clement Street can be as packed with Chinese people and markets as Chinatown. Parking can be extremely difficult here, so if you bring the car, bring your patience...or just take the bus.

Banks

- **Bank of America** · 600 Clement St
- **Bank of America** · 4141 Geary Blvd
- **Bank of the Orient** · 317 6th Ave
- **Bank of the West** · 801 Clement St
- **California Federal Bank** · 4455 Geary Blvd
- **East West Bank** · 4355 Geary Blvd
- **Gateway Bank** · 919 Clement St
- **National American Bank** · 622 Clement St
- **San Francisco Federal CU** · 4375 Geary Blvd
- **United Commercial Bank** · 498 Clement St
- **Washington Mutual** · 301 Clement St
- **Wells Fargo** · 599 Clement St

Car Rental

- **Hertz** · 3928 Geary Blvd
- **Toyota San Francisco** · 3901 Geary Blvd

Gas Stations

- **76** · 3898 California St
- **76** · 4135 California St
- **76** · 4850 Geary Blvd
- **Chevron** · 3675 Geary Blvd
- **Shell** · 4501 Geary Blvd

O Landmarks

- **Temple Emanu-El** · 2 Lake St

Libraries

- **Richmond Branch Library** · 351 9th Ave

Police

- **Richmond Police Station** · 461 6th Ave

Schools

- **Challenge to Learning** · 924 Balboa St
- **Frank McCoppin School** · 651 6th Ave
- **George Peabody Elementary** · 251 6th Ave
- **Laurel School** · 350 9th Ave
- **Roosevelt Middle School** · 460 Arguello Blvd
- **Star of the Sea Grammar School** · 360 9th Ave
- **Sutro Elementary** · 235 12th Ave
- **Zion Lutheran Church School** · 495 9th Ave

Supermarkets

- **CalaFoods** · 4041 Geary Blvd
- **Safeway** · 735 7th Ave

Presidio Golf Course

West Pacific Ave

Presidio Ter

Arguello Blvd

Chabot St

Mountain Lake

Mountain Lake Park

West Pacific Ave

PRESIDIO HEIGHTS

Park Blvd

West Pacific Ave

Wyman Ave

Brown St

Belles St

Hains St

Lake St
500

California St

Cornwall St

California St

A

Park Presidio Blvd

California St
4900

200

100

200

Arguello Blvd

22▶

Euclid

Palm Ave

Jordan Ave

Clement St

Clement St

100

1

Geary Blvd
400

Geary Blvd

3900

Geary Blvd

20

15th Ave

14th Ave

Funston Ave

12th Ave

11th Ave

10th Ave

9th Ave

8th Ave

7th Ave

6th Ave

5th Ave
400

4th Ave

3rd Ave

2nd Ave

Almond Ave

Loraine Ct

500

Anza St

1700

500

Edward St

B

1000

Balboa St

100

Golden Gate Ave

700

Cabrillo St

McAllister St

N Willard St

Fulton St

Arguello Blvd

Golden Gate Park

PAGE 166

Conservatory Dr W

Conservatory Dr E

John F Kennedy Dr

S Tea Garden Dr

Lilly Pond

1

2

Green Apple Books is a wonderful independent bookshop with creaky floors that seems to go on forever. Go to Last Day Saloon for live music. The food in this area is excellent and bare-bones. Try Burma Super Star for Burmese and Brothers for cook-it-at-your-table Korean. Clementine is a nice and reasonably priced French restaurant. Hong Kong Flower Lounge has great Chinese and dim sum.

Bars

- **Last Day Saloon** · 406 Clement St
- **Plough & Stars** · 116 Clement St
- **The Bitter End** · 441 Clement St

Coffee

- **Blue Danube Coffee House** · 306 Clement St
- **HRD Coffee Shop** · 521 3rd Ave
- **Little Paris Coffee Shop** · 444 Clement St

Copy Shops

- **Copy Max** · 3700 Geary Blvd

Hardware Stores

- **Home Hardware** · 335 Clement St
- **Standard Plumbing-Ace Hardware** · 1019 Clement St

Liquor Stores

- **Park Presidio Liquor** · 4400 California St
- **Pyramid Liquors** · 4401 Geary Blvd

Pet Shops

- **B & B Pet Supplies** · 4820 Geary Blvd
- **Sixth Avenue Aquarium** · 425 Clement St

Restaurants

- **Bella Trattoria** · 3854 Geary Blvd
- **Brother's Korean Restaurant** · 4128 Geary Blvd
- **Brother's Korean Restaurant** · 4014 Geary Blvd
- **Burma Super Star** · 309 Clement St
- **Café Riggio** · 4112 Geary Blvd
- **Clementine** · 126 Clement St
- **Coriya Hot Pot City** · 852 Clement St
- **Giorgio's Pizza** · 151 Clement St
- **Katia's Russian Tea Room** · 600 5th Ave
- **Le Soleil** · 133 Clement St
- **Royal Thai** · 951 Clement St

Shopping

- **Green Apple Books and Music** · 506 Clement St
- **Sloat Garden Center** · 327 3rd Ave

Video Rental

- **Mega World (Chinese)** · 848 Clement St
- **Movie Crazzz of San Francisco** · 242 Balboa St
- **Richmond Video & Laser (Hong Kong)** · 837 Clement St

Map 22 · **Presidio Heights / Laurel Heights**

This is a clean and upscale part of the city. The homes bordering the Presidio are gorgeous, and the Roos House is an excellent example of Bernard Maybeck architecture. Laurel Heights, south of California Street, offers more modest and uniform housing.

Banks

- **Bank of America** · 2345 Golden Gate Ave
- **Bank of America** · 3565 California St
- **Bank of America** · 2835 Geary Blvd
- **Bay View Bank** · 3550 Geary Blvd
- **First Republic Bank** · 3533 California St
- **Wells Fargo** · 3431 California St
- **Wells Fargo** · 3624 Geary Blvd

Car Washes

- **Shell Car Wash** · 3035 Geary Blvd

Gas Stations

- **76** · 3501 Geary Blvd
- **Shell** · 3035 Geary Blvd

Landmarks

- **Roos House** · 3500 Jackson St

Post Offices

- 3245 Geary Blvd

Schools

- **Claire Lillenthal Madison Cmps** · 3950 Sacramento St
- **Presidio Hill School** · 3839 Washington St
- **San Francisco Day School** · 350 Masonic Ave
- **Simpatico** · 100 Masonic Ave
- **University of San Francisco** · 2130 Fulton St

Supermarkets

- **Cal-Mart Supermarket** · 3585 California St

Go to charming Sacramento Street for high-end boutique shopping. Sue Fisher King has fancy housewares, and you can lunch with the ladies at Sociale. The Laurel Heights Shopping Center on California is where to go for most of the neighborhood's groceries and necessities. Bryan's is outstanding for meat, fish, and poultry. Don't miss Mel's Drive-In (American Graffiti anyone?) for diner fare.

23 24 25 29

Coffee

- **Peet's** · 3419 California St
- **Starbucks** · 1799 Fulton St
- **Starbucks** · 3595 California St

Copy Shops

- **Geary Print Shop** · 3452 Geary Blvd
- **Kinko's Copies** · 25 Stanyan St
- **Pro Image Printing** · 3216 Geary Blvd

Hardware Stores

- **Hardware Unlimited** · 3326 Sacramento St
- **Standard 5 & 10 Ace** · 3545 California St

Liquor Stores

- **Fulton Food Shop** · 1801 Fulton St
- **Park Walker** · 3500 Geary Blvd
- **Wine Impressions** · 3461 California St

Movie Theaters

- **Landmark Bridge** · 3010 Geary Blvd
- **UA Coronet** · 3575 Geary Blvd

Pet Shops

- **Dollard Martin** · 3429 Sacramento St
- **Drew's K-9 Korner** · 3518 Geary Blvd
- **Nippon Goldfish Co** · 3109 Geary Blvd
- **Pet Source** · 2900 Geary Blvd

Restaurants

- **Mel's Drive-In** · 3355 Geary Blvd
- **Sociale** · 3665 Sacramento St
- **Straits Café** · 3300 Geary Blvd

Shopping

- **AG Ferrari Fine Foods** · 3490 California St
- **Bryan's Quality Meats** · 3445 California St
- **Kindersport** · 3566 Sacramento St
- **Mom's the Word** · 3385 Sacramento St
- **The Grocery Store** · 3625 Sacramento St

Video Rental

- **Jasmin Oriental Grocery (Japanese TV)** · 3244 Geary Blvd
- **One Stop Video** · 3250 Geary Blvd
- **Wherehouse Music** · 3301 Geary Blvd

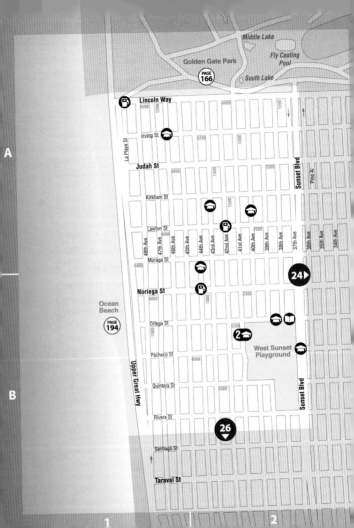

Two words: residential, foggy. Ocean Beach is the main destination. On rare sunny days, it gets crowded and beachy, but otherwise it stays pretty empty aside from a few guys fishing and the hard-core surfers. You can get more for your money in terms of housing out here, but you do have to deal with the relentless fog. Sunset Boulevard is good for jogging or biking.

Gas Stations

- **76** · 1200 La Playa St
- **76** · 3601 Lawton St
- **76** · 3701 Noriega St

Libraries

- **Ortega Branch Library** · 3223 Ortega St

Schools

- **AP Giannini Middle School** · 3151 Ortega St
- **Francis Scott Key Elementary** · 1530 43rd Ave
- **Holy Name School** · 1560 40th Ave
- **Independence Continuation School** · 1717 44th Ave
- **Mark Twain High School** · 1921 41st Ave
- **Rivendell School** · 4501 Irving St
- **St Ignatius College Preparatory School** · 2001 37th Ave
- **Sunset Elementary** · 1920 41st Ave

Map 23 · **Outer Sunset**

The original Thanh Long restaurant is here. It's known as Crustacean in Beverly Hills, and there's one on Polk & California in the city, but this Thanh Long is where it all began. Go for the infamous roasted crab and garlic noodles.

Hardware Stores

- **Chu Supply Ace Hardware** · 3644 Lawton St
- **Sunset True Value Hardware** · 3126 Noriega St

Liquor Stores

- **Arrow Market & Liquor** · 4541 Irving St
- **JM Liquors** · 3801 Noriega St
- **Lawton Liquors** · 3645 Lawton St

Pet Shops

- **A Exotic Pet Shop** · 3412 Judah St

Restaurants

- **Thanh Long** · 4101 Judah St

Video Rental

- **Neighborhood Video** · 3653 Lawton St
- **Top Video World** · 4035 Judah St
- **Video Galaxy (Chinese and English)** ·
  3911 Noriega St

Map 24 • **Sunset**

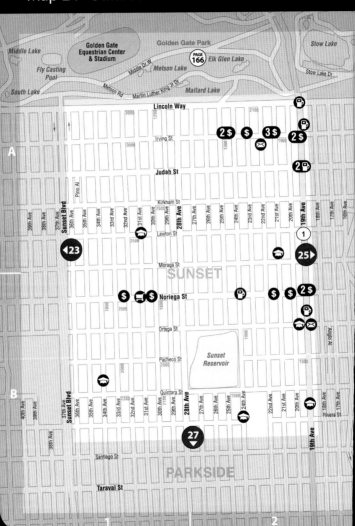

Still residential and foggy, this uniform and plain part of the city houses much of San Francisco's middle-class population.

28 33 34   Ma

$ Banks

· **Bank of America** · 1450 Noriega St
· **Bank of America** · 2325 Noriega St
· **Bank of America** · 1945 Irving St
· **Bank of Canton** · 2533 Noriega St
· **Bank of the Orient** · 2001 Irving St
· **Bay View Bank** · 1850 Irving St
· **Citibank** · 2000 Irving St
· **First Republic Bank** · 1809 Irving St
· **National American Bank** · 1250 Noriega St
· **United Commercial Bank** · 2219 Irving St
· **United Commercial Bank** · 1301 Noriega St
· **Washington Mutual** · 2323 Irving St
· **Washington Mutual** · 1811 19th Ave
· **Wells Fargo** · 2300 Irving St

Gas Stations

· **76** · 1400 19th Ave
· **76** · 1401 19th Ave
· **76** · 1700 Noriega St
· **Chevron** · 1288 19th Ave
· **Chevron** · 1890 19th Ave
· **Shell** · 1200 19th Ave

Post Offices

· 1199 Ortega St
· 1314 22nd Ave

Schools

· **Abraham Lincoln High School** · 2162 24th Ave
· **Adda Clevenger Junior Prep** · 1577 34th Ave
· **Anthony Schools** · 2145 19th Ave
· **Lawton Alternative School** · 1570 31st Ave
· **Robert Louis Stevenson Elementary** ·
  2051 34th Ave
· **San Francisco Conservatory** · 1201 Ortega St
· **Sunset Bible School** · 1690 21st Ave

Supermarkets

· **Safeway** · 2350 Noriega St

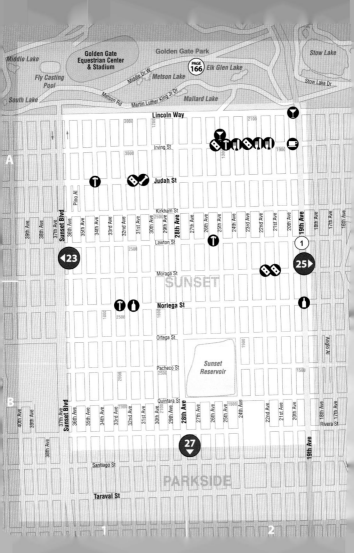

Irving Street is the main drag, where you'll find a smattering of ethnic restaurants. Most notably are the Southeast Asian places—Marnee Thai, Shangri-La Vegetarian, and Micado for sushi. Durty Nelly's Irish pub is here as well.

Bars

- **Durty Nelly's** • 2328 Irving St
- **Molly Malone's** • 1849 Lincoln Way

Coffee

- **Starbucks** • 1800 Irving St

Hardware Stores

- **9 PM Ace Hardware** • 2526 Noriega St
- **Taraval Hardware** • 2900 Judah St
- **U Save Plumbing & Hardware** • 1928 Lawton St
- **Win Long Hardware & Supply** • 2244 Irving St

Liquor Stores

- **Nineteenth Avenue Liquors** • 1800 19th Ave
- **Quarts & Pints Liquor Store** • 2434 Noriega St

Pet Shops

- **Animal Connection** • 2550 Judah St

Restaurants

- **Marnee Thai** • 2225 Irving St
- **Micado** • 2126 Irving St
- **Shangri La** • 2026 Irving St

Video Rental

- **Blockbuster Video** • 2400 Irving St
- **Hong Kong Video & Trading (Chinese, Mandarin and Korean)** • 1450 Noriega St
- **Lam's Video & Laser (Hong Kong)** • 2600 Judah St
- **Noriega Tapes Videos & Trading (Hong Kong)** • 1443 Noriega St
- **Tam's Video (Chinese, Taiwanese and English)** • 2204 Irving St

Map 25 · **Inner Sunset / Golden Gate Heights**

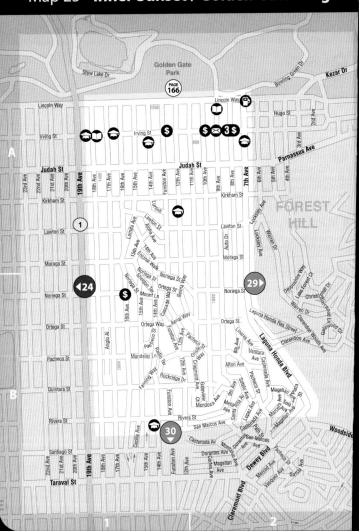

Although still foggy, this part of Sunset is vibrant. The neighborhood is filled mostly with families and grad students from the nearby UC San Francisco Medical Center. Parking can be challenging, especially around 9th and Irving. This is also where the Sunset starts to climb the hill up to Mt. Sutro. There are great views from the top of Golden Gate Heights at Grand View and Sunset Heights parks.

 ## $ Banks

- **Bank of America** · 800 Irving St
- **Bay View Bank** · 1200 Irving St
- **California Federal Bank** · 701 Irving St
- **California Federal Bank** · 900 Noriega St
- **Sterling Bank & Trust** · 825 Irving St
- **Wells Fargo** · 725 Irving St

 ## Gas Stations

- **Shell** · 601 Lincoln Way

Libraries

- **Helen Crocker Russell Library** · 9th Ave & Lincoln Way
- **Sunset Branch Library** · 1305 18th Ave

 ## Post Offices

- 821 Irving St

Schools

- **Alice Fong Yu Alternative Elementary** · 1541 12th Ave
- **Gateway High School** · 1350 7th Ave
- **Herbert Hoover Middle School** · 2290 14th Ave
- **Jefferson Elementary** · 1725 Irving St
- **St Anne's School** · 1320 14th Ave
- **Woodside International School** · 1555 Irving St

Map 25 · **Inner Sunset / Golden Gate Heights**

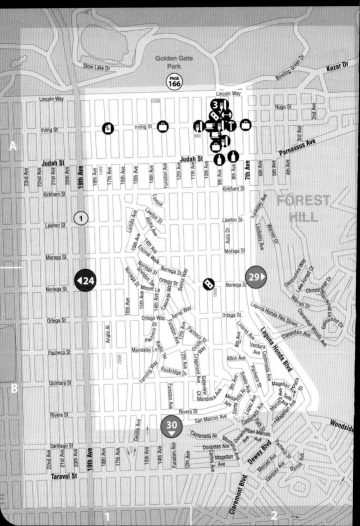

The area around 9th and Irving is where all of the action is. Ebisu is great for sushi, and Einstein's, with its fresh thick bread, makes great sandwiches and contributes to the community all at the same time. When it's really foggy, go to Park Chow for comfort food. Drop by Wishbone for unique personal and home stuff.

Coffee

- **Beanery** · 1307 9th Ave
- **Starbucks** · 744 Irving St

Copy Shops

- **Lauretta Printing & Copy** · 1600 Irving St

Gyms

- **Megaflex Gym & Fitness Center** · 1247 9th Ave

Hardware Stores

- **Progress True Value Hardware** · 724 Irving St

Liquor Stores

- **Judah Ninth Avenue Liquors** · 1400 9th Ave
- **Stand-By Market** · 1400 8th Ave

Restaurants

- **Ebisu** · 1283 9th Ave
- **Einstein's** · 1336 9th Ave
- **Park Chow** · 1240 9th Ave
- **Pasta Pomodoro** · 816 Irving St
- **PJ's Oyster Bed** · 737 Irving St

Shopping

- **Andronico's Market** · 1200 Irving St
- **Oriental Art Gallery** · 1340 9th Ave
- **Wishbone** · 601 Irving St

Video Rental

- **Gramophone Video** · 1799 10th Ave
- **Le Video** · 1231 9th Ave

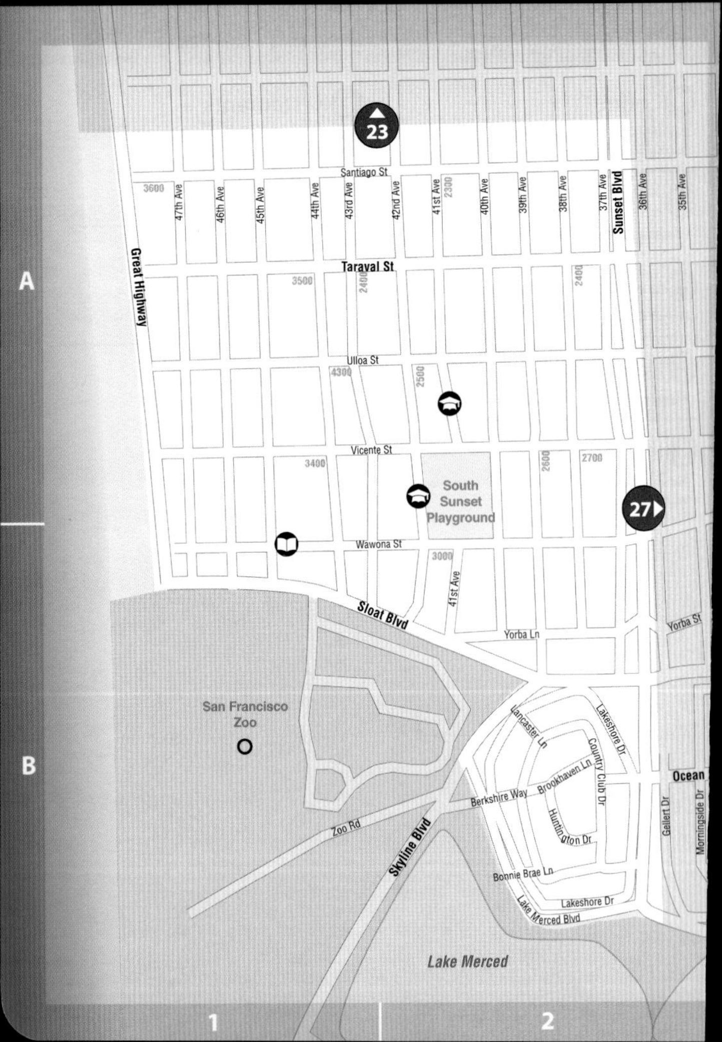

Map 26 · **Parkside (Outer)**

▲ 23

Santiago St

3600

47th Ave
46th Ave
45th Ave
44th Ave
43rd Ave
42nd Ave
41st Ave
2200
40th Ave
39th Ave
38th Ave
37th Ave
36th Ave
35th Ave

Sunset Blvd

Great Highway

A

Taraval St

3500
2400
2400

Ulloa St
4300
2500

2500

Vicente St
3400

South
Sunset
Playground

2600
2700

Wawona St
3000

41st Ave

Sloat Blvd

Yorba Ln

Yorba St

◀ 27

B

San Francisco
Zoo
○

Lancaster Ln
Lakeshire Dr

Brookhaven Ln
Country Club Dr

Berkshire Way

Huntington Dr

Ocean

Gellert Dr
Merningside Dr

Zoo Rd

Skyline Blvd

Bonnie Brae Ln

Lakeshore Dr

Lake Merced Blvd

Lake Merced

1

2

Just like its neighbor (the Sunset), Parkside is quiet, unassuming, residential, uniform, and foggy. It's bordered by Ocean Beach on the west and the San Francisco Zoo and Lake Merced on the south. The Lake Merced area offers running/biking trails, urban boating and fishing, and golf at Harding Park.

 28 33 34 Ma

O Landmarks

- **San Francisco Zoo** · 1 Zoo Rd

Libraries

- **United Irish Cultural Center** · 2700 45th Ave

Schools

- **St Gabriel School** · 2550 41st Ave
- **Ulloa Elementary** · 2650 42nd Ave

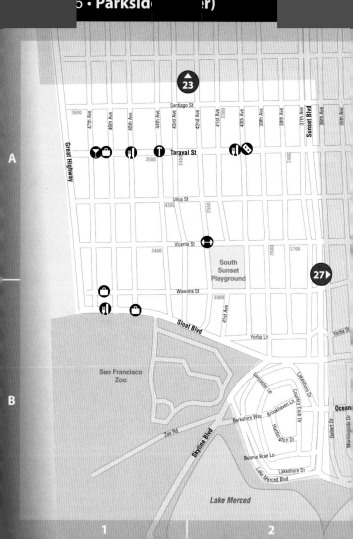

Santiago St

3600

47th Ave
46th Ave
45th Ave
44th Ave
43rd Ave
42nd Ave
41st Ave
40th Ave
39th Ave
38th Ave
37th Ave
36th Ave
35th Ave

2300

2400

Great Highway

Sunset Blvd

A

Taraval St

3500

2400

2400

Ulloa St

4300

2500

2600

2700

3400

Vicente St

South
Sunset
Playground

2600

Wawona St

3000

41st Ave

Sloat Blvd

Yorba Ln

Yorba St

San Francisco
Zoo

B

Zoo Rd

Lancaster Ln

Lakeshore Dr

Country Club Dr

Brookhaven Ln

Berkshire Way

Huntington Dr

Ocean

Gellert Dr

Morningside Dr

Skyline Blvd

Bonnie Brae Ln

Lakeshore Dr

Lake Merced Blvd

Lake Merced

1

2

Taraval is the main drag here, but unfortunately there's not a lot to offer this far out. If you take the kids to the zoo, check out the classic standby, the Doggie Diner (great sign). Free as a Bird is good for kites and wind-powered toys for the beach.

28 33 34   Ma

Bars

· **Sand Bar** · 3639 Taraval St

Gyms

· **Megaflex Gym & Fitness Center** · 3119 Vicente St

Hardware Stores

· **Lakeside Hardware & Lumber** · 3401 Taraval St

Restaurants

· **Bashful Bull Too!** · 3600 Taraval St
· **Doggie Diner** · 2750 Sloat Blvd
· **North Beach Pizza** · 3054 Taraval St

Shopping

· **Free as a Bird** · 3620 Wawona St
· **Occidental Power** · 3629 Taraval St
· **Sloat Garden Center** · 2700 Sloat Blvd

Video Rental

· **New Video Corner (Chinese)** · 3008 Taraval St

This is a quiet and modest neighborhood with well-known Stern Grove at its heart. During summer weekends this area gets jammed with people going to the free concerts at Stern Grove.

Banks

- **Bank of America** · 1007 Taraval St
- **Bank of America** · 1515 Sloat Blvd
- **Bank of America** · 245 Winston Dr
- **California Federal Bank** · 3146 20th Ave
- **Citibank** · 2400 19th Ave
- **First Bank & Trust** · 1000 Taraval St
- **Washington Mutual** · 926 Taraval St
- **Wells Fargo** · 599 Buckingham Way
- **World Savings & Loan Assn** · 1595 Sloat Blvd

Car Rental

- **Enterprise** · Winston Dr/Stonestown Mall · 415-337-9000

Gas Stations

- **76** · 1855 Taraval St
- **Olympian Oil** · 2301 19th Ave
- **Shell** · 2399 24th St

O Landmarks

- **Stern Grove** · 19th Ave @ Sloat Blvd
- **Stonestown Galleria** · 3251 20th Ave

Libraries

- **Parkside Branch Library** · 1200 Taraval St
- **Sutro Library** · 480 Winston Dr

Police

- **Taraval Police Station** · 2345 24th Ave

Post Offices

- · 1543 Sloat Blvd
- · 1800 Taraval St

Schools

- **Lakeshore Alternative Elemenary** · 220 Middlefield Dr
- **Lowell High School** · 1101 Eucalyptus Dr
- **Mercy High School** · 3250 19th Ave
- **St Stephen's School** · 401 Eucalyptus Dr

Map 27 • **Parkside (Inner)**

You'll find most of what you need on Taraval and Sloat. There are several good sporting goods stores on Taraval. Try El Burrito Express for burritos, Ming's Diner for Chinese, or Rick's for Hawaiian-style food.

Coffee

- **Starbucks** · 3251 20th Ave
- **Tully's Coffee** · 1509 Sloat Blvd

Copy Shops

- **Copy Circle** · 959 Taraval St
- **Kinko's** · 1597 Sloat Blvd

Gyms

- **Fitness USA Supercenters** · 3251 20th Ave
- **YMCA** · 333 Eucalyptus Dr

Hardware Stores

- **Great Wall Hardware** · 1821 Taraval St

Liquor Stores

- **Gene's Liquor** · 2201 Taraval St
- **Liquor Locker** · 1223 Taraval St

Pet Shops

- **Petcetera** · 2226 Taraval St
- **Petco** · 1591 Sloat Blvd

Restaurants

- **El Burrito Express** · 1601 Taraval St
- **Ming's Diner** · 2129 Taraval St
- **Rick's** · 1940 Taraval St

Shopping

- **Tower Records** · 3205 20th Ave

Video Rental

- **Blockbuster Video** · 1503 Sloat Blvd
- **Captain Video** · 233 Winston Dr
- **Kearny Video** · 1038 Taraval St
- **Lanxang Thai Video (Thai)** · 1043 Taraval St
- **Tower Records/Video/Books** · 3205 20th Ave
- **Video World** · 1241 Taraval St

Escolta Way

Wawona St

Pine Lake Park

Eucalyptus Dr

Gellert Dr

A

Lake Merced

Lake Merced

Lake Merced B

Winston Dr

20th Ave

Stonecrest Dr

Campus Dr

State Dr

Stonestown Galleria

Buckingham Way

27

PAGE 180

San Francisco State University

1

Harding Rd

Lake Merced Blvd

Font Blvd

Tapia Dr

Serrano Dr E

Juan Bautista Cir

Crespi Dr

Gonzalez Dr

Vega Dr

Varela Ave

Wyton Ln

Stratford Dr

Denslowe Dr

33

2 $

Pinto Ave

Acevedo Ave

Serrano Dr

Higuera Ave

Vidal Dr

Arballo Dr

Gonzalez Dr

Rivas Ave

Garces Dr

Vidal Dr

Fuente Ave

Burnell Dr

Grijalva Dr

Eucalyptus

Diaz Ave

Castelo Ave

Font Blvd

Banbury Dr

Cambon Dr

Felix Ave

$

Lake Merced

35

John Muir Dr

Garces Dr

Gonzalez Dr

Brotherhood Way

Thomas More Way

Chumasero Dr

B

N Lake Merced Hls

N Lake Merced Hls

S Lake Merced Hls

San Francisco Co.

San Mateo Co.

Congo St

1

2

This area is dominated by San Francisco State University and Lake Merced, which is a large urban lake that is great for running, biking, boating, and especially golf at the awesome newly-renovated Harding Park golf course. Fort Funston is also nearby; hang out and watch the hang gliders.

$ Banks

- **Bank of America** • 1645 Holloway Ave
- **Wells Fargo** • 35 Cambon Dr
- **Wells Fargo** • 1650 Holloway Ave

Schools

- **Brandeis Hillel Day School** •
  655 Brotherhood Way
- **Bridgemont Jr & Sr High** • 777 Brotherhood Way
- **Holy Trinity Orthodox School** •
  999 Brotherhood Way
- **Krouzian Zekarian Armenian School** •
  825 Brotherhood Way
- **School of the Arts** • 700 Font Blvd
- **St Thomas More Catholic School** •
  50 Thomas Moore Way

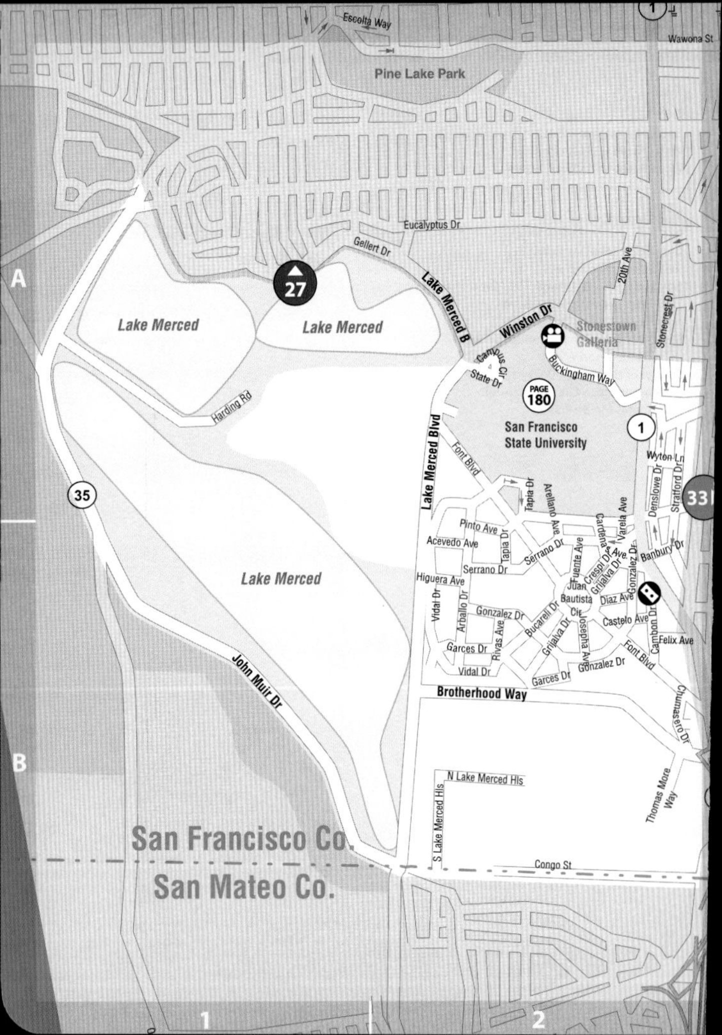

Map 28 · **SFSU / Park Merced**

Escolta Way

1

Wawona St

Pine Lake Park

Eucalyptus Dr

Gellert Dr

Lake Merced B

A

27

Lake Merced

Lake Merced

Winston Dr

20th Ave

Stonecrest Dr

Stonestown Galleria

Gonzalez Cir Dr

State Dr

Buckingham Way

PAGE
180

San Francisco
State University

1

Harding Rd

Lake Merced Blvd

Font Blvd

Wyton Ln

Denslowe Dr

Stratford Dr

33

35

Tapia Dr

Pinto Ave

Acevedo Ave

Tapia Dr

Serrano Dr

Arellano Ave

Serrano Dr

Fuente Ave

Crespi Dr

Cardenas Ave

Varela Ave

Gonzalez Dr

Banbury Dr

Lake Merced

Higuera Ave

Vidal Dr

Arballo Dr

Gonzalez Dr

Bucareli Dr

Juan
Bautista
Cir

Eucalyptus

Grijalva Dr

Cambon Dr

Diaz Ave

Rivas Ave

Castelo Ave

Font Blvd

Felix Ave

Garces Dr

Vidal Dr

Grijalva Dr

Garces Dr

Gonzalez Dr

Chumasero Dr

Brotherhood Way

Thomas More
Way

B

N Lake Merced Hls

San Francisco Co.

S Lake Merced Hls

Congo St

San Mateo Co.

1

2

If you're looking for a big mall, you've found it! Stonestown Galleria has all of your standard mall chain stores and a movie theater. Hours of fun.

Movie Theaters
· **UA Stonestown Twin** · 501 Buckingham Way

Video Rental
· **Movie Magic Park Merced** · 57 Cambon Dr

Map 29 • **Twin Peaks**

The area of Forest Hill and Twin Peaks is mostly residential. It's just about smack dab in the middle of the city, and the view from the top of Twin Peaks is the best in town. It's a bit of a drive to get up there, but it's worth it, especially at night. Count on it being windy and cold.

28 33 34 38

Banks

· **Bank of America** · 350 Parnassus Ave
· **Bank of America** · 500 Parnassus Ave
· **Wells Fargo** · 400 Parnassus Ave
· **Wells Fargo** · 510 Parnassus Ave

Libraries

· **Library & Center for Knowledge** ·
  530 Parnassus Ave

Schools

· **Clarendon Alternative Elementary** ·
  500 Clarendon Ave
· **Rooftop Alternative Elementary** ·
  443 Burnett Ave
· **Rooftop Middle School** · 500 Corbett Ave

Most of what this area has to offer can be found around Parnassus.

Coffee

· **Starbucks** · 350 Parnassus Ave

Gyms

· **Millberry Fitness Center - UCSF** ·
   500 Parnassus Ave

Liquor Stores

· **Holsum Market** · 4686 18th St

Restaurants

· **Pomelo** · 92 Judah St

Map 30 · **West Portal**

The development of the MUNI tunnel that connects West Portal to downtown brought this neighborhood to life. It's a laid-back, quiet, conservative, middle-class neighborhood.

Banks

- **Bank of America** · 288 West Portal Ave
- **Bank of the West** · 2606 Ocean Ave
- **Bay View Bank** · 2656 Ocean Ave
- **California Federal Bank** · 2499 Ocean Ave
- **Citibank** · 130 West Portal Ave
- **San Francisco Federal CU** · 2645 Ocean Ave
- **Washington Mutual** · 98 West Portal Ave
- **Wells Fargo** · 730 Taraval St
- **Wells Fargo** · 145 West Portal Ave

Gas Stations

- **76** · 800 Ulloa St
- **Chevron** · 301 Claremont Blvd

Libraries

- **Merced Branch Library** · 155 Winston Dr
- **West Portal Branch Library** · 190 Lenox Way

Post Offices

- · 317 West Portal Ave

Schools

- **Aptos Middle School** · 105 Aptos Ave
- **Commodore Sloat Elementary** · 50 Darien Way
- **Herbert Hoover Middle School** · 2290 14th Ave
- **St Cecilia School** · 660 Vicente St
- **West Portal Lutheran School** · 200 Sloat Blvd
- **West Portal Elementary** · 5 Lenox Way

Supermarkets

- **Safeway** · 730 Taraval St

Although the Eezy Freezy Market doesn't have anything extraordinary to offer, we love the sign that still says "We give S&H green stamps." It sets the tone. Stop by the old-time diner, the Manor Coffee Shop, or if you're in the mood for Mexican, try El Toreador. For Peruvian, go to Fresca. West Portal Station is the divey neighborhood watering hole. Hausen Home is a great place to buy things for the house.

Bars

- **Joxer Daly's** · 46 West Portal Ave
- **West Portal Station** · 824 Ulloa St

Coffee

- **Manor Coffee Shop** · 321 West Portal Ave
- **Peet's** · 54 West Portal Ave
- **Starbucks** · 100 West Portal Ave

Gyms

- **One Health & Fitness** · 850 Taraval St
- **Taraval Fitness Center** · 645 Taraval St

Hardware Stores

- **Papenhausen Hardware** · 32 West Portal Ave
- **West Portal Paint & Hardware** · 311 West Portal Ave

Movie Theaters

- **Century Empire 3** · 85 West Portal Ave

Pet Shops

- **Happy Pet** · 709 Taraval St

Restaurants

- **El Toreador** · 50 West Portal Ave
- **Fresca** · 24 West Portal Ave
- **Manor Coffee Shop** · 321A West Portal Ave

Shopping

- **Ambassador Toys** · 186 West Portal Ave
- **Hausen Home** · 80 West Portal Ave
- **Irish Delights** · 77 West Portal Ave

Video Rental

- **Dr Video** · 99 West Portal Ave
- **San Francisco Home Video** · 320 West Portal Ave

Map 31 • Mt Davidson

At 938 feet, Mt. Davidson is the highest point in San Francisco. Perched high above the city is the giant, controversial 103-foot-high Mt. Davidson Christian cross in Mt. Davidson Park. This is an unremarkable, hilly neighborhood, consisting mostly of modest single-family homes.

Banks

• **Sequoia National Bank** • 699 Portola Dr

Gas Stations

• **Shell** • 701 Portola Dr
• **Twin Peaks Car Care** • 598 Portola Dr

Schools

• **Archbishop Riordan High School** •
  175 Phelan Ave
• **J Eugene McAteer High School** • 555 Portola Dr
• **Miraloma Elementary** • 175 Omar Way
• **Montessori Teacher Training Ctr** • 678 Portola Dr
• **San Francisco Police Academy** • 350 Amber Dr
• **St Brendan's School** • 940 Laguna Honda Blvd
• **St Finn Barr School** • 419 Hearst Ave
• **Sunnyside Elementary** • 250 Foerster St

Supermarkets

• **Safeway** • 625 Monterey Blvd

Map 31 • **Mt Davidson**

Laguna Honda
Hospital and
Rehabilitation
Center

Portola Dr

Amethyst Way

Quartz Way

Cameo Way

Amber Dr

Duncan St

Turquoise Way

Coralino Ln

29

Vasquez Ave

Rock Al

Idora Ave

Sydney Way

Sydney Way

A

Rockwood Way

Woodman

Del Sur Ave

Charles Ave

O'Shaughnessy Blvd

Jade Pl

Ulloa St

30

Rock Ave

Juanita Way

Portola Dr

Agua Way

Rockdale Dr

Isola Way

Encline Ct

Van Dale A

Glen Canyon Park

Myra Way

Reposa Way

Marietta Dr

St Croix Dr

Teresita Blvd

Berkeley Way

**DIAMOND
HEIGHTS**

Marne Ave

Omar Way

Sequoia Way

Avoca

El Sereno C

Arroyo Way

Pio Ct

Mount
Davidson
Park

Dalewood Way

Molimo Dr

Bella Vista Way

Marietta Dr

Valenta Ct

32

Casitas Ave

Myra Way

Cresta Vista Dr

Molimo Dr

Cuba Al

Teresita Blvd

Mercato

Elk St

Robinhood Dr

Lansdale Ave

Coventry

Hillcrest Ct

Bella Vista Way

Dorcas Way

Foerster St

Los Palmos Dr

Lassen Al

Teresita

Congo St

Bosworth St

Globe

Los Palm os St

Lulu Al

Stanford Heights A

Verna St

Teresita

Conrad

Stillings Ave

Northcott

Hazelwood Ave

Cresta Vista Dr

Burlwood Dr

Melrose Ave

Melrose Ave

Brentwood Ave

Stafford Heights A

Congo St

Yerba Buena Ave

Hazelwood Ave

Colon Ave

Valdez Ave

Melrose Ave

Mangels Ave

Edna St

Detroit St

300

Plymouth Ave

Northwood Dr

Ridgewood Ave

Ginnessea

Joost Ave

Foerster St

Monterey Blvd

Montecito Ave

Hearst Ave

600

Edna St

200

Circular Ave

Colonial Way

Nantucket Ave

Westwood Dr

Eastwood Dr

Greenwood Ave

Flood Ave

Staples Ave

Judson Ave

Edna St

Arco Way

Araus Way

Paulding St

Plymouth Ave

34

Marston Ave

Balboa
Park

1   **2**

There is not really any reason to come up here unless you're exploring or maybe biking to Mt. Davidson. The businesses that are here merely service the neighborhood needs.

Bars

• **Tower Lodge** • 689 Portola Dr

Coffee

• **Railroad Ex Presso** • 705 Monterey Blvd
• **Starbucks** • 675 Portola Dr

Liquor Stores

• **Miraloma Liquor Store** • 683 Portola Dr
• **Viglizzo's Tower Market** • 635 Portola Dr

Map 32 · **Diamond Heights / Glen Park**

Diamond Heights is another really hilly area, which has cheaper housing due to its location. There are some really great views of the city from Diamond Heights, and that's just about it, except for lots of reasonably-priced nondescript apartments. Glen Park is better and more family-oriented with its share of Victorians and modern-style homes. Nearby Glen Canyon Park is great for hiking and playing with your pooch.

 28 33 34 38 3 | Ma

$ Banks

- **Bank of America** · 2810 Diamond St
- **Bank of America** · 5268 Diamond Heights Blvd
- **California Federal Bank** · 2895 Diamond St

Car Washes

- **Mission Shell** · 3550 Mission St

Community Gardens

Gas Stations

- **Shell** · 3550 Mission St
- **Shell** · 4298 Mission St

Libraries

- **Glen Park Branch Library** · 653 Chenery St

Post Offices

- 4083 29th St
- 5262 Diamond Heights Blvd

Schools

- **Fairmount Elementary** · 65 Chenery St
- **Glen Park Elementary** · 151 Lippard Ave
- **Kate Kennedy Children's Center** · 1670 Noe St
- **Mission Education Center** · 1670 Noe St
- **St John's School** · 925 Chenery St
- **St Paul's School** · 1690 Church St

Supermarkets

- **CalaFoods** · 4175 Mission St
- **Safeway** · 5290 Diamond Heights Blvd

Map 32

Chenery Park is a fantastic neighborhood restaurant and La Corneta Taqueria is good for tacos and burritos. Tyger's is popular and gets busy for breakfast on the weekends. If you need to wet your whistle, stop by the Glen Park Station bar or the R&R Cocktail Lounge.

28 33 34 38 3

Bars

- **Glen Park Station Bar** · 2816 Diamond St
- **R&R Cocktail Lounge** · 609 Chenery St

Coffee

- **Higher Grounds Coffee House** · 691 Chenery St

Gyms

- **Sol Gym** · 2838 Diamond St

Hardware Stores

- **Glen Park Hardware** · 685 Chenery St

Liquor Stores

- **Mission, Silver Market** · 4304 Mission St
- **Veteran's Liquor Store** · 1710 Church St

Pet Shops

- **Critter Fritters Pet Foods** · 670 Chenery St

Restaurants

- **Chenery Park** · 683 Chenery St
- **La Corneta Taqueria** · 2834 Diamond St
- **Pomelo** · 1793 Church St
- **Tyger's** · 2798 Diamond St

Video Rental

- **East-West Video** · 2810 Diamond St

This is a residential neighborhood populated mostly by detached single-family homes. Ingleside Terrace is more upscale with larger homes and yards.

Banks

- **Bank of America** · 1649 Ocean Ave

Car Rental

- **Enterprise** · 4050 19th Ave · 415-406-1164

Gas Stations

- **76** · 1490 Ocean Ave
- **Chevron** · 1100 Junipero Serra Blvd
- **Chevron** · 1799 Ocean Ave
- **Chevron** · 2998 San Jose Ave
- **Gas Outlet** · 1101 Junipero Serra Blvd

O Landmarks

- **Ingleside Terraces Sundial** · Borcia St & Entrado Ct

Libraries

- **Ingeside Branch Library** · 1649 Ocean Ave
- **Ocean View Branch Library** · 345 Randolph St

Schools

- **Jose Ortega Elementary** · 400 Sargent St
- **College of Theology and Urban Studies** · 200 Plymouth Ave
- **Koinonia University** · 1970 Ocean Ave
- **Sheridan Elementary** · 431 Capitol Ave
- **St Emydius School** · 301 De Montfort Ave
- **Voice of Pentecost Academy** · 1970 Ocean Ave

Map 33 • Ingleside

Coffee
· **Java of Ocean** · 1700 Ocean Ave

Copy Shops
· **Copy Edge** · 1508 Ocean Ave

Gyms
· **24 Hour Fitness** · 1850 Ocean Ave

Liquor Stores
· **Homran Liquors** · 1551 Ocean Ave
· **RC Package House** · 99 Broad St

Video Rental
· **Blockbuster Video** · 1770 Ocean Ave
· **Oceanview Video** · 1720 Ocean Ave

This is a totally residential outer neighborhood.

Banks

- **Bank of America** · 5150 Mission St
- **Wells Fargo** · 50 Phelan Ave

Gas Stations

- **76** · 999 Ocean Ave
- **Arco** · 5898 Mission St
- **Best Auto Care** · 2099 San Jose Ave
- **Econo Gas** · 5098 Mission St
- **Shell** · 2200 Alemany Blvd

Police

- **Ingleside Police Station** · 1 John Young Ln

Schools

- **Balboa High School** · 1000 Cayuga Ave
- **Bethel Center** · 2557 Alemany Blvd
- **James Denman Middle School** · 241 Oneida Ave
- **Leadership High School** · 300 Seneca Ave
- **Lick Wilmerding High School** · 755 Ocean Ave
- **Longfellow Elementary** · 755 Morse St
- **Ocean Avenue Campus of CCSF** · 50 Phelan Ave
- **SF Junior Academy After Care** · 66 Geneva Ave
- **San Francisco Christian School** · 25 Whittier St

Map 34 · **Oceanview**

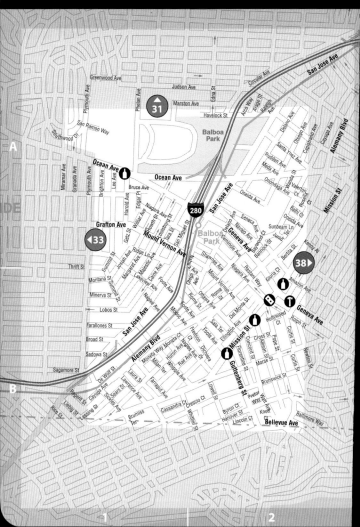

⊤Hardware Stores
· **J & J True Value Hardware** · 929 Geneva Ave

⍟Liquor Stores
· **Brothers Market** · 5501 Mission St
· **Mike's Liquor** · 5084 Mission St
· **United Liquor Market** · 5298 Mission St
· **Willey's Den** · 1015 Ocean Ave

◆Video Rental
· **Mission Video** · 5188 Mission St

The area surrounding Cortland Ave. gives this neighborhood sort of an inner-city village feeling. There is definitely a bohemian quality in the air. Tourists tend to avoid the area, and only a few buses head up here, so it hangs on to its local appeal.

$ Banks

- **Bank of America** · 3250 Mission St
- **Bank of America** · 433 Cortland Ave
- **Wells Fargo** · 3350 Mission St

⬤ Car Washes

- **Always Open Car Wash** · 2560 Marin St

⬤ Gas Stations

- **Chevron** · 101 Bay Shore Blvd
- **Shell** · 319 Bay Shore Blvd

✚ Hospitals

- **St Luke's Hospital** · 555 San Jose Ave

📖 Libraries

- **Bernal Heights Branch Library** ·
  500 Cortland Ave

✉ Post Offices

- · 45 29th St

🎓 Schools

- **Immaculate Conception Elementary** ·
  1550 Treat Ave
- **Junipero Serra Elementary** · 625 Holly Park Cir
- **Paul Revere Elementary** · 555 Tompkins Ave
- **Paul Revere Elementary Annex** ·
  610 Tompkins Ave
- **St Anthony / Immaculate Conception** ·
  299 Precita Ave

🛒 Supermarkets

- **Safeway** · 3350 Mission St

The big draw to Bernal Heights is the Liberty Café, which really is a great little restaurant (try the chicken pot pie), but we also like Blue Plate down the hill on Mission, and Emmy's Spaghetti Shack. Skip's Tavern is a bona-fide dive bar that captures the local quality of the neighborhood. Wild Side West is another good bet for an original local watering hole.

Bars

- **El Rio** · 3158 Mission St
- **Odeon Bar** · 3223 Mission St
- **Roccapulco** · 3140 Mission St
- **Skip's Tavern** · 453 Cortland Ave
- **The Wild Side West** · 424 Cortland Ave

Copy Shops

- **Bernal Boxes & Fax This** · 322 Cortland Ave
- **Copy Central** · 3181 Mission St

Farmer's Markets

- **Alemany Blvd** · 100 Alemany Blvd

Hardware Stores

- **Cole Hardware** · 3312 Mission St

Liquor Stores

- **Beverages & More** · 201 Bay Shore Blvd
- **DJ Liquors** · 3278 Mission St
- **Sam's Liquor** · 580 Precita Ave

Pet Shops

- **Bernal Beast** · 509 Cortland Ave

Restaurants

- **Blue Plate** · 3218 Mission St
- **Cottage Bakery** · 410 Cortland Ave
- **Dusit Thai** · 3221 Mission St
- **Emmy's Spaghetti Shack** · 18 Virginia Ave
- **Liberty Café & Bakery** · 410 Cortland Ave
- **Little Nepal** · 925 Cortland Ave
- **Maggie Mudd** · 903 Cortland Ave
- **Moki's Sushi & Pacific Grill** · 830 Cortland Ave
- **Palatino** · 803 Cortland Ave
- **Rock Soup** · 3299 Mission St
- **Valentina** · 419 Cortland Ave

Video Rental

- **Blockbuster Video** · 3125 Mission St
- **Front Lyne** · 402 Cortland Ave
- **Video Oasis** · 439 Cortland Ave

Map 36 · **Bay View / Silver Terrace**

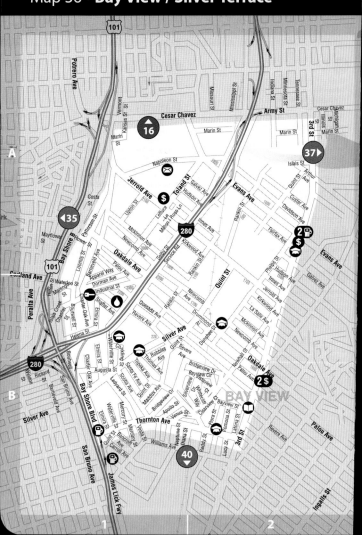

This is an industrial area surrounded by low-income housing. The only reason to come here is for the San Francisco Wholesale Produce Market, which supplies many San Francisco restaurants. Skip the scene at night.

$ Banks

- **Bank of America** · 5000 3rd St
- **Bank of America** · 2090 Jerrold Ave
- **Bay View Bank** · 4947 3rd St
- **Union Bank** · 3801 3rd St

Car Rental

- **S & C Ford** · 211 Industrial St · 415-553-4400

Car Washes

- **B & B Car Wash** · 2220 Revere Ave

Gas Stations

- **76** · 3800 3rd St
- **76** · 975 Bay Shore Blvd
- **Arco** · 2190 Carroll Ave
- **Shell** · 3750 3rd St

Libraries

- **Bayview - Anna E Waden** · 5075 3rd St

Post Offices

- 180 Napoleon St

Schools

- **Dr Charles R Drew Elementary** · 50 Pomona St
- **Joshua Marie Cameron Academy** · 3801 3rd St
- **Southeast Campus of CCSF** · 1800 Oakdale Ave
- **Thurgood Marshall High School** · 45 Conkling St
- **Twenty-First Century Academy** · 2055 Silver Ave

Map 36 • **Bay View / Silver Terrace**

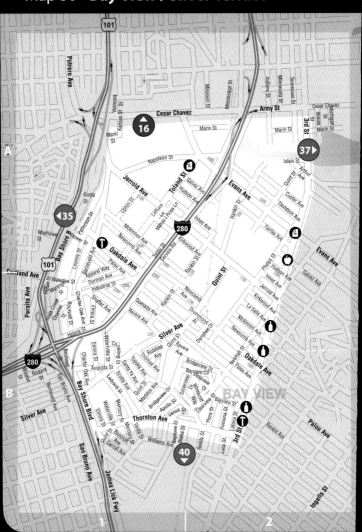

Copy Shops

- **Bay Copy Plus** · 3801 3rd St
- **Press Works** · 111 Toland St

Farmer's Markets

- **Bayview** · Walgreens at 3rd & Galvez

Hardware Stores

- **G Mazzei & Sons' Hardware** · 5166 3rd St
- **Lumberland Builders Supply** · 2590 Oakdale Ave

Liquor Stores

- **Bayview Liquors** · 4700 3rd St
- **Golden Eagle Liquors** · 5100 3rd St
- **Sav Mor Mart** · 4500 3rd St

Hunter's Point is a working shipyard and site of the US's first dry dock. The best thing about the area is the huge Artist's Community at Hunter's Point. The low-income housing here is plagued by unemployment and crime, so be very careful if you come and don't come at night.

 Community Gardens

 Post Offices

- 1570 Burke St
- 1300 Evans Ave

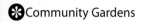 Schools

- **Burnett Nursery & School-Age** ·
  1520 Oakdale Ave
- **Evans Campus of CCSF** · 1400 Evans Ave
- **George Washington Carver Elementary** ·
  1360 Oakdale Ave
- **Gloria R Davis Middle School** · 1195 Hudson Ave
- **Malcolm X Academy** · 350 Harbor Rd

Map 37 • **Indian Basin / Hunter's Point**

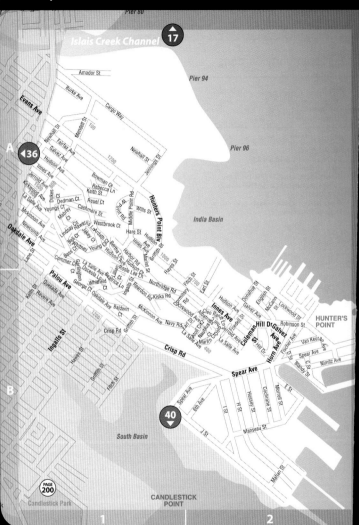

Pier 80

Islais Creek Channel

17

Amador St

Pier 94

Burke Ave

Cargo Way

Evans Ave

Newhall St

Fairfax Ave

A 36

Galvez Ave

Hudson Ave

Jerrold Ave

Innes Ave

Kirkwood Ave

Dukes Ct

La Salle Ave

Dedman Ct

Youngs Ct

Mabrey Ct

McKinnon Ave

Newcomb Ave

Westbrook Ct

Bowman Ct

Rebecca Ln

Keith St

Reuel Ct

Cashmere St

Hare St

Hunters Point Blvd

Wills St

Middle Point Rd

Hudson Ave

Innes Ave

India Basin

Pier 96

Oakdale Ave

Lindsay Ct

Baker Ct

Hawkins Ct

Whitney Ct

Young Ct

Harbor Rd

Hudson Rd

Rosie Lee Ln

Commer Ct

Garrington Ct

Bass Ct

George Ct

Oakdale Ave

Baldwin Ct

La Salle Ave

Osceola

Whitfield

Beatrice Ln

Palou Ave

Quesada Ave

Ingalls St

Keith St

Revere Ave

Crisp Rd

Griffith St

McKinnon Ave

Navy Rd

Northridge Rd

Kiska Rd

Brookwood Ave

Reardon Rd

Fitch St

Galt St

Cleo Rand

Jennings St

Newhall St

Coleman

Innes Ave

Hudson Ave

Galvez Ave

Donahue St

Earl St

Northridge Rd

La Shoot Ct

Nichols Way

Oakdale Ave

Martin

La Salle Ave

Crisp Rd

Innes Ave

Coleman-Hill Dr

Galvez Ave

Horn Ave

Hill Dr

Fisher Ave

English St

McCann

Robinson St

Lockwood St

HUNTER'S POINT

Spear Ave

Van Keur

Spear Ave

Bandy St

Nimitz Ave

B

Spear Ave

8th Ave

1st St

Husley Ave

Cochran Ave

H St

E St

Morrell St

C St

South Basin

40

Manseau St

PAGE 200

Candlestick Park

Mahan St

CANDLESTICK POINT

1   2

Map 38 • Excelsior / Crocker Amazon

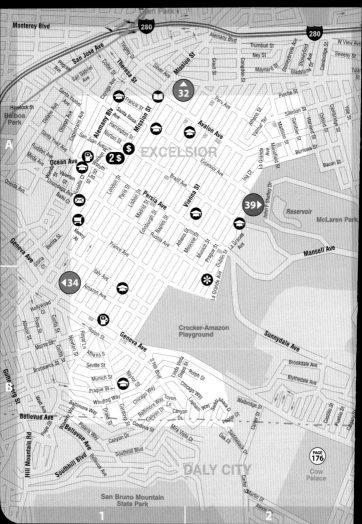

This is an outer residential neighborhood with quick and easy access to the freeway.

Banks

- **Bank of America** · 15 Ocean Ave
- **Bay View Bank** · 4610 Mission St
- **Wells Fargo** · 4648 Mission St

Community Gardens

🅿 Gas Stations

- **76** · 1798 Alemany Blvd
- **Arco** · 1200 Geneva Ave

📖 Libraries

- **Excelsior Branch Library** · 4400 Mission St

✉ Post Offices

- 15 Onondaga St

🏫 Schools

- **Cleveland Elementary** · 455 Athens St
- **Corpus Christi School** · 75 Francis St
- **Discovery Center School** · 65 Ocean Ave
- **Epiphany School** · 600 Italy Ave
- **Guadalupe Elementary** · 859 Prague St
- **Luther Burbank Middle School** ·
  325 La Grande Ave
- **Monroe Elementary** · 260 Madrid St
- **San Francisco Community Alternative School** ·
  125 Excelsior Ave

🛒 Supermarkets

- **Safeway** · 4950 Mission St

Map 38 • **Excelsior / Crocker Amazon**

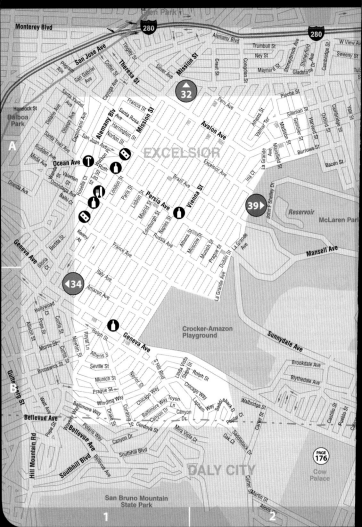

You'll find most of what you need along Mission Street. For entertainment, head into town.

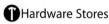Hardware Stores

- **Shic Hardware** · 58 Ocean Ave

Liquor Stores

- **D & D Liquor & Deli** · 1231 Geneva Ave
- **Frank's Market & Liquors** · 4799 Mission St
- **Snack & Bottle Shop** · 644 Persia Ave
- **Yick's Liquors** · 4701 Mission St

Restaurants

- **North Beach Pizza** · 4787 Mission St

Video Rental

- **Into Video** · 4907 Mission St
- **Movie Magic** · 4627 Mission St

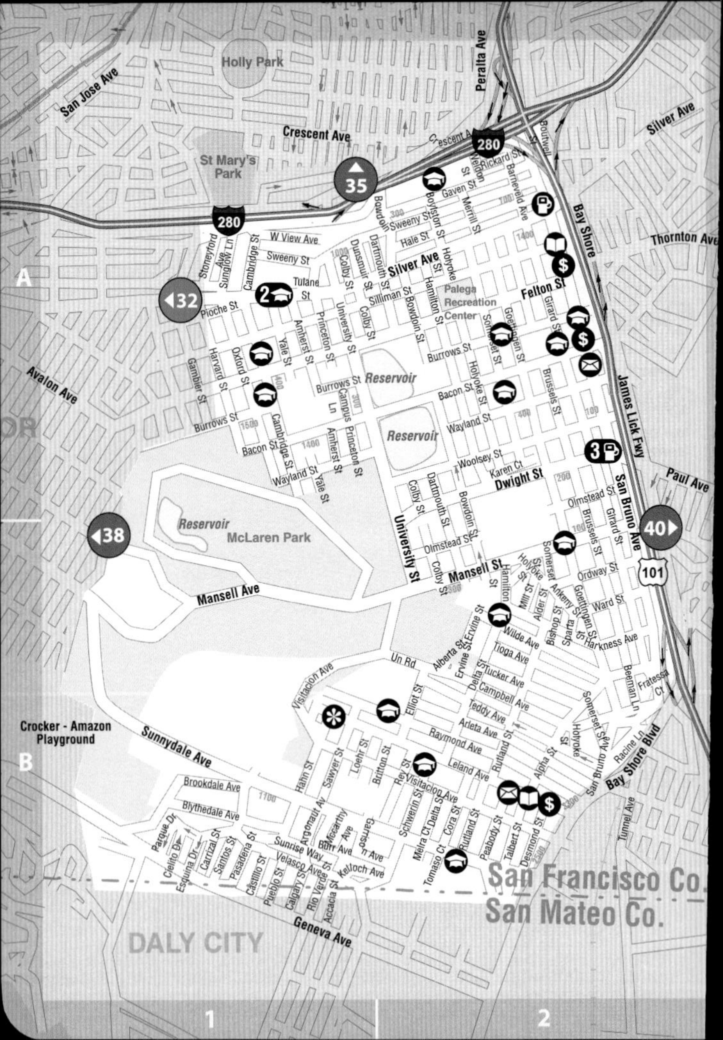

Map 39 · **Visitacion Valley**

Banks

- **Bank of America** · 6 Leland Ave
- **Bank of America** · 2485 San Bruno Ave
- **Bank of the West** · 2675 San Bruno Ave

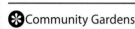## Community Gardens

Gas Stations

- **76** · 2895 San Bruno Ave
- **Art's Valerio** · 2985 San Bruno Ave
- **General Auto Services** · 2990 San Bruno Ave
- **Shell** · 2380 San Bruno Ave

Libraries

- **Portola Library** · 2450 San Bruno Ave
- **Visitacion Valley Library** · 45 Leland Ave

Post Offices

- 2755 San Bruno Ave
- 68 Leland Ave

Schools

- **Cornerstone Academy** · 501 Cambridge St
- **Cornerstone Academy** · 801 Silver Ave
- **Edward R Taylor Elementary** · 423 Burrows St
- **El Dorado Elementary** · 70 Delta St
- **Fellowship Academy & Preschool** · 495 Cambridge St
- **Hillcrest Elementary** · 810 Silver Ave
- **Martin Luther King Jr Middle School** · 350 Girard St
- **Our Lady of the Visitacion School** · 795 Sunnydale Ave
- **Phillip Burton Academic School** · 400 Mansell St
- **SR Martin College Preparatory** · 2660 San Bruno Ave
- **San Francisco School** · 300 Gaven St
- **St Elizabeth's School** · 450 Somerset St
- **Visitacion Valley Elementary** · 55 Schwerin St
- **Visitacion Valley Middle School** · 450 Raymond Ave

Map 39 · **Visitacion Valley**

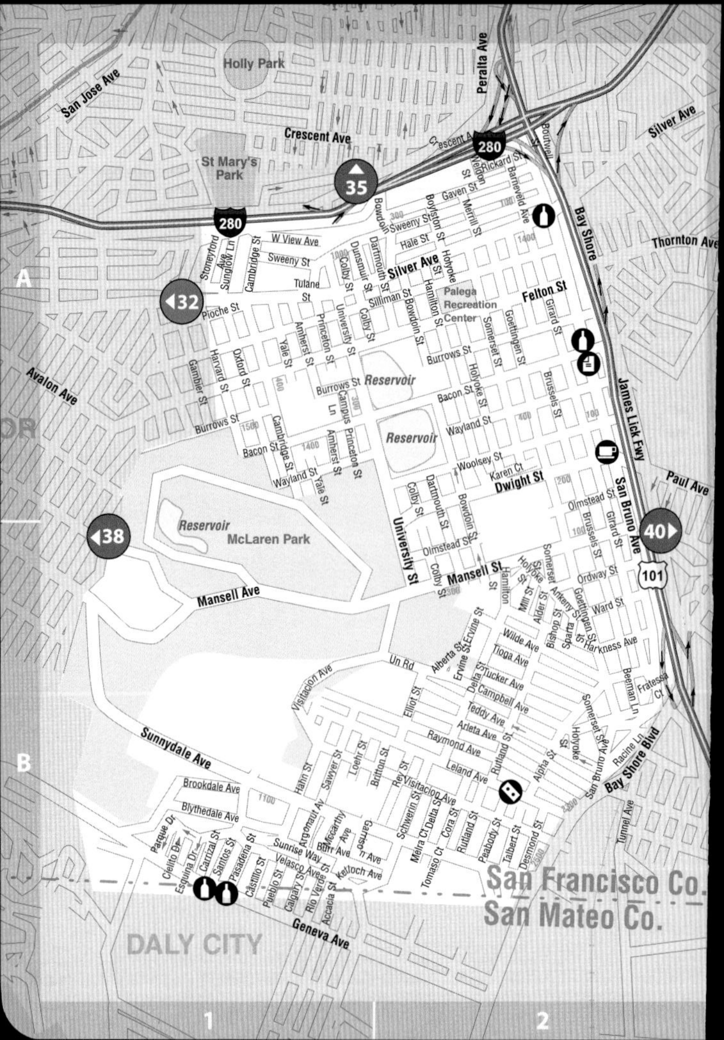

Holly Park

San Jose Ave

Crescent Ave

St Mary's Park

35

280

W View Ave

Sweeny St

Gaven St

Peralta Ave

Crescent

280

Silver Ave

Brickard Ave

Bay Shore

Silver Ave

Thornton Ave

32

Cambridge St

Sweeny St

Tulane

Pioche St

Hale St

Silver Ave

Felton St

Boylston St

Hoffman Ave

Merrill Ave

Gaven St

Barneveld Ave

Palega Recreation Center

A

Avalon Ave

Oxford St

Harvard St

Gambier St

Amherst St

Yale St

Princeton St

University St

Silliman St

Colby St

Bowdoin St

Bradford St

Girard St

Goettingen St

Somerset St

Brussels St

James Lick Fwy

Burrows St

Burrows St

Reservoir

Burrows St

Bacon St

Holyoke St

Bacon St

Somerset St

Brussels St

Cambridge St

Campus Ln

Princeton Ln

Reservoir

Wayland St

Karen Ct

Paul Ave

Wayland St

Woolsey St

Bacon St

Dartmouth St

Dwight St

Colby St

San Bruno Ave

Olmstead St

Girard St

University St

Reservoir

McLaren Park

38

Dartmouth St

Colby St

Bowdoin St

Mansell St

Olmstead St

Dwight St

Mansell St

40

101

Mansell Ave

Somerset St

Ardenwood

Girard St

Ward St

Ordway St

Hamilton St

Mill St

Alder St

Raymond Ave

Harkness Ave

Un Rd

Wilde Ave

Visitacion Ave

Alberta St

Eleanor St

Tioga Ave

Tucker Ave

Del Campbell Ave

Teddy Ave

Arleta Ave

Leland Ave

Beeman Ln

Sawyer St

Loehr St

Bruno Ave

Alpha St

Bay Shore Blvd

Elliot St

Burr St

Schwerin St

Re/Visitacion St

Sunnydale Ave

Brookdale Ave

Maria Dr

Delta St

Rutland St

Peabody St

Talbert St

Desmond St

Hahn St

Cora St

Pague Dr

Cielito Dr

Carter St

Pasadena St

Sunrise Way

Velasco Ave

Acacia St

Keith St

Racine Ln

Fratessa Ct

B

Blythedale Ave

Esquina Dr

Carpil St

Schwerin St

Tocoloma Ave

Kelloch Ave

Calgary St

Tioga Ave

Rutland St

Castillo St

Tumer Ave

San Francisco Co.
San Mateo Co.

Geneva Ave

DALY CITY

Geneva Ave

1   2

Somewhat scary residential area. Don't come at night unless the 49ers have a game at 3Com.

Coffee

• **P & M Coffee Shop** • 3007 San Bruno Ave

Copy Shops

• **Star Copier Electronics** • 2726 San Bruno Ave

Liquor Stores

• **Bus Stop Liquors & Deli** • 2698 San Bruno Ave
• **Easy Stop Market** • 2203 Geneva Ave
• **M & M Shortstop** • 2145 Geneva Ave
• **White Palace Liquor Store** • 1524 Silver Ave

Video Rental

• **Sin Fung Video (Chinese)** • 144 Leland Ave

Map 40 • **Bay View / Candlestick Point**

Candlestick Point State Recreation Area is popular with wind surfers. The name comes from the early pioneers who burned wooden ships off of the point—the last part sinking into the water looked like a candlestick.

 38 39 40 Ma

✳ Community Gardens

⬡ Police

- **Bayview Police Station** · 201 Williams Ave

✉ Post Offices

- 2111 Lane St

🎓 Schools

- **Bret Harte Elementary** · 1035 Gilman Ave
- **St Paul of the Shipwreck School** · 1060 Key Ave

Map 40 • **Bay View / Candlestick Point**

BAY VIEW

Silver Ave

Oakdale Ave

Hunters Point Blv

Palou Ave

36

37

Thornton Ave

Bay Shore

San Bruno Ave

Neptune St
Diana St
Reddy St
Ceres St
Lucy St

Mercury St
Venus St
Bancroft St
Newhall St

Williams Ave

Carroll Ave
Newhall St

Donner Ave
Egbert Ave

Fitzgerald Ave

Mendell St

Bancroft Ave

Lane St

Quesada Ave
Revere Ave
Shafter Ave
Thomas Ave
Underwood Ave
Van Dyke Ave
Wallace Ave

Key Ave

Ingalls St

Crisp Rd

Crisp Rd

39

Dwight St

Mansell St

Paul Ave

Lane St
Moscow St
Gould St
Exeter St
Carr St

Salinas Ave

Keith St
Key St
Keith St

3rd St

Donner Ave

Armstrong Ave

Bancroft Ave
Carroll Ave

Donner Ave
Egbert Ave
Fitzgerald Ave

Hollister Ave

Ingerson Ave

Jamestown Ave

Key Ave

Meade Ave

Gilman Ave

Yosemite Ave

Ingalls St

Hawes St
Griffith St
Fitch St

Coronado St

Jennings St

Armstrong Ave

Gilman Ave

Hawes St
Harney St
Nichols

Way

Griffith St

Bayview Park Rd

Bay View Park

Griffith St

Giants Dr

Jamestown Ave

Redondo

Le Conte Ave

Candlestick Park

Epbert Ave
Fitzgerald Ave
Gilman Ave

Fitch St

CANDLESTI
POINT

South Basin

PAGE
200

Hunters Point Exwy

Donner Ave

Candlestick Point
State Recreation
Area

CANDLESTI
POINT

Bay Shore Blvd

Wheeler Ave
Blanken Ave
Peninsula Ave
Tocoloma Ave

Tunnel Ave

Lathrop Ave

Visitacion Ave

Nueva Ave

Gillette Ave

Nibbi
Ct

Castaldi Rd

Raymond Ave

Executive Park Blvd

Thomas Mellon Cir

McKinnon

Harney Wy

Alana Wy

Alana Wy

Harney Way

San Francisco Co.

San Mateo Co.

A

B

101

1

2

Coffee
· **Bayside Coffee Shop** · 2011 Bay Shore Blvd

Copy Shops
· **Finest Printing** · 1555 Yosemite Ave

Liquor Stores
· **H & K Liquor & Deli** · 1300 Fitzgerald Ave
· **Smitty's Market** · 2610 Bay Shore Blvd

General Information

Phone: 415-831-2700
Website: www.parks.sfgov.org

Overview

One of the city's finest features, this panhandled swath of urban greenery is home to treasures that can surprise and delight even the most jaded San Franciscan. Each Sunday, J.F. Kennedy Drive, which snakes through the heart of the park, is closed to auto traffic, so cyclists, joggers, skaters, and general freaks (remember, this is near the Haight) have the pavement to themselves.

Bigger than New York City's Central Park, Golden Gate Park takes up 1,013 acres and is about 3 miles long and 1/2-mile wide. William Hammond Hall designed the park in 1870 and chose John McLaren to succeed him in 1887. McLaren worked for fifty years to improve the park by adding trees and plants from all over the world to beautify the vast recreational area. McLaren lived at McLaren Lodge (35), built in 1896, until he died at age 96 in 1943. The park boasts more than fifty ways to spend your day, from archery and lawn bowling (28) to horticultural museums (34) and barbecue pits (12).

Practicalities

Bordered by Lincoln Avenue to the south, Fulton Avenue to the north, Stanyan Street to the east, and the Great Highway to the west, the park is most easily accessed from 19th Avenue. Since parking is often difficult and meters have invaded whatever parking areas remain, public transportation is the best way to go. For bus, streetcar, and cable car service to Golden Gate Park, take the Muni #5, 7, 16AX, 16BX, 18, 21, 28, 28L, 29, 33, 44, 66, 71, and 71L. The free Golden Gate Shuttle picks up passengers at 15-minute intervals at 15 locations throughout the park on summer weekends and holidays only.

Attractions

The Dutch Windmill (1) is one of two originally constructed to irrigate the park. The California Academy of Sciences (23) is a library, research laboratory, planetarium, aquarium, and natural history museum all in one building. The M.H. de Young Memorial Museum is currently being rebuilt and will reopen in 2005. A unique feature of the Golden Gate Park is its number of bodies of water: nine lakes and a pond. Also, not every recreational park can boast a Buffalo Paddock (5), created in 1892.

Nature

The Conservatory of Flowers (34) houses huge palm trees, exotic orchids, and water lilies from around the world. The Garden of Shakespeare's Flowers (24) honors the plants and flowers mentioned in the Bard's poems and plays. The Strybing Arboretum (18) entices the senses with more than 6,000 plant species and is located near the Japanese Tea Garden (19), which features Asian foliage. In the middle of Stow Lake (15) is an island called Strawberry Hill (16), which is connected to the "mainland" by two bridges.

Architecture & Sculpture

The Japanese Tea Garden (19) features a very meditative teahouse, native Japanese and Chinese plants, and beautiful sculptures and birds. The Conservatory of Flowers is a great piece of Victorian architecture. For park information, go to the aforementioned McLaren Lodge (35), one of the oldest Mission-style buildings in San Francisco. The two-story Beach Chalet (2) houses some of the best murals in the city.

Open Spaces

Take your pooch along to one of the two dog runs (11, 37) to capture the feel of days when pre-domesticated dogs hunted in packs. The Children's Playground (30) and the Carousel (29) are sure to keep the kids occupied. If you're the type of person to "bring your own" food, then head to the barbecue pits (12) or picnic area (13) when your tummy starts growling.

Performance

In September, the San Francisco Shakespeare Festival presents Shakespeare in the Park, where free performances are held every weekend behind the Conservatory of Flowers (34). There's also the "Now and Zen Festival," a series of musical performances that usually takes place in late September at Sharon Meadows.

Sports

The San Francisco 49ers played in Kezar Stadium (32) from 1946 to 1970. Now it's used for high school football, among other things. An archery field lies just north of the public nine-hole golf course (4). The Fly Casting Pools (10) draw aspiring and expert fishermen alike. Soccer enthusiasts have their choice of two fields for practice and play (3, 8). Not to be left out, handball players have their choice of indoor or outdoor amusement (26). The San Francisco Lawn Bowling Club offers free lessons on the bowling greens (28). Twenty-one tennis courts are located at the eastern end of the park (33). Reservations for tennis are required for weekends and holidays. Playing fields and times must be reserved for most team sports. Call 415-831-5510 (for soccer, football, baseball, and softball) for pricing and available times.

Landmarks of Golden Gate Park

1. Dutch Windmill
2. Beach Chalet
3. Soccer Fields
4. Golf Clubhouse
5. Buffalo Paddock
6. Model Yacht Club
7. Spreckles Lake
8. Soccer & Polo Fields
9. Anglers Lodge
10. Fly Casting Pools
11. Dog Run
12. Barbecue Pits
13. Picnic Area
14. Boathouse / Boat Rentals
15. Stow Lake
16. Strawberry Hill
17. Playground
18. Strybing Arboretum
19. Japanese Tea Garden
20. M.H. de Young Memorial Museum
21. Music Concourse
22. California Academy of Sciences
23. Shakespeare Garden
24. Baseball Field
25. Handball Courts
26. AIDS Memorial Grove
27. Bowling Greens
28. Carousel
29. Children's Playground
30. Sharon Art Studio
31. Kezar Stadium
32. Tennis Courts
33. Conservatory of Flowers
34. McLaren Lodge
35. Horseshoe Pits
36. Dog Run

The Park Police Station is located by Kezar Drive and Waller Street.

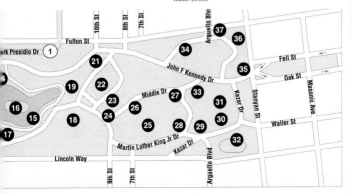

General Information

Website:	www.nps.gov/prsf
Mailing Address:	Golden Gate National Recreation Area, Building 201, Fort Mason, San Francisco, CA 94123
Phone:	415-561-4323 fax: 415-561-4310
Open:	Year-round, free entry.

Overview

Within spitting distance of the Golden Gate Bridge, offering spectacular views of the city and the Bay, the Presidio has some of the best real estate in the country. It's no surprise that private companies were

Parks and Places · **The Presidio**

area now known as the Presidio saw the arrival of Spanish soldiers and missionaries in 1776. The Presidio served as a military post under the flags of Spain, Mexico, and the United States. As a U.S. Army post, the Presidio protected commerce and trade and played a logistical role in every major U.S. military conflict over the last 150 years. In 1994, it became part of the Golden Gate National Recreation Area.

Encompassing 1,480 acres, it contains more than 500 historic buildings, a collection of coastal defense fortifications, a national cemetery, an historic airfield, a saltwater marsh, forests, beaches, native plant habitats, coastal bluffs, and miles dedicated to hiking and biking. Some of the eleven miles of hiking trails are the Golden Gate Promenade, the Coastal Trail, an ecology trail, portions of the Bay Area Ridge Trail, the Bay Trail, and the Anza National Historic Trail. Fourteen miles of paved roads provide smooth—albeit mostly uphill—biking for cyclists. There are also some unpaved parts of the Bay Area Ridge Trail if off-road is more your style. The park also contains numerous sports facilities, including a golf course, bowling alley, tennis courts, and athletic fields, as well as a campground. The recently re-landscaped Crissy Field area is another good reason to explore the park.

Facilities

Crissy Field Center, Building 603 on the corner of Mason and Halleck Streets, 415-561-7690; Open all year from 9 am to 5 pm, but closed on Mondays and Tuesdays. Houses a conservationist center that includes a café, bookstore, computer lab, and classrooms.

William Penn Mott Jr. Visitor Center, Presidio Officers' Club 50 Moraga Avenue, 415-561-4323. Open all year from 9 am to 5 pm, but closed on Thanksgiving, Christmas, and New Year's Day. Features rotating exhibits and a bookstore.

How to Get There–Driving

The Presidio can be reached from the north by crossing the Golden Gate Bridge (Highways 1 and 101); from the east by way of Lombard Street (Highway 101); and from the south via Highway 1.

How to Get There–Mass Transit

San Francisco Municipal Railway (Muni) buses serve the Presidio via the 28, 29, 43, and 82X lines. Bus service from the North Bay to the Golden Gate Bridge toll plaza is available through Golden Gate Transit. Commercial cable car buses are available from Fisherman's Wharf. The Presidio Trust provides free shuttle service within the Presidio and to nearby public transit stops.

eager to get in on the action when part of the Presidio was opened to development as an industrial park a couple of years ago. As a result, there's plenty of construction taking place on the grounds these days, but nothing that will mar the site's unique beauty. Once home to the Native American tribe the Ohlone, the

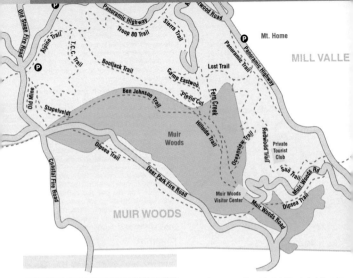

General Information

Website: www.nps.gov/muwo
Phone: 415-388-2596
Open: 8 am to sunset, including holidays.
Admission: $3 day fee or $15 for an annual pass.

Overview

This sanctuary of old-growth redwood trees is nothing short of a little bit of heaven. During the country's rapid industrialization in the 1800s, many once redwood-covered valleys were laid bare by development. However, some valleys weren't touched because they were hard to get to. Muir Woods was one of them. In 1905, following a conservationist fad, Congressman William Kent bought 295 acres for $45,000. To protect the redwoods, he donated the land to the federal government and President Theodore Roosevelt declared it a national monument in 1908. Although Roosevelt wanted the area to be named after Kent, Kent decided to memorialize conservationist John Muir.

For the less able (or inappropriately attired) park visitors, there's a paved walkway that takes you from the visitor center to the fourth bridge and back. Unless you like large crowds of loud people, plan to take any one of the dirt trails that wind their way through the redwoods.

Picnicking is not allowed in Muir Woods, but, if you're hungry, there is a café near the entrance. If you're lucky, you'll arrive at the right time to listen to an ecology talk by one of the knowledgeable park rangers.

Pets are prohibited, with the exception of guide or other service dogs. Although visitors cannot cycle in the woods, bikers are allowed on designated fire roads surrounding Muir Woods. For obvious reasons, smoking is not permitted.

How to Get There–Driving

From San Francisco, Peninsula, or South Bay, Take Highway 101 North across the Golden Gate Bridge. Exit Highway 1/Stinson Beach (there will be a sign for Muir Woods at this exit) and drive about 0.5 miles. At the stoplight, turn left. Drive about 2.7 miles. At the top of the hill, turn right towards Muir Woods/Mount Tamalpais. Follow posted signs to Muir Woods.

How to Get There–Mass Transit

No public transportation serves the park directly. Golden Gate Transit (415-923-2000) bus #63 runs on weekends and holidays and makes stops at the Mountain Home Inn, Pantoll, and Bootjack on Panoramic Highway. From any of these stops it is a 1- to 1.8-mile hike down to Muir Woods.

Overview

At 193 acres, with spectacular views of the Golden Gate Bridge and the Marin Headlands and a sprawling public golf course, Lincoln Park is one of the best park spaces in all of San Francisco. It's also probably the only one where you can play a round of golf and then take a brief stroll over to one of the finest art collections in the country, the Palace of the Legion of Honor.

Originally the site of the Golden Gate cemetery, city commissioners developed Lincoln Park in 1908, turning the Gold Rush graveyard into a posh 18-hole golf course. Many of the corpses were exhumed and moved as the plot was transformed, but hundreds of bodies remain buried beneath this picturesque park. If you've seen the film Poltergeist, you might want to avoid the area in the evening hours.

Practicalities

The park can be easily accessed by car from 34th Ave or El Camino del Mar. There is parking near the golf course (does this sound like a bad idea, anyone?), as well as near the Legion of Honor museum. The Muni bus #18 stops right at the Legion of Honor.

Golf

One of the main draws of Lincoln Park is undoubtedly the par-69 public golf course. The layout is not as challenging as the other two public 18-hole courses in town, Harding Park and the Presidio, but it benefited from a renovation unlike the others (even though it is a hundred years old). At the same time, the back nine at Lincoln offer challenges for even the most confident golfer, including a 240+ yard par three. It can be difficult to get advance tee times with the automated reservation system (at 415-750-GOLF), but the course usually accepts walk-ons. Take advantage of the cheaper weekday and twilight rates. Locals who pick up a Resident Golf Card at City Hall can play for $20 less. There is no driving range at Lincoln Park, and the putting green is a little lumpy, but the pro shop is fully equipped and conveniently connected to a bar and grill that frequently has draft beer specials. www.lincolnparkgc.com.

Art

The main cultural attraction of the park is the California Palace of the Legion of Honor. Modeled after the 18th century Palais de la Légion d'Honneur in Paris, this grand Beaux-Arts building has an excellent collection of ancient and European art. One of the notable pieces displayed here is Rodin's Thinker sculpture. The museum is open Tuesday through Sunday from 9:30 am to 5 pm. Adult admission is $8, but Tuesdays are free! The museum has an excellent café and a well-stocked museum store. Phone: 415-863-3330.

In addition to the scenic golf course and museum, this park is home to George Segal's controversial Holocaust Memorial sculpture, which is located near the Palace of the Legion of Honor. Installed in 1984, Segal's chilling work depicts a pile of emaciated, dead bodies next to one lone survivor gazing hopefully out over the Pacific.

Restaurants & Cafes

- Legion Cafe • California Palace of the Legion of Honor • 415-221-2233
- Lincoln Park Bar & Grill • 300 34th Ave • 415-221-2014

There are also numerous restaurants, bars, and cafes on Clement St. along the south end of the park.

General Information

Website: www.ghirardellisq.com
Address: 900 North Point St,
               San Francisco, CA 94109
Phone: 415-775-5500
Summer Hours: June 10–Sept 2, Mon–Sat 10 am–9 pm,
               Sun 10 am–6 pm.
Winter Hours: Sept 3–Apr 20, Mon–Thurs 11 am–7 pm,
               Fri–Sun 11 am–6 pm
Other Hours: Apr 21–June 9, Mon–Thurs 10 am–7 pm,
               Fri & Sat 10 am–8 pm, Sun 11 am–6 pm

Overview

Ghirardelli Square is right next to Fisherman's Wharf, so there are more tourists here than you can shake a crustacean at, but they're here with good reason: this cluster of shops, restaurants, and bars is a heck of a lot of fun. And did we mention the chocolate? If you're not into shopping and the weather is warm, the people-watching is great on the big steps facing the bay and Alcatraz.

Who, you may ask, put the "G" in Ghirardelli? In 1893, after two of those relentless San Francisco fires destroyed his lot, Italian goldrusher-cum-chocolatier Domingo Ghirardelli bought a block of property on North Point Street overlooking the San Francisco Bay, establishing his new factory site. In the 1960s, the chocolate factory moved across the Bay. What remains today is a brick-terraced courtyard of shops and fine restaurants on a site that has been granted National Historic Register status, a site that's considered the country's first successful adaptive reuse project. The original 1860 cast-iron chocolate grinder is located in the Lower Plaza, and other chocolate-making equipment is still operating on a small scale in the Ghirardelli Chocolate Manufactory. The famous "Ghirardelli" sign, 25 feet tall and 125 feet wide, brightly welcomes ships into the Bay and has become a San Francisco landmark.

Practicalities

Everything at Ghirardelli square is easy to locate, but if you need help, there is an information booth located at Fountain Plaza, which sells souvenirs, film, chocolate, and Muni passes, and gives out free maps.

The Square is made up of 7 principal buildings: the Clock Tower; the Mustard Building; the Cocoa Building; the Chocolate Building; Woolen Mill; Wurster; and the Power House. These were all part of the original Ghirardelli factory.

Parking is available at the California Parking Garage off Larkin Street or Beach Street. There is discounted parking with merchant validation. Rates are $1.50 per half-hour, $3 per hour, $15 for a 12-hour maximum, and $30 for a 24-hour maximum. With all the traffic that comes through here, your best bet is to avoid the parking issue altogether and take public transportation. For more information on parking, call 415-929-1665.

Activities

Ghirardelli Square is popular with tourists and locals because of its concentration of shops and restaurants. For the history buffs, there are free 20-minute walking tours offered on weekends between July 4 and September 1, from 2 pm to 5 pm, with docents dressed in Victorian costumes recalling the history of Domingo and his entire family. Sorry, no drag queens—at least not officially. Participants even get a free chocolate!

A big draw to the square is the annual Chocolate Festival, held on the first weekend in September. The event features chocolate treats from Ghirardelli Square establishments, as well as prominent restaurants, bakeries, and chocolatiers from around the Bay Area. Not to be missed is the "Earthquake" ice cream sundae-eating contest, where the winner receives his or her weight in Ghirardelli Chocolate.

Holidays are a time for family fun at Ghirardelli Square. On the Fourth of July, there is live musical entertainment and kid-related festivities. Christmas celebrations include the annual Tree Lighting Ceremony in late November, when there are a variety of caroling performances, a local celebrity emcee, and a visit from the Clauses. The 50-foot tree is decorated with, as you've probably guessed, chocolate bars. And in mid-December, the Jollyday celebration features children's entertainment and free face-painting.

Where to Eat

Eateries from across the dining spectrum abound at Ghirardelli Square. On the Fountain Plaza, Lori's Diner serves nostalgic American fare, and on the 1st floor of the Mustard Building, you'll find Mosaique, a lounge and café. Frjtz Fries is located on the 2nd floor of the Woolen Mill Building, offering Belgian fries and crepes. On the 3rd floor of the Chocolate Building is Gaylord India Restaurant, and on the 4th floor of the Woolen Mill Building is the Mandarin Restaurant. Along Beach Street in Wurster, there are a number of restaurants, including Pizza Chicago, McCormick and Kuleto's Seafood Restaurant, and Boudin Sourdough Bakery and Café, and modern Vietnamese cuisine is served at Ana Mandara in the Power House. However, if you have come to Ghirardelli Square for the food it is most famous for, Ghirardelli chocolate is not hard to find.

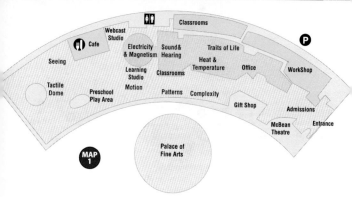

Webcast Studio
Classrooms
Cafe
Seeing
Electricity & Magnetism
Sound & Hearing
Traits of Life
Learning Studio
Heat & Temperature
Office
WorkShop
Classrooms
Motion
P
Tactile Dome
Preschool Play Area
Patterns
Complexity
Gift Shop
Admissions
Entrance
McBean Theatre
MAP 1
Palace of Fine Arts

General Information

Website: www.exploratorium.edu
Location: 3601 Lyon St., San Francisco, CA 94123
Phone: 415-EXP-LORE (415-397-5673)
Open: Tuesday through Sunday from 10 am to 5 pm. (Closed on Thanksgiving and Christmas.)
Entry: $12 for adults and $9.50 for children, students, and seniors. (The Tactile Dome is $15 for all, admission included.) Free admission on the first Wednesday of each month.

Overview

Want to see what happens to a building during an earthquake? How about shooting your body with enough static electricity to give you a Don King 'do? The Exploratorium, located in San Francisco's Palace of Fine Arts, includes over 650 science, art, and human perception exhibits. Founded in 1969 by Dr. Frank Oppenheimer, who was director until his death in 1985, the Exploratorium is a learning center that combines science and technology with nature and art.

Exhibits focus on how humans perceive light, color, sound, motion, electricity, heat, language, weather, and more. The not-to-be-missed Tactile Dome lets you crawl, climb, and slide through unusual textures in darkness, guided only by touch (which is not that different from a typical night on the town in San Francisco). The experience requires an extra fee with admission and a time reservation. We highly recommend making a reservation in advance of your visit by calling 415-561-0362.

The stately, classical looking Palace of Fine Arts might seem like an odd place for a scientific museum (it was built in 1915), but the Exploratorium continues to stay on par with the rapidly changing technological world. Its facilities include a multimedia Learning Center, wired classrooms, a biology laboratory, the 150-seat McBean Theater, and the Phyllis C. Wattis Webcast Studio. Attendance at a webcast is encouraged, and entrance is included in general admission.

How to Get There–Driving

From the North Bay, cross the Golden Gate Bridge, following signs indicating downtown San Francisco. Take the Marina exit on the left. (You'll see the Marina exit sign overhead.) Do not take the Lombard Street exit. Take a sharp right turn at the light at the end of the exit ramp. This is the entrance to the museum. The parking lot entrance is about 500 feet ahead on the right.

From the East Bay, cross the Bay Bridge. Follow the signs to the Ninth Street exit. Stay in the right-hand lane. Go one block and turn right onto Ninth. Stay in the left-hand lane. Immediately after Market, veer left onto Hayes Street. Make a right turn onto Van Ness Avenue. Take Van Ness to Lombard (look for signs to the Golden Gate Bridge). Turn left onto Lombard. Once on Lombard, get into the right-hand lane. Follow Lombard to Lyon Street. At Lyon Street turn right. At the "T", turn left onto Palace Drive. Follow it around the Palace of Fine Arts to the entrance of the parking lot, on your left.

From the South Bay or the Peninsula, take 101 North to the Market Street/Van Ness exit. Take Van Ness north (look for signs to the Golden Gate Bridge.) Turn left onto Lombard. Once on Lombard, get into the right-hand lane. Follow Lombard to Lyon Street. At Lyon Street turn right. At the "T", turn left onto Palace Drive. Follow it around the Palace of Fine Arts to the entrance of the parking lot, on your left.

How to Get There–Mass Transit

The Exploratorium has convenient access to public transportation. San Francisco Muni buses 30, 43, 28, and 29 go right to the door, while Muni bus lines 22, 41, and 45 also stop in the vicinity. From Fisherman's Wharf, take the 30 Stockton bus. If you're taking BART, get off at the Montgomery Street station, walk half a block up Market Street to Third Street and catch the #30 Stockton bus on the corner. Virtually all downtown-bound Golden Gate Transit buses stop near the Exploratorium.

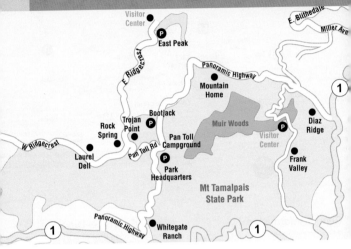

General Information

Website: www.parks.ca.gov
Mailing Address: 801 Panoramic Hwy, Mill Valley, CA 94941
Phone: 415-388-2070
Open: Daily: 7 am to sunset, with the hours fluctuating with the seasons.
Entry: Camping costs from $14.50. Reservations are required.

Overview

Just north of San Francisco's Golden Gate is Mt. Tamalpais (pronounced Tam-ill-pie-iss), which covers 6,300 acres of redwood and oak woodlands. The highlight is the spectacular view from the 2,571-foot peak. On a clear day, you can see as far as the Sierra Nevadas, some 200 miles away. Nearer views include downtown San Francisco, Tiburon, Mt. Diablo, the Marin Headlands, the Pacific Ocean, and the Farallon Islands. Originally, the peak was named—get ready for a mouthful—La Sierra de Nuestro Padre de San Francisco. Later, the name was changed to Tamalpais, in honor of the Miwok Indians who lived in the area for thousands of years before Europeans arrived. Locals just call it Mt. Tam.

Camping at Mt. Tamalpais is lots of fun, but you have to be very serious in your planning. If you're not up for camping, you can hike and bike in the area. There's a 200-mile-long trail system leading around and to the top of Tamalpais. Twisting roads to the peak challenge bicyclists. They can also be dangerous—bikers have been known to lose control and fall to their death over the cliffs, so cycle at your own risk. For the less athletically inclined, the Bootjack Picnic Area has tables, stoves, piped drinking water, and (oh what a relief!) flush toilets.

If you're taking your first excursion to Mt. Tamalpais, you should check out the visitor center on the East Peak Summit. There's also a refreshment stand that is open daily during the summer. Phones, picnic tables, and fully accessible restrooms are also available to bring you back to civilization.

The Mountain Theater (also called The Cushing Memorial Theater) has been in use since the early 1900s. In the 1930s, the Civilian Conservation Corps added seating, improved the stage, and landscaped the area. This natural-stone amphitheater seats 3,750 people and produces a play each spring.

Practicalities

During the summer months, when the weather heats up and the vegetation dries out, park authorities sometimes close parts of Mt. Tam due to a high potential for fires. You can get an update on park closings by calling the PanToll Station at 415-388-2070.

How to Get There–Driving

Mt. Tam is north of San Francisco's Golden Gate Bridge. From Highway 101 take Highway 1 to the Stinson Beach exit and follow signs up the mountain. If you happen to get distracted by incredible scenery, then let someone else do the driving so you can enjoy the view without risk of driving off a cliff. And watch out for the numerous cyclists.

General Information

Website: www.moscone.com
Location: 747 Howard Street, San Francisco, CA 94103
Phone: 415-974-4000
Fax: 415-974-4073

Overview

Notice a lot of bag-laden, name-tag-emblazoned people in "business casual" ambling around the streets? They're called conventioneers, and they're a form of wildlife typical to the habitat known as Moscone Center. The meeting and exhibition hall, which occupies two eleven-acre blocks and bordered by Mission, Folsom, Third, and Fourth Streets, is surrounded by shopping, dining, and nightlife options, as well as museums and new hotels. It's about to get even bigger. In 1996, the center received a large grant from the city to plan for the Moscone Center Expansion Project. The expansion will be near the original Moscone Center site on the northwest corner of Howard and Fourth Streets. The city also helped the center become greener, and not just in color—5,000 solar panels on the center's roof help it run more efficiently and cleanly.

The Moscone Center has ample rooftop facilities. On top of Moscone South is the Rooftop at the Gardens. It features the learning center Zeum, which teaches children about technology and the arts. The complex also features a unique 1906 carousel, a hands-on interactive children's garden, a café, and concession stands. Across the street, on top of Moscone North, the Yerba Buena Gardens includes two cafés and a memorial to Martin Luther King Jr.

The Moscone Center incorporates unique designs, including Moscone South's 16 post-tensioned steel and concrete arches arranged in pairs to support its roof. The north and south lobbies and the Esplanade ballroom outline more than a million square feet of overall building area. To maximize light dispersal, large expanses of glass were used for the exterior. Skylights also provide as much natural light as possible.

Facilities

There are two ATMs in the Moscone Center—one in the West building, the other in the North building.

How to Get There–Driving

Head north on Interstate 101 then take 80 East. Take the Fourth Street exit. Make a left on Bryant, a left on Third and a left on Howard. The Moscone Center is located on the 700 block of Howard Street. You'll find Moscone South on your left and Moscone North on your right.

Via the Bay Bridge, take the Fremont Street exit to Howard Street and turn left on Howard.

Via the Golden Gate Bridge, take the Lombard Street exit to Van Ness Avenue. Turn right on Van Ness. Travel south to Grove. This will be approximately two miles. Turn left on Grove Street. Continue to Market Street. Cross Market Street and travel south on Eighth Street to Folsom. Turn left on Folsom, left on Third, and left on Howard.

How to Get There–Mass Transit

If you're taking BART or Muni Metro, disembark at the Powell Street Station. Exit to Fourth and Market Streets and turn right onto Fourth. Walk two blocks south to Howard and turn left. The Moscone Center is located on the 700 block of Howard Street. You'll find Moscone South on your right and Moscone North on your left.

If Caltrain is more your speed, get off at Fourth & Townsend. Cross Fourth Street from the train station and catch the 15, 30, or 45 lines. Get off at Third and Folsom. Walk one block North up towards Howard St. Turn left onto Howard.

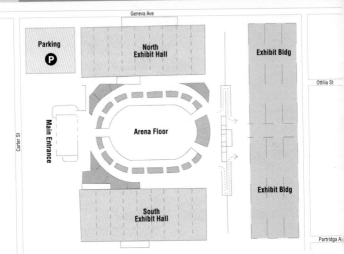

General Information

Website: www.cowpalace.com
Location: Geneva Ave and Santos St
Address: San Francisco Cow Palace, P.O. Box 34206, San Francisco, CA 94134-0206
Phone: 415-404-4100

Overview

Contrary to its name, the Cow Palace is not a residence for royal bovines, so there's no need to worry about stumbling over manure. The unusual name comes from one of its first events—a livestock exhibition. During the Great Depression, when the building was being planned, a newspaper commented: "Why, when people are starving, should money be spent on a 'palace for cows'?" The name stuck! Since opening in 1941, the Palace has welcomed more than 50 million visitors and now hosts fairs, expositions, and a circus—and even the famously raunchy "Exotic Erotic Ball," held each year near Halloween.

After World War II, during which the Palace was used as a garage for the federal government, it re-opened for the general public. The first sports event that the Cow Palace hosted was the U.S. Heavyweight Boxing Championship. Other sports-related shows that followed were roller derby, tennis, wrestling, professional basketball, and ice hockey. The Palace kept gaining in popularity and now holds political conventions, ice shows, the Grand National Rodeo, Ringling Bros. Barnum & Bailey Circus, the San Francisco Sport & Boat Show, and the Golden Gate Kennel Club Dog Show, not to mention many successful music concerts. In 1974, the Haight-Ashbury's own Grateful Dead unveiled one of the greatest P.A. systems ever, the "Wall of Sound."

How to Get There–Driving

From the Golden Gate Bridge, follow Highway 1 (19th Avenue) past S.F. State University. Take the Cow Palace/Alemany Blvd. loop and continue to Alemany. Turn left onto Alemany and continue to Geneva Ave. Turn right onto Geneva and follow the signs. The Cow Palace is on the right.

From Highway 101 N, take the Brisbane/Cow Palace exit, go straight to Geneva, and turn left. The Cow Palace is 10 blocks up on the left.

From Highway 101 S, take the Cow Palace/Third Street exit, and immediately merge to the right onto Bayshore. Follow Bayshore and turn right into Geneva. The Cow Palace is 10 blocks up on the left.

From Highway 280 N, take the Geneva/Ocean exit and turn right onto Geneva. Follow a few miles and the Cow Palace will be on the left.

From Highway 280 S, take the Geneva/Ocean exit and turn left onto Geneva. Follow a few miles and the Cow Palace will be on the right.

How to Get There–Mass Transit

Take the San Francisco/Daly City BART line to Balboa Park station. From Balboa Park station take the #15 Muni bus to the Cow Palace bus stop at Santos Street.

A good alternative to mass transit is the Daly City Cab service. Call 650-992-8865 for taxi transportation to or from the Cow Palace or to schedule taxi pickups at Balboa Park BART station.

General Information

Website: www.yerbabuenaarts.org
Location: 701 Mission St at 3rd St,
San Francisco, CA 94103-3138
Phone: 415-978-ARTS (2787)

Overview

Sandwiched between the wacky retail world of the Metreon Shopping Center and the even wackier world of 20th-century modern art displayed at the SFMOMA, the Yerba Buena Center and Gardens is a bright spot of San Francisco's SOMA neighborhood. The Yerba Buena Center for the Arts consists of two landmark buildings, both run by the nonprofit center: Galleries and Forum Building and the Theater. They are adjacent to the beautiful urban oasis of the Yerba Buena Gardens. The gardens offer an array of attractions, including restaurants, museums, public art, and, of course, nature space. You might be lucky and catch some outdoor performances from May through October.

The Center for the Arts features a 757-seat theater with two-tier seating. There are a variety of staged events, including theatrical presentations, concerts, lectures, and receptions for industry events. Another social gathering area is the Forum. Catch a program or lecture at the Center's screening room. For a special insight into the artwork in the galleries, take a tour with exhibiting artists, curators and other special guests on the first Thursday evening of each month. Check the website for current exhibitions.

The gardens include a butterfly garden that offers a relaxed habitat for a number of butterflies, as well as a sanctuary for humans (i.e., weary shoppers, stressed-out cubicle-land refugees, and anyone else who needs some urban relief). The Oché Wat Té Ou (Reflection), a tribute to the native Ohlone Indians, is a wood wall, patterned with Ohlone basket designs, behind a curved pool. The artists intend the piece to be used by poets, storytellers, and others adept at oral traditions. The Sister Cities Garden features flowering plants from thirteen cities around the world. On the terrace are two cafés. There's also sculpture, such as the "Shaking Man", a freaky, life-size bronze statue of a segmented businessman (he looks like he's been run through a paper shredder and glued back together) who offers a handshake for visitors. Have children? There's a bowling alley and ice-skating rink on the Rooftop Gardens. The Garden's centerpiece is the 22-foot-high, 50-foot-wide waterfall that leads to the impressive Martin Luther King Jr. Memorial. Twelve glass sections behind the waterfall are engraved with quotes from Dr. King's writings and speeches.

How to Get There–Driving

From the East Bay, take Interstate 80 and exit at Fremont Street. Turn left onto Fremont at the end of the ramp, and take another left onto Howard. Turn right on Fifth Street. Follow Fifth to Mission and turn right. Follow Mission to YBCA, between Fourth and Third Streets.

From the South Bay, take Highway 101 north and follow signs for I-80 East. Exit on Fourth Street, which will lead to Bryant. Turn left on Third Street. The Theater is on your left at the intersection of Third and Howard. The Galleries and Forum building are on your left at the intersection of Third and Mission.

From the North Bay, take Highway 101 south to the Lombard Street exit. Follow Lombard to Van Ness, turning right on Van Ness. Follow Van Ness until you reach Golden Gate then turn left. Golden Gate will take you across Market Street onto Sixth Street. Turn left onto Mission. Follow Mission to YBCA, between Fourth and Third Streets.

How to Get There–Mass Transit

If you're taking BART, exit at Montgomery Station or Powell Stations. Muni bus users can take all Market Street lines, plus 5 Fulton, 9 San Bruno, 14 Mission, 15 Third, 30 Stockton, 38 Geary, or 45 Union. If you're a Muni Metro rider, exit at Powell or Montgomery Street Stations.

Golden Gate Transit buses 10, 20, 50, 60, 70, and 80 stop on Mission at Third Street. The Caltrain stop closest to YBC & G is at Fourth and Townsend Streets.

Fisherman's Wharf / Pier 39

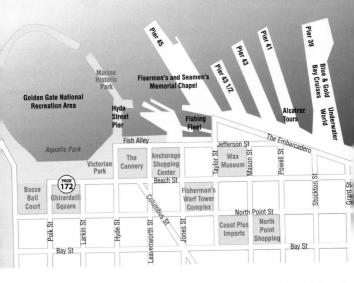

General Information

Website: www.fishermanswharf.org
Location: Northpoint St between
Van Ness and Grant
Phone: 415-974-6900

Overview

Ah, the Wharf—adored by tourists, loathed by residents. Or so they say. Even for jaded locals, the Wharf has its charms. Here you can gaze down at the boats in serene water or stop to watch fishermen fixing mesh nets broken by yesterday's catch. And let's not forget the seafood and nearby Ghirardelli Square. Sure, its souvenir-and-postcard shops make it seem pretty tacky, but if you get tired of looking at the tourists, you can always go and watch the sea lions in all their smelly, noisy glory as they lounge on the docks by Pier 39.

A busy port since the California Gold Rush, the Wharf has gone through three distinct changes. Originally, green Italian sailboats with patron saints painted on their backs frequented the Wharf. Later, stronger gasoline-powered boats, known as Monterey Hull boats, could be heard in the water, making it possible to fish more days of the year with better accessories, like machine-operated nets. Today, diesel-powered boats overshadow the vintage Monterey Hull boats in size as well as technology. The newest generation of boats is equipped with two-way radio telephones and sonar.

Attractions

The Blue & Gold Fleet is the exclusive operator of ferry service to Alcatraz as well as narrated Bay cruises (415-705-5555). Another ferry service, the Red & White Fleet, has been open since 1892 and features sailings under the Golden Gate Bridge and around Angel Island (877-855-5506). For a Sunday brunch buffet with champagne, visit the Pacific Marine Yachts' San Francisco Spirit (415-788-9100). The Wax Museum has Hollywood celebrities, presidents, and scientists—be sure to experience its Chamber of Horrors (800-439-4305).

Shopping

For forty-five distinctive shops, stop at the Anchorage Shopping Center. It also has one of the city's best microbreweries, as well as live entertainment every day (415-775-6000). The Cannery, which was originally an actual peach cannery, has been transformed into a marketplace with cafés and romantic restaurants (415-771-3112). The Fisherman's Wharf Tower Complex offers great shopping and gifts for your inner tourist (415-454-4328). The largest shopping center is Pier 39 with 110 specialty shops. If you don't feel like shopping, the views of San Francisco Bay from Pier 39 rival all postcards (415-705-5500). For galleries, a beautiful landscape, and famous chocolate, head to Ghirardelli Square (415-775-5500).

Restaurants

Alioto's Restaurant, 8 Fisherman's Wharf, offers great food with a great view (415-673-0183). For the penny-pinchers, free parking is included at the Franciscan Restaurant, 43 Fisherman's Wharf (415-362-7733), and Scoma's Restaurant, 47 Pier 47 (415-771-4385). For more than fifty years, Pompei's Grotto, 340 Jefferson St., has been presenting fresh seafood and Italian specialties in a casual, family-friendly environment (415-776-9265). For an interesting experience, the Rainforest Café, 145 Jefferson St, offers a realistic, but yes, artificial, rainforest (415-440-5610).

Accommodations

- Best Western Tuscan Inn • 425 Jones St • 415-561-1100
- Hilton • 2620 Jones St • 415-885-4700
- Holiday Inn • 1300 Columbus Ave • 415-771-9000
- Hyatt • 555 Northpoint St • 415-563-1234
- Radisson Hotel • 250 Beach St • 415-392-6700
- Marriott • 1250 Columbus Ave • 415-775-7555
- Sheraton • 2500 Mason St • 415-362-5500

How to Get There–Driving

From the south, take the 101 North towards San Francisco. Take 280 North towards Downtown San Francisco. Exit at King St. Follow King St. past Pacific Bell Park where King St. becomes Embarcadero. Continue down the Embarcadero staying in the middle lane. Turn left onto Bay St., right onto Mason St., then left onto Northpoint St.

From East Bay via the Bay Bridge, take 80 west to San Francisco, crossing the Bay Bridge. Exit at Harrison St/Embarcadero (this exit is on the left side). At the bottom of the exit, turn right onto Harrison St. At the end of Harrison St., take a left onto Embarcadero. Continue down Embarcadero staying in the middle lane. Turn left onto Bay St., right onto Mason St. then left onto Northpoint St.

How to Get There–Mass Transit

Take the F-line street car. A fun alternative is the Powell-Hyde cable car to Beach St or Powell-Mason cable car to Bay St. If BART is your mode of transportation, get off at Embarcadero.

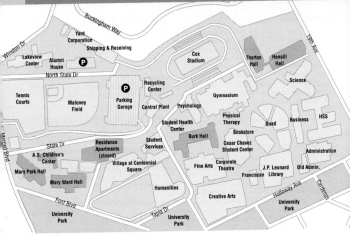

General Information

Mailing Address:	1600 Holloway Ave, San Francisco, CA 94132
Location:	1600 Halloway Ave between Cardenas and Varela
Phone:	415-338-1111
Website:	www.sfsu.edu
Opened:	1899
Present Enrollment:	28,378 (2,005 of whom come from overseas)
Type of School:	Public

Overview

Located near the city's posh and sylvan St. Francis Wood neighborhood, San Francisco State University's campus is an academic oasis bordered by the Stonestown shopping mall to the north, Lake Merced to the west, and tree-lined residential areas south and east. SFSU's student body represents an exceptional range of ethnic groups, cultures, ages, values, and life experiences. It's no wonder that SFSU ranks tenth in the nation in awarding degrees to minorities. The school's mix of people and cultures leads to stimulating discussions and academic offerings. The new Modern Jewish Studies program is just one example.

At SFSU, students don't just learn in classrooms and laboratories—they learn in the Bay Area itself. Through service learning programs and courses, SFSU students have worked to improve city housing projects, bring music instruction to city schools, help immigrants prepare for citizenship tests, and support health care for low-income residents. The students can also take advantage of San Francisco's attractions, authentic ethnic neighborhoods, parks and recreation areas, and the city's vibrant nightlife and entertainment attractions.

Tuition

As of spring 2003, undergraduate resident students who take up to 6.0 units of credit pay $702 per semester while undergraduate resident students who take more credits pay $1,002 per semester. Graduate resident students who accept up to 6.0 units pay $768 per semester and graduate resident students with more than 6.0 units pay $1,083 per semester. A nonresident student must add $282 per unit to the semester fees. Those taking advantage of the "Open University" program for non-matriculated students will pay a $175 per unit fee for lecture-discussion courses and $200 per unit for science lab courses.

Parking

The Lot 20 garage offers general paid public, visitor/guest, and student parking. It's open 24/7 and is $1 per hour with a $5 maximum. The roof level is restricted to staff and faculty between 7 am and 5 pm, Monday through Friday. Lot 25 is open everyday from 7 am to 10 pm and does not have the faculty and staff restriction. For those who bike to campus, the (free!) Bike Barn is open from 7:30 am to 10 pm weekdays, but it closes at 5 pm on Fridays.

ATMs

Washington Mutual ATMs are located on the main level of the Cesar Chavez Student Center. Bank of America and Wells Fargo ATMs are located outside the Student Center near the bookstore. CAL STATE 9 Credit Union ATMs are outside the Franciscan Building.

Cultural Events

In addition to regular music performances and exhibits at the Cesar Chavez Student Center, the university offers a number of annual cultural and arts-related events. Each May, the university's Cinema Department presents its Film Finals Showcase, a one-night gala event showcasing the work of young Bay Area filmmakers. Most of the films in the showcase go on to the national and international film festival circuit. Other events include community-service programs such as the annual African-American Community Health Fair, usually held in the spring.

Sports

The SFSU Department of Athletics has sixteen athletics teams, nine for women and seven for men. SFSU currently sponsors basketball, cross-country, soccer, track and field, and swimming for both men and women. Baseball and wrestling have men's teams, while indoor track and field, softball, tennis, and volleyball have women's squads. Intramural leagues, tournaments, and special events exist for students during the academic year. Workout facilities are available in the gym at noon and during certain evening hours for students, faculty, and staff. On July 1, 1998, San Francisco State University became an official member of the California Collegiate Athletic Association, which was founded in 1939.

Intercollegiate athletics is an integral component of the academic experience at SFSU. On-campus athletic facilities include Cox Stadium, Main Gymnasium, Maloney Field, Stephenson Field, the main pool, and tennis courts. Also, the Gator Conditioning Center is a fitness facility for all student-athletes. Intramural leagues, tournaments, and special events are offered in the fall and spring semesters. The program consists of men's, women's, and coed sports, including basketball, volleyball, indoor soccer, swimming, bowling, ultimate Frisbee, water polo, softball, badminton, tennis, and flag football.

Department Contact Info

Undergraduate Admissions 415-338-7238
Graduate Admissions 415-338-7238
College of Behavioral & Social Studies .. 415-338-1846
College of Business 415-338-1276
College of Creative Arts .... allarts@sfsu.edu
College of Education 415-338-2687
College of Ethnic Studies 415-338-1693
College of Extended Learning 415-405-7700
College of Health & Human Services . 415-338-3326
College of Humanities 415-338-1541
Interdisciplinary Studies 415-338-6927
College of Science and Engineering . 415-338-1571
Division of Information Technology . 415-338-1420
Disability Resource Center 415-338-2472
Student Health Center 415-338-1251
Recreation Program 415-338-3363
Lost and Found 415-338-2306

University of California, San Francisco

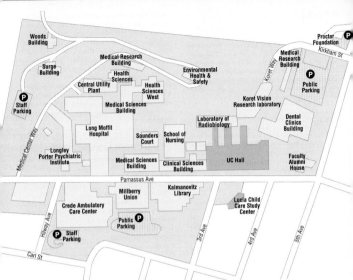

Parnassus Campus

General Information

Mailing Address:	The University of California, San Francisco, CA 94143
Location:	513 Parnassus Avenue
General Phone:	415-476-9000
Website:	www.ucsf.edu

Overview

The University of California, San Francisco offers graduate and professional programs in the areas of health sciences, education, and patient care. It has been part of the University of California for 130 years. UCSF places a strong emphasis on the diversity of its student body, as well as a commitment to public service amongst its students. The UCSF Homeless Clinic is completely run by students, providing free medical care to homeless people in San Francisco. There is also a dental clinic with the same goal. The Medical Effectiveness Research Center for Diverse Populations (MERC) conducts research on the barriers that impede various groups' access to quality health care.

UCSF students train at three main teaching hospitals in the city: San Francisco General Hospital, UCSF-Mount Zion Medical Center, and the Department of Veterans Affairs Medical Center.

At the Parnassus Campus, many services for students are located in the Millberry Union building at 500 Parnassus Avenue. There you'll find the bookstore; food services such as the Courtyard Café, Palio Coffee Bar, and Panda Express; the Recreation Fitness Center; Golden 1 Credit Union; Reprographics/Quick Copy; conference centers; The Source Computer Services; and faculty housing.

Tuition

Tuition varies depending upon which of the five schools you are admitted to. For the Medical School, California residents pay $11,500 and non-residents pay $22,500. Dental School students pay $11,000 (residents) and $22,000 (non-residents). For the School of Pharmacy, tuition is $9,000 (residents) and $20,000 (non-residents). Nursing School tuition is $7,500 (residents) and $18,700 (non-residents). (All fees are estimates and do not include housing.) Fees for the Graduate Division vary depending on your field of study. Visit http://saawww.ucsf.edu/admission/fees.htm for more information.

Parking

At the Parnassus Heights Campus, parking is available in public garages. Millberry Union Public Garage is located at 500 Parnassus Avenue and Irving Street. The first two hours are $2.50 each, with an additional hour costing $2.00. The 24-hour maximum is $20.00. The Westside/Kirkham Surface Lot is located behind the School of Dentistry at 707 Parnassus Avenue, and the rates are the same as at Millberry Union, but are only in effect from 7 am to 6 pm on weekdays. At all other times, a 24-hour flat rate of $1.25 is in effect. At Beckman/Koret Surface Lot, fees are the same as above, with the same hours as Westside/Kirkham. After 6 pm and on weekends, the lot is for permit parking only.

For parking information at the other four campuses, visit http://www.cas.ucsf.edu/ParkingandTrans/pg_publicparkingALL.html.

UCSF provides shuttles at some of the campuses, primarily between the Parnassus Campus and other campuses and places in San Francisco, including the student apartments on Turk Street and the transportation station at Powell Street.

Sports

UCSF does not have a competitive sports team, but does offer a wide variety of recreational sports, including clubs, leagues, and drop-in practice. The Millberry Recreation & Fitness Center is located in Millberry Union, 500 Parnassus Avenue, I Level East.

Department Contact Info

Dentistry 415-476-2737
Nursing 415-476-1435
Pharmacy 415-476-2733
Physical Therapy 415-476-3146
Medicine 415-476-4044
UCSF-UCB Joint Medical Program ... 510-642-5671
Medical Scientist Training Program .. 415-476-4423
Graduate Studies 415-502-4460

Other Campuses

- Laguna Honda School, 1350 Seventh Ave
- Laurel Heights, 3333 California St
- UCSF/Mount Zion Medical Center, 1600 Divisadero St
- Buchanan Dental Center, 100 Buchanan St
- Mission Center, 1855 Folsom St
- Harrison Street Building, 3130 20th St
- San Francisco General Hospital (Affiliation), 1001 Potrero Ave
- Hunters Point Facility, 830 Palou St
- San Francisco Executive Park, 250 Executive Park Blvd
- Oyster Point Facility, 612 Forbes Blvd
- Veterans Affairs Medical Center (Affiliation), 4150 Clement St

University of California, Berkeley

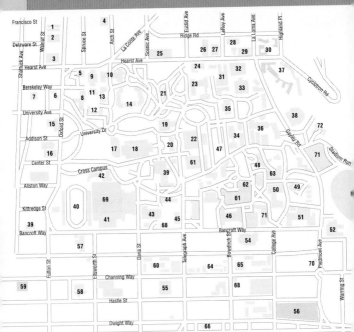

1 Oxford Research Unit
2 Natural Resources Laboratory
3 Insectary
4 McEnerney
5 Barker
6 University Garage
7 UC Press
8 Warren
9 Koshland
10 Tolman
11 Genetics and Plant Biology
12 Mufford
13 Morgan
14 Wellman Courtyard
15 University Hall/ Visitor Services
16 UC Printing
17 Life Sciences
18 Valley Life Sciences
19 Moffitt Library
20 California

21 Haviland
22 Bancroft Library
23 McCone Earth Sciences
24 North Gate Hall
25 Tennis
26 Etcheverry
27 Soda
28 Cloyne Court
29 Tennis
30 Foothill Student Housing
31 Naval Architecture
32 Cory
33 Hearst Mining
34 Birge/ Campbell
35 Evans
36 Latimer
37 Stern
38 Hearst Greek Theatre
39 Dwinelle
40 Edwards Track Stadium
41 Recreational Sports Facility

42 Callaghan
43 Zellerbach
44 Cesar E Chavez Student Center
45 King Student Union
46 Hearst Gym
47 Sather Tower
48 Faculty Club
49 Calvin Laboratory
50 Wurster
51 Law Building
52 International House
53 California Memorial Stadium
54 UC Berkeley Art Museum
55 Haste Student Housing
56 Residence Halls Unit 2
57 Tang Center/ University Health Services
58 Jones Child Study Center
59 Manville Apartments

60 Residence Halls Unit 1
61 North Field
62 Morrison
63 Minor/ Senior Hall
64 Parking and Transit Operations Office
65 Residence Halls Unit 3
66 Dwight Way House
67 Hearst Museum
68 Community Living Office
69 Evans Field
70 Casa Joaquin Murieta
71 Kleeberger Field
72 Parking and Transit

General Information

Mailing Address: 101 University Hall,
2200 University Ave,
Berkeley, CA 94720-4206

Location: 2200 University Ave at Oxford St
Phone: 510-642-5215
Website: www.berkeley.edu

Overview

The University of California, Berkeley is considered one of the world's leading intellectual centers. Widely known as "Cal," the sprawling, attractively wooded 178-acre campus is renowned for its architectural and historic landmarks, as well as for the size and quality of its libraries and laboratories, the scope of its research and publications, and the distinction of its faculty and students. National rankings consistently place Berkeley's undergraduate and graduate programs among the best.

The campus and surrounding city of Berkeley also offer a welcome respite, and cultural haven, for San Franciscans looking to get out of the city. Ample shops, bookstores, museums, theaters, and attractions like the Pacific Film Archive (which showcases rare and neglected examples of cinema history) make UC Berkeley a great destination for visitors as well as students.

Tuition

The proposed 2003-2004 budget for a student living off-campus with relatives comes to $11,800 for California residents and $24,800 for non-residents. A student who resides in on-campus housing will have estimated costs of $19,700 for California residents and $32,700 for non-residents.

Parking

If you are traveling to the campus for a visit, do not park in any University Parking Facilities, as these are reserved for students and faculty. You can try your luck at street parking, but, if you're arriving on a weekend, particularly in the summer, good luck! You might be searching for a long time. Otherwise there are lots at Oxford Street, Durant Ave., and Center Street (this lot is closest to University Hall). There is also the University of California Student Union Garage on Bancroft.

If you're coming over the Bay from San Francisco, you might want to leave the car at home and take BART. The downtown Berkeley stop will put you on the town's main street, just a short walk from campus. Note: If you make the trip on a Saturday or Sunday, there's no direct BART service to Berkeley—check station postings for directions on where to transfer.

Sports

Berkeley offers a full range of men's and women's intercollegiate sports, as well as a comprehensive intramural sports program. The Golden Bears' teams, which are ranked nationally in the top-ten, include softball, men's and women's water polo, men's and women's crew, rugby, men's and women's swimming, men's gymnastics, men's and women's tennis, and women's golf. For up-to-date news and schedule information and to purchase tickets, visit the official athletics website at www.calbears.com.

Department Contact Info

Undergraduate Admissions 510-642-3175
Graduate Admissions 510-642-7405
College of Letters & Science 510-642-4487
Boalt Hall Law School 510-642-1741
College of Chemistry 510-642-5060
College of Engineering 510-642-5771
College of Natural Resources 510-642-7171
Graduate School of Education 510-642-5345
Graduate School of Journalism 510-642-3833
Haas School of Business 510-642-7989
School of Information and 510-642-1464
  Management Systems
School of Optometry 510-642-9537
School of Public Health 510-642-6531
School of Social Welfare 510-642-4341
The Richard and Rhoda Goldman 510-642-4670
  School of Public Policy

Overview

With a population of over 102,743, Berkeley is the fourth most populated city in Alameda County, following Oakland, Fremont, and Hayward. The University of California draws a diverse group of people to Berkeley and, as a result, you'll find a variety of arts, sports, and recreation on offer.

Culture

The Pacific Film Archive, which is located on the UC, Berkeley campus, is home to an excellent collection of films from all over the world. They screen roughly 600 films a year, including rare and rediscovered prints of movie classics, new and historic works by the world's great film directors, restored silent films, and independently made fiction and documentary films. The progressive radio station KPFA-FM was the world's first listener-sponsored station, and it remains a role model for public radio and television today. Many neighborhood theatre companies exist in Berkeley, including the senior theater group Stagebridge, cutting edge Shotgun Players, Aurora, Nightletter, Central Works, Actors Ensemble, Darvag Persian Theater, and the Black Repertory Group. The most renowned of the groups is the highly acclaimed Berkeley Repertory Theatre. You'll find a variety of museums and galleries in Berkeley, and if you like classical music, you can't go past the Berkeley Symphony Orchestra for a great night out!

Festivals & Events

Cal Day—www.berkeley.edu/calday, 510-642-5215. On a Saturday in mid-April. Annual UC Berkeley open house for the community; performances, exhibits, lectures, tours, sports events, etc.
Earth Day—www.bayareaearthday.net, 510-548-2220. Saturday closest to April 22. Festival and Eco-Motion Parade downtown.
Berkeley Bay Festival—www.ci.berkeley.ca.us/marina/marinaexp/bayfest.html. On a Saturday in late April or May. Food, music, entertainment, boat tours, free sailing at the Berkeley Marina, 510-644-8623.
People's Park Anniversary Street Fair and Concert—www.dnai.com/~hi_there/people's_park.html, 510-644-7729. Late April or early May at the People's Park.
Berkeley Arts Festival—www.berkeleyartsfestival.com, 510-665-9496. First two weeks in May.
Live Oak Park Fair—www.liveoakparkfair.com, 510-898-3282 or 510-526-7363. June 12th and 13th.
Fourth of July Celebration—510-548-5335. http://www.ci.berkeley.ca.us/news/2000/00jun/062900safety.html. On July 4th at the Berkeley Marina.

Berkeley Kite Festival—www.highlinekites.com/Berkeley_Kite_Festival. 510-235-5483. Last weekend in July at the Cesar Chavez North Waterfront Park.
"How Berkeley Can You Be?" Parade/Festival—www.howberkeleycanyoube.com. Fourth Sunday in September in Downtown and North Berkeley, 510-849-4688.
Berkeley Artisans Holiday Open Studios—http://homepage.mac.com/rickeisner/bahos/bahos.html, Four weekends, Thanksgiving into December, 510-845-2612.

Restaurants

- **Mondo Gelato** • 2106 Shattuck Ave
- **Zachary's Pizza** • 1853 Solano Ave
- **Blondie's Pizza** • 2340 Telegraph Ave
- **Chez Panisse** • 1517 Shattuck Ave

Bars

- **Thalassa Bar & Billiards** • 2367 Shattuck Ave

Shopping

- **Ohmega Salvage** • 2407 & 2400 San Pablo Ave
- **Omego Too** • 2204 San Pablo Ave
- **Horticultural Nursery** • 1310 McGee Ave
- **Sharffen Berger** • 914 Heinz Ave
- **Sur La Table** • 1806 4th St
- **Hear Music** • 1809B 4th St

How to Get There

Berkeley sits approximately 13 miles from San Francisco and can be reached by car via the Bay Bridge (I-80 E). After crossing the bridge, stay in one of the left lanes and follow signs to Berkeley. Take the University Ave. exit towards Berkeley and turn right onto University Ave. The orange and red BART lines to Richmond both make stops at the Downtown Berkeley and North Berkeley stations.

Buckelew

Drake

Park

Bridgeway

Eureka

Turners

Donahue

Drake

Drake

Terrace

Cole

Redwood Highway

Stanford

Olima

Coloma

Butte

Cypress

Gate 5

Harbor

Lincoln

Tomales

Buchanan

Willow

Nevada

Testa

Richardson Bay

Lincoln

Nevada

Woodward

Marinship

Rodeo

Spring

Easterby

101

Marie

Napa

Bea

Bridgeway

Rodeo

Toyon

Currey

Platt

Scenic

Bonita

Girard

Litho

Locust

Caledonia

Alta Ave.

Crecienta

Monte Mar

George

Currey

Cazneau

Turney

Pine

Johnson

Bobcat

Glen

Glen

Santa Rosa

Girard

Bunkley

Bay

Spinnaker

Excelsior

Spencer

Spencer

San Carlos

Harrison

Atwood

Bridgeway

Golden Gate National Recreation Area

Wolfback Ridge

Wolfback Ridge

Cloudview

Ridge

Monte Mar

Prospect

Sausalito

Central

Noble

Sausalito

Crescent

North

West

4th

Richardson

Wolfback Ridge

Crescent

West

Main

2nd

Valley

Hecht

South

Bunker

Marion

Edwards

Just 2 miles north over the Golden Gate Bridge from San Francisco, lies the picturesque village of Sausalito. Boasting a mere 7,500 residents, it is, by most standards, a small town. However its numbers swell during the summertime as tourists arrive by the ferryload and day trippers fill the narrow sidewalks.

Sausalito is a beautiful spot, enjoying unsurpassed views of the City over the bay, an eclectic community, and something for just about everybody. While the south part of town along Bridgeway is chockablock with souvenir shops, boutiques and overpriced cafés, the local scene can be found a short walk away on Caledonia Street.

Sausalito is host to many street fairs and festivals throughout the year, from art shows to chili cook-offs. The town is also home to a unique community of floating homes—approximately 400 in all—some tiny one-room abodes, others magnificent mansions on the water.

$ Banks

- **Bank of America** · 750 Bridgeway
- **Wells Fargo** · 715 Bridgeway
- **West America Bank** · 1 Harbor Dr

Bars

- **No Name Bar** · 757 Bridgeway
- **Paterson's Bar** · 739 Bridgeway
- **Smitty's Bar** · 214 Caledonia St

Coffee

- **Bridgeway Cafe** · 633 Bridgeway
- **Cafe Lucca** · 1001 Bridgeway
- **Cafe Soleil** · 37 Caledonia St
- **Cafe Trieste** · 1000 Bridgeway
- **Cafe Tuttu** · 12 El Portal
- **Lighthouse Cafe** · 1311 Bridgeway
- **Sausalito Bakery & Cafe** · 571 Bridgeway
- **Sausalito Espresso** · 27 Braun Ct
- **Starbucks** · 14-16 Princess St
- **Waterfront Cafe** · 85 Libertyship Way

Movie Theaters

- **Marin Theater** · 101 Caledonia St

Restaurants

- **Avatars** · 2656 Bridgeway
- **Feng-Nian Chinese Restaurant** · 2650 Bridgeway
- **Fred's Place** · 1917 Bridgeway
- **Sartaj India Cafe** · 43 Caledonia St
- **Sushi Ran** · 107 Caledonia St

Shopping

- **Great Overland Book Co** · 215 Caledonia St
- **Pinestreet Papery** · 42 1/2 Caledonia St
- **Sausalito Ferry Company** · 688 Bridgeway

General Information

Website: www.ferrybuildingmarketplace.com
Mailing Address: Ferry Building Marketplace, One Ferry
Building, San Francisco, CA 94111
Phone: 415-693-0996
Times: 10 am to 6 pm Mondays through Fridays, 9 am to 6
pm on Saturdays, and 11 am to 5 pm on Sundays. There
are some slight variances from shop to shop.

Overview

Thanks to a recent repair to the long-broken Ferry Building clock, the bells toll once more, and they toll for thee…but in a good way. This newly refurbished building is the jewel of the San Francisco waterfront and is a testament to San Francisco's can-do, survivor spirit. In 1898, the Ferry Building opened over the older, wooden Ferry House. The architect, A. Page Brown, used steel to frame the new building. The foundation for the edifice is the largest for an over-water building, and with good reason—the steel-framed structure has survived two major earthquakes. In 1989, when the old Embarcadero freeway next to it crumbled in the earthquake, the Ferry Building stood firm. The 240-foot-tall clock tower is modeled after the 12th-century bell tower in the Seville Cathedral in Spain. Regular walking tours of the Ferry Building are free and start at noon on Saturdays, Sundays, and Tuesdays when you can sample fresh foods, produce, and plants at the Farmers' Market.

At the base of the Ferry Building is the three-story Nave, which includes shops, restaurants, cafés, and plazas. Behind the Nave are two open market halls. They offer an array of meats, fish, wines, cheeses, bread, pasta, and cookware. The Ferry Plaza Farmers' Market sells the best of the area's produce and regional specialties on Saturdays, Tuesdays, Thursdays, and Sundays. The wide esplanade on the water-side of the building has pedestrians en route to and from the adjacent Downtown Ferry Terminal. The popular Saturday Ferry Plaza Farmers' Market now has a permanent home on the large plaza on the southeast side of the building.

How to Get There–Driving

From the Bay Bridge, take the Main St./Embarcadero exit, turn right onto Harrison St. then turn left onto the Embarcadero.

From the Golden Gate Bridge, take the Marina Blvd. exit, proceed on Marina Blvd. around the Safeway. Turn left onto Bay Street for approximately 2 miles then turn right onto the Embarcadero.

From the South Bay, take Highway 101 towards the Bay Bridge (I-80), then take the Fourth Street exit and stay right on Bryant Street. Turn left onto the Embarcadero. The alternative is to take Hwy 280 towards Downtown and take the Sixth Street exit, staying right on Brannan Street. Turn left on the Embarcadero.

How to Get There–Mass Transit

The F Market above-ground vintage streetcar line goes right to the Ferry Building. If you're taking the Muni underground, get off at the Embarcadero and take the escalators to Market St. The Ferry Building is about a block and a half away.

General Information

Website: www.stinsonbeachonline.com
Ranger Station: 415-868-0942
Surf and Parking Report: 415-868-1922
Mailing Address: P.O. Box 413,
Stinson Beach, CA 94970

Overview

In the early 1800s, part of Stinson Beach was used to raise cows for milking. To improve access between the strip and its surroundings, the first dirt road along the coast from Sausalito was completed in 1870. Soon, tent camps sprang up and a community, known then as Willow Camp, formed. But the real birth of Stinson Beach happened in 1906, when refugees from the San Francisco Earthquake found shelter there. In 1916, with the opening of the first post office, the area was named Stinson Beach, in honor of the largest landowners. New residents arrived during World War II and, after the war, unused land was developed, resulting in today's Stinson Beach. In 1972, the beach became part of the Golden Gate Recreation Area. Although nudity is tolerated at many Bay Area beaches, Stinson isn't one of them—so keep your suit on.

A unique feature of Stinson Beach is its public alarm system. The regular blasts (at noon and at 5 pm) are hard to miss. If all is well, two short blasts will sound. If not, a 15 second blast means, roughly translated, "Get the hell out of there!"

If alarming siren blasts are not your cup of tea, you can also hear the mellifluous sounds of the Queen's English during "Shakespeare at Stinson," which offers performances of the Bard's plays at the beach's 155-seat theater. The company puts on classical plays to inspire future actors, directors, playwrights, and/or stage crew. The company maintains low ticket prices so that large numbers of people can experience its live theater. All previews are "pay what you will." There's also a family night, and Fridays are $14.

Accomodations

Lodging at Stinson Beach:
• The Sandpiper • 1 Marine Bay • 415-868-1632
• Ocean Court Motel • 18 Arena Ave • 415-868-0212
• Stinson Beach Motel • 3416 State Route #1 • 415-868-1712

Sports

Although sunbathing is hardly an athletic event, the Stinson Beach website lists it as a sporting activity. For those who want to do more than lie down and burn in ultraviolet radiation, Stinson Beach offers hang-gliding, kayaking, and surfing. If you're more terrestrial-bound, then try hiking, biking, and volleyball.

How to Get There–Driving

After crossing the Golden Gate Bridge, take Highway 101 North approximately three miles to the Highway 1/Stinson Beach exit. Follow the signs and enjoy your drive down one of the most scenic highways in the nation. Stinson Beach is approximately 20 miles from San Francisco.

If you're after a more scenic route, look for signs to Muir Woods and Mt. Tamalpais State Park while you're traveling along Highway 1. Turn right and take Panoramic Highway through the park. It will take you back to Highway 1 and ends only blocks south of Stinson Beach.

How to Get There–Mass Transit

Take Golden Gate 10, 20 or 50 from Transbay Transit Terminal, Civic Center BART, or Golden Gate Bridge Toll Plaza to Marin City Transfer Center (combined frequency 10-15 min). Transfer to Golden Gate bus 63 (only 3 morning trips). Return the same way in reverse (5 afternoon trips on Golden Gate bus 63).

General Information

Crissy Field Center: 415-556-0560
Address: 603 Mason St at Halleck St
Website: www.crissyfield.org

Overview

Once the host of the 1915 Panama Pacific International Exposition, this waterfront open space became an Army Air Corps airstrip from 1919 to 1936. Today, Crissy Field is used for public events and as a viewing area for events on the Bay. A recent environmental restoration project has Crissy Field looking downright splendid these days, and it's drawing more visitors than ever. The area offers an excellent view of the Golden Gate Bridge (especially from Fort Point), and it's not a bad place to watch the Bay Area's summer fireworks displays. Joggers, skaters, dog walkers, hikers, sail boaters, and windsurfers turn the field into a much-loved recreational spot for San Franciscans at play, and the paved Golden Gate Promenade is a favorite for joggers or those on skates and wheels. The Crissy Field Center, a new community environmental facility, helps to preserve these 100 acres of nature and restore the natural estuary, including the Tidal Marsh, beaches, and dunes.

Restrooms

There are restrooms at the west end of Crissy Field, at the Fort Point Mine Depot Warming Hut, near Historic Field at the Marine Sanctuary Visitor Center, near the marsh at Crissy Field Center, and at the east end near East Beach. So if you have to go, there are plenty of options.

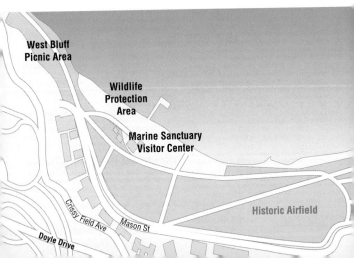

Sports

The field is part of the popular bike route that runs from the Golden Gate Bridge at Fort Point to Aquatic Park and the seaside town of Tiburon. Picking up the Golden Gate Promenade, you can enjoy the views of the Golden Gate and boats on the Bay while strolling, rollerblading, or skating. Windsurfing and flying kites are also common activities due to fairly strong winds along the Bay front. Fishing is also allowed, but don't try to trap any of the orange Dungeness Crabs that use the Bay as a nursery—it's illegal.

Practicalities

The Muni routes come directly into the Presidio and drop off at the Main Post Parking area, from which you can walk to Crissy Field: Route 28 (19th Ave), 29 (Sunset), 43 (Masonic). If you need one, all-terrain wheel chairs are available at the Crissy Field Center (415-561-7752). If you're planning on hosting a big group event (50 people or more), you'll need to acquire a permit from the National Parks Service by calling 415-561-4300.

Cafes & Bookstores

At Crissy Field Center you'll find not only information about the park but a cool café overlooking the marsh and a bookstore, which is open from 9 am until 5 pm. If you're interested in the environmental theme of sustainability, check out the Warming Hut Bookstore near Torpedo Wharf. The Warming Hut Café serves organic food in a delightful setting.

• Crissy Field Center Café • 415-561-7756
• Crissy Field Center Bookstore • 415-561-7761
• Warming Hut Café • 415-561-3042
• Warming Hut Bookstore • 415- 561-3040

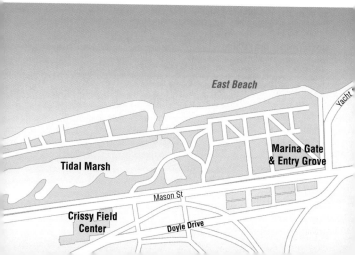

Overview

At four miles wide, this is the city's largest beach, but cold waters, cold winds, dangerous rip tides, and an absence of lifeguards discourage most swimmers. If that's not enough to keep the bronzed bods out of the salt drink, there have also been sharks spotted in the vicinity. The awesome currents and marine wildlife, however, are no deterrent for Bay area surfers (ultra-cool pop crooner Chris Isaak is known to be a regular). Despite the blustery weather and hazardous waters, this beach is usually filled with joggers, dog walkers, and, on warm days, sunbathers. It is one of the few beaches in the area that still tolerates bonfires (check out the National Park Service's rules and regulations first), making it a popular spot for picnicking and cookouts. Don't miss a chat with the tempestuous sea lions at the Seal Rocks at the northern end of the beach.

Practicalities

Despite the treacherous surf, the beach is free and open to the public at all times. It is conveniently located along the Great Highway and there is plenty of free parking along the road. Although the park service allows dogs on the beach, there is a very strict leash policy to protect the population of endangered western snowy plovers, which inhabit the beach ten months out the year. Ocean Beach can be accessed by bus or metro. Take bus 38, 31, 5 or the Muni to the N stop (Judah St.).

Restrooms

Although scarce, there are a few restrooms and changing rooms located along the beach, mostly around the southern end near the zoo. Most surfers simply change in and out of their wetsuits right in the parking lot, adding another aspect to the scenery on view at Ocean Beach. There are outdoor showers at Sloat Blvd.

Sports

This is an extremely popular and scenic spot for surfing, body surfing, kayaking, and fishing. Fledgling surfers take caution, for these currents are ruthless and there are no lifeguards. The path that runs parallel to the shore and next to the highway is an ideal stretch for walking, running, biking, and blading. Check out the Ocean Beach 5K and 10K marathon runs during the summer, which benefit an AIDS outreach project.

Restaurants and Cafes

- Beach Chalet · 1000 Great Hwy · 415-386-8439
- Cliff House (Seafood, American) · 1090 Point Lobos Ave · 415-386-1170
- St Joubert's Restaurant (South African) · 4115 Judah St · 415-753-5448
- Win's Restaurant (Chinese) · 3040 Taraval St · 415-759-1818

Overview

Nestled between Sea Cliff and the Golden Gate Bridge, Baker Beach is one of the most popular beaches among locals and tourists. In fact, it's one of the most popular urban beaches in the country. Less windy than Ocean Beach, this stretch of sandy real estate is the premier spot for catching some rays, and we're talking serious sun worship here—bathing suits are optional at the northern end of the shore! On some days you'll see more gawkers than nudists, but if the weather is particularly warm, be prepared for a major flesh parade.

Although the undertow is extremely dangerous, San Franciscans flock to Baker Beach for the beautiful views, surfing, nude bathing, and hiking trails. The undertow isn't the only danger here—in 1959 Baker Beach was the sight of the Bay Area's first shark attack. There haven't been any since, however.

The shoreline is dotted with several interesting rock formations, some of which can be climbed, and some of which are dangerous to scale, depending on the tide (think slippery surface, jagged rocks, and treacherous slopes). The nearby gun batteries are a great (and safer) spot to explore a bit of local history. Built in 1904 to protect the harbor's minefields, they offer a stellar view of the beach and the Bay. Baker Beach also has picnicking facilities with tables and grills at the east end of the parking lot. Beyond the northern tip of Baker Beach, and over the rocky hill, is another beach alternately known as North Baker Beach, Golden Gate Bridge Beach, and the Gay Beach—the nudity is more prevalent here, as are various x-rated shenanigans that we'll leave to the imagination.

Practicalities

The Baker Beach parking lot on Bowley St. (off of Lincoln Blvd.) is free, but fills up very quickly in the summer time. If you must drive, be prepared to look for parking blocks away from the main parking lots. Go north on 25th Avenue to Lincoln Blvd. Turn right on Lincoln, then take the second left, Bowley St. Take Bowley to Gibson Road and turn right. Gibson leads to the east parking lot. If you're biking it, there are ample bike racks around the parking areas. You can also take the Muni 29 bus. The beach closes at 7 pm during the winter (October to April) and is open until 10 pm the rest of the year.

Please note that clothing is required in the parking lot and may only be shed in specified areas (the nude area begins near the brown and yellow "Hazardous Surf" sign at the northern end of the beach).

Restrooms

Restrooms are located near the parking lot.

Sports

Swimming is discouraged, but surfing and boardsailing are very popular at this beach. The water becomes very deep very quickly and is therefore a great spot for fishing. Aside from water activities, this beach is famous for its winding hiking trails around the sloping cliffs off the Presidio. This area is filled with indigenous vegetation (including poison oak, so be careful what you touch). There are also rare birds and amazing views. The main trail is 5.5 miles long and is pretty hilly, so wear appropriate hiking shoes.

Overview

Just across the Golden Gate Bridge from San Francisco, and (on a clear day) within view of Baker Beach, Black Sands Beach offers a more exclusive retreat for those who enjoy nude sunbathing and who crave a view of San Francisco from the other side of the Bay. This 100-foot-wide beach's black volcanic sand is coarser and harder to walk on than the more traditional sand found on Baker, but the overall vibe at Black Sands is distinctly more casual and low key. Unlike Baker Beach, Black Sands is difficult to get to. Parking is limited, and the steep, poison oak-lined trail leading down to the beach is a challenge, but the journey is worth it. Just make sure you stay on the main path—the cliffs are steep and can be dangerous if you veer away from the well-worn trail.

Practicalities

Driving directions to trailhead: Cross the Golden Gate Bridge toward Marin and take the Alexander Avenue exit off Highway 101 (the exit will come up quickly on the right as soon as you cross the bridge). Rather than following the signs to Sausalito, go through the tunnel that runs under the highway on your left and follow Conzelman Road about 3.6 miles into the Marin Headlands. The road will become one-way and run downhill (offering amazing views of the Golden Gate). As soon as the road begins to flatten, look for a guardrail on the left. Soon after the guardrail, and near some old military fortifications, there will be a parking lot with a restroom. The lot is easy to miss, so keep your eyes peeled.

There is no public transit available to Black Sands Beach. People do bike into the Marin Headlands, but do so with care, and wear protective gear—the roads there are incredibly steep and potentially dangerous for bikers.

Sports

You won't see many surfers at Black Sands Beach (probably because the trail down is hard to navigate with a surfboard in hand), but fishermen do frequent the area. The most popular sports here, however, are nude sunbathing and Frisbee-throwing.

Restaurants/Accommodations/Gas, etc.

The nearest restaurants, hotels, motels, and other amenities are in Sausalito. There are picnicking areas and restrooms near the parking lot and along the road that leads away from Black Sands Beach.

Overview

Locals, in reference to the Chinese fishermen who docked their junks at the spot and camped there, originally called this area China Beach. It was briefly renamed Phelan Beach after former San Francisco Mayor and U.S. Senator James D. Phelan, who set in place a discriminatory law against fishermen of Chinese descent. Some maps still refer to China Beach as Phelan State Beach, but most locals refer to it by its original name.

China Beach is popular for its great views of the Golden Gate Bridge and the Marin Headlands and for its facilities. As with most Bay Area beaches, the unpredictable surf near Baker Beach and China Beach makes swimming risky, so if you do go out, don't go alone. Located west of Baker Beach, between Baker Beach and Land's End, China Beach offers amenities such as changing rooms, barbeque pits, and an enclosed sundeck. At the head of the trail down to the beach is a large trapezoidal stone marker placed there by Chinese Americans in 1981 to commemorate their unwarranted hardships when immigrating to America.

Sports

Common recreational activities include surfing, fishing, picnicking, volleyball, and boardsailing. Large waves from the northwest provide excellent surfing conditions. General swimming and wading are discouraged due to the cold water temperatures and strong tidal currents. If you do enter the water, be aware of undertows and rocks.

Restrooms

Restrooms are located near the changing area at China Beach Station.

How to Get There–Driving

The beach is accessible from Seacliff and 28th Avenue, near El Camino del Mar. Be prepared for a rather steep hike downhill to access this beach. A cul-de-sac off El Camino Del Mar near 28th Avenue in San Francisco leads to a lovely stretch of publicly owned coastline.

How to Get There–Mass Transit

The Muni 29 bus, which goes to Baker Beach, will drop you off at 25th Ave. and Camino Del Mar. From there, it's about a four-block walk west to Seacliff Ave., then down the slope to the beach.

San Francisco Marina & Marina Green

Overview

The San Francisco Marina is overseen by the San Francisco Parks & Recreation Department and is composed of two harbors: West Harbor and East Harbor, which is also known as Gashouse Cove. Marina Green, a popular spot for locals and tourists alike, separates the two harbors. A large, rectangular lawn with a seawall on the Bay side, it includes a paved walkway and a remarkable view of the Bay.

The Marina has 686 boat slips and houses the St. Francis Yacht Club, the Golden Gate Yacht Club, and the City Yachts boat sales (10 Marina Boulevard—415-567-8880). At Mean Lower Low Water (MLLW), the depth of the west entrance channel is usually between 10 and 20 feet, while the MLLW in the east channel is between 10 and 15 feet.

A recent proposal to build two new breakwaters in the Bay has created controversy—environmentalists and locals believe the barriers would disrupt tidal patterns and increase sedimentation and erosion of the shore, not to mention ruining the view of the Bay from Marina Green. Critics of the project believe that a complete environmental review needs to be conducted before the project begins. Most concerns about the breakwaters project stem from the belief that the overhaul is unnecessary and is being pushed to accommodate the owners of large, expensive boats.

Until 1912 the Marina Green area was dominated by fishermen's hovels. The 1915 Panama-Pacific International Exposition created fairgrounds from 635 acres of marshland. Now the Green is primarily a residential area. Because it's built mostly on landfill, the area is particularly vulnerable to earthquake damage—it was one of the hardest-hit neighborhoods in the 1989 earthquake.

Latitude 37° 48' N
Longitude 122° 24' W

Practicalities

You'll find ample parking anywhere along the Bay side except in spaces marked as permit parking only. On weekends, though, parking can be hard to find—so get to the lots early if you plan on making a day of it.

Guest Slips

Guests slips (as in boating slips) are available in three different locations. The San Francisco Yacht Harbor has temporary berthing docks. Call them on 415-292-2013 to check availability.

The St. Francis Yacht Club also has guest docking facilities for yachts, ranging in price from 80c to $1.50 per foot, per day and extra ($12) for power hookups. You can call to book on 415-563-6363 or fax 415-563-8670. The VHF radio channels for the St. Francis Yacht Club dockmaster are 68 or 69.

The Golden Gate Yacht Club also offers reciprocal privileges, including docking, to members of other yacht clubs. Call the Club Manager at 415-346-2628 or the Port Captain at 415-263-0282 to make a reservation and check in with the Assistant Manager on the 2nd floor when you arrive. Rates for docking are $20 per calendar day plus 40c per foot over 30 feet. Power hookups are $4 per day.

No Boat?

Why not get your body in shape? Exercise equipment and a Parcourse stop are at the southeast corner of the green. The Parcourse is so-named because, at each stop, there are a suggested number of repetitions of the exercise based on your level of fitness. The kite-flying crowd comes here often to take advantage of the prevailing winds that make this site ideal for the sport.

Restrooms

Restrooms can be found near the Harbormaster Building and also in the Marina Green Park.

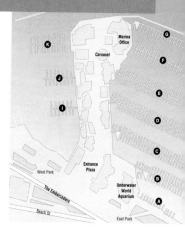

Overview

Whether you're there to watch the sea lions or shop, or you're catching a ferry to visit one of the Bay's many attractions (such as Angel Island or Alcatraz) or nearby Sausalito and Tiburon, Pier 39 is your gateway to the Bay, and it's one of the most popular spots in the city. On a good day, Pier 39 is a great place to stop as you walk from the Ferry Building and downtown to the Wharf (or vice versa).

The Pier 39 Marina is located on the San Francisco waterfront, between the two bridges, below Coit Tower. Pier 39 houses a 300-berth marina with slips available for rental and guest docking. The Marina offers a variety of ways to experience the Bay. You can venture out on a sailboat or powerboat rides or take one of the many tour boats. If you're lucky, you might even be able to get an overnight stay on a private yacht.

Latitude: 37° 48′ N
Longitude: 122° 24′ W

Docking Info

Lease prices for permanent docking range between $294 a month for a 36′ x 13′ slip and $488 for a 60′ x 20′ slip.

Guest Slips

Boaters are welcome to use the guest slips for a few hours during the day but must make reservations on 415-705-5556. Facilities include ice, water and electrical hookup, restrooms, 6 private shower rooms, and pump-a-head. Check in is at noon and check out is at 11:30 am. A key deposit is required, and overnight docking fees range from $35 to $50, depending on the size of your vessel.

Getting There–Driving

From the East Bay, take the Bay Bridge to SF, exit at Main Street/Embarcadero, turn right on Harrison, go three blocks to The Embarcadero, turn left. Pier 39 is on your right.
Driving from the South Bay, take Highway 101 North and follow the signs to the Bay Bridge, exit at Fourth St. and turn left on Bryant St. to the Embarcadero.
Driving from the North Bay, take 101 South, cross Golden Gate Bridge, exit at Lombard St., turn left on Van Ness Ave. and right on Bay St. to the Embarcadero.

Parking

The Pier 39 Garage, located across the street from Pier 39, allows one hour of free parking before 6 pm or two hours free parking after 6 pm.

Getting There–Mass Transit

Take BART to the Embarcadero Station. Go upstairs and cross the Embarcadero to the Ferry Building. In front of the Ferry Building, take the "F" line trolley to Pier 39. The "F" line trolley travels to Fisherman's Wharf from Castro/Market. The Muni buses that serve the Pier are 47, 15, and 10.

General Information

49ers Website: www.sf49ers.com
Phone: 415-656-4900

Overview

The San Francisco 49ers have the distinction of being the first major league professional sports franchise on the West Coast. Named after the gold prospectors who flocked to the Bay Area in the late 1840s (much like the dot-commers who flocked to San Francisco 150 years later), the team has never been called anything else, and San Francisco is the only city in which it has resided. In 1971, the 49ers moved from Kezar Stadium to Candlestick Park. The stadium was named in 1970 by fans via ballot, in reference to Candlestick Point, the chilly bayside locale where the stadium resides. The playing surface is natural grass and the stadium currently seats 70,207. San Francisco sold the naming rights to 3Com Corporation in 1995 for $500k for 6 months. In 1996, the deal was extended to January 2000 for $3.9 million. The right of 3Com to name the park ended in January 2002. Since 1981, the 49ers have won 13 division titles, five conference championships, and five Super Bowl championships.

How to Get There–Driving

The 3Com Park exit from 101 N takes you to the park. In the last two hours before a game, it is quicker to use the Third Street exit from the 101 freeway instead of the 3Com Park exit. Go north on Third Street. If you have a pre-paid parking pass, turn right on Gilman Avenue. If you do not have a pre-paid parking pass, turn right on Carroll Avenue and use the dirt parking lots.

Avoid post-game congestion on southbound 101 by using the 280 freeway. Avoid post-game congestion on northbound 101 through downtown San Francisco by using Third Street or the northbound 280 freeway.

Parking

Parking is available in exterior dirt lots just outside the stadium. Parking for cars and motorcycles costs $25, and you'll need to take Third St. to Ingerson and the entrance to the bus lot is on your left. Limo and RV parking is $40 and you enter the lot via Gilman Ave.

How to Get There–Mass Transit

Direct bus service to the stadium is available for all games on the Muni, Santa Clara Valley Transportation Authority, or Sam Trans buses. Connections from BART, Caltrain, Golden Gate Transit, and AC Transit can be made to the Muni and Sam Trans ballpark routes.

For home games, the following express Muni services are offered: 9X from Sutter & Montgomery via Sutter, Stockton, Fourth to Folsom then express to Candlestick; 28X limited stop service from Funston & California to Candlestick Park via Funston, California, Park Presidio and regular route to 19th Ave. and Sloat, then via Sloat, Junipero Serra, Ocean, Geneva to Mission, then express to Candlestick; 47X from California & Van Ness via Van Ness to S. Van Ness & Mission, then express to Candlestick. Adult fare for this special express service is $5 and $3 discounted fare. With a valid Muni pass, it's only $2. Muni also runs a $1 shuttle from Bacon & San Bruno to Paul and Third St (Caltrain) then express to the ballpark on game days. SamTrans also runs bus lines 810, 820, 840, 850, 851, 880 to the park on game days. A season pass will set you back $60, while a four-game pass is $35. A single round-trip ticket is $12.

How to Get Tickets

If you'd like to become a 49ers season ticket holder, you'll have to join the waitlist by calling 415-656-4900 or writing to Ticket Office, 3Com Park, Room 400, San Francisco, CA, 94124. Single tickets for $58 can be purchased through Ticketmaster, with the usual highway robbery charge of $6 per ticket "convenience fee" and a postage and handling fee of $3 per order. www.ticketmaster.com.

Lower Box $26
View Box $20
Arcade $20
View Res $16
Bleacher $10
Club Level
Field Club
Luxury Suites

General Information

Address: 24 Willie Mays Plz, San Francisco, CA 94107
Phone: 415-972-2000
Giants Website: www.sfgiants.com

Overview

They do build them like they used to. This stately new stadium in downtown San Francisco is a sight to behold, and it's breathed new life into the area, not to mention a lot of increased maritime traffic in McCovey Cove. It's also been the cause for more than a few 'sick days' in downtown cubicle land. After playing at Polo Grounds III, Seals Stadium, and the much maligned Candlestick Park, the SF Giants finally found a home of their own at Pacific Bell Park, thanks to the persistence and dedication of local businessman Peter Magowan. The Giants played the first official game at Pacific Bell Park in April 2000, hosting the Los Angeles Dodgers.

How to Get There–Driving

From the Peninsula/South Bay: Take I-280 north (or I-101 N to I-280 N) to the Mariposa St. exit. Turn right on Mariposa Street, then left on Third Street to get to the parking lots.

From the East Bay: Take I-80/Bay Bridge to the Fifth Street exit. Exit onto Harrison Street then turn left onto 6th Street and continue onto I-280 South. Take the first exit at 18th Street and turn left onto 18th Street. Go over freeway and turn left onto Third Street, where you'll find the parking lots.

From the North Bay: take Highway 101 S/Golden Gate Bridge to the Marina Blvd. exit. Drive past Fort Mason and turn left onto Bay Street then right onto the Embarcadero. Continue on the Embarcadero under the Bay Bridge until it turns into King Street. Turn left onto Third Street and look for the parking lots.

Parking

Pacific Bell Park has over 5,000 parking spaces in Parking Lots A (Charter Seat Holder parking), B and C. The lots are located on the south side of the China Basin Channel across the Lefty O'Doul Bridge from the ballpark. For season parking call 415-972-2000.

How to Get There–Mass Transit

Take the Muni Metro N line/inbound (or specially marked Metro trains on game days) directly to the ballpark by getting of at the Second and King Muni Metro station. You can also catch the regular Muni bus services 10 (Townsend), 15 (Third Street), 30 (Stockton), 42 (Downtown Loop), 45 (Union), and 47 (Van Ness), which will drop you within one block of Pacific Bell Park. If Caltrain is your mode of transportation, the San Francisco stop at Fourth and King Streets is one block from the ballpark. Or take BART from Colma, Daly City, Millbrae, SFO, San Bruno and South San Francisco to downtown San Francisco. Then transfer to Muni N-Line at Civic Center, Powell, Montgomery or Embarcadero to the ballpark. Remember to buy a $1 return BART-Muni transfer before you leave the BART station.

If you're coming from Alameda and Contra Costa, take BART to Embarcadero or Montgomery Stations and transfer to Muni Metro. The Alameda/Oakland Ferry Service provides direct service to the ballpark for most games. AC Transit also provides bus service from many East Bay cities to the Transbay Terminal, which is within walking distance of the ballpark. From Marin and Sonoma, take Golden Gate Transit's Larkspur Ferry directly to the park.

How to Get Tickets

Individual tickets range in price from $10 to $70 and can be purchased through the Giants website. If you're interested in season tickets, you can call 415-972-2298 or email seasontickets@sfgiants.com.

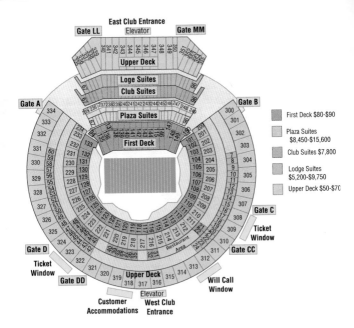

East Club Entrance
Gate LL Elevator **Gate MM**

Upper Deck

Loge Suites

Club Suites

Gate A **Gate B**

Plaza Suites

First Deck

Restaurant Area

Gate C

Gate D **Ticket Window**

Ticket Window **Gate CC**

Gate DD Upper Deck

Will Call Window

Elevator
Customer **West Club**
Accommodations **Entrance**

First Deck $80-$90

Plaza Suites
$8,450-$15,600

Club Suites $7,800

Lodge Suites
$5,200-$9,750

Upper Deck $50-$70

General Information

Address: 7000 Coliseum Way,
                  Oakland, CA 94621
Phone: 510-561-2121
A's Website: www.oaklandathletics.com
Raiders' Website: www.raiders.com

Overview

They used to call it the Oakland-Alameda County Coliseum. But we live in an age where corporate sponsorship dictates the majority of stadium names. So is it any surprise that Network Associates shelled out $5.8 million to put their name on the stadium for 5 years? Built at an initial cost of $25.5 million in 1966, the 1996 renovation budget ballooned from $100 million to $200 million by the time it was complete. But hey, it was money well spent…after all, the renovated Coliseum lured the Raiders back from a 12-year stint in Los Angeles. The Coliseum also plays home to the Oakland Athletics (you might have heard them called the Oakland A's).

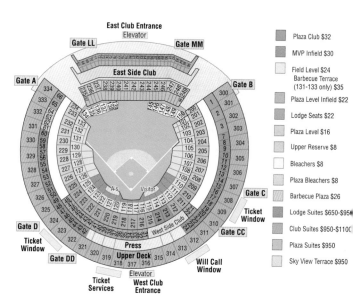

East Club Entrance
Elevator

Gate LL   Gate MM

East Side Club

Gate A   Gate B

Gate C
Ticket Window

Gate CC

Gate D
Ticket Window   West Side Club

Gate DD   **Press**
Upper Deck

Will Call Window

Ticket Services   Elevator
West Club Entrance

	Plaza Club $32
	MVP Infield $30
	Field Level $24 Barbecue Terrace (131-133 only) $35
	Plaza Level Infield $22
	Lodge Seats $22
	Plaza Level $16
	Upper Reserve $8
	Bleachers $8
	Plaza Bleachers $8
	Barbecue Plaza $26
	Lodge Suites $650-$95(
	Club Suites $950-$110(
	Plaza Suites $950
	Sky View Terrace $950

How to Get There–Driving

From San Francisco, take the Bay Bridge to I-580 East toward Hayward, exit at I-980 going toward Downtown Oakland. Continue on I-980, which becomes I-880 South. Exit at 66th Avenue and follow signs to the Coliseum.

Parking

There is ample parking for fans on all sides of the Coliseum, with many choosing to arrive ahead of schedule for tailgate parties. Bus and RV parking is located directly south of the stadium. Parking is $12 for cars, $20 for limousines, and $25 for buses.

How to Get There–Mass Transit

Take the Fremont BART to the Coliseum/Oakland Airport stop. AC Transit also runs buses 45, 46, 49, 56, 58, and 98 to the Coliseum BART stop.

How to Get Tickets

For Raiders season tickets, call 1-888-44-RAIDERS. For individual game tickets call 510-762-2277 or purchase them online from www.tickets.com. Athletics prices range from $8–$33 for individual games and may be purchased through tickets.com or by calling 510-762-BALL. If you're after season or group tickets, call 510-638-4627.

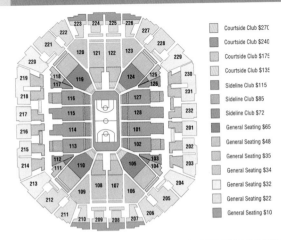

Courtside Club $270
Courtside Club $240
Courtside Club $175
Courtside Club $135
Sideline Club $115
Sideline Club $85
Sideline Club $72
General Seating $65
General Seating $48
General Seating $35
General Seating $34
General Seating $32
General Seating $22
General Seating $10

General Information

Address: 7000 Coliseum Way,
                    Oakland, CA 94621
Phone: 510-986-2233
Lost and Found: 510-383-4660
Website: www.gs-warriors.com
Warriors Website: www.warriors.com

Overview

While the new Arena in Oakland plays host to a variety of sporting events, concerts and circuses, its full-time tenant is the Golden State Warriors basketball team, the Bay Area's only NBA team.

The Golden State Warriors began as the Philadelphia Warriors, earning the honor of being the first NBA champions in the league's inaugural 1947 season. They moved to San Francisco in 1962 and changed their name to Golden State after relocating to Oakland in 1971. The Warriors can boast the NBA's first superstar in Joe Fulks, who averaged 23.2 point per game in the first season of the NBA (originally called the BBA). The only player to ever score 100 points in a single game was the Warriors' Wilt Chamberlain. One of the best free throw shooters ever was Rick Barry, whose underhanded tosses connected 89.3 percent of the time.

How to Get There–Driving

Go east over the Bay Bridge to 880 South. Take the 66th Avenue exit. Turn left at the end of ramp and follow signs to the Arena. The Arena is right next door to the Network Associates Coliseum.

Parking

North and South parking lots open two hours prior to tip-off. Parking fees are $12 for cars, $20 for limos, and $40 for buses.

How to Get There–Mass Transit

Take the Fremont or the Dublin/Pleasanton train from SF to the Coliseum/Oakland Airport stop (fares vary; $2.75 from Embarcadero). AC Transit also runs buses 45, 46, 49, 56, 58, and 98 to the Coliseum BART stop.

How to Get Tickets

For Warriors season tickets, call 1-888-479-4667. For single game tickets or any other performances at the Arena, buy tickets from Ticketmaster—www.ticketmaster.com.

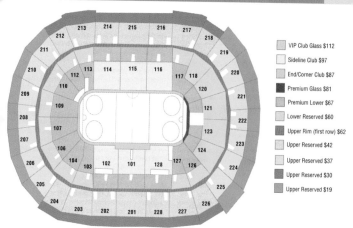

VIP Club Glass $112
Sideline Club $97
End/Corner Club $87
Premium Glass $81
Premium Lower $67
Lower Reserved $60
Upper Rim (first row) $62
Upper Reserved $42
Upper Reserved $37
Upper Reserved $30
Upper Reserved $19

General Information

Address: 525 W. Santa Clara St, San Jose, CA 95113
Phone: 408-287-7070
Website: www.sj-arena.com
San Jose Sharks Website: www.sj-sharks.com

Overview

In 1991, the San Jose Sharks paid the $50 million entrance fee to the NHL. The construction of a brand new stadium soon .followed, with the San Jose Sharks playing their first game in the San Jose Arena on September 30th, 1993. The spiffy new Pavilion also plays host to a variety of other entertainment, including music, tennis, wrestling and boxing. Hey, the place was good enough for Cher—could you get a better endorsement than that?

Regardless of what you're watching at the Pavilion, you're not allowed to throw objects onto the stage or playing surface or into the stands. However, there is one exception to the rule—"…when, during a hockey game, a player scores a 'hat trick' (three goals in a game); in this case, throwing of hats is customary and has been deemed appropriate." So make sure to take along that sombrero.

How to Get There–Driving

Take the US-101 and exit at CA-87 Guadalupe Parkway. Bear right on Guadalupe Parkway and continue until the Julian Street exit. Turn right onto W Julian St. and left on Stockton Ave. If you take 280, take the Bird Ave. exit and continue until it becomes Autumn St. Follow the signs to the parking lots.

Parking

There are over 6,000 parking spaces located within a 1/2-mile radius of the Pavilion. The charge for parking ranges from $8 to $13 for most events.

How to Get There–Mass Transit

Caltrain is the best public transportation option, with the San Jose Diridon located just across from the stadium. A one-way fare from any of the SF Zone stations is $6. VTA bus lines 63, 64, 65, 68, 180, and the DASH all stop at the San Jose Diridon Station.

How to Get Tickets

For Sharks season passes call 408-999-5757 or check their website for order form details. Single game tickets cost between $18 and $108 and can be purchased via ticketmaster.com and all Ticketmaster outlets including Wherehouse Music, Tower Records, Ritmo Latino and select Rite-Aid stores.

Sports • Golf

San Francisco is home to a broad spectrum of golf courses—from nondescript municipal courses to some of the country's most scenic and heralded links. At the high end are two of the best courses in the nation, The San Francisco Golf Club and The Olympic Club. The SFGC claims only 250 members (you'd probably have better luck swimming to shore from Alcatraz than trying to get into this club). For those who do manage get a tee time, it is a truly remarkable experience—the course offers a classic layout with empty fairways and pristine greens.

While the private courses are some of the most famous, there are numerous public options in and around San Francisco. The Presidio Golf Course has hosted the U.S. Open and is a much improved course since the Arnold Palmer Golf Company took over management. There are several interesting par threes on the course, and the 9th and 18th holes are great finishers. The food at the Presidio Café is also some of the best at any golf course in the area, particularly on the weekends, when they serve brunch. If you want to play, call early, as tee times are hard to get. Be prepared for a five- to six-hour round on weekends.

Perhaps the most exciting development in San Francisco golf is the renovation of Harding Park. Harding is over 80 years old and, like many public courses, it fell victim to overplay (160,000 rounds per year) and was under management by the Parks & Recreation department for several decades. Over the last two years, however, various agencies have invested roughly $15 million to renovate the course, and the early reviews suggest that it has been returned to greatness.

There are also several options in San Francisco for golfers looking to save money or avoid crowds. Lincoln Park is an inexpensive municipal course boasting terrific views from several holes. Another economical choice is Glen Eagles, a nine-hole course that Lee Trevino once described as the hardest nine holes in golf. The course has several unique attributes, including a tree in a bunker on the sixth hole (a six-hundred-plus-yard par five). You may also be treated to hip hop music coming from the adjacent neighborhood on holes four and five and, if you're lucky, you may actually see a burning vehicle or two.

Golf Courses

Name	Address	Phone	Par	Fees
Golden Gate Park	47th Ave & Fulton	415-751-8987	27	$20 weekdays; $26 weekends
Lincoln Park	34th Ave & Clement	415-221-9911	68	$23 weekdays; $27 weekends
Presidio	300 Finley Rd	415-561-4663	72	$42 weekdays; $72 weekends
Harding Park	99 Harding Rd	415-661-1865		$26 weekdays; $31 weekends
San Francisco Club	Thomas Moore Way & Brotherhood Way	415-469-4122	71	$150 all times
Glen Eagles	2100 Sunnydale	415-587-2425	72	$17 weekdays; $24 weekends
Montclair	2477 Monterey Blvd, Oakland	510-482-0422	27	$4 weekdays; $4.50 weekends
Claremont Country Club	5295 Broadway Terrance, Oakland	510-653-6789		$40 weekdays; $50 weekends
Tilden Park	Grizzly Peak & Shasta Rd, Berkeley	510-848-7373	70	$25 weekdays; $40 weekends
Mill Valley	280 Buena Vista Ave, Mill Valley	415-388-9982	33	$20 weekdays; $23 weekends

Driving Ranges

Mission Bay Golf Ctr	1200 Sixth St		415-431-7888	$8/bucket; clubs on loan

Bowling Alleys

			Fees
Yerba Buena Ice Skating & Bowling Center	750 Folsom	415-777-3727	M–F $3.50 per game before 5pm and $5 after 5pm. Weekends $3.50 before 1pm and $5 after.
Presidio Bowling Center	Presidio Bldg 93	415-561-2695	$2.75–$4/game $2.50/shoes

Swimming Pools

			Type	Fees
Central YMCA	220 Golden Gate Ave	415-885-0460	Indoor	membership
24-Hour Fitness	1645 Bryant St	415-437-4188	Indoor	membership
24-Hour Fitness	1850 Ocean Ave	415-334-1400	Indoor	membership
Balboa Pool	San Jose Ave & Havelock	415-3374701	Indoor	adults $3 / kids 50¢
Boy's & Girl's Club	1950 Page St	415-221-6100	Indoor	$3/day
Cathedral Hill Plaza	1333 Gough St	415-346-3868	Indoor	$15/day
Central YMCA	220 Golden Gate Ave	415-885-0460	Indoor	membership
Chinatown YMCA	855 Sacramento St	415-576-9622	Indoor	$12/day
Club One	535 Union St	415-337-1010	Indoor	$20/day
Club One	350 3rd St	415-512-1010	Outdoor	membership
Club One	1755 O'Farrell	415-749-1010	Indoor	$20/day
Coffman Pool	Visitacion and Hahn	415-337-4702	Indoor	adults $3 / kids 50¢
Embarcadero YMCA	169 Steuart St	415-957-9622	Indoor	$15/day
Garfield Pool	26th St & Harrison St	415-695-5001	Indoor	adults $3 / kids 50¢
Golden Gateway	370 Drumm St	415-616-8800	Outdoor	membership
Hamilton Pool	Geary Blvd and Steiner	415-292-2001	Indoor	adults $3 / kids 50¢
Herbst Natatorium	2001 37th Ave	415-731-2522	Indoor	$4/day
Koret Health & Rec	2130 Fulton	415-422-6820	Indoor	$15/day
Letterman Pool	Funston Ave at Lincoln	415-447-9680	Indoor	$12/day
Mission Pool	19th St and Linda	415-695-5002	Outdoor	adults $3 / kids 50¢
MLK Jr. Pool	5701 3rd St	415-882-2807	Indoor	adults $3 / kids 50¢
Olympic Club	524 Post St	415-775-4400	Indoor	membership
Physis	1 Post St	415-781-6400	Indoor	$15/day
Rossi Pool	Arguello and Anza	415-666-7014	Indoor	adults $3 / kids 50¢
San Francisco Bay Club	150 Grenwich St	415-433-2550	Indoor	membership
Sava Pool	19th Ave and Wawona	415-753-7000	Indoor	adults $3 / kids 50¢
Sheehan Hotel	662 Sutter St	415-775-6500	Indoor	$10/day
Stonestown YMCA	333 Euclayptus	415-242-7100	Indoor	$10/day
The Sports Club	747 Market St	415-633-3900	Indoor	membership

Tennis Courts

	Address	Type	# of Cts	Surface	School/Public/Private
Alamo Square Park	1000 Hayes St	Outdoor	1	hard	public
Hayes Valley	700 Hayes St	Outdoor	1	hard	public
Margaret Hayward	1000 Golden Gate Ave	Outdoor	2	hard	public
Jackson	1700 17th St	Outdoor	1	hard	public
Potrero Hill	1600 22nd St	Outdoor	2	hard	public
San Francisco Tennis Club	645 Fifth St	Indoor/Outdoor	24		
Chinese Playground	800 Sacramento St	Outdoor	1	hard	public
Alice Marble	1200 Greenwich St	Outdoor	3	hard	public
Helen Willis	1400 Broadway	Outdoor	1	hard	public
Lafayette Sq	2200 Washington St	Outdoor	2	hard	public
Dolores Park	500 Dolores St	Outdoor	6		
Folsom	3000 21st St	Outdoor	1	hard	public
Holly Park	290 Highland Ave	Outdoor	1	hard	public
James Jr Rolph	1400 Potrero Ave	Outdoor	2	hard	public
Mission Playground	3550 19th St	Outdoor	2	hard	public
Bay Club	150 Greenwich	Outdoor	2	clay	private
Golden Gateway Tennis	370 Drumm	Outdoor	9	clay	private
Alice Chalmers	750 Brunswick St	Outdoor	1	hard	public
Balboa	350 Ocean Ave	Outdoor	4	hard	public
Cayuga Park	1850 Cayuga St	Outdoor	3	hard	public
Crocker Amazon	1100 Geneva Ave	Outdoor	1	hard	public
Excelsior	400 Russia Ave	Outdoor	1	hard	public
Ocean View	300 Plymouth Ave	Outdoor	2	hard	public
St Mary's	200 Crescent Ave	Outdoor	3	hard	public
Corona Hts Park	50 States St	Outdoor	2	hard	public
Eureka Valley	200 Collingwood St	Outdoor	1	hard	public
Noe Valley Courts	1000 Douglass St	Outdoor	1	hard	public
Sidney Peixotto	100 Roosevelt Way	Outdoor	1	hard	public
Alta Plaza	2500 Jackson St	Outdoor	3	hard	public
Ella Hill Hutch Community Center	1050 MacAllister	Outdoor	4	hard	public
Hamilton	1900 Geary Blvd	Outdoor	2	hard	public
Golden Gate Hts	2000 12th Ave	Outdoor	2	hard	public
James B Moffet	1500 Vicente St	Outdoor	4	hard	public
John P Murphy	1960 9th Ave	Outdoor	3	hard	public
Larsen Park	800 Vicente St	Outdoor	1	hard	public
McCoppin Sq	1400 Taraval St	Outdoor	2	hard	public
South Sunset	3000 Wawona St	Outdoor	1	hard	public
Buena Vista Park	1200 Haight St	Outdoor	2	hard	public
Gratlan	1200 Stanyon St	Outdoor	1	hard	public
Angelo Rossi	650 Arguello Blvd	Outdoor	3	hard	public
Golden Gate Park	37 Belcher St	Outdoor	21	hard	public
Julius Kahn	1 Spruce St	Outdoor	4	hard	public
Laurel Hill	300 Euclid Ave	Outdoor	1	hard	public
Mountain Lake	1100 Lake St	Outdoor	4	hard	public
Argonne	5400 Geary Blvd	Outdoor	1	hard	public
Cabrillo	3300 Cabrillo St	Outdoor	1	hard	public
Fulton	4800 Fulton St	Outdoor	1	hard	public
Margaret O Dupont	300 30th Ave	Outdoor	4	hard	public
Richmond	1700 Lake St	Outdoor	1	hard	public
Rochambeau	2300 Lake St	Outdoor	1	hard	public
Sunset	2300 Lawton St	Outdoor	2	hard	public
West Sunset	3200 Ortega St	Outdoor	2	hard	public
George Moscone	3400 Buchanan St	Outdoor	4	hard	public
Aptos	2250 Ocean Ave	Outdoor	1	hard	public
Joseph Lee	1600 Oakdale Ave	Outdoor	1	hard	public
Silver Terrace	5200 Bayshore Blvd	Outdoor	1	hard	public
Youngblood Coleman	500 Mendell St	Outdoor	2	hard	public
Miraloma	50 Omar Way	Outdoor	1	hard	public
Sunnyside	Forester & Melrose Sts	Outdoor	1	hard	public
George Christopher	5210 Diamond Hts Blvd	Outdoor	2	hard	public
Midtown Terrace	600 Clarendon Ave	Outdoor	4	hard	public
Peter Folger	90 Elk St	Outdoor	2	hard	public
Upper Noe	300 Day St	Outdoor	1	hard	public
West Portal	1000 Ulloa St	Outdoor	1	hard	public
Junipero Sierra	300 Stonecrest Dr	Outdoor	1	hard	public
Merced Heights	800 Shields St	Outdoor	1	hard	public
Stren Grove Annex	300 Sloat Blvd	Outdoor	2	hard	public
North Beach	700 Lombard St	Outdoor	3	hard	public
Francis J Herz	1700 Visitacion Blvd	Outdoor	1	hard	public
Louis Sutter	500 University St	Outdoor	2	hard	public
McLaren Park	1000 Mansell St	Outdoor	6	hard	public
Portola	500 Felton St	Outdoor	2	hard	public
Hunter's Point Boys & Girls Club	729 Kirkwood Ave				

General Information

Local hiking website: www.bahiker.com
Nature Hotline: 415-472-0911
San Francisco Hiking Club: www.sfhiking.com

Mount Davidson Park

Lansdale & Dalewood • 0.44 miles • Easy
With a peak at 927 feet, Mount Davidson constitutes the city's highest point. The trail to the top is short (0.5 miles) and moderately steep. Views from the top are obstructed by trees and a gigantic 100-foot concrete cross. The city of San Francisco was forced to sell the top of the park when residents complained that the gargantuan cross violated the separation of church and state. Aside from local controversy, this peak was also the site of a famous scene from Dirty Harry. To get to the park from downtown, take 101 South to 280 West and exit on Monterey Blvd. There is a small parking area on Portola. Bus number 36 conveniently stops right in front of the park. Dogs and bikes are allowed.

Crissy Field

Presidio East Beach entrance • 3.3 miles • Easy—flat
With 100 acres of open space, Crissy Field is a very popular spot for locals to escape urban life. Aside from the splendors of wildlife, the relatively flat path provides a much-needed respite from the steep city streets. The main trail, which was restored in 1998, weaves through picturesque marshland, meadows, and shoreline peppered with native flora and fauna. At 3.3 miles long, the beautiful scenery and smooth trail distinguish Crissy Field as an ideal place for walking, jogging, biking, blading, and dog walking. Crissy Field can be reached by three bus lines: 28, 29 and 43.

Inspiration Point

**Presidio Arguello Gate entrance •
1.78 miles • Easy—some hills**
Located in the Presidio, this trail offers yet another rustic escape from the sights and sounds of the city. Due to the surrounding non-native vegetation and urban development, this area has been dubbed an "ecological island." The Point houses the only serpentine grassland in the entire Golden Gate National Recreation Area, in addition to many other native bunch grasses. The flourishing plant life has much to do with an intensive three-year grassland restoration project which ran from 1995 to 1998.

The trail starts near Mountain Lake and continues for 1.78 miles. Although there are a few hills (it is San Francisco after all), the path is fairly easy. Inspiration Point is dog friendly, but be sure to observe the National Park Service's strict leash policy.

Glen Canyon

Bosworth & Elk • 0.9 miles • Moderate—short but steep
Positioned between Glen Canyon Park and Mount Davidson, the steep and gravelly trails in Glen Canyon are mostly used by nearby residents. Although there is an entrance on Bosworth Street, the entrance off Diamond Heights Blvd, has better parking. Park in the Diamond Heights Shopping Center and enter the park through the Christopher Playground behind the shopping center. The park may also be accessed by the number 44 bus (Elk Street stop) or the Glen Park BART station. The trails are short and riddled with poison oak, but the canyon is rarely crowded and has some rewarding views. The park is also home to several interesting rock formations, that offer some of the best bouldering in San Francisco.

Twin Peaks

Twin Peaks Blvd • 0.64 miles • Moderate—some hills
Twin Peaks has some of the best views in all of San Francisco. Located near the center of the city, this neighborhood affords some incredible panoramic vistas, provided there's no fog creeping down the mountain. This is a very touristy area, so if you're seeking solitude, look elsewhere. To get to the trails, travel along Bosworth, which becomes O'Shaughnessy Boulevard heading uphill. Take O'Shaughnessy to the junction with Portola at the top of the hill. Turn right, and immediately get into the left lane. Wait at the light, then turn left onto Twin Peaks Blvd. Drive uphill and park at the first pullout on the left (just past the first sharp curve). If that's full, continue uphill on Twin Peaks to the lot just past the north peak. The two hills of Twin Peaks are easily navigated, with moderate but short ascents and descents. The entire trail through the hills is short (0.64 miles), but some sections are very steep, so wear appropriate footwear. There's a portable toilet but no drinking water and, while there is handicapped parking, the trails over the peaks are not wheelchair accessible. Dogs are allowed.

Fort Funston

Skyline & John Muir Dr • 1.52 miles • Easy—some elev. gain
Fort Funston has several trails, all of which vary in difficulty and terrain type. Most trails are sandy and hard to navigate in hiking shoes; however, the main trail (Sunset Trail) is paved and wheelchair accessible. Despite the sandy terrain, the beautiful ocean views and bounteous vegetation make this an extremely popular spot to get away from it all, or at least most of it. Many of the trails access the beach, making Fort Funston a favorite among dog walkers as well. To reach the park by car, take Highway 35 to John Muir Drive and follows signs to the Fort Funston parking lot. For more information contact the Fort Funston Ranger Station at 415-239-2366.

McLaren Park

Cambridge & John F. Shelly Dr • 1.6 miles • Easy
This multi-faceted park has a plethora of paved trails, which are ideal for walking or jogging.

Bay Trail

Once finished, the Bay Trail will extend over 400 miles through the Bay Area, covering nine counties and 41 cities. This massive route will weave through commercial, residential, rural, and coastal areas, making this trail a scenic haven for bikers, joggers, bladers, and walkers. Aside from the aesthetic appeal of the path, the Bay Trail will provide alternative commute routes for cyclists, as well as link several public transportation facilities. The majority of the trail will be paved. Some areas will even overlap with city sidewalks, but some sections will be more rustic. For more information, check the official website www.abag.ca.gov/bayarea/baytrail/baytrail.html.

Muir Woods National Monument

This Marin County redwood preserve contains some of the most enchanting scenery in the entire country. Declared a national monument in 1908, today it is a quintessential San Francisco stop for both tourists and locals and is visited by over a million people every year. The best times to visit are on weekdays in the early morning or after 4pm. Parking at all other times will be an adventure in itself. In order to maintain the pristine conditions of the park, dogs, bikes, and picnics are not permitted. To get to the park by car, cross the Golden Gate Bridge, get off at the first exit, and follow the signs for Muir Woods National Monument. For more information on rules and directions visit the official website at www.nps.gov/muwo or call the information hotline at 415-388-2596.

Bike Information

San Francisco Bicycle Coalition: 415-431-BIKE, www.sfbike.org
San Francisco Mountain Biking: www.sfmtb.com
Bay Area Transit Authority: www.transitinfo.org
Critical Mass: www.critical-mass.org

Despite the brutally steep hills, biking is a very popular way to get around in San Francisco. This city was the birthplace of Critical Mass—a monthly bicycle ride which celebrates alternative, environmentally friendly modes of transportation. Forty-eight people participated in the first ride in 1992 and today thousands of people around the globe have joined this infectious movement. In addition to Critical Mass, the San Francisco Bike Coalition (SFBC), a non-profit organization which formed in 1971, has done much to improve cycling conditions in San Francisco. Some of their achievements include new legislation requiring bicycle racks in every parking garage, as well as the implementation of new bike lanes all over the city.

Bikes Onboard Mass Transit

Taking bikes on BART is a little more complicated. Be sure to consult the All About BART pamphlet to determine the rules and regulations concerning bikes. In general, bikes are allowed on all trains except during rush hour (refer to BART schedules), and they are not allowed on crowded cars or the first car of the train at all times. An adult must accompany cyclists under the age of 14. All BART stations are equipped with lockers. For information on availability call 510-464-7136.

All AC buses are equipped with front-mounted bicycle racks, which can accommodate 2 bikes at a time. Be sure to strap it in tightly – AC transit claims no responsibility for bikes that get damaged en route. For more information on AC's bicycle rack policies call 510-839-2882. Bikes are allowed at all times on the following MUNI routes: 17, 35, 36, 39, 53, 56, 66, 76, 91.

Caltrain has a capacity for 32 bikes per train. Some trains will even offer an additional bike car, holding a total of 64 bikes, but don't count your chickies before they hatch. This second car is never guaranteed. The designated bike car is always the one closest to San Francisco.

If you're traveling by water, the following ferry services accommodate bikes: Blue & Gold, Alameda/Oakland, Golden Gate, and Vallejo/Baylink. Sorry folks, no bikes allowed on cable cars or historic streetcars.

Bike Shops

- Adventure Bicycle Company · 968 Columbus Ave · 415-771-8735
- American Cyclery · 510 Fredrick St · 415-664-4545
- American Cyclery Too · 858 Stanyan St · 415-876-4545
- Avenue Cyclery · 756 Stanyan St
- Bicycle Warehouse · 428 S Airport Blvd · 415-558-1714
- Big Swingin Cycles · 1122 Taraval St · 415-661-2462
- The Bike Hut · Pier 40 Embarcadero & Townsend · 415-543-4335
- Bike Nook · 3004 Taraval St · 415-731-3838
- Blazing Saddles Bike Rental · 1095 Columbus
- By the By (on-call bike maintenance) · 415-527-9204
- Castro Cycle Crafters · 4023 18th St · 415-863-8337
- City Cycles · 3001 Steiner St
- DD Cycles · 4049 Balboa · 415-752-7980
- Fog City Cycles · 3430 Geary Blvd · 415-221-3031
- Foxy Flyer Bicycle Company · 3330 Steiner St · 415-674-1910
- Fresh Air Bicycles · 1943 Divisadero
- Freewheel Bicycle Shop · 980 Valencia · 415-643-9213
- Freewheel Bicycle Shop · 1920 Hayes St · 415-752-9195
- Mahayana Foundation Cyclery · 218 Fillmore St · 415-863-7404
- Noe Valley · 4193 24th St
- Nomad Cyclery · 2555 Irving St
- Ocean Cyclery · 1915 Ocean Ave · 415-239-5004
- Open Road · 1352 Irving St
- Park Cyclery · 1865 Haight St
- Pedal Revolution · 3085 21st St · 415-641-1264
- Roaring Mouse Cycles · 1352 Irving St · 415-753-6272
- Road Rage Bicycles · Folsom & 7th St
- Sports Basement · 1301 6th St
- Vision Cyclery · 772 Stanyan St · 415-221-9766

Skate Information

Skating Club of San Francisco: www.scsf.com
California Outdoor Rollerskating Association: www.cora.org

Golden Gate Park

There are no official skate parks at the moment, so Golden Gate Park will have to suffice as a haven for the roller folk. Every Sunday a two-mile section of Kennedy Blvd. is closed off for the exclusive use of pedestrians and skaters/bikers. It's pretty much a free-for-all, so keep your eyes open if you're on a bike, especially for the little kids on bikes and skates. On Saturdays a one-mile stretch of Middle Drive is closed to vehicular traffic. Thousands of people on bikes, rollerskates, rollerblades, and skateboards gather weekly to flaunt their new tricks. This park has everything from a roller-dancing area (6th Avenue and Kennedy Blvd) to organized skating events, such as the Lake Merced Loop. This seventeen-mile group skating event takes place every Sunday. The trip starts at 1 pm from 6th Ave and Kennedy Blvd and is not recommended for novice skaters. If you don't have your own gear, you can rent skates from Skates on Haight located a few blocks east of the park at 1818 Haight St., 415-752-8375. Aside from Golden Gate Park, the smooth paths around the Marina Green are another popular spot for skaters of all breeds.

Midnight Rollers

Looking for something to do on a Friday night? Why not take a cruise with the Midnight Rollers—a weekly organized event which brings hundreds of skaters to the streets of San Francisco. The party starts every Friday at 8 pm at the Ferry Building. At 8:30 pm sharp the party takes off for a 12.5-mile adventure through the city streets. Happy skating!

Yerba Buena Gardens

750 Folsom St., 415-777-3727
Admission $4.50-6.50; Skate Rental $2.50
Website: www.skatebowl.com.

The temperate climate of the Bay Area precludes any outdoor ice skating, however, the indoor rink in Yerba Buena Gardens is fully equipped for all your ice skating needs. Join a figure skating class, or try out for the Faultline Hockey Program. This facility offers several classes ranging from ballet on ice to skate day camp during the summer. You can pick up any skating gear at the fully equipped Yerba Buena Pro Shop, 415-820-3521.

Gear

For skateboard or rollerblade gear check out San Francisco's oldest skate shop, Skates on Haight at 1818 Haight St., 415-752-8375. Don't miss their extensive online catalog at www.skatesonhaight.com. Also check out the Purple Skunk at 5820 Geary Blvd., 415-668-7905 or DLX Skateboards & Clothing at 1831 Market St., 415-626-5588.

General Information

Airport Information: 650-821-8211
Airport Website: www.sfoairport.com
Ground Transportation (Bay Area Transit Information):
817-1717 (Bay Area only, no area code is required)
Lost & Found: 650-821-7014
Parking: 650-821-7900
Police (Non-Emergency): 650-821-7111
US Customs: 650-624-7200
US Immigration and Naturalization Service:
650-837-2800

Overview

This is fog city, remember? Airports and fog don't usually mix well, and San Francisco International Airport (SFO) is no exception. With just a couple of closely spaced runways, the airport is particularly prone to weather-related delays. Still, SFO served just over 41 million passengers in 2000, making it the 5th largest airport in U.S. and the 9th largest in the world. The two most popular destinations remain Los Angeles, with 80 flights daily, and New York, with 42 flights per day. While other local airports have been giving SFO some stiff competition for those and other destinations, recent improvements might help it win back passengers. The newly remodeled international terminal, for one, has earned rave reviews with its ultra stylish design and art-filled space. Another welcome addition is the newly opened BART connection to SFO, which will ease the commute for thousands of travelers.

Mayor Brown and others want to give SFO another boost with new runways to ease congestion and delays, but the now five-year old runway expansion plan is itself delayed. The new runways would fill in 1.5 square miles of open water in the bay—a prospect (think churning mud, lots of nasty chemicals, dying fish) that has environmentalists worried. For now, the economic downturn and the resulting reduction in air traffic have the expansion on hold, but discussion is expected to heat up again when air travel increases.

How to Get There–Driving

So you really want to drive to the airport? You probably don't want to do it during the morning rush hour, at least not without giving yourself plenty of extra time. Traffic is generally a lot more manageable than it used to be, particularly since the bursting of the dot-com bubble took a lot of commuters off the road. If you're driving from San Francisco, take 101 South and get off at the SF International Airport Exit. If you're coming along Highway 380, travel east to the 101 South exit towards San Jose. Take the SF Intl Airport exit. The exits and signs directing you to the various terminals are well placed and easy to follow.

How to Get There–Mass Transit

There are really three options for public transportation and the best option for you will depend on where you're going and how much baggage you have. SamTrans runs a few bus routes out of SFO including the KX Express bus, which provides service between San Francisco, SFO, and Palo Alto. You'd better be travelling light though, because the KX doesn't allow luggage! Route 292 is a local bus that makes many stops in the communities between San Francisco, SFO, and San Mateo. Route 397 runs an overnight "owl" service between San Francisco, SFO, and Palo Alto. Route 193 operates on a limited schedule between the Stonestown Galleria in San Francisco, Daly City BART Station, and SFO. KX Express will set you back $3.50, while the local buses cost $1.25.

Caltrain runs a service from Millbrae Station to 4th & King Street ($2.25) and free shuttles run between the station and the airport approximately every 20-30 minutes except on weekends. The new BART service also offers a cross-platform transfer at Millbrae.

BART is probably going to be the most effective and efficient way of transferring you and your luggage to San Francisco International Airport. The blue line runs all the way into SFO. It's amazing that it took until 2003 to finally get BART into SFO, but hey, it was worth the wait.

How to Get There–Really

If you'd rather not drive and you don't relish the prospect of lugging your bags to the nearest BART station or bus stop, there are a number of shuttle services that can get you to SFO from the city for around $20 (a bargain, compared to the typical cab fare). Most shuttles will pick you up at your front door in plenty of time to make your flight, but you'll share your ride with 2 to 3 others. See Shuttles, page 218.

Parking

For domestic flights, if you're leaving from Terminal 1, park in Sections A/B, B or C. Terminal 2 flights should head to Section D, and if you're going from Terminal 3, park in Sections E, F, or F/G. Rates for parking are $1 per 12 minutes, $28 maximum for the first 24 hours, and $35 maximum per additional 24 hours.

If your destination is abroad, use Garage A for Air France, Alaska Airlines (Mexico flights), British Airways, Cathay Pacific, China Airlines, Japan Airlines, KLM, Korean Air, LACSA, Northwest (International), Philippine Airlines, TACA and Virgin Atlantic. Garage G serves Aeroflot, Air Canada, AirChina, ANA, Asiana, EVA, Lufthansa, Mexicana, Singapore Airlines, and United (International). Parking costs $1 per 12 minutes and $22 per 24-hour period.

For two hours of free parking in any terminal garage, you need to spend $20 at participating shops and restaurants in the International Terminal to have your ticket validated. You can also print out discount parking coupons via the airport website at www.flysfo.com.

If your budget doesn't cover long-term parking in the domestic lots, an alternative is the cheaper long-term lot located off the U.S. 101/San Bruno Avenue-East exit. You can park there for up to 30 days and a free shuttle service will take you to and from the terminals every 5 minutes. Parking is $1 for each 12 minutes, $13 for 24 hours through day 7 and $11 per 24 hours thereafter. The website offers a "7th day free" coupon so if you'll be there for a week, print it out and take it with you. If the long-term lot happens to be full, get a voucher to park right at the terminals for the same long-term rate!

Cabs

Typical fare from the airport to Cow Palace is around $29, downtown will set you back roughly $37, and the Wharf will be around $44.

Rental Cars

Alamo	650-875-8403
Avis	650-877-6777
Budget	650-877-0998
Dollar	650-244-4131
Enterprise	650-697-9200
Hertz	650-876-1745
National	650-616-3000
Thrifty	650-259-1313

Hotels

- La Quinta Inn · 20 Airport Blvd · San Francisco · 650-583-2223
- Radisson San Francisco Airport · 5000 Sierra Point Pkwy · San Francisco · 415-467-4400
- Sheraton Gateway, 600 Airport Blvd · Burlingame · 650-340-8500
- Summerfield Suites by Wyndham · 1350 Huntington Ave · San Bruno · 650-588-0770
- Clarion San Francisco Airport · 401 East Millbrae Ave · Millbrae · 650-692-6363
- Ramada Airport · 245 S Airport Blvd · San Francisco · 650-873-3550
- Hampton Inn Airport · 300 Gateway Blvd · San Francisco · 650-876-0200
- Best Western Grosvenor Hotel · 380 South Airport Blvd · San Francisco · 650-873-3200
- Travelodge Airport · 326 S. Airport Blvd · S an Francisco · 650-583-9600
- Holiday Inn San Francisco · 275 S. Airport Blvd · 877-877-3342
- Hyatt Regency San Francisco Airport · 1333 Bayshore Highway · Burlingame · 650-347-1234

Terminal 1

Air Canada
Alaska Airlines
America West
ATA
Continental
Delta
Frontier Airlines
Hawaiian Airlines
Midwest Express
National Airlines
Northwest (domestic)
US Airways

Terminal 3

American
United Airlines (domestic)

International Terminal

Aeroflot
Air China
Air France
All Nippon
Asiana
British Airways
Cathay Pacific
China Airlines
Eva Airways
Japan Airlines
KLM
Korean Air
LACSA
Lufthansa
Mexicana
Northwest (international)
Philippine Airlines
Singapore Airlines
TACA
United Airlines (international)
Virgin Atlantic

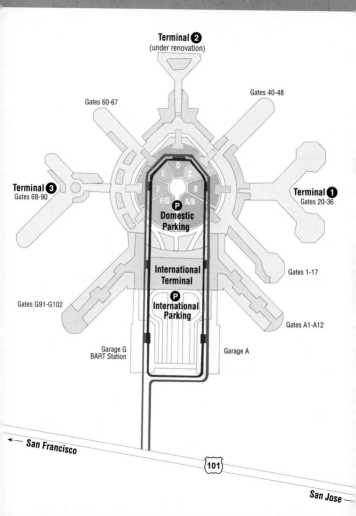

Terminal ❷
(under renovation)

Gates 40-48

Gates 60-67

Terminal ❸
Gates 68-90

Terminal ❶
Gates 20-36

E D
F C
B
F/G A/B
Ⓟ
Domestic Parking

Gates 1-17

International Terminal

Ⓟ
International Parking

Gates G91-G102

Gates A1-A12

Garage G
BART Station

Garage A

← San Francisco

101

San Jose →

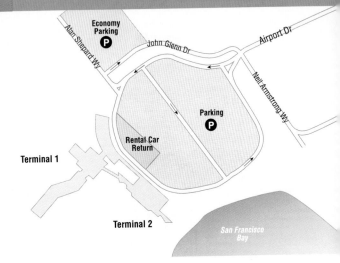

Terminal 1

Alaska
Aloha
America West
American
Continental
Delta
JetBlue
United/Express

International Terminal

Aloha
Allegro
Mexicana
North American
Ryan International
SunTrips

Terminal 2

Southwest

General Information

Airport Phone: 510-563-3300
Airport Website: www.oaklandairport.com
Parking: 1-888-IFLYOAK
Lost and Found: 510-563-3982
Friendly Cab Service: 510-536-3000
Veteran's Cab Service: 510-533-1900

Overview

Gertrude Stein said famously of Oakland, "there's no *there* there." These days, though, a lot of people have been going *there* to get everywhere else. Oakland International Airport's preponderance of low-fare carriers has actually led to a recent increase in passengers.

Oakland might not be the biggest Bay Area airport, but it's rich in history. Amelia Earhart took off from Oakland on her ill-fated flight—but don't worry, navigation is a bit more reliable these days. The original airport at North Field was built in 1927 and is still in operation today for air cargo, general aviation, and corporate jet activities. Commercial passenger and cargo jet aircraft operate from South

Field, which opened in 1962. Oakland Airport is a thriving business, handling more than 10 million passengers per year and employing approximately 10,700 airport-related workers.

How to Get There–Driving

If you're coming to Oakland from San Francisco, give yourself a little extra time for possible Bay Bridge delays, especially if you're traveling during the morning or evening rush hours. Travel south on Hwy 880 and exit at Hegenberger Road. Merge onto Hegenberger Road and continue straight ahead to the airport. Use the right lane for Terminal 1/International, the economy parking lot and cargo facilities. Use the left lane for Terminal 2 and the hourly and daily parking lots and all rental car returns.

How to Get There–Mass Transit

The best way to get from San Francisco to the Oakland Airport is via the Orange, Blue, and Green BART lines. Hours of operation to the Coliseum/Oakland Airport station are Monday-Friday, 4 am until midnight; Saturday, 6 am until midnight; Sunday, 8 am until midnight. From the Coliseum/Airport station, the airBART shuttle to the airport departs every 15 minutes and costs $2 for adults and 50¢ for those entitled to discounts.

If you're arriving to the area by Amtrak (Jack London Square Station), Alameda/Oakland Ferry, or BART, local AC Transit bus 58 will take you right to the airport for $1.50 or 75¢ discounted fare.

How to Get There–Really

You really don't want to drive to Oakland if you can avoid it—not unless you really like the views from the Bay Bridge. Signage is somewhat confusing in the parking areas, and recent construction there makes getting around the lots somewhat tricky these days. Save yourself the money and hassle by taking BART. It's about the cheapest and most efficient way to get to there.

Parking

Oakland airport parking is logically organized by letter with Lot H accommodating hourly parking, Lot D housing daily parkers, and Lot E assigned for economy parking. All lots are $2 per 30 minutes for short-term parking. If you park in the hourly lots, parking is $27 for the first 24 hours and $32 for each day after that. The daily parking lots are $20 per day for up to 6 days and $17 per day after that. The economy lot is $17 per day for up to 6 days and $14 per day thereafter.

Rental Cars

- Avis • 510-577-6370 or 800-331-1212
- Budget • 510-568-6150 or 800-527-0700
- Dollar • 866-434-2226 or 800-800-4000
- Enterprise • 510-567-1760 or 800-736-8222
- Hertz • 510-639-0200 or 800-654-3131
- National • 510-632-2225 or 800-227-7368
- Thrifty • 510-568-1279 or 800-847-4389

Hotels

- Best Western • 170 Hegenberger Rd • 510-633-0500
- Holiday Inn Oakland Airport • 500 Hegenberger Rd • 510-562-5311
- Comfort Inn and Suites • 8452 Edes Ave • 510-568-1500
- Holiday Inn Express • 66 Airport Rd • 510-569-4400
- Courtyard by Marriott • 350 Hegenberger Rd • 510-568-7600
- Hilton Oakland Airport • One Hegenberger Rd • 510-635-5000
- Days Inn Oakland Airport • 8350 Edes Ave • 510-568-1880
- Oakland Airport Ramada • 8471 Enterprise Way • 510-562-4888
- Hampton Inn Oakland Airport • 8466 Enterprise Way • 510-632-8900
- Park Plaza Hotel • 150 Hegenberger Rd • 510-635-5300

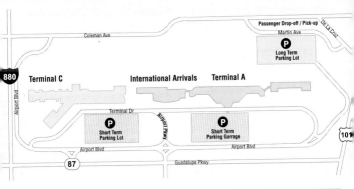

Terminal A

American/American Eagle
Southwest

Terminal C

Alaska
America West
ATA
Continental
Delta
Frontier
Horizon Air
Mexicana
Northwest
United/United Express

General Information

General Airport Info: 408-277-4SKY
Airport Website: www.sjc.org

Overview

San Jose likes to boast that it's the biggest city in Northern California—well, okay, so maybe it is, but their airport isn't! Still, Norman Y. Mineta San José International Airport (SJC) is not a bad place to fly out of or into. And, like Oakland, it can sometimes offer more affordable flights than SFO (if you don't mind driving a while to get there, that is). They're working on making SJC more accessible by adding freeway routes and new interchanges (see "How to Get There—Driving" below). It might be a tad messy right now, but it'll get better.

Located two miles north of downtown San jose, SJC is a completely self-supporting enterprise, owned and operated by the City of San Jose. Passenger totals last year exceeded 11.1 million, with the airport averaging 388 commercial and 335 general aviation flights daily.

How to Get There–Driving

"Do You Know the Way to San Jose?" croons Dionne, but you might not be singing along if you're stuck in the morning commute to Northern California's biggest burg. Silicon Valley traffic can turn the trip from San Francisco into a two-hour (or more) affair, so if you have to drive to or from the city, particularly during the rush hours, give yourself plenty of time.

From San Francisco, begin on I-80 west, which eventually becomes US-101 south. Stay on US-101 south and take the CA-87/Guadalupe Parkway exit on the right. Merge onto Guadalupe Parkway then turn right onto Airport Parkway. If you're coming down I-880, take the Brokaw Road exit. Drive along O'Toole Ave and make a right on E. Brokaw Road, which becomes Airport Parkway.

Construction projects are currently underway to create a new Skyport Drive/Airport Boulevard Interchange, so be prepared for detours and watch the signs. Caltrans is also building the Route 87 freeway just east of SJC.

How to Get There–Mass Transit

There are a few public transportation options that will take you close to the airport and then you'll need to take a bus or a shuttle to the terminals. Caltrain riders should get off at Santa Clara and take the VTA Airport Flyer (Route 10) to the airport. The Route 10 bus also makes a stop at the VTA Metro Light Rail Station. From there, it's a convoluted route to get you there: Take the light rail to the Civic Center stop and board the VTA 180 Express Bus, which will take you right to the Fremont BART stop. If you're traveling from further afield, Greyhound and Amtrak both stop roughly 3 miles from the airport but you'll have to take a taxi from there.

How to Get There–Really

Sure, the traffic can be a nightmare if you go at the wrong time, but if you don't like transferring from buses to trains and back again, and you'd rather not pay for cabs or shuttles, get a ride if you can, or drive yourself. Just remember to give yourself plenty of time.

Parking

There are really only two options for parking at San Jose Airport—short-term or long-term parking. If you're going to Terminal A or International arrivals, head to the short-term parking garage, and if Terminal C is your destination, try the short term parking lot across the roadway from the terminal. Short-term parking is $1 per 20 minutes with a maximum daily fee of $30. For longer stays, park in the long-term lot on Martin Avenue, which is only $15 per day. A free shuttle is provided to and from the terminals.

Cabs

Yellow Cab (408-293-1234) departs from Terminal A and United Cab (408-971-1111) from Terminal C. A fare to San Francisco Airport will set you back $65-$70, while a longer trip to downtown SF will cost you between $90 and $100.

Rental Cars

- Alamo · 408-980-5249
- Avis · 408-993-2224
- Budget · 408-286-7850
- Dollar · 408-999-6567
- Enterprise · 408-452-1100
- Fox · 408-436-1990
- Hertz · 408-437-5700
- National · 408-288-4662
- Payless · 408-781-5690
- Thrifty · 408-453-3344

Hotels

- Hyatt Saint Claire · 302 S Market St · 408-271-3399
- Crown Plaza Downtown · 282 Almaden Blvd · 408-998-0400
- Hilton San Jose and Towers · 300 Almaden Blvd · 408-287-2100
- Travelodge Sports Arena · 1041 The Alameda · 408-295-0159
- Adlon Hotel · 1275 N 4th St · 888-452-3566
- Holiday Inn Express Airport · 1350 N 4th St · 408-467-1789
- Best Western San Jose Lodge · 1440 N 1st St · 408-453-7750
- Radisson Plaza Hotel Airport · 1471 N 4th St · 408-452-0200
- Travelodge Convention Center · 1415 Monterey Rd · 408-993-1711
- Homestead San Jose · 1560 N 1st St · 408-573-0648
- Courtyard San Jose Airport · 1727 Technology Dr · 408-441-6111
- Hotel De Anza · 233 W Santa Clara · 800-843-3700

(217)

Airlines

Airlines	Phone	SFO	OAK	SJC
Aeroflot	650-821-0504	■		
Air Canada	888-247-2262	■		
Air China	800-986-1985	■		
Air France	800-237-2747	■		
Alaska Airlines	800-426-0333	■	■	■
All Nippon	800-235-9262	■		
Allegro	877-443-7585	■		
Aloha	800-367-5250		■	
America West	800-235-9292	■	■	■
American Airlines	800-433-7300	■		■
Asiana	800-227-4262	■		
ATA	800-435-9282	■	■	■
British Airways	800-247-9297	■		
Cathay Pacific	800-233-2742	■		
China Airlines	800-227-5118	■		
Continental	800-525-0280	■	■	■
Delta	800-221-1212	■	■	■
Eva Airways	800-695-1188	■		
Frontier Airlines	800-432-1359	■		■
Hawaiian Airlines	800-367-5320	■		
Horizon Air	800-547-9308			■

Airlines	Phone	SFO	OAK	SJC
Japan Airlines	800-525-3663	■		
Jet Blue	800-538-2583		■	
KLM	800-447-4747	■		
Korean Air	800-438-5000	■		
LACSA	800-225-2272	■		
Lufthansa	800-645-3880	■		
Mexicana	800-531-7921	■	■	■
Midwest Express	800-452-2022	■		
National Airlines	888-757-5387	■		
North American	718-656-2650		■	
Northwest	800-225-2525	■		
Philippine Airlines	800-435-9725	■		
Ryan International				■
Singapore Airlines	800-742-3333	■		
Southwest	800-435-9792	■	■	■
Sun Trips	800-SUN-TRIPS		■	
TACA	800-535-8780	■		
United Airlines	800-241-6522	■	■	■
US Airways	800-428-4322	■		
Virgin Atlantic	800-862-8621	■		

Shuttle Services

Shuttle Services	Phone	SFO	OAK	SJC
A-1 Shuttle Services	888-698-2663		■	
Advanced Airporter	415-550-1112	■		
Airport Interlink	916-372-6615	■		
Airport Shuttle	510-653-1500	■	■	
Air-Transit Shuttle	510-568-3434	■		
American Airporter Shuttle	800-282-7758	■		
AM-PM Airporter	510-547-2155		■	
Apollo Shuttle	925-676-9146	■	■	■
Atlas Express Airport Connection	510-569-5982	■	■	■
Atlas Express Airport Shuttle	408-249-7777	■	■	■
Avon Airporter Express	707-643-5778	■	■	
Bay Area Express	510-234-9759	■	■	
Bay Area Shuttle	800-960-1992	■	■	
Bayporter Express	800-287-6783	■	■	
Bay Shuttle	415-564-3400	■		
Best Way Shuttle	925-363-7711	■	■	
Bridge Airporter Express	800-300-1661	■	■	
California Airporter	800-225-6316	■		
Chamber Airport Express	510-569-5445	■	■	
City Express Shuttle & Limo	888-874-8885	■	■	
Citywide Shuttle	877-336-0090	■	■	■
Comfort Shuttle	510-774-6833	■	■	

Shuttle Services	Phone	SFO	OAK	SJC
Door-to-Door Shuttle	415-775-5121	■		
East Bay Connection	800-675-3278		■	
Lorrie's Airport Shuttle	415-334-9000	■		
Lucky Shuttle	510-303-8773	■	■	■
Luxor Shuttle	510-562-7222	■	■	■
M & M	415-552-3200	■	■	
Pacific Airport Shuttle	415-681-6318	■		
Peter's Airport Shuttle	650-871-8315	■		
Pyramid Airporter	510-562-0822	■		
Quake City Shuttle	415-255-4899	■		
Safety Express Shuttle	510-388-2029	■	■	
San Jose Express	408-370-0701	■	■	■
Santa Clara Airporter	800-771-7794			■
SF City Shuttle	650-876-0789	■		
SFO Airporter (major hotels)	800-532-8405	■		
Shuttle Pro	866-499-2447	■		
South Bay Airport Shuttle	408-559-9477			■
South & East Bay Shuttle Inc.	800-548-4664	■	■	■
SuperShuttle	800-BLUE-VAN	■	■	■
The Shuttle	415-971-9031	■	■	
USA Shuttle & USA Charter	408-441-6337	■	■	■
VIP Airport Shuttle	408-885-1800	■	■	■

Alameda/ Oakland Ferry

415-705-5555 • www.eastbayferry.com
This ferry provides commuter routes from the East
Bay to the city, as well as direct service to Pacific Bell
Park for Giants' games. Tickets may be purchased on
board and fares vary from $1 to $12 according to
where you traveling. This ferry makes stops at Angel
Island on weekends during the summer.

Angel Island-Tiburon Ferry

415-435-2131 • www.angelislandferry.com
This family-owned ferry offers an array of services,
including sunset cruises (reservations
recommended), Giants game cruises, and trips to
Angel Island and Tiburon. These vessels may also be
chartered for special occasions, such as weddings or
birthday parties.

Blue & Gold Fleet

415-705-5555 • www.blueandgoldfleet.com
Located at Pier 41, Blue & Gold provides service to
Alcatraz. It is highly recommended that you
purchase tickets in advance by calling 705-5555,
because tours frequently sell out. Tickets start at $13.
Blue & Gold also offers narrated historical tours of
the Bay.

Golden Gate Ferry

415-923-2000 • www.goldengate.org
Makes stops at Larkspur, Sausalito, and Tiburon. The
fare is $5.60 each way. Buy a frequent rider ticket
book and it's $3.50/$3 each way. This ferry also
makes stops at Pacific Bell Park for Giant's games.
Great views of San Quentin too! Buy tickets ahead of
time at the terminal or by calling 478-2277.

Harbor Bay Ferry

510-769-5500 • www.harborbayferry.com
Provides convenient commuter service between San
Francisco and Alameda. Fares are $5 each way, but
commuter rates and monthly passes are available.
This service also offers a river cruise up the
Sacramento Delta on weekends with live music and
lunch.

Red & White Fleet

415-673-2900 • www.redandwhite.com
This service also offers tours of Alcatraz as well as
narrated tours of the Bay in six different languages.
Tickets start at $15 and the boat leaves from Pier 43.

Vallejo Baylink Ferry

www.baylinkferry.com
Makes stops at Vallejo, Fisherman's Wharf, and the
San Francisco Ferry Building. The fare is $9.50 each
way for adults, but monthly passes are available.

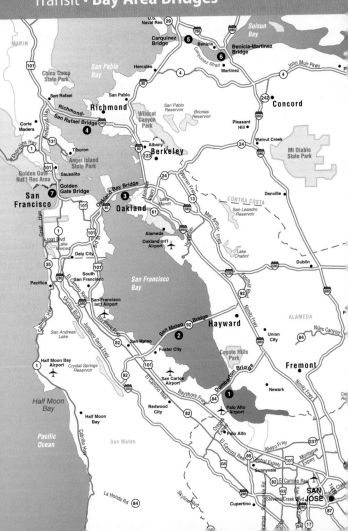

The Bay Area's bridges, especially the Golden Gate and the Bay Bridge, are the undisputed icons of the city's romantic allure. Both bridges have appeared in countless movies. The Golden Gate even fell apart in the recent sci-fi thriller "The Core," a sight that would bring tears to any longtime resident's eyes. Dustin Hoffman drove across the Bay Bridge (but the wrong way!) in "The Graduate." But don't let these star bridges eclipse their lesser-known, but nonetheless hardworking, counterparts; the San Francisco area actually has seven toll bridges.

The Golden Gate Bridge is the only one in California that is not under state jurisdiction. It takes seven years to paint the span its distinctive reddish-orange hue and, once they finish, they start all over again.

The Dumbarton Bridge was the first vehicular crossing of the San Francisco Bay. The original San Mateo-Hayward Bridge was the longest bridge in the world when it was completed in 1929, but today a portion of that bridge is used as a fishing pier, since the bridge was completely replaced in the '60s. The Carquinez Bridge consists of two parallel suspension bridges, one built in 1927 and the other in 1958. The 1927 bridge is currently being rebuilt and should open this year. The Oakland Bay Bridge, consisting of two crossings connected by a tunnel on Yerba Buena Island, consumed over six percent of the total steel output of the nation in 1933. The eastern span, between Oakland and Yerba Buena Island, is currently being rebuilt and should be open to traffic sometime within the next three to four years.

		Toll	# of lanes	Pedestrian/Bicyclists?	# of Vehicles/Day (in thousands)	Original Cost (in millions)	Engineer	Main Span/Length	Operated by	Opened to Traffic
1	Dumbarton Bridge	$2	6	Yes	61	2.25		8600'	DOT	1/15/27
2	San Mateo-Hayward Bridge	$2	6		81	70		9500'	DOT	10/31/67
3	Oakland Bay Bridge	$2	10	No	270	77	Charles C. Purcell	23,000'	DOT	11/12/36
4	Richmond – San Rafael Bridge	$2	4		60	66		24,000'	DOT	9/1/56
5	Carquinez Bridge	$2	7	Yes	116	8	Aven Hanford & Oscar Klatt	4200'	DOT	5/21/27
6	Benicia-Martinez Bridge	$2	6		100	25		6300'	DOT	9/16/62
7	Golden Gate Bridge	$5	6	Yes	125	33	Joseph Baermann Strauss	6450'	*	5/27/37

* Golden Gate Bridge Highway and Transportation District

Web resources

Excellent bridges URL: www.dot.ca.gov/dist4/calbrdgs.htm
Another site to check: www.subwaymark.bravepages.com/bridges/ca-sfo.htm
Bridge toll increase story: sanfrancisco.bizjournals.com/sanfrancisco/stories/2003/04/21/daily4.html
Golden Gate Bridge Website: www.goldengatebridge.org/fastraktolls/index.html

City of San Francisco Dept. of Parking and Traffic
Address: 25 Van Ness Ave, Suite 410
San Francisco, CA 94102
Phone: 415(recorded info)
Website: www.sfgov.org (official)
www.sfbaytraffic.info
www.sfgate.com/traffic

California Dept. of Transportation (Caltrans)
Traffic hotline: In CA: 800-427-ROAD (7623)
Outside CA: 916-445-7623
Website: www.dot.ca.gov/hq/roadinfo

Golden Gate Bridge
Phone: 415-921-5858
FasTrak: 1-877-442-8655

Bay Bridge Traffic
www.dot.ca.gov/hq/roadinfo

Radio traffic info KGO 810 AM
KQED 88.5 FM
KALW 91.7

Orientation

The 46 square miles of streets, lanes, alleys, and winding roads that are crammed onto the tip of the San Francisco Peninsula will make even occasional commuters in the city sing bitterly, "I Left My Maalox in San Francisco" (apologies to Tony Bennett). Aside from the relatively orderly layout of avenues out in the Sunset, some of the city's thoroughfares make it look like Jackson Pollock was on the job when they were laying out the streets of San Francisco. Let's not forget that this city is home to Lombard Street, "the crookedest street in the world." You'd think the city's small area would be an easy space to navigate—but it's crowded, so driving in the city is usually a challenge, and it gets even worse during rush hours (roughly from 7:00 am to 10:30 am and 3:30 pm to 7:00 pm on weekdays). And if there's a parade or construction going on—well, maybe you should just go to the Haight and sample some of its famous herbal remedies.

A word or two about San Francisco's steep hills: If you're driving a stick-shift, make sure you're comfortable with your shifting and hill-start skills—they will be tested. Some intersections are on inclines so fierce, you'll think you're airborne before you actually see the cross-street, so don't go driving like Steve McQueen in *Bullit*. And be mindful of the cable car lines that run up and down Powell St. and along California St.—there's plenty of pedestrian traffic as cable car passengers board and disembark.

Icon- and color-coded signs mark famous tourist areas like North Beach, Fisherman's Wharf, and Chinatown (A crab for the wharf, pagoda for Chinatown…get it?).

Bridges

On any given day the Golden Gate Bridge, which connects the city to Marin County in the north, and the Bay Bridge, which runs to Treasure Island and Oakland/Berkeley in the east, can be either smooth sailing or a grid-locked mess. It all depends on the stars. On weekends, particularly if the weather is good, the Golden Gate Bridge tends to be full of residents fleeing the city for Marin. The Bay Bridge tends to back up most during weekday rush hours. Check local traffic reports for up-to-the-minute bridge traffic updates.

Major Bay Area Freeways

Highway 101: Runs north-south through the city, ending in Oregon (to the north) and Los Angeles (to the south).

I-280: Runs parallel and just to the west of Highway 101. This route tends to be less crowded to the 101, and it's a bit easier on the eyes.

Highway 1: Like a wayward lover, this pretty bit of road merges briefly with Highway 101 as they cross the Golden Gate Bridge together, then ambles off on its own again. Highway 1's scenic, winding route is one of the prettiest in the nation—but don't drive it if you're in a hurry.

I-80: Runs north-south through Berkeley and connects the East Bay with San Francisco via the Bay Bridge.

I-280: Connects the East Bay with I-5, which runs through the Central Valley and provides the fastest route south to Los Angeles. Be warned: the 390-mile, six-to-seven hour drive isn't exactly scenic—lots of flat farmland. You'll think you're in Iowa.

Major Construction Projects and Alternate Routes

The closing of the Central Freeway's Fell St. off-ramp has presented San Francisco drivers with their biggest challenge since the elevated portion of the Embarcadero came down after the 1989 earthquake. With the Fell St. ramp gone, Mission St. is now the last Central Freeway exit. It provides access to Civic Center and the designated detour route at Van Ness Avenue.

Drivers wishing to avoid Central Freeway congestion can use alternate surface street routes, or I-280. To quote a Zen master, it all depends on where you're going. If you're coming into the city from the Bay Bridge (I-80), your best bet is to get off the freeway as soon as you can. Use the Harrison St., Fremont St., Fifth St., or Ninth St. exits, depending on your destination. If you're coming in to the city from the Peninsula or the South Bay on Highway 101, use the Ninth St. exit on US 101, or the Seventh St. exit on I-80 as alternatives to Mission St. You can also take the I-280 and exit at Sixth St. to reach downtown San Francisco, the Richmond District, or the Western Addition.

Parking Stickers and Permits

If you live in an established Residential Permit Parking area (identified by a sign displayed on your block), then you need a permit. Sounds simple, right? The catch is even some metered streets are RPPs, and there aren't always signs posted, so your best bet is to call one of the phone numbers listed below. If you actually do reside in the area, you can get an application for a permit by visiting the 1380 Howard St office, by calling 255-3900, or by downloading it from www.sfgov.org. Be warned—the lines at 1380 Howard St. can be long, so you're better off mailing or e-mailing it in.

City of San Francisco Dept. of Parking and Traffic

Residential Parking Permit Office (RPP)
Address: 1380 Howard Street, San Francisco, CA 94103
Phone: 415-255-3900 or 415-554-5000 (recorded info)
Enforcement Division
Address: 505 7th St, San Francisco, CA 94103
Phone: 415-553-1631
Traffic Engineering Division
Address: 25 Van Ness Avenue, Suite 345, San Francisco, CA 94102
E-mail: rpp_engineering@ci.sf.ca.us

Of Tickets, Tow-trucks, and Other Lovely Things

If your life suddenly turns into "Dude, Where's My Car?" chances are you've been towed. Here are some phone numbers (and options) you need to know about:

City of San Francisco Dept. of Parking and Traffic
Tow Line (basic information): 415-553-1235
Tow Desk (if you're not sure your
    car has been towed): . . . . . .415-553-1239 or 553-1240
S.F. Police (to report a stolen vehicle): 415-553-0123
To protest a towing (Hearing Division):
. 415-255-3967
If the S.F.P.D. towed your car: 415-553-1619
If your car is booted: .415-553-1634
    (Boot-removal fee is $75)

Getting Your Car Back

City Tow (Towing yard)
Location of yard: 415 Seventh St, at Harrison
City Tow offices: 850 Bryant St, Room 145
S.F.P.D. Towing: 850 Bryant St, Room 154

For Parking Citations and Hearings

Address: 1380 Howard St, Suite 1000,
                San Francisco, CA 94103
Phone: 415-255-3900 (citations/permits)
                415-255-3964 (hearings)

Parking Meters

Check the parking meter for hours. Meters usually operate from 9 am to 6 pm Monday through Saturday, but in some areas the hours start as early as 7 am and run to as late as 9 pm. On Port property, meters also operate on Sundays and holidays.

Hourly Rates for Selected Areas:
Downtown: $2.00 hourly/25¢ for motorcycles
Downtown Periphery: $1.50 hourly/15¢ motorcycles
Fisherman's Wharf: $1.50 hourly/15¢ motorcycles
All other areas: $1.00 hourly/10¢ motorcycles

Curb Colors

If you've ever wondered what the various curb colors mean, this list will give you a pretty good idea of where you're entitled to park and for how long.

Green: Limited time parking—10 minutes from 9 am–6 pm Monday through Saturday.

Yellow: Commercial loading and unloading; vehicles with commercial plates may park up to 30 minutes from 9 am–6 pm Monday–Saturday. Some yellow zones are restricted to trucks with commercial plates only. Violators will be towed. Usually accompanied by a sign; check for hours of enforcement.

Blue: Parking for vehicles with special disabled person plates or placards only. Always enforced; violators will be fined $275. (Shame on you for even contemplating it!)

Red: No parking at any time. Vehicles in bus stops will be towed and subject to $250 additional fine.

White: Passenger loading zone (usually in front of churches, restaurants, hotels, etc.). Vehicles may not be left unattended for any length of time during enforcement hours; attended vehicles may stand for up to 5 minutes. Hours of enforcement may be painted on the curb or posted on a sign. If not, check to see if the business in front of the white zone appears to be in operation.

Street Cleaning

San Francisco streets are swept on a rotating weekly schedule between the hours of 6 am and 3 pm. Unless a posted sign says "Every day including holidays", the following holidays are exempt from street cleaning:

• New Years Day
• Martin Luther King Jr.'s Birthday
• Presidents' Day
• Memorial Day
• Independence Day
• Labor Day
• Columbus Day
• Veterans' Day
• Thanksgiving and Day after Thanksgiving
• Christmas Day

Transbay Terminal

Address:	425 Mission St
	San Francisco, CA 94105
Phone:	415-495-1569
Baggage:	415-495-1555
Customer Service:	415-495-1575

Transbay Terminal is in the midst of a remarkable and quite costly restoration project. The former bus terminal is being transformed into a techno-savvy, multi-purpose facility with a long-awaited 6-track train station. The new 600,000-square-foot depot will integrate retail, residential, and commercial space into one big happy transit utopia. Aside from enhancing the volume of local commuter service (AC Transit, GGT, SamTrans, and Muni), the new terminal will accommodate the downtown extension of Caltrain. Is your mouth watering yet? Unfortunately this massive project will not be finished until 2007, so hold off on that jig.

AC Transit

Website:	www.actransit.org
Phone:	510-891-4700
Lost and Found:	510-891-4706

The Alameda-Contra Coast bus line provides convenient commute routes from or to the East Bay. AC operates 37 Transbay lines to San Francisco and 104 local lines within the East Bay area. Route Y makes frequent trips from Transbay to the Amtrak Terminal in Emeryville. The fare from the East Bay to the Transbay Terminal is $3 each way and $1.50 each way within the East Bay area. Monthly passes and senior/ youth discounts are available. Most of the AC fleet is equipped with front-mounted bicycle racks which hold a maximum of two bikes. An additional two bikes are allowed on board if the bus is not too crowded. The cyclist is completely responsible for loading and unloading. For more information on schedules and routes refer to the AC Transit website.

Golden Gate Transit

Website:	www.goldengate.org
Phone:	415-923-2000
Lost and Found:	415-925-5565

GGT provides flexible bus service between San Francisco, Marin, and Sonoma Counties. It also runs an express bus service to 49ers home games from three different locations: Larkspur Ferry Terminal, Santa Rosa, and Broadway Market. Fares range from $1.50 to $6.60 according to how far you travel. The bus drivers do not supply change, so make sure that you have the exact amount for your fare. For commuters, the Ride Value Discount Ticket Book provides a 20% discount. Each book varies according to travel distance, so refer to the Ride Value Table to determine what Ticket Book is appropriate for you. Tickets may be purchased by phone or at a number of venues listed on their website. If you travel by both bus and boat, the transfer from the GGT bus to the Golden Gate Ferry is free. Most, but not all, of the GGT buses have bicycle racks which hold up to two bikes. The cyclist is completely in charge of loading and unloading.

SamTrans

Website:	www.samtrans.com
Phone:	800-660-4287

This San Mateo-based bus company provides service from San Francisco to several outlying towns such as Palo Alto, San Bruno, and Redwood City. Fares for SamTrans vary according to how far you are traveling and whether or not the bus makes express or local stops. Youth and monthly passes are available for purchase by phone or from several vendors, which are listed on their website. In addition to its regular routes, SamTrans provides special service routes to 49ers games and also to the Año Nuevo State Reserve near Santa Cruz during seal breeding season (January and February). Consult the website for more information on schedules and fares. Every SamTrans bus has a bike rack which can accommodate up to two bikes. The cyclist is completely in charge of loading and unloading. If the bus isn't too crowded two additional bikes are permitted on board.

Greyhound

Phone: 1-800-229-9424
Website: www.greyhound.com

Greyhound is the rock-bottom travelers' best friend. Called "The Dog" by its patrons, Greyhound offers dirt-cheap fares, the flexibility drifters prefer, basic station amenities (toilets and vending machines), and the gritty, butt-busting experience of traveling America's scenic blue-line highways and rural by-ways along with some very colorful characters.

Here are some tips on taking "The Dog" out of town:
• Even though bathrooms are onboard, pack your own toilet paper and Wet Ones.
• Air freshener, deodorant, a pillow, and earplugs make being bused more bearable.
• Pack a cooler. Then padlock it.
• Wear padded bicycle shorts or bring a cushion.
• Get your shots.

Stations: Transbay terminal is the Greyhound hub of the Bay area. Some Greyhound buses do make other stops at the San Francisco Airport, the Caltrain depot, the Ferry Building, Hyatt Regency hotel, and the San Francisco Shopping Center. These are limited service bus stops, however, so be sure to consult the Greyhound website to ascertain which buses stop at those locations. There are no ticketing or baggage amenities at limited service stops.

Shipping Services: Greyhound Package Express offers commercial and personal shipping services and is available at the Transbay terminal. Packages are held at the station for pick-up. Call the stations for shipping office hours and rates at 415-495-1555.

Fares: To purchase tickets, call the toll-free number and pay by credit card, book online with a credit card through Greyhound's website, or visit the Transbay station where cash, travelers checks, and major credit cards are accepted.

Regular fare pricing applies for both individual advance ticket sales and minutes-before-departure sales as Greyhound does not reserve seats. Tickets can be used for travel to the designated destination on any day or at any departure time. Boarding is first-come-first-served, so get in line at the boarding zone for a choice seat. However, Greyhound's bark is bigger than its bite—if a significant number of passengers are abandoned, Greyhound rolls another bus, or two, or three out on the spot. Good dog.

Discounts are given for children under 12 (40%), seniors 62 and older (10%), military (10%), and patients of Veteran's Administration Hospitals (25%). The cost for an individual return ticket is deeply discounted if it is purchased at the same time as a departure ticket.

Traveling companions can save money. Purchase a ticket three days in advance and earn a free ticket for your companion (no age restrictions). Passengers accompanying someone with a disability always ride free.

Super Friendly Fares offer the greatest savings for travelers who can purchase seven days in advance of travel. For example, a regular one-way ticket from San Francisco to Los Angeles is $42 and a regular fare round-trip ticket costs $82. However, if you book a round-trip Super Friendly Fare, the ticket costs only $69. You do the math.

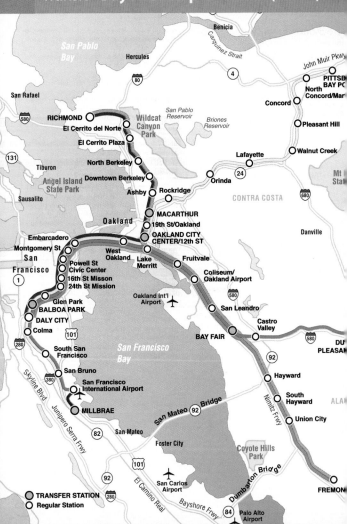

San Pablo
Bay

Benicia

Carquinez Strait

Hercules

John Muir Pkwy

PITTSB
BAY PC

North
Concord/Mar

Concord

San Rafael

Pleasant Hill

RICHMOND

El Cerrito del Norte

Wildcat
Canyon
Park

San Pablo
Reservoir

Briones
Reservoir

Walnut Creek

El Cerrito Plaza

Lafayette

North Berkeley

Tiburon

Downtown Berkeley

Orinda

CONTRA COSTA

Mt
Sta

Angel Island
State Park

Ashby

Rockridge

Sausalito

MACARTHUR

Danville

Oakland

19th St/Oakland

OAKLAND CITY
CENTER/12th ST

Embarcadero

Montgomery St

West
Oakland

Lake
Merritt

Fruitvale

San
Francisco

Powell St
Civic Center
16th St Misson
24th St Mission

Coliseum/
Oakland Airport

Oakland Int'l
Airport

San Leandro

Glen Park

BALBOA PARK

Castro
Valley

DALY CITY

BAY FAIR

Colma

San Francisco
Bay

DU
PLEASAN

South San
Francisco

Hayward

San Bruno

South
Hayward

San Francisco
International Airport

Union City

MILLBRAE

ALA

San Mateo

San Mateo

Bridge

Foster City

Coyote Hills
Park

Dumbarton
Bridge

San Carlos
Airport

El Camino Real

Palo Alto
Airport

FREMON

Bayshore Frwy

TRANSFER STATION

Regular Station

General Information

Website: www.bart.gov
Mailing Address: PO Box 12688,
                 Oakland CA 94606-2688
Phone: 510-464-7134

Overview

The Bay Area Rapid Transit system evolved out of the need to ease congestion on the Bay Bridge following the post-war increase of migration to the Bay Area and the subsequent boom of the auto industry. The proposed solution was an underwater tube, devoted solely to high-speed electrical trains. After years of research and planning and the gaining of public approval, the transbay tube structure was completed in August 1969. Constructed in 57 sections and sitting as deep as 135 feet beneath the surface on the bay floor, the $180 million structure took six years to design and less than three years to construct. Today, the BART system provides efficient train transit between San Francisco and the East Bay cities and suburbs of Contra Costa and Alameda counties.

Hours

Mondays through Fridays, BART service begins at 4:00 am, Saturdays at 6:00 am, and Sundays at 8:00 am. BART service may extend past midnight, but not much farther. Most of the time, the last train leaves at midnight.

Fares and Tickets

BART fares are based on distance traveled. You can determine the cost of your trip by using the BART Fare Calculator or one of the fare charts located at each station. For ballpark figures, the minimum is $1.15 and the maximum is $5.50. Children under 4 ride for free. All vending machines accept nickels, dimes, quarters, $1, $5, and $10 bills. If you place more money on the ticket than is needed for the ride, the ticket can be used for several trips. Discount tickets for seniors, children, and persons with disabilities are sold online, not at vending machines. There's a special Excursion Fare for $4.00. It allows anyone to go anywhere, as long as you enter and exit at the same station within three hours.

To enter the BART system, insert your ticket into the fare gate. The ticket will be returned to you, and then the fare gate will open. Use the same ticket when you exit the station. The correct fare will automatically be deducted, and a ticket with any remaining value will be returned to you. If you have too little money, then use an Addfare machine to exit.

Pets

Pets are only allowed if they are in carrying cases, but service animals (guide dogs, police dogs, etc.) can ride unimpeded.

Lost and Found

The Lost and Found office is located at the 12th Street City Center Station in Oakland near the 14th street exit. It's open on Mondays, Wednesdays, and Fridays from noon to 2 pm and 3 pm to 6 pm. Call 510-464-7090 for more information.

Parking

Customers parking at Daly City, Colma, South San Francisco, San Bruno, and Millbrae Stations will be required to pay a daily ($2.00) or monthly parking fee ($42 for unreserved or $63 for reserved parking). There is a 24-hour limit to all parking.

Seniors and People with Disabilities

All BART stations have escalators and elevators. All trains have a sign located above some seats suggesting that passengers make those seats available to seniors and persons with disabilities. Specific C2 cars have flip-up seats, which are near each set of doors, to allow room for wheelchairs. All restrooms are designed for those using wheelchairs in mind.

Bicycle Rules

BART has very extensive rules for people who take bicycles on trains. Bikes are allowed on all trains except during peak hours. Check the BART schedules for permitted bike traveling times. Regardless of any other rule, bikes are never allowed on crowded cars. Bikes can never occupy the first car of any train. Bicyclists must use the elevator or stairs, not escalators and always walk bikes. Gas-powered vehicles are not permitted. If you chain your bike to a pole, fence, or railing in any BART station, you may return to find that is has been removed.

Transit • **Muni Metro**

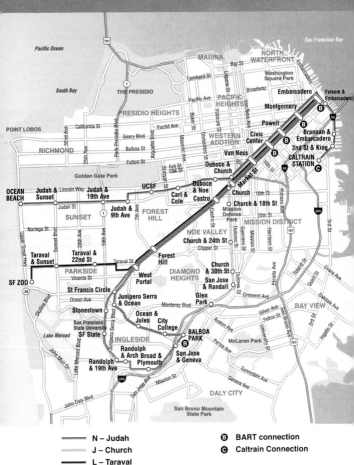

Pacific Ocean

San Francisco Bay

South Bay

THE PRESIDIO

Point Lobos

THE PRESIDIO

PRESIDIO HEIGHTS

MARINA

NORTH WATERFRONT

Bay St

Lombard St

Washington Square Park

Broadway

Pacific Ave

PACIFIC HEIGHTS

Embarcadero

Montgomery

Folsom & Embarcadero

RICHMOND

California St

Geary Blvd

Euclid Ave

Balboa St

Fulton St

WESTERN ADDTION

Powell

Civic Center

Van Ness

Brannan & Embarcadero

2nd St & King

CALTRAIN STATION

Golden Gate Park

UCSF

Duboce & Church

Market St

Church

OCEAN BEACH

Judah & Sunset

Lincoln Way

Judah & 19th Ave

Judah St

Carl & Cole

Duboce & Noe

Castro

Church & 18th St

16th St

Mission Dolores Park

MISSION DISTRICT

20th St

SUNSET

Judah & 9th Ave

FOREST HILL

NOE VALLEY

Church & 24th St

Clipper St

Noriega St

Taraval & Sunset

Taraval & 22nd St

Taraval St

Forest Hill

DIAMOND HEIGHTS

Church & 30th St

San Jose & Randall

Glen Park

BAY VIEW

PARKSIDE

Vicente St

West Portal

SF ZOO

St Francis Circle

Ocean Ave

Stonestown

Junipero Serra & Ocean

Ocean & Jules

City College

Monterey Blvd

BALBOA PARK

San Jose & Geneva

San Francisco State University

SF State

INGLESIDE

Randolph & Arch Broad & Plymouth

Randolph & 19th Ave

Lake Merced

John Muir Dr

John Daly Blvd

DALY CITY

Mission St

Geneva Ave

San Bruno Mountain State Park

McLaren Park

Sunnydale Ave

—— **N – Judah**
—— **J – Church**
—— **L – Taraval**
—— **M – Clearwater**
—— **K – Ingleside**

B BART connection
C Caltrain Connection

General Information

Website: www.sfmuni.com
Mailing Address: 949 Presidio Avenue, #243,
                  San Francisco, CA 94115
Phone: 415-673-6864

Overview

Oh, that clunky, cantankerous Muni. Most residents can recall at least one time when the city's subway has broken down. That's right, it sometimes just stops working. Blame that on the older model Muni cars that are so flimsy and archaic you can almost see the wind-up key that powers them. The buses can be a challenge too. But after years of being one of the city's most frustrating and laughed about services, city officials finally seem to have gotten the message. They're getting better at making Muni run. Here are the facts you need to know to get around San Francisco on Muni trains and buses.

Hours

Muni operates 24 hours on these specific lines: L Taraval, N Judah, 5 Fulton, 14 Mission, 2 Fillmore, 24 Divisadero, 38 Geary, 90 San Bruno Owl (a combination of routes 9 San Bruno and 47 Van Ness), 91 Owl (a combination of routes K Ingleside, 15 Third St, 30 Stockton, and 28 19th Avenue), and 108 Treasure Island. All night "owl" service operates every 30 minutes, with the exception of route 108.

Fares and Tickets

For buses, Metro, and historic streetcars, adults pay $1.25, seniors and youth pay $.35, and children four and under ride free. Exact fares required—drivers cannot provide change. Transfers are available and are generally good for 90 minutes from time of issue.

On cable cars, the fare is $3 each way. Transfers are not given or accepted on cable car lines.

Speed up your trip by boarding at any door of any Metro streetcar with your proof of payment. Your valid Muni pass, passport, ticket, or transfer is your proof of payment. Keep it for your entire ride on all five Muni Metro lines, including anywhere inside the fare gates and on the platforms at the Muni Metro subway stations, from the Embarcadero Station to the West Portal Station. Don't throw your proof of payment away while traveling within the Muni Metro system. Muni Fare Inspectors may ask you for proof of payment on board any J, K, L, M, or N streetcar or on subway station platforms between the Embarcadero and West Portal stations. If you don't have proof of payment, they can issue a citation for up to $250.

Safety

Smoking, eating, drinking, littering, or playing sound equipment without earphones is not allowed on Muni vehicles or at Metro stations. Please notice that under Muni regulations, passengers are not allowed to put their feet on the seats and children are not allowed to stand on the seats.

Between 8:30 p.m. and 6:30 a.m., additional passenger stops will be made either for persons waiting for a transit vehicle or for passengers on a transit vehicle at their request, at the nearside corner of any street intersection located between the regular stops.

Working dogs, including guide dogs, signal dogs, and service dogs may ride free at any time. These dogs do not have to be muzzled, but must be on a leash. People entering with an animal that is not a working dog must pay the same fare for the animal that they do for themselves. These animals are allowed to ride on Muni vehicles from 9 am to 3 pm and from 7 pm to 5 am on weekdays, and all day on Saturdays, Sundays, and holidays. Only one of these animals may ride per vehicle. Dogs must be muzzled and on a short leash or in a closed container, and other animals must be carried in closed containers.

Lost and Found

Call 415-923-6168 for lost and found information.

Airport Connections

Muni does not serve the San Francisco International Airport. The airport is located 14 miles south of downtown San Francisco, in San Mateo County. For public transit information to the airport, contact BART, SamTrans, or Caltrain. For shuttles and other services, call the San Francisco Transportation Hotline at 1-800-736-2008 or select "Ground Transport" on the San Francisco International Airport Web site.

Seniors and People with Disabilities

Most Muni vehicles are fully accessible to the elderly and handicapped. Cable cars are not wheelchair accessible. At this time only the 5, 14, 22, 24, 30 and 31 trolley bus lines are wheelchair accessible. All of the underground stations are easy to get to by elevator, escalator (except for Forest Hill, which has no escalators), and West Portal, which has ramps). If you're using Muni elevators, you might want to wear a surgical mask—the devices are not always clean, and the aroma inside the elevators can be less than welcoming.

Bicycle Rules

Bikes are allowed on Muni on the following lines: 17 Parkmerced, 35 Eureka, 36 Teresita, 37 Corbett, 39 Coit, 53 Southern Heights, 56 Rutland, 66 Quintara (neighborhood service), 66 Quintara (limited-hour downtown service), 76 Marin Headlands (Sundays and selected holidays), 91 Owl, and 108 Treasure Island. There are racks on the front of the buses that allow two bikes to be carried on each bus. Note that Muni operators will allow bicyclists to take bikes on any bike-rack equipped bus, whether or not that bus is in service on one of the designated lines. If a Muni vehicle does not have a bike rack, then bikes are not allowed. Metro vehicles, historic streetcars, and cable cars do not have bike racks.

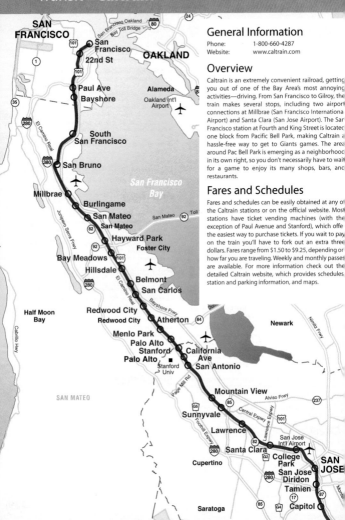

General Information

Phone: 1-800-660-4287
Website: www.caltrain.com

Overview

Caltrain is an extremely convenient railroad, getting you out of one of the Bay Area's most annoying activities—driving. From San Francisco to Gilroy, the train makes several stops, including two airport connections at Millbrae (San Francisco International Airport) and Santa Clara (San Jose Airport). The San Francisco station at Fourth and King Street is located one block from Pacific Bell Park, making Caltrain a hassle-free way to get to Giants games. The area around Pac Bell Park is emerging as a neighborhood in its own right, so you don't necessarily have to wait for a game to enjoy its many shops, bars, and restaurants.

Fares and Schedules

Fares and schedules can be easily obtained at any of the Caltrain stations or on the official website. Most stations have ticket vending machines (with the exception of Paul Avenue and Stanford), which offer the easiest way to purchase tickets. If you wait to pay on the train you'll have to fork out an extra three dollars. Fares range from $1.50 to $9.25, depending on how far you are traveling. Weekly and monthly passes are available. For more information check out the detailed Caltrain website, which provides schedules, station and parking information, and maps.

Overview

Whether you're looking for some good music, serious cinema, or half-naked fun, San Francisco has plenty to offer all year round. With one of the most socially and ethnically diverse populations in the country, San Francisco offers a seemingly endless stream of cultural parades and neighborhood street fairs. Holidays like St. Patrick's Day, Cinco de Mayo, and Halloween are serious business—dress, or undress, appropriately (especially if you're bound for—and we do mean "bound"—the Exotic Erotic Ball or the Folsom Street Fair). Of course you might be looking for something a bit more artistic when the lights go down; there are plenty of nationally known film festivals to choose from. Whatever you end up doing, there's likely to be good food and drink nearby. Enjoy!

- **SF International Art Exposition** · January · www.sfiae.com
  What can we say? Lots and lots of art.
- **Chinese New Year Celebration and Parade** · Mid-February · www.chineseparade.com
  A venerable San Francisco tradition.
- **St. Patrick's Day Parade** · on or around March 1
  A green party, not The Green Party.
- **The San Francisco International Asian American Film Festival** · March · www.naatanet.org/festival
  Showcasing one of the Bay Area's most vibrant ethnic communities.
- **Cherry Blossom Festival** · April
  Is it Spring yet?
- **San Francisco International Film Festival** · Late April–Early May · www.sffs.org
  The stars come out for this one…get your tickets early.
- **Cinco de Mayo Celebration** · May 5 · www.sfmission.com
  Not to be missed. The Mission in all of its glory.
- **Bay to Breakers** · Mid-May · www.baytobreakers.com
  As many gawkers as runners (maybe more) and more jiggling naked flesh than you'll probably ever want to see.
- **Carnaval Celebration** · Late May · www.sfmission.com
  Think Cinco de Mayo with a lot more skin, and sin.
- **Haight Street Fair** · June
  Haight. Hemp. Hippies. Hordes.
- **San Francisco Gay & Lesbian Film Festival** · Mid-June · www.frameline.org/festival
  Queer cinema at its most intriguing. Just in time for Pride.
- **San Francisco Gay Pride Week** · Last Week of June · www.sfpride.org
  Somewhere over the rainbow is here. Come see for yourself.
- **SF Silent Film Festival** · July · www.silentfilm.org
  Check it out at the Castro Theatre.

- **San Francisco Jewish Film Festival** · July–August · www.sfjj.org
  You'd have to be meshuga to miss it.
- **North Beach Jazz Festival** · July–August · www.nbjazzfest.org
  Cool neighborhood. Cool music.
- **San Francisco Fringe Festival** · Early September · www.sffringe.org
  Release your inner freak (or at least see what some of the best freaky artists are up to).
- **San Francisco Opera in the Park** · Early September · www.chroniclecalendar.com/opera/
  Arias aplenty, and a blanket for two.
- **San Francisco Blues Festival** · Late September · www.sfblues.com
  Bring your own shades. Lost-love-induced angst included.
- **Folsom Street Fair** · Late September · www.folsomstreetfair.com
  Not your mother's street fair—this is all whips, chains, and leather, baby.
- **Castro Street Fair** · Early October · www.castrostreetfair.org
  Shop in the sun under the Big Rainbow flag.
- **Marin Italian Film Festival** · Early-to-mid-October · www.marin.org
  A bit of recent Italian cinema across the Golden Gate.
- **San Francisco Open Studies** · Weekends in October · camille@artspan.org
  Like a scavenger hunt for the best local artists. Bring your street map.
- **Exotic Erotic Ball** · Late October · www.exoticeroticball.com
  Inhibitions be damned! One of the Bay Area's hottest parties.
- **Halloween Party** · October 31
  Official party at Civic Center, but the real fun is in the Castro.
- **Dia de los Muertos (Day of the Dead)** · October 31-November 2 · www.sfmission.com
  Come purge all your Catholic demons.

Overview

The roughly 46 square miles that comprise the city of San Francisco contain a distinct collection of diverse and lively neighborhoods and people. It's hard to reduce all that to facts and figures, but what the hell—we're going to try.

Statistics

San Francisco city population:	776,733*
San Francisco Bay Area population:	7,039,362
	(source: CityRating.com)
Area (sq. miles):	46
(source: San Francisco Convention & Visitors Bureau)	

Population Demographics

Gender

Male:	394,828	50.83%
Female:	381,905	49.17%

Age

Median:	36.5 years	
18 years and over:	663,931	85.48%
21 years and over:	640,952	82.52%
62 years and over:	123,704	15.93%
65 years and over:	106,111	13.66%

Race

One race	743,478	95.72%
Caucasian	385,728	49.66%
Asian	239,565	30.84%
African American	60,515	7.79%
American Indian/Alaskan Native	3,458	0.45%
Native Hawaiian/Pacific Islander	3,844	0.49%
Hispanic or Latino	109,504	14.1%
Some other race	50,368	6.48%
Two or more races	33,255	3.0%

*All numbers from U.S. Census Bureau data unless otherwise noted

Reference Books

Herb Caen's San Francisco: 1976-1991, by Herb Caen and Irene Mecchi (Chronicle Books, 1992)
The late Chronicle columnist's best pieces about the city he loved.
San Francisco Then & Now, by Bill Yenne (Thunder Bay Press, 2003)
Collection of historical and contemporary photographs of the city's neighborhoods and landmarks.
Streets and San Francisco: The Origins of Street and Place Names , by Louis K. Loewenstein, Penny Demoss (Wilderness Press, 1996)
The stories behind the city's streets and landmarks.
The Barbary Coast: An Informal History of the San Francisco Underworld, by Herbert Asbury (Thunder's Mouth Press, 2002)
San Francisco has always had its share of sin—here's a tour of the city's darker side.

Stairway Walks in San Francisco, by Adah Bakalinsky (Wilderness Press, 2003)
The third edition of this popular guidebook lists just about all of the city's stairway walks, from the well-known to the hard-to-find.
Imperial San Francisco: Urban Power, Earthly Ruin, by Gary A. Brechin (University of California Press, 2001)
A study of the rich and powerful who helped make San Francisco.

Television

2 KTVU	(FOX)	www.ktvu.com
4 KRON	(NBC)	www.kron.com
5 KPIX	(CBS)	www.kpix.com
7 KGO	(ABC)	www.abc7news.com
9 KQED	(PBS)	www.kqed.org
11 KNTV	(ABC)	www.kntv.com
14 KDTV	(Univision)	www.univision.net
20 KSWB	(WB)	www.wb20.com
25 WNYE	(Public)	www.wnye.nycenet.edu
26 KTSF	(Independent)	www.ktsf.com
30 KBI	(HSN)	www.kbitv.com
32 KMTP	(PBS)	www.gy.com
44 KBHK	(UPN)	www.upn44.com
48 KSTS	(Telemundo)	www.ksts.com
50 KFTY	(Clear Channel)	www.kfty.com
54 KTEH	(PBS)	www.kteh.org
60 KCSM	(PBS)	www.kcsm.com

AM Radio

560	KSFO	Talk radio
610	KFRC	Oldies
680	KNBR	Sports
740	KCBS	News
810	KGO	News, traffic, talk radio
910	KNEW	Talk radio
960	KBAL	Oldies/Top 40
1050	KNBR	Sports
1450	KEST	Inspirational

FM Radio

88.5	KQED	News, public radio
90.3	KUSF	Alternative music
91.1	KCSM	Jazz
91.7	KALW	New, public radio
93.3	KYCY	Country
94.1	KPFA	Community radio, variety
94.9	KYLD	Hip-hop
97.3	KLLC	Top 40
98.1	KISS	R&B, classic soul, disco
99.7	KFRC	Oldies
101.3	KIOI	80s
102.1	KDFC	Classical
103.7	KKSF	Easy listening
104.5	KFOG	Adult-contemporary rock
105.3	KITS	Modern rock
106.1	KMEL	Hip-hop
106.9	KEAR	Christian
107.7	KSAN	Classic rock

Magazines

Bitch • An edgy, irreverent, feminist response to pop culture. • 1611 Telegraph Ave, #515 • 510-625-9390

Mother Jones • The grandmother of progressive news, culture, and politics (bi-monthly). • 731 Market St, 6th Fl • 415-665-6637

Noodle • Trendy mouth of gay Asian culture—politics, entertainemnt, and fashion (with great photo spreads. • PO Box 31028 • 415-202-8524

San Francisco • This monthly glossy offers news and features, fashion, restaurant reviews, and more. • 243 Vallejo St • 415-398-2800.

7x7 • A monthly glossy with an edgier take on the city's dining, fashion, and entertainment scenes. • 59 Grant Ave • 415-362-7797

QSF • Art, entertainment and fashion, San Francisco-style, for the LGBT community.

Newspapers

Asian Week • 809 Sacramento St • 415-397-0220
East Bay Express • 1335 Stanford Ave, #100 • 510-879-3700
El Tecolote • 2601 Mission St, #700 • 415-648-1045
Frontlines • 3311 Mission St, #135 • 415-452-9992
Jewish Bulletin • 225 Bush St, #1480
Noe Valley Voice • 1021 Sanchez St • 415-821-3324
Papercity • 30 Grant Ave, #300 • 415-901-1365
San Francisco Bay Guardian • 135 Mississippi • 415-255-3100
San Francisco Business Times • 275 Battery St • 415-999-2522
The San Francisco Call • PMB 31 322 Cortland Ave • 415-826-0414
San Francisco Chronicle • 901 Mission St • 415-777-1111
San Francisco Examiner • 988 Market St • 415-359-2600
San Francisco Weekly • 185 Berry, Lobby 4 • 415-536-8100

Websites

www.sfvisitor.org—The official Convention & Visitors Bureau site—loads of useful information.

www.craigslist.org—Easily the most popular site for hooking up in San Francisco, whether that means hooking yourself up with a new job, a new apartment, news about what's going on, or a companion.

www.sfstation.com—An entertainment-oriented city guide that offers a weekly calendar of events, info on clubs, music, film, special events, literary happenings, and the like.

www.sfgate.com—The San Francisco Chronicle's site—news about San Francisco and the Bay Area, as well as national news, classifieds, weather and traffic updates, etc.

www.sanfrancisco.citysearch.com—A comprehensive, up-to-date listing of restaurants, clubs, and other entertainment venues. Includes ratings of popular hot spots, photos of each venue, and links to related sites.

12 Essential San Francisco Books

The Maltese Falcon, by Dashiell Hammett
Sam Spade, in perhaps the most famous noir detective story.

Tales of the City, by Armistead Maupin
Six-volume series about San Francisco in the 1970s and beyond.

The Works of Philip K. Dick, by Philip K. Dick
The man who gave us *Blade Runner* set nearly all his novels and stories in the Bay Area.

Flower Drum Song, by C.Y. Lee
A young Chinese immigrant strives to make it in San Francisco's Chinatown.

McTeague, by Frank Norris
A crazy dentist in 19th-century San Francisco.

Our Lady of Darkness, by Fritz Leiber
Wonderfully creepy supernatural thriller that pays loving homage to the city.

Bombardiers, by Po Bronson
Perhaps *the* novel of the dot-com boom.

Lonesome Traveler, by Jack Kerouac
The famous Beat wanders around San Francisco and elsewhere.

The Mayor of Castro Street, by Randy Shilts
Novelistic report about the assassinations of Mayor George Moscone and Supervisor Harvey Milk.

Golden Gate, by Vikram Seth
A novel set in verse about the lives and loves of '80s-era San Francisco singles.

The Joy Luck Club, by Amy Tan
Four immigrant families mingle generations of memories.

A Rush of Dreamers, by John Cech
A novel based on the life of real-life eccentric Joshua "Emperor" Norton in 19th-century San Francisco.

Essential San Francisco Movies

Greed (1925)	Harold and Maude (1971)
The Thin Man (1934)	The Conversation (1974)
San Francisco (1936)	The Towering Inferno (1974)
The Maltese Falcon (1941)	High Anxiety (1977)
Dark Passage (1947)	Foul Play (1978)
The House on Telegraph Hill (1951)	Invasion of the Body Snatchers (1978)
Vertigo (1958)	Time After Time (1979)
Flower Drum Song (1961)	Chan Is Missing (1982)
Point Blank (1967)	The Joy Luck Club (1993)
The Graduate (1967)	Mrs. Doubtfire (1993)
Bullitt (1968)	The Rock (1996)
Dirty Harry (1971)	Romeo Must Die (2000)

Songs About San Francisco

I Left My Heart in San Francisco – Tony Bennett
San Francisco – Judy Garland
Dock of the Bay – Otis Redding
Frisco Blues – John Lee Hooker
San Francisco Days – Chris Isaak
Lights – Journey
San Francisco – Scott McKenzie
We Built This City – Starship
San Francisco (You've Got Me) – Village People
Little Boxes (Ticky, Tacky) – Pete Seeger

(233)

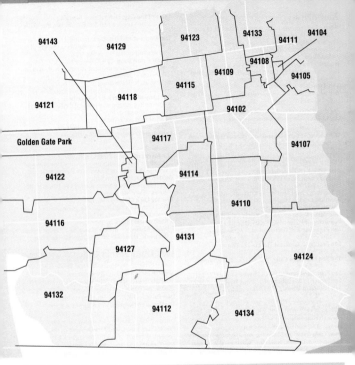

Post Offices

	Address	Zip	Phone	Map
18th Street Station	4304 18th St	94114	415-431-2701	10
Bayview Station	2111 Lane St	94124	415-822-7157	40
Bernal Heights Finance Station	45 29th St	94110	415-550-8569	35
Brannan Street Finance	460 Brannan St	94107	415-882-4690	8
Bryant Street Station	1600 Bryant St	94103	415-431-3407	11
Chinatown Station	867 Stockton St	94108	415-433-1202	7
Civic Center Box Unit / Pacific Center	101 Hyde St	94142	415-563-7284	7
Clayton Street Station	554 Clayton St	94117	415-621-5816	9
Diamond Heights Carrier Annex	1570 Burke St	94131	415-641-0183	37
Diamond Heights Finance	5262 Diamond Heights Blvd	94131	415-550-8373	32
Embarcadero Postal Center	226 Harrison St	94105	415-536-6413	8
Excelsior Finance Station	15 Onondaga St	94112	415-334-1057	38

Post Offices——continued

	Address	Zip	Phone	Map
Federal Building Finance Station	450 Golden Gate Ave	94102	415-487-8981	7
Fox Plaza Finance Station	1390 Market St	94102	415-931-1053	11
Geary Station	5654 Geary Blvd	94121	415-752-0113	20
Golden Gate Station	3245 Geary Blvd	94118	415-751-9739	22
Irving Street Postal Store	821 Irving St	94122	415-665-1355	25
Lakeshore Plaza Station	1543 Sloat Blvd	94132	415-564-0258	27
Marina Green Retail Store	3749 Buchanan St	94123	415-440-4390	2
Marina Station	2055 Lombard St	94123	415-351-1875	2
McLaren Station	2755 San Bruno Ave	94134	415-467-5026	39
Mission Station	1198 S Van Ness Ave	94110	415-648-0155	15
Napoleon St Carrier Complex	180 Napoleon St	94124	415-285-0872	36
Noe Valley Station	4083 29th St	94114	415-821-3914	14
North Beach (Carrier) Station	2200 Powell St	94133	415-986-3494	4
North Beach (Finance) Station	1640 Stockton St	94133	415-362-3128	4
Number 57 Station (Macy's)	170 O'Farrell St	94108	415-956-0131	7
Pacific Carrier Annex	1199 Ortega St	94122	415-665-1355	24
Parkside Station	1800 Taraval St	94116	415-759-0150	27
Pine Street Station	1400 Pine St	94109	415-351-2435	7
Potrero Retail Store	1655 Bryant St	94103	415-861-8130	11
Presidio Station	950 Lincoln Blvd	94129	415-563-0126	Presidio
Rincon Finance	180 Steuart St	94105	415-896-0762	8
San Francisco P+DC	1300 Evans Ave	94188	415-550-5134	37
Steiner Street Station	1849 Geary St	94115	415-931-1053	5
Sunset Finance Station	1314 22nd Ave	94122	415-665-1355	24
Sutter Street Postal Store	150 Sutter St	94104	415-765-1761	8
Visitation Station	68 Leland Ave	94134	415-333-4629	39
West Portal Station	317 West Portal Ave	94127	415-759-0158	30

Police

	2001	2002	% Change
Homicide	46	58	26.08%
Rape	253	227	- 10.27%
Robbery	3,786	3,269	- 13.65%
Aggravated Assault	2,487	2,417	- 2.81%
Burglary	6,706	6,092	- 9.15%
Other Larceny	14,181	13,681	- 3.52%
Auto Boosting	10,702	11,647	8.83%
Motor Vehicle Theft	6,593	6,536	- .86%
Citywide Total:	44,754	43,927	- 1.84%

Police Station	Address	Map
Bayview Police Station	201 Williams Ave	40
Central Police Station	766 Vallejo St	4
Ingleside Police Station	1 John Young Ln	34
Mission Police Station	630 Valencia St	11
Northern Police Station	1125 Fillmore St	5
Park Police Station	1699 Waller St	9
Richmond Police Station	461 6th Ave	21
Southern Police Station	850 Bryant St	12
Taraval Police Station	2345 24th Ave	27
Tenderloin Police Station	301 Eddy St	7

Map 1	Address	Last pick-up
Drop Box	2301 Lombard St	5:00

Map 2	Address	Last pick-up
Drop Box	2055 Lombard St	5:00
Drop Box	3749 Buchanan St	5:00
Kinko's	3225 Fillmore St	5:00
Post Box	1592 Union St	5:00
The Postal Chase	3053 Fillmore St	5:00
Drop Box	2001 Union St	4:45
Mailbox & Company	1517 North Point St	4:45

Map 3	Address	Last pick-up
Drop Box	1300 Columbus Ave	5:15
Drop Box	900 North Point St	5:00
Jona's on Hyde	1800 Hyde St	4:30

Map 4	Address	Last pick-up
Drop Box	80 Francisco St	5:00
Drop Box	55 Francisco St	5:00
Postal Annex	350 Bay St	4:30

Map 5	Address	Last pick-up
Drop Box	1849 Geary St	4:45
Drop Box	2404 California St	4:30
HWC Packaging Store	2525 California St	4:15
Jet Mail	2130 Fillmore St	4:15

Map 6	Address	Last pick-up
Drop Box	1255 Post St	5:15
Drop Box	1700 California St	5:10
Drop Box	727 Van Ness Ave	5:00
Drop Box	1388 Sutter St	5:00
Kinko's	1800 Van Ness Ave	5:00
Drop Box	2333 Buchanan St	4:30
Mail Box Plus	1450 Sutter St	4:30

Map 7	Address	Last pick-up
Drop Box	1355 Market St	5:15
Drop Box	870 Market St	5:15
Drop Box	1 Hallidie Plz	5:15
Drop Box	490 Post St	5:10
Drop Box	965 Mission St	5:10
Drop Box	901 Market St	5:10
Drop Box	530 Bush St	5:10
Drop Box	360 Post St	5:10
Drop Box	291 Geary St	5:00
Drop Box	455 Golden Gate Ave	5:00
Drop Box	450 Golden Gate Ave	5:00
Drop Box	909 Hyde St	5:00
Mail Boxes for U	1230 Market St	5:00
Postal Grafix	1040 Hyde St	5:00
Drop Box	1400 Pine St	4:45
Cyber Copy	272 O'Farrell St	4:30
Print Mate	1051 Bush St	4:00

Map 8	Address	Last pick-up
Service Center	120 Bush St	5:30
Service Center	555 California St	5:30
Service Center	350 Sansome St	5:30
Service Center	50 Fremont St	5:30
Service Center	71 Spear St	5:30
Service Center	127 Kearny St	5:30
Service Center	724 Battery St	5:30
Service Center	520 Washington St	5:30
Service Center	220 Battery St	5:30
Drop Box	703 Market St	5:15
Drop Box	246 1st St	5:15
Drop Box	301 Howard St	5:15
Drop Box	631 Howard St	5:15
Drop Box	201 Spear St	5:15
Drop Box	180 Steuart St	5:15
Drop Box	685 Market St	5:15
Drop Box	650 California St	5:15
Drop Box	655 Montgomery St	5:15
Drop Box	303 2nd St	5:15
Drop Box	333 3rd St	5:15
Drop Box	785 Market St	5:10
Drop Box	71 Stevenson St	5:10
Drop Box	90 New Montgomery St	5:10
Drop Box	222 Kearny St	5:10
Copy Mat	705 Market St	5:05
Drop Box	221 Main St	5:05
Drop Box	760 Market St	5:00
Drop Box	201 3rd St	5:00
Drop Box	225 Bush St	5:00
Drop Box	120 Montgomery St	5:00
Drop Box	433 California St	5:00
Drop Box	44 Montgomery St	5:00
Drop Box	550 California St	5:00
Drop Box	351 California St	5:00
Drop Box	456 Montgomery St	5:00
Drop Box	580 California St	5:00
Drop Box	135 Main St	5:00
Drop Box	120 Howard St	5:00
Drop Box	140 2nd St	5:00
Drop Box	160 Spear St	5:00
Drop Box	345 Spear St	5:00
Drop Box	100 Spear St	5:00
Drop Box	333 Market St	5:00
Drop Box	525 Market St	5:00
Drop Box	595 Market St	5:00
Drop Box	33 New Montgomery St	5:00
Drop Box	605 Market St	5:00
Drop Box	475 Brannan St	5:00
Drop Box	625 3rd St	5:00
Drop Box	139 Townsend St	5:00
Drop Box	601 California St	5:00
Drop Box	600 California St	5:00
Drop Box	88 Kearny St	5:00
Drop Box	560 Davis St	5:00
Drop Box	790 Sansome St	5:00
Drop Box	1 Maritime Plz	5:00
Drop Box	1005 Sansome St	5:00
Drop Box	1 Embarcadero Ctr	5:00
Drop Box	600 Montgomery St	5:00
Drop Box	550 Montgomery St	5:00
Drop Box	101 California St	5:00
Drop Box	1 California St	5:00
Drop Box	600 Harrison St	5:00
Drop Box	501 2nd St	5:00
Drop Box	340 Brannan St	5:00
Drop Box	388 Market St	5:00
Drop Box	444 Market St	5:00
Drop Box	111 Pine St	5:00
Kinko's	369 Pine St	5:00
Kinko's	201 Sacramento St	5:00
Postal Annex	100 1st St	5:00
Service Center	3 Embarcadero Ctr	5:00
Speedway Copy	210 Sansome St	5:00
Speedway Copy	475 4th St	5:00
Drop Box	150 Sutter St	4:30
Drop Box	651 Bryant St	4:30
Handle With Care Pkg	200 Pine St	4:30
Drop Box	460 Brannan St	4:15
At Your Service	247 3rd St	4:00

Map 9

	Address	Last pick-up
The Postal Chase	915 Cole St	4:30
Express Photo & Mail	1388 Haight St	4:15
Haight Natural Foods	1621 Haight St	4:00

Map 10

	Address	Last pick-up
Kinko's	1967 Market St,	5:00
PO Plus	584 Castro St	5:00
Mail Access	2261 Market St	4:45
Drop Box	2390 Market St	4:30
Post All Center	530 Divisadero St	4:30
Drop Box	4304 18th St	4:00
Drop Box (Copy Central)	2336 Market St	4:00

Map 11

	Address	Last pick-up
Drop Box	1390 Market St	5:15
Drop Box	25 Oak St	5:15
Office Max	1750 Harrison St	5:15
Cyber Copy & Design	3128 16th St	5:00
Service Trade	1550 Bryant St	4:45
Drop Box	100 Van Ness Ave	4:30
Drop Box	1855 Folsom St	4:30
Drop Box	1655 Bryant St	4:30
Drop Box	550 15th St	4:30
Drop Box	2169 Folsom St	4:30
Drop Box	555 Florida St	4:00

Map 12

	Address	Last pick-up
Service Center	1150 Harrison St	5:40
The Showplace	2 Henry Adams St	5:15
The Gift Center	888 Brannan St	5:00
Drop Box	1000 Brannan St	5:00
Drop Box	101 Henry Adams St	5:00
Drop Box	600 Townsend St	5:00
Drop Box	444 De Haro St	4:00
Drop Box	555 De Haro St	4:40
The Packaging Store	1255 Howard St	3:30

Map 13

	Address	Last pick-up
Drop Box	185 Berry St	5:00
Drop Box	340 Townsend St	5:00
Drop Box	330 Townsend St	5:00
Potrero Mail-n-More	1459 18th St	4:30

Map 14

	Address	Last pick-up
Mail Boxes Etc	4104 24th St	5:00
Drop Box	4083 24th St	4:15
Jensen's Mail & Copy	5214 Diamond Heights Blvd	4:00

Map 15

	Address	Last pick-up
Mail Carrier Fasc	3288 21st St	4:15
Drop Box	1198 S Van Ness Ave	4:00

Map 16

	Address	Last pick-up
Drop Box	200 Kansas St	5:15
Drop Box	1001 Potrero Ave	5:00
Drop Box	1314 22nd St	4:00

Map 17

	Address	Last pick-up
Drop Box	2343 3rd St	5:15

Map 19

	Address	Last pick-up
Media Pro	3739 Balboa St	4:00

Map 20

	Address	Last pick-up
AA Travel & Tours	2219 Clement St	4:00
Drop Box	5654 Geary Blvd	4:00
Union Post	5432 Geary Blvd	4:00

Map 21

	Address	Last pick-up
Box Brothers	4644 Geary Blvd	4:30
CopyMax	3700 Geary Blvd	4:00

Map 22

	Address	Last pick-up
PO Plus	3450 Sacramento St	5:00
Mail Boxes Etc	3701 Sacramento St	4:30
Drop Box	3245 Geary Blvd	4:00
Drop Box	3333 California St	4:00
Kinko's	25 Stanyan St	4:00
Mail Boxes Etc	3145 Geary Blvd	4:00

Map 24

	Address	Last pick-up
Drop Box	2655 Judah St	4:00

Map 25

	Address	Last pick-up
Drop Box	821 Irving St	4:00

Map 27

	Address	Last pick-up
Drop Box	1800 Taraval St	4:30
Kinko's	1597 Sloat Blvd	4:30
Drop Box	1543 Sloat Blvd	4:15
Drop Box	3251 20th Ave	4:00

Map 28

	Address	Last pick-up
Drop Box	1600 Holloway Ave	4:00

Map 29

	Address	Last pick-up
Drop Box	350 Parnassus Ave	5:00

Map 30

	Address	Last pick-up
Drop Box	2499 Ocean Ave	5:00
The Postal Chase	58 West Portal Ave	4:45
Drop Box	317 West Portal Ave	4:00

Map 32

	Address	Last pick-up
Glen Park Mail Depot	2912 Diamond St	4:45

Map 33

	Address	Last pick-up
Ocean View Village	3931 Allemeny Blvd	4:00

Map 34

	Address	Last pick-up
Geneva Mail Box Ctr	910 Geneva Ave	4:15

Map 35

	Address	Last pick-up
Drop Box	3181 Mission St	4:30

Map 36

	Address	Last pick-up
Drop Box	1875 Marin St	5:30
Drop Box	20 Dorman Ave	4:45
Drop Box	2200 Jerrold Ave	4:45
Baycopy Plus	3801 3rd St	4:30

Map 37

	Address	Last pick-up
Drop Box	50 Mendell St	5:00

Map 40

	Address	Last pick-up
Drop Box	150 Executive Park Blvd	5:00
Drop Box	5 Thomas Mellon Cir	5:00
Drop Box	250 Executive Park Blvd	5:00
Drop Box	1485 Bay Shore Blvd	4:30

Presidio

	Address	Last pick-up
Drop Box	1014 Lincoln Blvd	3:45
Drop Box	215 Lincoln Blvd	3:30
Drop Box	39 Mesa Ave	3:30

Hospitals

From the top-ranked UCSF/Mt. Zion Medical Center to the smaller, community-based facilities like Chinese Hospital, San Francisco isn't that bad a place in which to get sick. It's also home to some of the best AIDS treatment centers in the country.

Hospital	Address	Phone	Map
California Pacific Medical Center Davies Campus	Castro St & Duboce St	415-565-6060	10
California Pacific Medical Center Pacific Campus	2333 Buchanan St	415-600-3333	6
Chinese Hospital	845 Jackson St	415-677-2300	7
Kaiser Permanante Medical Center	2425 Geary Blvd	415-833-3304	5
San Francisco General Hospital	1001 Potrero Ave	415-206-8111	16
San Francisco VA Medical Center	4150 Clement St	415-750-2052	18
St Francis Memorial Hospital	1150 Bush St	415-353-6300	7
St Luke's Hospital	555 San Jose Ave	415-641-6625	35
St Mary's Medical Center	450 Stanyan St	415-750-5700	9
UCSF/Mt Zion Medical Center	505 Parnassus Ave	415-567-6600	29

Libraries

Sure, the big, modern Main Library gets all the attention (check out the café and library bookstore), but the far-flung branches offer special collections that cater to neighborhood residents, like Chinatown's impressive selection of Asian books and videos, and the Eureka Valley/Harvey Milk Branch's gay & lesbian titles, as well as back issues of neighborhood newspapers.

Library	Address	Phone	Map
Anza Branch Library	550 37th Ave	415-355-5717	19
Bayview - Anna E Waden	5075 3rd St	415-715-4100	36
Bernal Heights Branch Library	500 Cortland Ave	415-695-5160	35
Chinatown Branch Library	1135 Powell St	415-274-0275	7
City and County Law Library	1390 Market St	415-554-6821	11
Eureka Valley / Harvey Milk Memorial Library	3555 16th St	415-554-9445	10
Excelsior Branch Library	4400 Mission St	415-337-4735	38
Foundation Center, San Francisco	312 Sutter St	415-397-0903	8
Glen Park Branch Library	653 Chenery St	415-337-4740	32
Golden Gate Valley Library	1801 Green St	415-292-2195	2
Helen Crocker Russell Library	9th Ave & Lincoln Way	415-661-1514	25
Ingeside Branch Library	1649 Ocean Ave	415-355-2898	33
Library & Center for Knowledge	530 Parnassus Ave	415-476-8293	29
Main Library	100 Larkin St	415-557-4400	7
Marina Branch Library	1890 Chestnut St	415-292-2150	2
Merced Branch Library	155 Winston Dr	415-337-4780	30
Mission Branch Library	300 Bartlett St	415-695-5090	15
Municipal Railway Library	949 Presidio Ave	415-923-6089	5
Noe Valley Branch Library / Sally Brunn	451 Jersey St	415-695-5095	14
North Beach Branch Library	2000 Mason St	415-274-0270	4
Ocean View Branch Library	345 Randolph St	415-337-4785	33
Ortega Branch Library	3223 Ortega St	415-753-7120	23
Park Branch Library	1833 Page St	415-666-7155	9
Parkside Branch Library	1200 Taraval St	415-753-7125	27
Portola Library	2450 San Bruno Ave	415-715-4090	39
Potrero Library	1616 20th St	415-695-6640	16
Presidio Branch Library	3150 Sacramento St	415-292-2155	5
Richmond Branch Library	351 9th Ave	415-666-7165	21
San Francisco Law Library	400 McAllister St	415-551-3647	7
Sunset Branch Library	1305 18th Ave	415-753-7130	25
Sutro Library	480 Winston Dr	415-731-4477	27
United Irish Cultural Center	2700 45th Ave	415-661-2700	26
Visitacion Valley Library	45 Leland Ave	415-337-4790	39
West Portal Branch Library	190 Lenox Way	415-753-7135	30
Western Addition Library	1550 Scott St	415-292-2160	5

Map 1 · Marina / Cow Hollow (West)

Exploratorium	3601 Lyon St	415-397-5673	Experimental hands-on museum of science, art, and human perception at the Palace of Fine Arts. Check out the tactile dome.
Marina Green	Marina Blvd (between Scott & Webster)		
Palace of Fine Arts	Marina Blvd & Lyon St		Bernard Maybeck's "ruin" designed for the 1915 Panama-Pacific International Exposition. Desperately in need of repair, but we love it.
Wave Organ	At the end of the jetty on Yacht Rd (St Francis Yacht Club)		Trippy ocean-powered musical instrument and sculpture created by artists in the '80s.

Map 2 · Marina / Cow Hollow (East)

Fort Mason Center	Buchanan & Marina Blvd	415-441-3400	Former military base that now houses galleries, museums, theaters, and the restaurant "Greens."
MatrixFillmore	3138 Fillmore St	415-563-4180	Glam hipsters galore. Cool lounge space. Are you checking me out?
Octagon House	2645 Gough St	415-441-7512	1861 house with decorative arts. Open 3 days a month, $3.

Map 3 · Russian Hill / Fisherman's Wharf

Bimbo's 365 Club	1025 Columbus Ave	415-474-0365	1931 North Beach nightclub with a groovy undersea theme.
Fisherman's Wharf	From Aquatic Park to Pier 39		Tacky tourist trap, but the sea lions love it. Historic boats, fresh crabs, the ferry to Alcatraz, etc.
Ghiradelli Square	900 North Point St	415-775-5500	Site of the original Ghiradelli chocolate factory; touristy shops and cafes.
Lombard Street	Between Hyde St & Leavenworth St		Unofficially known as "the world's crookedest street"; avoid it on the weekends.
Macondray Lane	Jones St between Green St & Union St		Hidden gem on Russian Hill. Influenced Armistead Maupin's "Barbary Lane" in Tales of the City. No cars allowed.
National Maritime Museum	900 Beach St	415-561-7100	Museum of everything seaworthy— ship models, figureheads, maritime paintings, photos, and artifacts. Free.
San Francisco Art Institute	800 Chestnut St	415-771-7020	Spanish mission-style building with Diego Rivera mural.

Map 4 · North Beach (East) / Telegraph Hill

Coit Tower	1 Telegraph Hill Blvd	415-362-0808	Art Deco memorial on Telegraph Hill, built in 1933, & funded by Lilie Hitchcock-Coit. Stellar WPA murals and great views.
Filbert Steps	Filbert St, just past Sansome		Telegraph Hill stairway surrounded by private gardens and homes. A flock of wild parrots lives in the trees here.
Saints Peter and Paul Church	666 Filbert St	415-421-0809	Catholic church at Washington Square in North Beach. Masses given in English, Italian, and Chinese.

Map 5 · Pacific Heights / Western Addition

Japan Center Peace Pagoda	Geary St & Webster St		Five-tiered structure at the entrance to Japan Center.
Lyon Street Stairs	Lyon St & Broadway		One of the nicest spots in all of San Francisco.
The Fillmore	1805 Geary St	415-346-6000	1912 dance hall, operated by Bill Graham in the '60s and '70s. An excellent place to see a show.
The Painted Ladies	Steiner St between Grove St & Fulton St		That classic view on Alamo Square of the six Victorians against the San Francisco skyline.

Map 6 · Pacific Heights / Japantown

Hass-Lilienthal House	2007 Franklin St		1886 Victorian home.
Spreckel's Mansion	2080 Washington St		Orgiinallly built in 1912 for Adolph and Alma de Bretteville Spreckels. Currently owned by Danielle Steel.
St John Coltrane African Orthodox Church	930 Gough St	415-673-3572	Jazz-inspired services and a John Coltrane memorial.
St Mary's Cathedral	1111 Gough St	415-567-2020	Modern funky-looking cathedral with a hyperbolic paraboloid that forms a cross. Designed by Peter Luigi Nervi 1971.

Map 7 · Nob Hill / Chinatown / SOMA

450 Sutter Medical Building	450 Sutter St		Amazing Art Deco building, Timothy Pfleuger.
Asian Art Museum	200 Larkin St	415-581-3500	Extensive Asian art collection in the old Beaux Arts style library building—a little claustrophobic in the galleries, but well worth your time.
Cable Car Museum	1201 Mason St	415-474 1887	Museum of all things cable car and how they work. Free.
Chambord Apartments	1298 Sacramento St		Beaux Arts building by James Francois Dunn (1921)
City Hall	1 Dr Carlton Goodlett Pl	415-252-2568	Administrative services, art exhibits, events.
Civic Center	Franklin to Leavenworth, & Turk to Hayes	415-904-7100	Includes City Hall, Court House, state and federal buildings, main library, Asian Art Museum, Davies Symphony Hall, War Memorial Opera House, Bill Graham Civic Auditorium.
Fleur de Lys	777 Sutter St	415-673-7779	French fine dining institution.
Glide Memorial Church	330 Ellis St	415-674-6000	Excellent gospel choir and contributions to the community.
Grace Cathedral	1100 California St	415-749-6300	Grand Episcopalian cathedral on Nob Hill.
Imperial Tea Court	1411 Powell St	415-788-6080	The best place for tea in Chinatown and in all of San Francisco.
Masonic Auditorium	1111 California St	415-776-4702	Theater on top of Nob Hill, seats about 2,000.
Pacific Union Club	1000 California St		Private men's club. Former home to James C Flood. Brownstone builit in 1885 and survivor of the 1906 earthquake and fire.

Map 7 · Nob Hill / Chinatown / SOMA — continued

San Francisco Main Library	100 Larkin St	415-557-4400	Very modern, very organized public library.
The Huntington Hotel	1075 California St	415-474-5400	Luxury hotel, Old San Francisco style. The Big 4.

Map 8 · Union Square / Embarcadero / South Beach

Bank of America Building	555 California St		761' tall. Really cool views from the hokey Carnelian Room upstairs.
Caltrain Station	4th St & King St	800-660-4287	Runs down the Peninsula linking San Francisco to San Jose.
City Lights Bookstore	261 Columbus Ave	415-362-8193	North Beach bookstore & center of the '50s Beat scene. A very cool place. Check out the poetry room upstairs.
Cupid's Span	Rincon Park		The giant bow and arrow on the Embarcadero by Claes Oldenburg and Coosje van Bruggen.
Ferry Building	Embarcadero & Market St		Built in 1850 and still in use today. Newly remodeled and home to the amazing Ferry Plaza Farmer's Market.
Hallidie Building	130-150 Sutter St		Early modern architecture; first glass-curtain wall building in America, 1918.
Justin Herman Plaza	Market St & Embarcadero		A good place to meet for a protest, or better yet Critical Mass. Also a favorite lunch spot for the downtown crowd.
Lotta's Fountain	Kearny/Geary @ Market St		Meeting point for separated families during the 1906 eathquake.
Portsmouth Square	Kearny St between Clay St & Washington St		Chinatown's "living room" and center of social activity. Historical significance as the early heart of the city.
Sea Change sculpture	Embarcadero at 2nd St & Townsend St		60-ft stainless steel Mark di Suvero sculpture on the Embarcadero, 1995.
Sentinel Building	916 Kearny St		Beautiful 1905 flatiron with green copper-clad windows (aka: the Coppola building).
SFMOMA	151 3rd St	415-357-4000	Modern Art Museum. Mario Botta design.
Sing Chong and Sing Fat Buildings	Grant St & California St		Great examples of Chinese pagoda-style architecture, built in 1908.
Sony Metreon	101 4th St	415-369-6000	Sony entertainment center; movies, shopping, dining, events.
Transamerica Pyramid	600 Montgomery St		San Francisco's tallest (853') and most distinctive building, William Pereira, 1972.
VC Morris Building (Circle Gallery)	140 Maiden Ln		1948 Frank Lloyd Wright-designed building with interior spiral.
Yerba Buena Center for the Arts	701 Mission St	415-978-2700	Fumikiko Maki-designed exhibition and performance space.

Map 9 · Haight Ashbury / Cole Valley

Grateful Dead House	710 Ashbury St		Corner of Haight & Ashbury, circa 1890s Cranston-Keenan building. We miss you Jerry.
Haight-Ashbury	Haight St & Ashbury St		1960's hippie haven and early home to the Grateful Dead. Great Victorians, cool shops, disillusioned youth, and drugs.

Map 10 · Castro / Lower Haight

Café du Nord	2170 Market St	415-861-5016	Former speakeasy with Victorian interiors. Great place to see live music.
Castro Theatre	429 Castro St	415-621-6120	Historic Art Deco single-screen movie palace.
Harvey Milk Memorial Plaza	400 Castro St		Castro St plaza built in memory of Harvey Milk.
Harvey's	500 Castro St	415-431-4278	Bar and Castro Street institution at the former site of the Elephant Walk and the 1979 White Night riots.
Mission Dolores	3321 16th St	415-621-8203	1776 Spanish mission and Catholic church.
Mission Dolores Park	Church St & 18th St		City park adjacent to Mission Dolores.

Map 11 · Hayes Valley / The Mission

Maestrapeace	18th St & Valencia St		Mural by 7 women painters depicting women at work, play, etc. on the side of the Women's Center Building.

Map 12 · SOMA / Potrero Hill (North)

Anchor Brewing Company	1705 Mariposa St	415-863-8350	All of the Anchor brews are still produced here—yum. Small group tours daily, make a reservation.
Defenestration	6th & Howard St		That great empty building South of Market with the furniture and home appliances stuck all over the outside of it. Brian Goggin 1997.
End Up	401 6th St	415-357-0287	SOMA bar/dance club with theme nights.
Flower Mart	640 Brannan St		The best place to buy flowers—open to the public after 10 am.

Map 13 · SOMA East

Caltrain Depot			This renovated train station is much improved since the original depot, constructed in the 1960s.

Map 15 · Mission (Outer)

Good Vibrations	601B Valencia St	415-974-8980	A SF institution; where to shop for all things safe-sex.

Map 18 · Outer Richmond (West) / Ocean Beach

Cliff House	1090 Point Lobos Ave	415-386-3330	3 erections—1863, 1896, and 1909. Currently houses touristy restaurants and bars with great ocean views.
Fort Miley	El Camino Del Mar & Clement St	415-556-8371	Ruins of old defense batteries. San Francisco State University Adventure Rope Courses.
Palace of The Legion of Honor	34th Ave & Clement St	415-863-3330	Our prettiest museum. Ancient, European, and Decorative Arts. Classic old paintings, Rodin sculpture, and lots of old furniture.
Sutro Baths	Just west of Cliff House on Point Lobos Ave		Ruins of Alfred Sutro's massive indoor swimming pool complex, 1896.

Map 19 · Outer Richmond (East) / Seacliff

Lincoln Park Golf Course	300 34th Ave	415-750-4653	Public golf course, built in 1908. Stellar views.

Map 21 · Inner Richmond

Temple Emanu-El	2 Lake St	415-751-2535	Jewish temple built in a Byzantine-Roman fusion style.

Map 22 · Presidio Heights / Laurel Heights

Roos House	3500 Jackson St		Classic Bernard Maybeck house in Pacific Heights.

Map 26 · Parkside (Outer)

San Francisco Zoo	1 Zoo Rd	415-753-7080	Zoo; info on www.sfzoo.org/visit/

Map 27 · Parkside (Inner)

Stern Grove	19th Ave & Sloat Blvd	415-252-6252	Free concerts in the summer, Sundays at 2.

Map 33 · Ingleside

Ingleside Terraces Sundial	Borcia St & Entrado Ct		Massive white sundial built in 1913.

Golden Gate Park

Beach Chalet	1000 Great Hwy	415-386-8439	Golden Gate Park's Visitor Center is on first floor. Restaurant/ Brew Pub on 2nd floor. Great ocean views and murals.
Conservatory of Flowers	Golden Gate Park		One of the oldest existing wood-frame municipal greenhouses in the US; built in 1878 and newly restored in 2003.
Dutch & Murphy Windmills	Great Hwy @ Fulton & Lincoln		Historic windmills on the northwest and southwest corners of Golden Gate Park, created btwn 1902-1905.
Japanese Tea Garden	Tea Garden Dr	415-752-4227	Descendant of the Japanese Garden of 1894 Exhibition.
M H DeYoung Memorial Museum	75 Tea Garden Dr	415-682-2481	Fine Art—American, African, Oceanic, and the Americas. New building will open 2005.
Morrison Planetarium	55 Concourse Dr	415-750-7141	Trippy light shows.
Steinhart Aquarium	55 Concourse Dr	415-750-7145	California Academy of Sciences' Aquarium.
Strybing Arboretum & Botanical Gardens	9th Ave & Lincoln	415-661-1316	Botanical Gardens in Golden Gate Park.

The Presidio

Fort Point	Long Ave & Marine Dr, Presidio of San Francisco	415-556-1693	Anybody see Vertigo? Fort built during the Civil War, historic site since 1970. Popular destination for runners along the Marina.
Golden Gate Bridge	US Highway 101	415-556-1693	Bridge built between 1933-1937. Walk or bike it for free, $5 toll to drive it. Parking south of bridge.
Presidio Golf Course	300 Finley Rd	415-561-4661	Great public golf course founded in 1895, formerly operated by the military.
The Presidio		415-561-4323	1776 Spanish military post; 1,480 acres of buildings and grounds.

Overview

When it comes to sexuality, San Francisco has something for everyone, and we do mean everyone. While the gay ghetto used to be located on Polk St., most agree that it's now centered in the Castro. In this city, though, the only thing you can be sure of is that every bar or club is "mixed"—even in the land of the rainbow flag. So if you're a boy looking for a boy, a girl looking for a girl, or some variation of the two, you're likely to find what you want in San Francisco.

Websites

- **Craig's List—www.craigslist.org**
  General community site (for straights, gays, and everyone else) that offers heavily trafficked "men seeking men" and "women seeking women" sections, as well as other community-related listings and information.
- **Hillgirlz—www.hillgirlz.com**
  Online lesbian resource featuring a calendar of events, bookshop, services listing, advice, music info, and stars.
- **Out in San Francisco—www.outinsanfrancisco.com**
  Excellent resource for local news, discussion forums, classifieds, personals, and travel.
- **Passport Magazine—www.passportmagazine.com**
  Gay and lesbian travel magazine.
- **Queery—www.queery.com**
  Prominent news stories and a comprehensive gay and lesbian web directory.
- **SFGate—www.sfgate.com/eguide/gay**
  The gay and lesbian section of the sfgate.com website with local stories and extensive reviews of nightlife venues.

Publications

- **The Bay Area Reporter**—Weekly newspaper for San Francisco's lesbian, gay, bisexual, transgender, queer, and questioning community. Look for it on Thursdays.
- **The Bay Times**—Monthly newspaper with extensive arts and entertainment listings.
- **Girlfriends Magazine**—www.girlfriendsmag.com Lesbian culture, politics and entertainment.
- **Odyssey Magazine**—www.odysseymagazine.net Excellent resource for nightlife information, with fun stories, photos, and amusing horoscopes. Published every other Friday.
- **QSF**—www.qsfmagazine.com
  Monthly print magazine that highlights all things queer in San Francisco. Luscious cover boys and gals.
- **SF Frontiers Magazine**—
  www.frontiersnewsmagazine.com. Published every other Thursday with news articles, commentary, arts and entertainment, and a calendar of events.
- **San Francisco Spectrum**—www.sfspectrum.org Monthly newspaper. Offers community news and entertainment listings, as well as columns on a variety of topics and for specific LGBT communities (bears, leather, etc.).

Bookstores

- **A Different Light.** The only specifically gay and lesbian book store in San Francisco, located at 489 Castro St., 415-431-0891. They have excellent readings so check their website for the schedule. www.adlbooks.com.
- **Books, Inc.** This general bookstore is located in the Castro and has a decent selection of gay and lesbian books. 2275 Market St., 415-864-6777, www.booksinc.net.
- **Modern Times.** In the Book Buzz section of their website, Seeley's Starter List for Transgender and Queer Issues sits comfortably amongst Monthly Staff Picks, Children's Books, and Ideal Books for a Lazy Sunday. Located in the Mission at 888 Valencia St., 415-282-9246, www.mtbs.com.
- **City Lights Bookstore.** In North Beach, Lawrence Ferlinghetti's City Lights Bookstore has an excellent selection of fiction, including many foreign titles. Queer beats include Ginsberg, Kerouac, Burroughs, Orlovsky, and bi fave Diane DiPrima. 261 Columbus Ave. at Broadway, 415- 362-8193, www.citylights.com.

Health Centers and Support Organizations

- **Asian & Pacific Islander Wellness Center**, 730 Polk Street, 4th floor, San Francisco, CA 94109, 415-292-3400—www.apiwellness.org—HIV-related and general health services for the Asian LGBT community.
- **California AIDS Hotline**—800-367-AIDS, www.aidshotline.org
- **CUAV (Community United Against Violence)**, 160 14th Street, San Francisco, CA, 94103, 415-777-5500, 24-hour support line: 415-333-HELP. CUAV offers counseling and legal assistance for victims of hate crimes and domestic violence, as well as education programs, and programs for queer youth.
- **Gay and Lesbian Medical Association**, 459 Fulton Street, Suite 107, San Francisco, CA 94102—www.glma.org—A 501(c)3 non-profit organization working to end homophobia in health care. If you're looking for a gay, lesbian, bisexual, transgender, or LGBT-friendly chiropractor, dentist, therapist, or doctor they have an online referral service and will point you in the right direction.
- **Gay Health Care in San Francisco**, 45 Castro Street, Suite 402, San Francisco, CA 94114-1027, 877-693-6633, www.owenmed.com—Bill Owen, MD's practice places emphasis as the primary health care of adults. As a gay doctor, Bill has a special focus on primary care of gay men and lesbians, including patients with HIV/AIDS.
- **Lesbian, Gay, Bisexual and Transgender Support Center**, 1800 Market Street—San Francisco, CA 94102, 415-865-5555, www.sfcenter.org—Center provides regular support groups, workshops, drop-in services, and recreational activities for LGBT San Franciscans.

- **LYRIC (Lavender Youth Recreation and Information Center)**, 127 Collingwood Street, San Francisco, CA, 94114, 415-703-6150, lyric@lyric.org. Youth Talkline: 800-246-PRIDE. Peer-based education, advocacy, recreation, information, and leadership for queer youth, 23 and under.
- **Rainbow Flag Health Services**, 510-521-7737, www.gayspermbank.com—A bank that provides known-donor insemination, Rainbow Flag Health Services actively recruits gay and bisexual sperm donors.
- **San Francisco AIDS Foundation**, 995 Market St, #200, San Francisco, CA 94103.

Annual Events

- **San Francisco Pride**, June 26 and 27, 2004—www.sfpride.org
- **Lesbian and Gay Film Festival**, usually held in June each year—www.frameline.org/festival/, 415-861-1404
- **Castro Street Fair**, usually in October—www.castrostreetfair.org
- **Folsom Street Fair**, usually in September—www.folsomstreetfair.com

Venues

Lesbian

26 Mix (1st & 3rd Thurs)	3024 Mission St	415-825-7378
550 Barneveld (2nd Sat)	550 Barneveld	415-550-8286
Blondie's Bar and No Grill	540 Valencia St	415-864-2419
Cherry Bar	917 Folsom St	888-5-SKIRTS
El Rio (4th Saturday)	3158 Mission St	415-282-3325
Endup (Saturdays)	401 6th St	415-357-0827
Gangway	841 Larkin St	415-776-6828
Lexington Club	3464 19th St	415-863-2052
N'Touch (Wednesday)	1548 Polk St	415-441-8413
Pendulum (Thursday)	4146 18th St	415-863-4441
Wild Side West	424 Cortland St	415-647-3099

Gay

1015 Folsom	1015 Folsom St	415-431-1200
26 Mix	3024 Mission St	415-825-7378
Asia SF	201 Ninth St	415-255-2742
Aunt Charlie's Lounge	133 Turk St	415-441-2922
Back Flip	601 Eddy St.	415-771-3547
Badlands	4121 18th St	415-626-1061
Cinch Saloon	1723 Polk St	415-776-4162
Club Rendez-Vous	1312 Polk St	415-673-7934

Daddy's	440 Castro St	415-621-8732
Detour	2348 Castro St	415-861-6053
Divas	1081 Post St	415-474-DIVA
Eagle Tavern	12th St	415-626-0880
Edge	4149 18th St	415-863-4027
Endup	401 6th St	415-357-0827
Esta Noche	3079 16th St	415-861-5757
Expansion Bar	2124 Market St	415-863-4041
Ginger's Too	43 6th St	415-543-3622
Ginger's Trois	246 Kearny St	415-989-0282
Harvey's	500 Castro St	415-431-4278
Hob Nob	700 Geary St	415-771-9866
Hole in the Wall Saloon	289 8th St	415-431-4695
Joy	2925 16th St	415-431-8889
Loading Dock	1525 Mission	415-864-1525
Lone Star Saloon	1354 Harrison St	415-863-9999
Marlena's	488 Hayes St	415-864-6672
Martuni's	4 Valencia St	415-241-0205
Men's Room	3988 18th St	415-861-1310
Metro	3600 16th St	415-703-9750
Midnight Sun	4067 18th St	415-861-4186
Moby Dick	4049 18th St	415-235-3136
The Mix	4087 18th St	415-431-8616
My Place	1225 Folsom St	415-863-2329
N'Touch	1548 Polk St	415-441-8413
Pendulum	4146 18th St	415-863-4441
Pilsner Inn	225 Church St	415-621-7058
Powerhouse	1347 Folsom St.	415-552-8689
Reflections	1160 Polk St	415-771-6262
SF Badlands	4121 18th St	415-626-9320
The Bar on Castro	456 Castro St	415-626-7220
Transfer	198 Church St	415-861-7499
Twin Peaks	401 Castro St	415-864-9470
Whiskey Lounge	4063 18th St	415-255-2RED
Wooden Horse	622 Polk St	415-928-4046

Mixed

Cafe du Nord	2170 Market St	415-861-3846
El Rio	3158 Mission St	415-282-3325
Jezebel's Joint	510 Larkin	415-345-9832
Lucky 13	2140 Market St	415-884-1525
Lush Lounge	1092 Post St	415-771-2022
Mint	1942 Market St	415-626-4726
Noc Noc	557 Haight St	415-861-5811
Phone Booth	1398 S Van Ness	415-648-4683
Pow	101 Sixth St	415-278-0940
Sadie's Flying Elephant	491 Potrero	415-551-7988
The Cafe	2367 Market St	415-861-3846
The Stud Bar	399 9th St	415-252-7883
Trax	1437 Haight St	415-864-4213

General Information · **Hotels**

All area codes are 415 unless otherwise noted.

Map 1 · Marina / Cow Hollow (West)

Best Inn	2707 Lombard St	567-2425	$70-$85	★★
Chateau Tivoli Bed & Breakfast	1057 Steiner St	776-5462	$135-$160	
Days Inn	2358 Lombard St	922-2010	$75-$105	★★★★★
Edward II Bed & Breakfast Inn	3155 Scott St	922-3000	$95	
Gold Rush Inn	2230 Lombard St	922-3900	$59	
Greenwich Inn	3201 Steiner St	921-5162	$65	★★
Marina Motel	2576 Lombard St	921-9406	$89	
Presidio Inn	2361 Lombard St	931-7810	$99	
Sands Motor Inn	2440 Lombard St	922-0244	$99	
Sea Captain Motel	2322 Lombard St	921-4980	$69	
Super 8 Motel	2440 Lombard St	922-0244	$99	
Surf Motel	2265 Lombard St	922-1950	$79	
Travelodge	2755 Lombard St	931-8581	$99	

Map 2 · Marina / Cow Hollow (East)

Best Inn	2850 Van Ness Ave	776-3220	$79-$99	
Buena Vista Motor Inn	1599 Lombard St	923-9600	$89-$139	◆◆◆
Capri Motel	2015 Greenwich St	346-4667	$70	◆◆◆◆
Chelsea Motor Inn	2095 Lombard St	563-5600	$86-$98	
Comfort Inn by the Bay	2775 Van Ness Ave	928-5000	$145.95	
Coventry Motor Inn	1901 Lombard St	567-1200	$105	★★★
Cow Hollow Motor Inn	2190 Lombard St	921-5800	$125	★★★★
Francisco Bay Motel	1501 Lombard St	474-3030	$85	◆◆◆
Hotel Del Sol	3100 Webster St	921-5520	$145	★★★
Lombard Motor Inn	1475 Lombard St	441-6000	$86	
Lombard Plaza Motel	2026 Lombard St	921-2444	$59	
Marina Inn	3110 Octavia St	928-1000	$75	
Pacific Heights Inn	1555 Union St	776-3310	$98	
Ramada Limited	1940 Lombard St	775-8116	$99	
Redwood Inn	1530 Lombard St	776-3800	$75	
SF Motor Inn	1750 Lombard St	921-1842	$75	
Sherman House	2160 Green St	563-3600	$300	★★★★
Star Motel	1727 Lombard St	346-8250	$99	
Town House Motel	1650 Lombard St	885-5163	$85	
Travelodge	1450 Lombard St	673-0691	$89	
Union Street Inn	2229 Union St	346-0424	$169	

Map 3 · Russian Hill / Fisherman's Wharf

Columbus Motor Inn	1075 Columbus Ave	885-1492	$135-$180	★★★
Courtyard by Marriott	580 Beach St	775-3800	$179	★★★★
Hilton	2620 Jones St	885-4700	$179	★★★
Holiday Inn	1300 Columbus Ave	771-2463	$139	★★★
Holiday Inn	550 North Point St	409-4600	$159	★★★★
Hyatt Hotels & Resorts	555 North Point St	563-1234	$189	
Marriott Hotels & Resorts	1250 Columbus Ave	775-7555	$179	★★★
Suites at Fisherman's Wharf	2655 Hyde St	771-0200	$229	
Travelodge	1201 Columbus Ave	776-7070	$119	

Map 4 · North Beach (East) / Telegraph Hill

Casa Melissa	615 Union St	391-8365	$100
Castro Hotel	705 Vallejo St	788-9709	$70
Dockside Boat & Bed	39 Pier 39	392-5526	$125-$375

Entella Hotel	905 Columbus Ave	929-7195	$30	
Hotel Boheme	444 Columbus Ave	433-9111	$149	
Radisson Hotel Fisherman's	250 Beach St	392-6700	$179	◆◆◆
San Remo Hotel	2237 Mason St	776-8688	$55	
Sheraton	2500 Mason St	362-5500	$229	★★★
Triangle Hotel	524 Columbus Ave	433-5122	$57	
Tuscan Inn Fisherman's Wharf	425 North Point St	561-1100	$159	★★★
Washington Square Inn	1660 Stockton St	981-4220	$145	
Wharf Inn	2601 Mason St	673-7411	$185	

Map 5 · Pacific Heights / Western Addition

Archbishop's Mansion	1000 Fulton St	563-7872	$165-$355	★★★★1/2
Artists Inn	2231 Pine St	346-1919	$170	
Best Western Miyako Inn	1800 Sutter St	921-4000	$79-$119	◆◆
Hotel Drisco	2901 Pacific Ave	346-2880	$175	★★★★
Laurel Inn	444 Presidio Ave	567-8467	$155	◆◆◆
Monte Cristo Hotel	600 Presidio Ave	931-1875	$98	

Map 6 · Pacific Heights / Japantown

Broadway Manor Inn	2201 Van Ness Ave	776-7900	$59-$69	★★1/2
Cathedral Hill Hotel	1101 Van Ness Ave	776-8200	$129-$450	★★★
Holiday Inn	1500 Van Ness Ave	441-4000	$124	
Jackson Court Bed & Breakfast	2198 Jackson St	929-7670	$180	
Majestic Hotel	1500 Sutter St	441-1100	$90	
Oasis Inn	900 Franklin St	885-6865	$65	
Queen Anne Hotel	1590 Sutter St	441-2828	$95	★★★
Radisson Miyako Hotel	1625 Post St	922-3200	$159	★★★
Red Coach Motor Lodge	700 Eddy St	771-2100	$79	
Richelieu Hotel	1050 Van Ness Ave	673-4711	$89	
Rodeway Inn	860 Eddy St	474-4374	$79.99	
Sonoma Inn	1485 Bush St	928-8540	$45	

Map 7 · Nob Hill / Chinatown / SOMA

Abigail Hotel	246 Mcallister St	626-6500	$69	
Acer Hotel	280 O'Farrell St	956-9939	$140-$150/wk	
Adelaide Hostel & Hotel	5 Isadora Duncan Ln	359-1915	$24-$65	★★★
Admiral Hotel	608 O'Farrell St	885-4989	$200/wk	
Air Travel Hotel	655 Ellis St	771-3000	$59 +tax	
Albergo Hotel Verona	317 Leavenworth St	775-1641	$49	
Aldrich Hotel	439 Jones St	885-6604	$55	
			+$5 key deposit	
Amsterdam Hotel	749 Taylor St	673-3277	$79	
Andrews Hotel	624 Post St	563-6877	$99	
Ansonia Hotel	711 Post St	673-2670	$66	
Balmoral Residence Club	1010 Bush St	673-5070	$275/wk	
Bel Air Hotel	344 Jones St	771-3460	$60	
Beresford Hotel	635 Sutter St	673-9900	$89	★★★
Beresford Hotel-Arms	701 Post St	673-2600	$99	◆◆◆
Beresford Hotel-Manor	860 Sutter St	673-3330	$54	
Biltmore Hotel	735 Taylor St	775-0630	$59-$99	
			after summer weekly only	
Bristol Hotel	56 Mason St	296-0980	$65	
Campton Place Hotel	340 Stockton St	781-5555	$395-445	★★★★
Cartwright Hotel	524 Sutter St	421-2865	$89-$209	★★

All area codes are 415 unless otherwise noted.

Map 7 · Nob Hill / Chinatown / SOMA — continued

Castle Inn Motel	1565 Broadway	441-1155	$79-$89	◆◆
Chancellor Hotel	433 Powell St	362-2004	$148-$175	◆◆◆
Chase Hotel	1278 Market St	861-9720	$45	
Clift Hotel	495 Geary St	775-4700	$195-$575	
Columbia Hotel	411 O'Farrell St	673-8007	$50	
Commodore Hotel	825 Sutter St	923-6800	$100	
Cornell Hotel	715 Bush St	421-3154	$85-$120	
Crowne Plaza	480 Sutter St	398-8900	$129-$279	★★★★
Dakota Hotel	606 Post St	931-7475	$65	
Days Inn	895 Geary St	441-8220	$79	★★★
Donatello Hotel	501 Post St	441-7100	$179-$200	★★★★
Edgeworth Hotel	770 O'Farrell St	931-0723	$50	
Elk Hotel	670 Eddy St	776-0767	$55	
Elm Hotel	364 Eddy St	673-5636	$50	
Embassy Suites Hotel	610 Polk St	673-1404	$109	★★
Empress Hotel	144 Eddy St	674-8100	$79	
Essex Hotel	684 Ellis St	474-4664	$59	★★
European Guest House	761 Minna St	861-6634	$30-$90	
Fairmont San Francisco	950 Mason St	772-5000	$209-$349	★★★★
Fitzgerald Hotel	620 Post St	775-8100	$79-$99	
Foley's Inn	235 O'Farrell St	397-7800	$59	
Gates Hotel	140 Ellis St	781-0430	$60	
Gateway Motel	438 O'Farrell St	749-1888	$65	
Glenwood Hotel	717 Sutter St	292-1422	$35	
Golden Gate Hotel	775 Bush St	392-3702	$115	
Grand Hyatt on Union Square	345 Stockton St	398-1234	$139	★★★1/2
Grant Hotel	753 Bush St	421-7540	$70	
Grosvenor Suites	899 Pine St	421-1899	$149	
Handlery Union Square Hotel	351 Geary St	781-7800	$119	◆◆◆
Harcourt Hotel	1105 Larkin St	673-7721	$59	
Haveli Hotel	37 6th St	957-9900	$45	
Hilton	333 O'Farrell St	771-1400	$179	★★★★
Holiday Inn	480 Sutter St	398-8900	$159	★★★★
Hotel Adagio	550 Geary St	775-5000	$119	★★★★
Hotel Bedford	761 Post St	673-6040	$89	★★★
Hotel Bijou	111 Mason St	771-1200	$89	★★★
Hotel Carlton	1075 Sutter St	673-0242	$79	★★★
Hotel Diva	440 Geary St	885-0200	$115	★★★
Hotel Huntington & Nob Hl Spa	1075 California St	474-5400	$190	★★★★
Hotel King George	334 Mason St	781-5050	$79	◆◆◆
Hotel Metropolis	25 Mason St	775-4600	$85	★★1/2
Hotel Milano	55 5th St	543-8555	$89	★★★
Hotel Monaco	501 Geary St	292-0100	$189	★★★★
Hotel Nikko San Francisco	222 Mason St	394-1111	$139	★★★★
Hotel Rex	562 Sutter St	835-0300	$129	★★★
Hotel Serrano	405 Taylor St	885-2500	$259	★★★★
Hotel Union Square	114 Powell St	397-3000	$89	★★1/2
Hotel Verona	317 Leavenworth St	771-4242	$49	
Hyatt Hotels & Resorts	345 Stockton St	398-1234	$139	★★★★
Inn At Union Square	440 Post St	397-3510	$159	◆◆◆

Hotel	Address	Phone	Price	Rating
Juliana Hotel	590 Bush St	392-2540	$109	★★★
Kean Hotel	1018 Mission St	621-0105	$50	
Kensington Park Hotel	450 Post St	788-6400	$115	★★★
Layne Hotel	545 Jones St	441-9317	$89.99	
Marilyn Inn	27 Dashiell Hammett St	392-6102	$55	
Marines' Memorial Club	609 Sutter St	673-6672	$149	★★★
Mark Hopkins Inter-Continental	1 Nob Hill	392-3434	$169	★★★★
Mary Elizabeth Inn	1040 Bush St	673-6768	$49	
Maxwell Hotel	386 Geary St	835-0300	$120	★★★
Mayflower Hotel Apartment	975 Bush St	673-7010	$80	
Mithila Hotel	972 Sutter St	441-9297	$69-$129	★★★
Monarch	1015 Geary St	673-5232	$89	
Monticello Inn	129 Ellis St	392-8800	$109	★★★
National Hotel	1139 Market St	864-9343	$50	
Navareth Hotel	556 Jones St	771-2006	$60	
Nob Hill Hotel	835 Hyde St	885-2987	$99	
Nob Hill Inn	1000 Pine St	673-6080	$165	
Nob Hill Lambourne	725 Pine St	433-2287	$169	
Nob Hill Motel	1630 Pacific Ave	775-8160	$94	
Olympic Hotel	140 Mason St	982-5010	$89	
Orchard Hotel	665 Bush St	362-8878	$139	★★★
Orlando Hotel	995 Howard St	495-9706	$50	
Pan Pacific Hotel	500 Post St	771-8600	$169	★★★★
Petite Auberge	863 Bush St	928-6000	$139	
Phoenix Hotel	601 Eddy St	776-1380	$99	★★★
Pickwick Hotel	85 5th St	421-7500	$89	
Pontiac Hostel Hotel	509 Minna St	863-7775	$51.30	
Post Hotel	589 Post St	749-1285	$55	
Powell Hotel	28 Cyril Magnin St	398-3200	$99	◆◆◆
Powell Place	730 Powell St	362-7022	$145	
Prescott Hotel	545 Post St	563-0303	$139	★★★
Quality Inn	610 Geary St	673-9221	$89.95	★★★
Ramada Mark Twain	345 Taylor St	673-2332	$80-$120	★★★
Ramada Plaza	1231 Market St	626-8000	$89.95	◆◆◆1/2
Renaissance Hotels & Resorts	55 Cyril Magnin St	392-8000	$179	★★★★
Renaissance Stanford Court Htl	905 California St	989-3500	$199	★★★★
Renoir Hotel	45 McAllister St	626-5200	$89	★★★
Ritz-Carlton San Francisco	600 Stockton St	296-7465	$295	★★★★★
Royal Pacific Motor Inn	661 Broadway	781-6661	$89.10	
San Francisco Residence Club	851 California St	421-2220	$78	
San Francisco Traveler's Inn	374 5th St	882-4555	$40	
Savoy Hotel	580 Geary St	441-2700	$89	★★★
Sheehan Hotel	620 Sutter St	775-6500	$75	
Sir Francis Drake Hotel	450 Powell St	392-7755	$129	★★★
Sonny Hotel	579 O'Farrell St	441-9636	$50	
Spalding Hotel	240 O'Farrell St	397-4924	$55	
St Moritz Hotel	190 O'Farrell St	397-4639	$40	
Stratford Hotel	242 Powell St	397-7080	$89	
Sunnyside Hotel	135 6th St	777-2491	$45	
Super 8 Motel	415 O'Farrell St	928-6800	$69.95	
Taylor Hotel	615 Taylor St	775-0780	$55	
Union Sq Back Packers Hostel	70 Derby St	775-7506	$42	
Union Square Plaza Hotel	432 Geary St	776-7585	$79	★★★

General Information · **Hotels**

All area codes are 415 unless otherwise noted.

Map 7 · Nob Hill / Chinatown / SOMA — continued

Villa Florence Hotel	225 Powell St	397-7700	$189
Vintage Court Hotel	650 Bush St	392-4666	$105
Warwick Regis Hotel	490 Geary St	928-7900	$129 ★★★★
Westin St Francis	335 Powell St	397-7000	$219 ★★★★
White Swan Inn	845 Bush St	775-1755	$180
Winton Hotel	445 O'Farrell St	885-1988	$55
YMCA	220 Golden Gate Ave	885-0460	$62.16
York Hotel	940 Sutter St	885-6800	$89 ★★★★

Map 8 · Union Square / Embarcadero / South Beach

Argent Hotel San Francisco	50 3rd St	974-6400	$179-$309 ★★★★
Baldwin Hotel	321 Grant Ave	781-2220	$79 +tax
Balmoral Hotel	706 Kearny St	956-8858	$160-$200
Basque Hotel	15 Romolo Pl	398-1359	$200/wk ★
Bay City Suites	88 Howard St	543-9925	$3500 studio apt/month
Courtyard By Marriott	299 2nd St	947-0700	$109-$229 ★★★★
Europa Hotel	310 Columbus Ave	391-5779	$55
Four Seasons Hotel-SF	757 Market St	633-3000	$300 ★★★★★
Galleria Park Hotel	191 Sutter St	781-3060	$120 ★★★
Golden Eagle Hotel	402 Broadway	781-6859	$40
Grant Plaza Hotel	465 Grant Ave	434-3883	$89
Harbor Court Hotel	165 Steuart St	882-1300	$189 ★★★
Holiday Inn	750 Kearny St	433-6600	$129 ★★★
Hotel Alisa	447 Bush St	956-3232	$89
Hotel Astoria	510 Bush St	434-8889	$65 ★★
Hotel Palomar	12 4th St	348-1111	$215 ★★★★
Hyatt Hotels & Resorts	333 Battery St	392-1234	$210 ★★★★
Hyatt Regency Hotel	5 Embarcadero Ctr	788-1234	$194 ★★★★
Mandarin Oriental Hotel	222 Sansome St	276-9888	$325 ★★★★★
Mosser	54 4th St	986-4400	$129 ★★★
Omni San Francisco Hotel	500 California St	677-9494	$249 ★★★★
Palace Hotel	2 New Montgomery St	512-1111	$219 ★★★★
San Francisco Marriott Downtown	55 4th St	896-1600	$199 ★★★★
St Paul Hotel	935 Kearny St	986-9911	$50
Triton Hotel	342 Grant Ave	394-0500	$159 ★★★
W San Francisco	181 3rd St	777-5300	$279
YMCA	855 Sacramento St	576-9622	$35

Map 9 · Haight Ashbury / Cole Valley

Carl Hotel	198 Carl St	661-5679	$75-$85
Inn 1890	1890 Page St	386-0486	$89
Red Victorian Bed & Breakfast	1665 Haight St	864-1978	$100
Stanyan Park Hotel	750 Stanyan St	751-1000	$145 ★★★

Map 10 · Castro / Lower Haight

Alamo Square Bed & Breakfast	719 Scott St	922-2055	$95-$210
Beck Motor Lodge	2222 Market St	621-8212	$85-$125 ★★
Grove Inn	890 Grove St	929-0780	$95
Metro Hotel	319 Divisadero St	861-5364	$66
Twin Peaks Hotel	2160 Market St	863-2909	$62.70
Willows Bed & Breakfast Inn	710 14th St	431-4770	$109

Map 11 · Hayes Valley / The Mission

Albion House	135 Gough St	621-0896	$110-$265	
All Star Hotel	2791 16th St	864-7478	$45	
			+$5 key deposit	
Ascot Hotel	1657 Market St	864-9034	$55	
			+$5 key deposit	
Days Inn	465 Grove St	864-4040	$95	★★★
Edwardian San Francisco Hotel	1668 Market St	864-1271	$89-$119	★★★
Hayes Valley Inn	417 Gough St	431-9131	$61	
Hotel Sunrise	447 Valencia St	431-2211	$50	
Ivy Hotel	539 Octavia St	863-6388	$53	
New Central Hotel & Hostel	1412 Market St	703-9988	$40	
Travelodge	1707 Market St	621-6775	$89	

Map 12 · SOMA / Potrero Hill (North)

Bay Bridge Inn	966 Harrison St	397-0657	$65-$120	
Best Western Civic Center Inn	364 9th St	621-2826	$99-$109	
Best Western Inn	114 7th St	621-0701	$125	★★
Best Western Inn	121 7th St	626-0200	$155	★★★
Best Western Inn	140 7th St	552-8600	$159	★★★
Britton Hotel	112 7th St	621-7001	$139-$145	★★
Ho Jo Inn	385 9th St	431-5131	$89-$129	
Holiday Inn	50 8th St	626-6103	$99	★★★
Ramada Inn	240 7th St	861-6469	$79	
Rodeway Inn	101 9th St	621-3655	$85	
Soma Inn Hotel-Hostel	1082 Folsom St	558-8555	$36	

Map 15 · Mission (Outer)

Inn San Francisco	943 S Van Ness Ave	641-0188	$95	★★★

Map 23 · Outer Sunset

Beach Motel	4211 Judah St	681-6618	$55-$65
Oceanview Motel	4340 Judah St	661-2300	$75

Map 26 · Parkside (Outer)

Days Inn	2600 Sloat Blvd	665-9000	$80-$125	★★★★★
Ocean Park Motel	2690 46th Ave	566-7020	$75	
Roberts-at-the-Beach-Motel	2828 Sloat Blvd	564-2610	$85	

Map 30 · West Portal

Sunset Motel	821 Taraval St	681-3306	$92.34

Map 34 · Oceanview

Amazon Motel	5060 Mission St	334-1533	$75
Mission Inn	5630 Mission St	584-5020	$65

Map 35 · Bernal Heights

Graywood Hotel	3308 Mission St	550-9315	$55

Map 40 · Bay View / Candlestick Point

Franciscan Motel	6600 3rd St	467-9710	$50
San Francisco Bayside Trvldg	2011 Bay Shore Blvd	467-8811	$65

Golden Gate Park

Great Highway Inn	1234 Great Hwy	800-624-6644	$110

Car Rental

AVIS	SF International Airport	650-877-6780	
Budget	574 McDonnell Rd	1-800-527-7000	
National Car Rental	SF International Airport	650-877-4745	

Car Wash

Allways Open Car Wash	2560 Marin St	415-648-8335	35
Self Service Car Wash	2895 Geary Blvd	415-824-9500	22
Self Service Car Wash	346 Potrero Ave	415-824-9500	12

Copying

American Legal Copy	28 2nd St	415-777-4449	8
Kinko's	1800 Van Ness Ave	415-292-2500	6
Midnight Run Copy	98 Battery St	415-989-7922	8

Delivery and Messengers

Express Delivery	1-800-400-7874
Flash Messenger Service	415-621-7603
Silver Bullet	415-777-5100
Sunny Express	888-786-6939
Western Messenger Services	415-487-4100

Gas Stations

Arco	2190 Carroll Ave	415-468-0446	36
Chevron	1799 Ocean Ave	415-334-4842	33
Richmond Super Shell	4501 Geary Blvd	415-221-0424	21
Shell	2890 3rd St	415-821-0998	17
Shell	1070 Oak St	415-864-3231	10
Shell	4298 Mission St	415-334-2610	32

Gyms

24 Hour Fitness	2145 Market St	415-864-0822	10
24 Hour Fitness	1645 Bryant St	415-437-4188	11
24 Hour Fitness	303 Second St	415-543-7808	8
24 Hour Fitness	1200 Van Ness Ave	415-776-2200	6
24 Hour Fitness	100 California St	415-434-5080	8
24 Hour Fitness	350 Bay St	415-395-9595	4
24 Hour Fitness	3741 Buchanan St	415-563-3535	2

Locksmith

24-Hour Locksmith	1195 Church St	415-821-1030	14
24-Hour Locksmith Emergency		415-441-8700	
A Aardvark Locksmith	236 Hugo St	415-386-1174	
All City Locksmith		415-495-7217	
America's Locksmith		415-989-0990	
Castro Locksmiths		415-864-2521	
Golden Gate Locksmiths		415-391-7833	
The Lock Doctor		415-648-1247	

Pharmacies

Safeway pharmacy	2020 Market St	415-861-7660	10
Walgreens	3201 Divisadero St	415-931-6415	1
Walgreens	498 Castro St	415-861-3136	10

Plumbers

24 Hour Rooter	2300 26th St	925-838-7280	
AAA Discount Rooter		415-550-0356	
Plug Busters		415-252-7584	
Roto-Rooter Plumbers		415-221-2710	

Private Investigator

Denver B Moore	588 Sutter St	415-978-9755	7
Je Gann	2194 Edison Ave	510-568-1465	

Veterinarian

Pets Unlimited Veterinary Hospital	2343 Fillmore St	415-563-6700	5
Presidio Way Veterinary Hospital	3619 California St	415-387-6752	22

Overview

The San Francisco Recreation & Park Department has just begun a 10-year, $400 million capital plan for the development and renovation of city parks. Considerations are underway to incorporate more off-leash dog facilities into the parks in order to recognize the strength, character, and influence the pet-owning community brings to neighborhood parks. The Recreation and Park Commission approved the Dog Advisory Committee's dog policy in May 2002, and they have been aiming to meet their dog-friendly goals since. For questions regarding off-leash dog policy, contact the Department at 415-753-7180 or www.parks.sfgov.org. Another great website with city-specific dog information is www.dogfriendly.com.

Alta Plaza Park

Bordered by Jackson, Clay, Steiner, and Scott Streets. 650-666-7200. This on-leash/off-leash pending dog park celebrates Pug Day on the first Sunday of every month. At the gathering, which takes place between 3:30 and 5 pm, there can be up to 50 pugs in the park.

Golden Gate National Recreation Area

415-556-0560. Starting at the coastline south of San Francisco and stretching 76,500 acres to the area north of the Golden Gate Bridge, this dog-friendly recreation area includes many San Francisco parks and beaches, some with off-leash areas.

Golden Gate Park Dog Runs

Golden Gate Park has 4 off-leash areas: Southeast section bounded by Lincoln Way, King Drive, and 2nd and 7th Avenues; Northeast section at Stanyan and Grove Streets; Southcentral area bounded by King Drive, Middle Drive, and 34th and 38th Avenues; and a fenced training area in the North-central area near 38th Avenue and Fulton Street.

Mountain Lake Park

8th Avenue and Lake Street, 650-666-7200. A strong local dog community utilizes this off-leash park, which has a canine water fountain at 9th Avenue.

St. Mary's Park

Located at Murray Street and Justin Drive, 415-206-9233. This park has a recreation center with a fenced-in dog park on the lower tier below the playground, including canine water fountains.

Beaches

San Francisco has a handful of dog-friendly beaches. However, dogs must remain on the leash most of the time.

Baker Beach is located in the Golden Gate National Recreation Area from Lincoln Blvd to Bowley Street and has a great view of the Golden Gate Bridge. It is located approximately 1.5 to 2 miles south of the Golden Gate Bridge. It is dog-friendly but does not have off-leash areas. (650-556-8371)

Fort Funston/Burton Beach is very popular with the dogs, with trails that run through the dunes, and a water faucet and trough for thirsty dogs at the parking lot at Skyline Boulevard and John Muir Drive. (Skyline Blvd/Hwy 35)

Ocean Beach is 4 miles long and runs parallel to the Great Highway. There is a mix of off-leash and leash-required areas. Dogs must be on leash on Ocean Beach between Sloat Blvd and Fulton. Dogs may be off-leash north of Fulton to the Cliff House and south of Sloat for several miles. (415-556-8642)

General Information

Website: www.sfmoma.org
Location: 151 Third Street (between Mission and Howard Streets), San Francisco, CA 94103
Phone: 415-357-4000
Opening Times: Thursday through Tuesday from 10 am to 6 pm (extended to 9 pm on Thursdays). Closed on Thanksgiving, Christmas, and New Year's Day.
Entry: $10 for adults, $7 for seniors, $6 for students, free for children 12 and under. Free admission offered on the first Tuesday of each month.

Overview

How about sharing your mid-day with Mondrian? Or taking an afternoon break with Diebenkorn? For those who work in downtown San Francisco, the San Francisco Museum of Modern Art offers an easy-to-reach oasis of calm and creativity. When it opened in 1935 (in another location, and without the "modern" in its name) under the direction of Grace L. McCann Morley, it was the first museum on the West Coast devoted solely to 20th-century art. In January 1995, SFMOMA opened a new museum facility in the burgeoning South of Market district, designed by renowned Swiss architect Mario Botta. Across the street from Yerba Buena Center, the SFMOMA is the centerpiece of a growing cluster of downtown and SOMA-area museums, with a permanent collection that includes more than 22,000 objects. Museum membership now exceeds 44,000.

The extensive painting and sculpture collection contains works by distinguished artists such as Jackson Pollock and Henri Matisse, and includes genres such as American Post-Minimalism, German Expressionism, and Fauvism. It also showcases the work of San Francisco Bay Area artists such as David Park and Wayne Thiebaud. More than 50 years ago, the museum was one of the first to recognize photography as an art form. Today, its Department of Photography has international stature. SFMOMA has a state-of-the-art education center adjacent to the permanent collection galleries on the second floor. Its library, open by appointment only, comprises more than 50,000 catalogued items, including monographs, exhibition catalogues, and 1,600 periodical titles.

How to Get There–Driving

From the East Bay: Take Interstate 80 and exit at Fremont Street. Take an immediate left from Fremont onto Howard Street and get into the right lane. Go two blocks and turn right onto Third Street.
From the Peninsula: Take Highway 101 until it connects to Interstate 80 and exit at Fourth Street; Fourth immediately leads onto Bryant Street. Take a left from Bryant onto Third Street and follow it until you reach the Museum.
From the North Bay: Take Highway 101 to Lombard Street. Follow Lombard to Van Ness Avenue and turn right; follow Van Ness until you reach Golden Gate Avenue and turn left. Follow Golden Gate as it crosses Market Street onto Sixth Street. Turn left from Sixth Street onto Folsom Street and follow Folsom up to Third Street; turn left onto Third.

How to Get There–Mass Transit

BART will take you to Montgomery Street or Powell Street Stations, both close to SFMOMA. Muni bus lines 5 Fulton, 9 San Bruno, 14 Mission, 15 Third, 30 Stockton, 38 Geary, and #45 Union run to the Museum and Muni Metro Lines J-Church, K-Ingleside, L-Taraval, M-Oceanview, N-Judah will take you to either Montgomery Street or Powell Street Stations.

Golden Gate Transit buses 10, 20, 50, 60, 70, and 80 stop on Mission and Third Streets in front of Yerba Buena Center for the Arts and Caltrain will get you to Fourth and King Streets.

Sutter and Geary Streets have one of the larger concentrations of art galleries in the city, but don't miss quirky, contemporary spots like New Langton Arts, Balmy, and the showplaces along Hayes St and in the Mission. (The San Francisco Center for the Book on De Haro is another local treasure.) *All area codes are 415 unless otherwise noted.*

Map 2 • Marina / Cow Hollow (East)

Hespe Gallery	1764 Union St	776-5918

Map 4 • North Beach (East)

Campbell-Thiebaud Gallery	647 Chestnut St	441-8680

Map 5 • Pacific Heights/W Addition

Thomas Reynolds Gallery	2291 Pine St	441-4093

Map 6 • Pacific Heights / Japantown

San Francisco Arts Commission Gallery	402 Van Ness Ave	554-6080

Map 7 • Nob Hill/Chinatown/SOMA

Alliance Francaise	1345 Bush St	775-7755
Baxter Chang Patri Fine Art	222 Mason St	397-2000
Braunstein/Quay Gallery	430 Clementina St	278-9850
Castle Fine Arts	454 Sutter St	956-5000
Eleonore Austerer Gallery	540 Sutter St	986-2244
Frey Norris Gallery	456 Geary St	346-7812
HANG	556 Sutter St	434-4264
Jenkins Johnson Gallery	464 Sutter St	677-0770
Jewett Gallery	100 Larkin St	557-4277
John Pence Gallery	750 Post St	441-1138
Martin Lawrence Galleries	366 Geary St	956-0345
Maxwell Galleries	559 Sutter St	421-5193
Meridian Gallery	545 Sutter St	398-7229
Skylight Gallery	100 Larkin St	557-4277
Songlines Aboriginal Art	619 Post St	614-1223
The Luggage Store	1007 Market St	255-5971
Weinstein Gallery	383 Geary St	362-8151

Map 8 • Union Sq / Embarcadero

111 Minna Gallery	111 Minna St	974-1719
871 Fine Arts	49 Geary St	543-5155
Brian Gross Fine Art	49 Geary St	788-1050
Caldwell Snyder Gallery	341 Sutter St	392-4609
Catharine Clark	49 Geary St	399-1439
Compositions Gallery	317 Sutter St	693-9111
Crown Point Press	20 Hawthorne St	974-6273
Dolby Chadwick Gallery	266 Sutter St	956-3560
Dorothy Weiss Gallery	256 Sutter St	397-3611
Ebert Gallery	49 Geary St	296-8405
Erickson & Elins Gallery	345 Sutter St	981-1080
Fraenkel	49 Geary St	981-2661
George Krevsky Gallery	77 Geary St	397-9748
Gregory Lind Gallery	49 Geary St	296-9661
Hackett-Freedman Gallery	250 Sutter St	362-7152
Haines Gallery	49 Geary St	397-8114
Heather Marx Gallery	77 Geary St	627-9111
Jernigan Wicker Fine Arts	161 Natoma St	512-0335
John Berggruen Gallery	228 Grant Ave	781-4629
Larry Evans	77 Geary St	398-7545
Lizabeth Oliveria Gallery	49 Geary St	229-1138
Meyerovich Gallery Contemporary	251 Post St	421-7171
Modernism Gallery	685 Market St	541-0461
Montgomery Gallery	353 Sutter St	788-8300
Olga Dollar Gallery	210 Post St	398-2297
Patricia Sweetow Gallery	49 Geary St	788-5126
Robert Koch Gallery	49 Geary St	421-0122
Scott Nichols Gallery	49 Geary St	788-4641
Shapiro Gallery	760 Market St	398-6655
Space 743 and the Clay Studio	743 Harrison St	777-9080
Spencer Smyth Gallery	495 Jackson St	391-5969
Stephen Wirtz Gallery	49 Geary St	433-6879
Toomey-Tourell Fine Art	49 Geary St	989-6444
Xanadu Gallery	140 Maiden Ln	392-9999

Map 10 • Castro / Lower Haight

Atelier Gallery	2354 Market St	861-8216
Creativity Explored	3245 16th St	863-2108

Map 11 • Hayes Valley / The Mission

364 Hayes Street	364 Hayes St	431-0364
66balmy Annex	591 Guerrero St	522-0502
Art Options	372 Hayes St	252-8334
Cell Space	2050 Bryant St	648-7562
Culture Cache	1800 Bryant St	626-7776
ESP Gallery	305 Valencia St	252-8191
Glama-rama	417 S Van Ness Ave	861-4526
Intersection for the Arts	446 Valencia St	626-2787
Jack Hanley Gallery	395 Valencia St	522-1623
LGBT Community Center	1800 Market St	554-4297
Linc Real Art	1632 Market St	503-1981
Lo-Fi Customs Gallery	1776 Mission St	626-1434
Octavia's Haze	498 Hayes St	255-6818
Paxton Gate	824 Valencia St	824-1872
Peres Project	1800 Bryant St	861-2692
Pond	214 Valencia St	437-9151
Punch Gallery	155 10th St	522-5555
San Francisco Women Artists Gallery	370 Hayes St	552-7392
Southern Exposure	401 Alabama St	863-2141
Spanganga	3376 19th St	821-1102
Start Soma	270 14th St	505-4734
Studio Z Gallery	314 11th St	252-7666
The Lab	2948 16th St	864-8855
Velet da Vinci	508 Hayes St	626-7478
Vorpal Gallery	393 Grove St	397-9200

Map 12 • SOMA/Potrero Hill (North)

Atrium Gallery	600 Townsend St	559-7774
Cameraworks Gallery and Bookstore	1246 Folsom St	863-1001
CCAC Wattis Institute	1111 8th St	551-9210
Crafts-Logan Galleries	111 8th St	551-9210
FiftyCrows Gallery	1074 Folsom St	551-0091
Gallery 16	1616 16th St	626-7495
Joseph Chowning Gallery	1717 17th St	626-7496
New Langton Arts	1246 Folsom St	626-5416
San Francisco Center for the Book 565-0545	300 De Haro St	

Map 13 • SOMA East

| Limn Gallery | 292 Townsend St | 977-1300 |

Map 15 • Mission (Outer)

66 Balmy Gallery	66 Balmy Alley	648-1760
aov	3328 22nd St	431-8341
Artists' Television Access	992 Valencia St	824-3890
Balazo/Mission Badlands Gallery	2811 Mission St	920-0896
Balmy Alley	24th St, between Folsom & Harrison	
Galleria de la Raza	2857 24th St	826-8009
Lola Gallery	2519 Mission St	401-6800
Mission Cultural Center for Latino Arts	2868 Mission St	821-1155
Precita Eyes Mural Arts Ctr	2981 24th St	285-2287
The Warehouse	3075 21st St	235-9552

Map 17 • Potrero Hill (Southeast)

| Ambersand International Arts | 1001 Tennessee | 285-0170 |
| Sublounge | 628 20th St | 552-3603 |

Map 18 • Outer Richmond (West)

| Gallery Paule Anglim | 14 Geary St | 433-2710 |

Map 22 • Presidio Hgts/Laurel Hgts

| Thacher Gallery | 2130 Fulton St | 422-2660 |

Map 25 • Inner Sunset

| The Canvas Cafe Gallery | 1200 9th Ave | 504-0060 |

Museums

The SFMOMA's collection has made important acquisitions in recent years, and the Palace of the Legion of Honor has arguably the best location in the city. But don't forget fun spots like the Cable Car Museum, the Cartoon Museum, the Tattoo Art Museum, and, dare we say it, the Sanitary Landfill Sculpture Garden.

Museums	Address	Phone	Map
African-American Historical & Cultural Society	Fort Mason Center, Building C	415-441-0640	2
Asian Art Museum	200 Larkin St	415-379-8800	7
Cable Car Museum	1201 Mason St	415-474-1886	7
California Academy of Sciences	55 Concourse Dr	415-750-7145	GGP
California Palace of the Legion of Honor	Lincoln Park	415-750-3600	18
Cartoon Art Museum	655 Mission St	415-227-8666	8
Chinese Historical Society of America	965 Clay St	415-391-1188	7
Exploratorium	3601 Lyon St	415-563-7337	1
Golden Gate Railroad Museum	Hunters Point Naval Shipyard	415-822-8728	37
Haas-Lilenthal House	2007 Franklin St	415-441-3000	6
Maritime Museum	900 Beach St	415-561-7100	3
Meandra San Francisco Design Museum	382 Mission St		8
Mexican Museum	Fort Mason Center, Building D	415-202-9700	2
Musee Mechanique	Pier 45 at the end of Taylor St	415-386-1170	7
Museum of Craft & Folk Art	Fort Mason Center, Building A	415-775-0991	2
Museum of Russian Culture	2450 Sutter St	415-921-7631	5
National Japanese American Historical Society	1684 Post St	415-921-5007	6
Octagon House	2645 Gough St	415-441-7512	2
Pacific Heritage Museum	608 Commercial St	415-362-4100	8
Randall Museum	199 Museum Way	415-554-9600	9
San Francisco Museum of Modern Art	151 3rd St	415-357-4000	8
Sanitary Landfill Sculpture Garden	401 Tunnel Ave	415-330-1415	40
Society of California Pioneers	300 4th St	415-957-1849	8
Tattoo Art Museum	841 Columbus Ave	415-775-4991	4
The Wax Museum	145 Jefferson St	800-439-4305	4
The Yerba Buena Center for the Arts	701 Mission St	415-978-2787	8
Wells Fargo History Museum	420 Montgomery St	415-396-2619	8
Zeum	221 4th St	415-777-2800	8

City Lights in North Beach is a worthy first stop. Don't miss Green Apple Books on Clement St (and don't forget the fiction annex just a few doors down). Acorn Books on Polk St is great for used and rare books. Kayo Books on Post has one of the best selections of pulps and paperbacks anywhere. A Clean Well Lighted Place for Books on Van Ness is the place for new titles—and author readings.

All area codes are 415 unless otherwise noted.

Map 1 · Marina / Cow Hollow (West)

Books Inc	2251 Chestnut St	931-3633	General new.

Map 2 · Marina / Cow Hollow (East)

Anonymous Place	1885 Lombard St	923-0248	12-step.
Book Bay	Fort Mason #C	771-1076	Used general donated books, non-profit.
Great Overland Book Co	2848 Webster St	351-1538	General used.
Robert Dagg Rare Books	2087 Union St	474-7368	Used modern literature by appointment.
Vedanta Society Bookshop	2323 Vallejo St	922-2323	Spiritual, metaphysical books.

Map 3 · Russian Hill / Fisherman's Wharf

Barnes & Noble Booksellers	2550 Taylor St	292-6762	Chain.
Builders Booksource	900 N Point St	440-5773	Architecture, design, kids, cook.
Maritime Store	2905 Hyde St	775-2665	Maritime, historical, nature, non-fiction.
Pampanito Store	45 Pier	351-3105	Books on WWII.
Russian Hill Bookstore	2234 Polk St	929-0997	General used.

Map 4 · North Beach (East) / Telegraph Hill

Cavalli Italian Book Store	1441 Stockton St	421-4219	Italian books.
Eastwind Books & Arts Inc	1435 Stockton St	772-5877	Chinese and English.
Golden Gate National Park Store	75 Jefferson St	434-4622	Guidebooks, travel, educational books.

Map 5 · Pacific Heights / Western Addition

Browser Books	2195 Fillmore St	567-8027	General.
Kinokuniya Book Stores-America	1581 Webster St	567-7625	Japanese books, English books, Asian culture and history.
Marcus Book Stores	1712 Fillmore St	346-4222	African-American books.

Map 6 · Pacific Heights / Japantown

A Clean Well Lighted Place	601 Van Ness Ave	441-6670	General.
Alan Wofsy Fine Arts	1109 Geary Blvd	292-6500	Used, out-of-print art books.

Map 7 · Nob Hill / Chinatown / SOMA

Acorn Books	1436 Polk St	563-1736	Hard to find out of print.
Argonaut Book Shop	786 Sutter St	474-1692	Used and rare.
Arkipelago Philippine Books	953 Mission St	777-0108	Filipino books.
Borders Books & Music	400 Post St	399-0522	Chain.
European Book Co	925 Larkin St	474-0626	French, German, Spanish.
Fields Book Store	1419 Polk St	673-2027	Metaphysical, mind-body-spirit, world religion.
Kayo Books	814 Post St	749-0554	Specialize in old paperbacks '30-'70s, used.
Magazine	920 Larkin St	441-7737	Magazines, out of print and used only.
McDonald's Book Shop	48 Turk Street	673-2235	Used books only.
Thomas A Goldwasser Rare Books	486 Geary St	292-4698	Rare books.

Map 8 · Union Square / Embarcadero / South Beach

Alexander Book Co	50 2nd St	495-2992	General new.
B Dalton Bookseller	1 Embarcadero Ctr	982-4278	Chain.
Black Oaks Books	540 Broadway	986-3872	General, mainly used.
Books Inc	160 Folsom St	442-0982	General new.
Brick Row Book Shop	49 Geary St # 235	398-0414	Rare 18th-19th century lit.
Cafe De La Presse	352 Grant St	398-2680	International magazines and newspapers.
Califia Books	20 Hawthorne St	284-0314	Tues-Fri-Sat, noon-5 or by appt.
Chronical Books	101 4th St	369-6271	Only books published by Chronicle
City Lights Bookstore	261 Columbus Ave	362-8193	General new.
Discovery Channel Store	4 Embarcadero Ctr	956-4911	General, science.
Eight-Seventy One Fine Arts Gallery and Bookstore	49 Geary St	543-5155	Art books only.
Emmett Harrington Fine Books	251 Post St	646-0060	Rare books by appointment only.
Gumps	135 Post St	982-1616	Department store with stationary department.
Jeffrey Thomas Fine & Rare Bks	49 Geary St	359-9486	Fine and rare books.
John Windle Antiquarian Bksllr	49 Geary St	986-5826	Old and rare.
Louie Brothers Book Store	754 Washington St	391-8866	Chinese books.
New China Book Store	642 Pacific Ave	956-0752	Chinese books.
Outlet Store	160 Folsom St	442-4830	General new.
Pacific Book Auction Galleries	133 Kearny St	989-2665	Book auctions of rare books, maps, manuscripts, photos.
Rand McNally Map & Travel	595 Market St	777-3131	Maps, travel, everything for the traveller.
SFMOMA Museum Store	151 3rd St	357-4035	Art, architecture, painting, photography, design.
Sino-American Books & Arts	751 Jackson St	421-3345	Chinese books.
Stacey's Bookstore	581 Market St	421-4687	General new and used.
Treasure Books	848 Clay St	362-8818	Chinese books.
Waldenbooks	4 Embarcadero Ctr	397-8181	Chain.
William K Stout Architectural	804 Montgomery St	391-6757	Architecture, design, art, landscape.

Map 9 · Haight Ashbury / Cole Valley

Anubis Warpus	1525 Haight St	431-2218	Magazines & counter culture.
Booksmith	1644 Haight St	863-8688	General new.
Bound Together Book Collective	1369 Haight St	431-8355	Anarchist books.
Forever After Books	1475 Haight St	431-8299	General used, true crime, psych, health, history, sci-fi.
Great Expectations Bookstore	1500 Haight St	863-4639	
Recycled Records	1377 Haight St	626-4075	Music, entertainment, movie books.

Map 10 · Castro / Lower Haight

A Different Light Bookstore	489 Castro St	431-0891	Gay and lesbian.
Aardvark Books	227 Church St	552-6733	Primarily used.
Books Inc	2275 Market St	864-6777	General new.
Crystal Way	2335 Market St	861-6511	Spiritual, metaphysical, recovery, yoga.

Arts and Entertainment · **Bookstores**

Map 11 · Hayes Valley / The Mission

Abandoned Planet Bookstore	518 Valencia St	861-4695	General new and used.
Adobe Book Shop	3166 16th St	864-3936	General used, specialize in philosophy Greek and Roman lit.
Bolerium Books	2141 Mission St	863-6353	Mostly used American social movements.
Borderlands Books	866 Valencia St	824-8203	Sci-fi, fantasy, horror new/used.
California Institute of Intergral Studies Bookstore	1453 Mission St	575-6100	Textbooks, spiritual books.
Forest Books	3080 16th St	863-2755	General used, poetry, eastern religion, art.
Get Lost Travel Books	1825 Market St	437-0529	Travel books.
Limelight Film & Theatre Bookstore	1803 Market St	864-2265	Film and theater, new and used.
Meyer Boswell Books	2141 Mission St # 302	255-6400	History of law.
Psychic Eye Book Shops	301 Fell St	863-9997	Metaphyhsical, astrology, herbs, eastern religion.
Valencia Books	569 Valencia	552-7200	General new.
Valhalla Books	2141 Mission St # 202	863-9250	Used and rare —Literature, mysteries, kids'.

Map 12 · SOMA / Potrero Hill (North)

Camerawork Gallery & Bookstore	1246 Folsom St	863-1001	Photography books .

Map 13 · SOMA East

Christopher's Books	1400 18th St	255-8802	General new.

Map 14 · Noe Valley

Cover To Cover Booksellers	1307 Castro	282-8080	General new children's and fiction.
Phoenix Books & Records	3850 24th St	821-3477	General new and used.
San Francisco Mystery Books	4175 24th St	282-7444	Mysteries.

Map 15 · Mission (Outer)

Dog Eared Books	900 Valencia St	282-1901	General new and used.
La Casa Del Libro	973 Valencia St	285-1399	Spanish books.
Libreria Cristiana Ebenezer	3224 1/2 22nd St	642-9959	Spanish books.
Modern Times Bookstore	888 Valencia St	282-9246	General, progressive, political new.
Nueva Libreria Mexico	2886 Mission St	642-0759	Spanish only.
Pathfinder Bookstore	3284 23rd Street	584-2135	
Scarlet Sage Herb Co	1173 Valencia St	821-0997	Healing books.

Map 17 · Potrero Hill (Southeast)

Mariuccia Iaconi Book Imports	970 Tennessee St	821-1216	Spanish literature, some Italian

Map 19 · Outer Richmond (East) / Seacliff

Bookmonger	2411 Clement St	387-2332	Used.
Educational Exchange	600 35th Ave	752-3302	Educational materials for classroom.

Map 20 • Richmond

Arlekim Russian Bookstore	5909 Geary Blvd	751-2320	Russian books.
Korean Book Ctr & Gifts	5633 Geary Blvd	221-4250	Korean books.

Map 21 • Inner Richmond

Green Apple Books & Music	506 Clement St	387-2272	General interest.
Pacific Books & Arts	524 Clement St	751-2238	General Chinese bookstore.
Thidwick Books	11 Clement St	831-1600	General new.
Znanie Bookstore	4720 Geary Blvd	752-7555	Russian books.

Map 22 • Presidio Heights / Laurel Heights

Books Inc	3515 California St	221-3666	General new.
Follett Campus Bookstore	2130 Fulton St	422-6493	General.

Map 24 • Sunset

Music Rack-SF Conservatory	1201 Ortega St	759-3440	Music books.

Map 25 • Inner Sunset / Golden Gate Heights

Black Oak Books	630 Irving St	564-0877	General mainly used.
Chelsea Book Shop	637 Irving St	566-0507	General used.
Elsewhere Books	260 Judah St	661-2535	Mystery and sci- fi.
Strybing Botanical Gardens	9th Ave & Lincoln Way	661-1316	Plant books.

Map 27 • Parkside (Inner)

Borders Books & Music	233 Winston Dr	731-0665	Chain, in Stonestown Galleria.
Unity Christ Church Bookstore	2690 Ocean Ave	566-4122	Spiritual, Unity books.

Map 28 • SFSU / Park Merced

SFSU Bookstore	1650 Holloway Ave	338-2665	Textbooks, general books.

Map 29 • Twin Peaks

UCSF Bookstore	500 Parnassus Ave	476-1666	Medical, general.

Map 30 • West Portal

Mark Post, Bookseller	2555 Ocean Avenue	586-2363	Literature, history, art, Scottish studies mostly used.
Waldenbooks	255 West Portal Ave	664-7596	Chain.
West Portal Books	111 West Portal Ave	731-5291	General used.

Map 32 • Diamond Heights / Glen Park

Bird & Beckett Books & Records	2788 Diamond St	586-3733	General new and used.

Let's put it this way. In the eyes of most market researchers, San Franciscans are known for two things: buying books, and buying drinks. There are plenty of venues where you can read while you imbibe. Quaff a few under the watchful gaze of James Joyce and other Celtic bards at O'Reilly's Irish Bar & Restaurant in North Beach. Or just quaff. No matter what bar you decide to read in, don't forget, thanks to California State Law, you'll have to leave your pipe at home. *All area codes are 415 unless otherwise noted.*

Map 2 • Marina / Cow Hollow (East)

Blue Light Café	1979 Union St	922-5510	Yuppie bar.
Bus Stop	1901 Union St	567-6905	Casual Cow Hollow hangout.
City Tavern	3200 Fillmore St	567-0918	One third of the "triangle." Good for afternoon sidewalk drinkin'.
Matrix Fillmore	3138 Fillmore St	563-4180	Cool lounge for the beautiful people.
Mauna Loa	3009 Fillmore St	563-5137	Low key Cow Hollow hang out.

Map 3 • Russian Hill / Fisherman's Wharf

2211 Club	2211 Polk St	434-1220	
Bacchus Wine & Sake Bar	1954 Hyde St	928-2633	
Bimbo's 365 Club	1025 Columbus Ave	474-0365	Famous live music venue with cool undersea murals.
Greens Sports Bar	2239 Polk St	775-4287	Great sports bar with tons of TV's.
Royal Oak	2201 Polk St	928-2303	Young crowd lookin' for love.

Map 4 • North Beach (East) / Telegraph Hill

Grant and Green	1371 Grant Ave	693-9565	North Beach classic, good live blues.
Hawaii West	729 Vallejo St	362-3220	North beach dive.
Lost and Found Saloon	1353 Grant Ave	392-1545	Live music.
North Star Café	1560 Powell St	397-0577	North Beach dive.
O'Reilly's Irish Bar & Restaurant	622 Green St	989-6222	Traditional Irish pub.
Pier 23 Café	Pier 23	362-5125	Live music, great deck, on the water.
Savoy Tivoli	1434 Grant Ave	362-7023	Cool Euro scene.

Map 5 • Pacific Heights / Western Addition

Boom Boom Room	1601 Fillmore St	673-8000	Great live music every night, mostly blues.
Frankie's Bohemian Café	1862 Divisadero St	921-4725	Beer bar, pub food.
Harry's on Fillmore	2020 Fillmore St	921-1000	Pac Heights crowd. Casual.
Lion's Den	2062 Divisadero St	567-6565	Used to be gay, now it's completely mixed.
Solstice	2801 California St	359-1222	
Storyville	1751 Fulton St	441-1751	Former jazz club, turned hip hop and funk. Still has the jazz club vibe.
The Fishbowl	1854 Divisadero St	775-3631	

Map 7 • Nob Hill / Chinatown / SOMA

Bambuddah	601 Eddy St	771-3547	Trendy bar at the Phoenix.
Blind Tiger	787 Broadway	788-4020	Trendy Chinatown cocktails.
Blue Lamp	561 Geary St	885-1464	Great live music in the Tenderloin.
Bobby's Owl Tree	601 Post St	776-9344	Really... there's an owl theme, and it's low-lit and lounge-y.
Club 181	181 Eddy St	673-8181	Dance club with theme nights. Sometimes it's good, sometimes it's not.
Edinburgh Castle	950 Geary Blvd	885-4074	Great divey Scottish bar.
Gold Dust Lounge	247 Powell St	397-1695	Dixieland. Getting touristy.
Harry Denton's Starlight Room	Sir Francis Drake Hotel, 21st fl, 450 Powell St	395-8595	Swanky cocktails and dancing with a view.
Julip	839 Geary St	474-3216	Nice lounge in the Tenderloin.
Ruby Skye	420 Mason St	693-0777	Terribly hip and trendy club.
Shanghai Kelly's	2064 Polk St	771-3300	Laid back Russian Hill saloon.

Arts and Entertainment • Bars

The Cinch Saloon	1723 Polk St	776-4162	Gay and western.
The Red Room	827 Sutter St	346-7666	Like it says, it's all red inside and lounge-y.
The Redwood Room	Clift Hotel, 495 Geary St	775-4700	Upscale trendy hotel bar for the beautiful people.
Tonga Room	Fairmont Hotel, 950 Mason St	772-5278	Excellent tiki bar with dancing and thunderstorms.

Map 8 • Union Square / Embarcadero / South Beach

7-11 Club	711 Market St	777-4455	Downtown dive.
850 Cigar Bar	850 Montgomery St	291-0850	Fancy, clubby cigar bar.
Bamboo Hut	479 Broadway	989-8555	Tiki bar amongst the strip clubs.
Bix	56 Gold St	433-6300	Remarkable martinis, beautiful bar.
Buddha Lounge	901 Grant Ave	362-1792	Chinatown classic.
Carnelian Room	Bank of America Bldg, 52nd fl, 555 California St	433-7500	Cheesy and expensive, but the view is worth a visit.
Frankie's Bohemian Café	443 Broadway	788-7936	Beer bar, pub food.
Gordon Biersch	2 Harrison St	243-8246	Brew pub, good patio, financial district, and bridge & tunnel crowd.
Harry Denton's	161 Steuart St	882-1333	Swanky cocktails and dancing. It's getting cheesy.
Hi-Ball Lounge	473 Broadway	397-9464	Swing in the red light district.
Hotel Utah Saloon	500 4th St	421-8308	Live music.
House of Shields	39 New Montgomery St	392-7732	Financial crowd decompressor.
Jazz at Pearl's	256 Columbus Ave	291-8255	North Beach institution.
Kate O'Brien's	579 Howard St	882-7240	Average busy Irish pub.
Li Po Cocktail Lounge	916 Grant Ave	982-0072	Cool Chinatown dive.
Royal Exchange	301 Sacramento St	956-1710	Financial district pub.
San Francisco Brewing Company	155 Columbus Ave	434-3344	North Beach beer bar, grab a table on the sidewalk.
South Beach Billiards	270 Brannan St	495-5939	Big, nice pool hall.
Spec's 12 Adler Museum Café	12 Adler Way	421-4112	Great, hard to find, Beat-era bar.
The Condor Sports Bar	300 Columbus Ave	781-8222	Sports bar in the former Condor strip club with the blinking nipples.
The Irish Bank Bar & Restaurant	10 Mark Ln	788-7152	Financial district watering hole.
The Saloon	1232 Grant Ave	989-7666	North Beach institution, great live music.
The Thirsty Bear	661 Howard St	974-0905	Brew pub and tapas by Moscone.
Tosca Café	242 Columbus Ave	986-9651	Oozes old-world San Francisco magic—a North Beach classic.
Vesuvio Café	255 Columbus Ave	362-3370	North Beach literati bar.

Map 9 • Haight Ashbury / Cole Valley

Club Deluxe	1511 Haight St	552-6949	Art deco swing-era lounge.
Finnegan's Wake	937 Cole St	731-6119	Cole Valley dive with ping pong.
Kezar Bar & Restaurant	900 Cole St	681-7678	Sports bar.
Martin Mack's	1568 Haight St	864-0124	Haight street pub.
Murio's Trophy Room	1811 Haight St	752-2971	Great rock and roll dive.
Persian Aub Zam Zam	1633 Haight St	861-2545	Former home of the "Martini-nazi." They're alot nicer now, but not as cool.

Map 10 • Castro / Lower Haight

Café Du Nord	2170 Market St	979-6545	Former speak-easy. Excellent live music, pool tables.
Detour	2348 Market St	861-6053	Gay bar with a dangerous 2 for 1 happy hour.
Harvey's	500 Castro St	431-4278	A Castro institution. Considered touristy by the locals.

Map 10 · Castro / Lower Haight — continued

Justice League	628 Divisadero St	289-2038	Popular divey hip-hop club.
Lucky 13	2140 Market St	487-1313	Hard rock and punk bar for the tattooed and pierced.
Mad Dog in the Fog	530 Haight St	626-7279	Great beer bar.
Midnight Sun	4067 18th St	861-4186	Gay bar with big TVs and sitcoms.
Nickie's BBQ	460 Haight St	621-6508	Grungy Lower Haight dancin'.
Noc Noc	557 Haight St	861-5811	Cool cavey alternative bar.
Pilsner Inn	225 Church St	621-7058	Gay bar with a pool table, darts, and pinball.
The Badlands	4121 18th St	626-9320	Gay bar.
The Bar on Castro	456B Castro St	626-7220	
The Café	2367 Market St	861-3846	Legendary gay bar and dance club.
The Metro Bar & Restaurant	3600 16th St	703-9750	Good balcony for checking out the Castro scene. The restaurant serves Chinese food.
The Transfer	198 Church St	861-7499	Daily happy hour 3-7 and pool. Mixed crowd.
The Twin Peaks	401 Castro St	864-9470	One of the oldest gay bars in the Castro.
Toronado	647 Haight St	863-2276	The best beer bar in the city. They've got an amazing selection.

Map 11 · Hayes Valley / The Mission

Beauty Bar	2299 Mission St	285-0323	Cocktail lounge, manicures, and martinis.
Dalva	3121 16th St	252-7740	Nice Mission lounge. Check out the jukebox.
DNA Lounge	375 11th St	626-1409	Dance club. It's back and happening again.
Doctor Bombay's	3192 16th St	431-5255	Low key Mission haunt.
Elbo Room	647 Valencia St	552-7788	Legendary alternative music joint.
Este Noche	3079 16th St	861-5757	Bisexuals and drag queens.
Hayes & Vine	377 Hayes St	626-5301	Wine bar.
Kilowatt	3160 16th St	861-2595	Small and divey.
Lexington	3464 19th St	863-2052	Cozy lesbian bar.
Liquid	2925 16th St	431-8889	Mission club.
Martuni's	4 Valencia St	241-0205	Show tunes anyone? Great piano bar, mostly gay crowd.
Paradise Lounge	1501 Folsom St	861-6906	Live music, poetry readings, pool tables, alternative crowd.
Slim's	333 11th St	552-0333	Big name live music.
The Albion	3139 16th St	552-8558	
Twenty Tank Brewery	316 11th St	255-9455	Brew pub.
Zeitgeist	199 Valencia St	255-7505	Biker bar with a big yard.

Map 12 · SOMA / Potrero Hill (North)

Asia SF	201 9th St	255-2742	Gender illusionists. Go for the entertainment.
Cat Club	1190 Folsom St	431-3332	DJ dance club.
Endup	401 6th St	357-0827	Open til forever and notorious for the Sunday T dance. Watch for theme nights.
Lingba Lounge	1469 18th St	826-3611	
Mars Café	798 Brannan St	621-6277	Jetsons-like lounge.
Ten15 Folsom	1015 Folsom St	431-1200	Club scene.
The Stud	399 9th St	252-7883	Gay, duh.

Map 13 • SOMA East

Bottom of the Hill	1233 17th St	621-4455	Great live music of all kinds.
Sno-Drift	1830 3rd St	431-4766	DJ dance club.
The Ramp	855 China Basin St	621-2378	Hit the deck on Saturday/Sunday afternoons.

Map 14 • Noe Valley

Noe's Bar	1199 Church St	282-4007	Sports bar.
Rat and Raven	4054 24th St	285-0674	Check out the beer garden in back.
The Dubliner	3838 24th St	826-2279	Casual local Irish bar.

Map 15 • Mission (Outer)

26 Mix	3024 Mission St	248-1319	Sound lounge.
Latin American Club	3286 22nd St	647-2732	Kick back Mission bar.
Lone Palm	3394 22nd St	648-0109	Laid back Mission dive.
The Make-Out Room	3225 22nd St	647-2888	Trendy bar.

Map 17 • Potrero Hill (Southeast)

Sublounge	628 20th St	552-3603	Popular dance club.

Map 19 • Outer Richmond (East) / Seacliff

Trad'r Sam's	6150 Geary Blvd	221-0773	Unpretentious tiki bar.

Map 20 • Richmond

Tommy's Mexican Restaurant	5929 Geary Blvd	387-4747	Legendary margaritas.

Map 21 • Inner Richmond

Last Day Saloon	406 Clement St	387-6343	Great for live music.
Plough & Stars	116 Clement St	751-1122	Traditional Irish bar, live music.
The Bitter End	441 Clement St	221-9538	Cozy, neighborhood Irish bar. Fireplace, pool tables, pinball, darts.

Map 24 • Sunset

Durty Nelly's	2328 Irving St	664-2555	Country-style Irish pub.
Molly Malone's	1849 Lincoln Way	681-3820	Irish pub.

Map 30 • West Portal

Joxer Daly's	46 West Portal Ave	564-1412	Neighborhood Irish pub.
West Portal Station	824 Ulloa St	753-9554	Good divey bar.

Map 31 • Mt. Davidson

Tower Lodge	689 Portola Dr	564-9501	Locals bar.

Map 32 • Diamond Heights / Glen Park

Glen Park Station Bar	2816 Diamond St	333-4633	Neighborhood bar.
R&R Cocktail Lounge	609 Chenery St	333-3030	Neighborhood bar.

Map 35 • Bernal Heights

El Rio	3158 Mission St	282-3325	Latin dive, racially and sexually mixed.
Odeon Bar	3223 Mission St	550-6994	Alternative club.
Roccapulco	3140 Mission St	648-6611	One of the oldest Latin clubs in town, great for salsa.
Skip's Tavern	453 Cortland Ave	282-3456	Exceptional bar with live music.
The Wild Side West	424 Cortland Ave	647-3099	Western and Victorian stuff, but not country. Fireplace. Check out the backyard.

Sausalito

No Name Bar	757 Bridgeway	332-1392
Paterson's Bar	739 Bridgeway	332-1264
Smitty's Bar	214 Caledonia St	332-2637

Arts and Entertainment • **Clubs & Cabarets**

From the dark, shadowy corners of Jezebel's Joint and the Cat Club, to the bright, sun-drenched summer Sunday afternoons on the patio at El Rio, San Francisco has favorite haunts for just about every mood. Feeling posh? Go mingle with the well-dressed at the Redwood Room. Serious itch to dance? Try Ruby Skye or Glas Kat. *All area codes are 415 unless otherwise noted.*

Club	Address	Phone	Map
1100 Club	1100 Polk St	771-2022	7
111 Minna Gallery	111 Minna St	974-1719	8
26 Mix	3014 Mission St	826-7378	15
330 Ritch Street	330 Ritch St	541-9574	8
Amber	718 14th St	626-7827	10
An Sibin DJ Bar	1176 Sutter St	929-1992	7
Anu	43 6th St	543-3505	7
Arrow	10 6th St	255-7920	7
Asia SF Bar	201 9th St	255-2742	12
Atlas Cafe	3049 20th St	648-1047	15
Aunt Charlie's Lounge	133 Turk St	441-2922	7
Backflip	601 Eddy St	771-3547	7
Badlands	4121 18th St	626-9320	10
Bambuddha Lounge	601 Eddy St	885-5088	7
Bas	383 Bay St	399-9555	4
Beauty Bar	2299 Mission St	285-0323	11
Bigfoot Lounge	1750 Polk St	440-2355	7
Bimbo's 365 Club	1025 Columbus Ave	474-0365	3
Blind Tiger Lounge	787 Broadway	788-4020	7
Bliss	4026 24th St	826-6200	14
Bohemia Lounge	1624 California St	474-6968	7
Border Cantina	1192 Folsom St	626-6043	12
Broadway Studios	435 Broadway	291-0333	8
Butter	354 11th St	863-5964	11
Buzz 9	139 8th St	255-8783	12
Cafe Cocomo	650 Indiana St	824-6910	13
Cafe Mars	798 Brannan St	621-6277	12
Cat Club	1190 Folsom St	431-3332	12
Cherry Bar & Lounge	917 Folsom St	974-1585	7
Cinch Saloon	1723 Polk St	776-4162	7
City Nights	715 Harrison St	546-7938	8
Cityscape	333 O'Farrell St	923-5002	7
Cloud 9	34 7th St	355-9991	7
Club Bien Bien	333 Bay St	399-9555	4
Club Caliente	298 11th St	255-2232	11
Club NV	525 Howard St	339-8686	8
Club Rendez-Vous	1312 Polk St	673-7934	7
Club Six	60 6th St	863-1221	7
Dalva	3121 16th St	252-7740	11
Decibel	699 Market St	543-0191	8
Delirium Cocktails	3137 16th St	552-5525	11
Deluxe	1509 Haight St	552-6949	9
Divas	1081 Post St	928-6006	7
DNA Lounge	375 11th St	626-1409	11
El Rio	3158 Mission St	282-3325	35
Esta Noche	3079 16th St	554-8436	11
Factory 525	525 Harrison St	339-8686	8
Fiddler's Green	1333 Columbus Ave	441-9758	3
Fuse	493 Broadway	788-2706	8
G Bar	488 Presidio Ave	409-4227	5
Galaxy Club	1840 Haight St	387-2996	9
Galia	2565 Mission St	970-9777	15
Glas Kat	520 4th St	957-9318	8
Harry Denton's Starlight Room	450 Powell St, 21st Floor	395-8595	7
Hi-Fi Lounge	2125 Lombard St	345-8663	2
Hole in the Wall Saloon	289 8th St	431-4695	12
Holy Cow	1535 Folsom St	621-6087	11
Hush Hush Lounge	496 14th St	241-9944	11
Il Pirata	2007 16th St	626-2626	12
Jelly's Cafe	295 China Basin St	495-3099	13
Jezebel's Joint	510 Larkin St	345-9832	7
Jillian's	101 4th St	369-6100	8
Julip Cocktail Lounge	839 Geary St	474-3216	7
Justice League	628 Divisadero St	289-2038	10
Kate O'Brien's	579 Howard St	882-7240	8
Kelly's Mission Rock	817 China Basin St	625-5355	13
Laszlo	2534 Mission St	648-7600	15
Le Colonial	20 Cosmo Pl	931-3600	7
Li Po Lounge	916 Grant St	675-9955	8
Liquid	2925 16th St	431-8889	11
Mad Dog in the Fog	530 Haight St	626-7279	10
Make-Out Room	3225 22nd St	647-2888	15
Marlena's	488 Hayes St	864-6672	11
Martuni's	4 Valencia St	241-0205	11
McCarthy's on Mission	2327 Mission St	648-0504	11
mezzanine	444 Jessie St	820-9669	7
'N Touch	1548 Polk St	441-8413	7
Nickie's BBQ	460 Haight St	621-6508	10
Odeon	3223 Mission St	550-6994	35
Oxygen Bar	795 Valencia St	255-2102	11
Phoenix Bar	811 Valencia St	695-1811	11
Piyassa	1686 Market St	864-3700	11
Polly Esther's	181 Eddy St	882-1977	7
Pow!	101 6th St	278-0940	7
Rasselas on Fillmore	1534 Fillmore St	346-8692	5
Rawhide II	280 7th St	621-1197	12
Red Devil Lounge	1695 Polk St	921-1695	7
Red Eye	1337 Mission St	888-286-2581	12
Redwood Room	495 Geary St	775-4700	7
Roccapulco	3140 Mission St	648-6611	35
RoHan Lounge	3809 Geary St	221-5095	21
Ruby Skye	420 Mason St	693-0777	7
Sacrifice	800 S Van Ness Ave	641-0990	11
Sitio	1151 Folsom St	626-2388	12
Skylark	3089 16th St	621-9294	11
Sno-drift	1830 3rd St	431-4766	13
Soluna	272 McAllister St	621-2200	7
Space 550	550 Barneveld Ave	550-8286	36
Storyville	1751 Fulton St	441-1751	5
Studio-Z	314 11th St	252-7666	11
sublounge	628 20th St	552-3603	17
Ten 15	1015 Folsom St	431-1200	12
The Attic	3326 24th St	643-3376	15
The Bamboo Hut	479 Broadway	989-8555	8
The Bar on Castro	456 Castro St	626-1061	10
The Cafe	2367 Market St	861-3846	10
The Cellar	685 Sutter St	441-5678	7
The Eagle Tavern	398 12th St	626-0880	11
The Stud	399 9th St	863-6623	12
The Top	424 Haight St	864-7386	10
Tropi-Gala Night Club	358 Ocean Ave	596-7972	34
Tunnel Top	601 Bush St	986-8900	7
Velvet Lounge	443 Broadway	788-0228	8
Voodoo Lounge	2937 Mission St	285-3369	15
Whisper Nightclub	535 Florida St	356-9800	11
Wish Bar and Lounge	1539 Folsom St	278-9474	11
Zebulon	83 Natoma St	975-5705	8

You haven't lived until you've watched "The Women" (catcalls and all) at the venerable Castro Theater. Don't miss the chance to dine while you view at the Foreign Cinema, and keep your eyes on The Roxie for some truly quirky cinematic offerings. There are plenty of multiplexes too (try the AMC at 1000 Van Ness or Loew's Sony Metreon next to Yerba Buena Gardens). Don't be fooled into thinking the UA Stonestown Twin is **in** the Stonestown Galleria—it's actually a totally separate building far across the parking lot behind the mall.

Movie Theater	Address	Phone	Map
AMC 1000 Van Ness	1000 Van Ness Ave	415-922-4AMC	6
AMC Kabuki 8	1881 Post St	415-922-4AMC	5
Balboa Theater	3630 Balboa St	415-221-8184	19
Castro Theater	Castro St & Market St	415-621-6120	10
Century Empire 3	85 West Portal Ave	415-661-2539	30
Century Presidio	2340 Chestnut St	415-921-6720	1
Foreign Cinema	2534 Mission St	415-648-7600	15
Four Star	2200 Clement St	415-666-3488	20
Landmark Bridge	3010 Geary Blvd	415-352-0810	22
Landmark Clay	2261 Fillmore St	415-352-0810	5
Landmark Embarcadero	1 Embarcadero Ctr	415-352-0810	8
Landmark Lumiere	1572 California St	415-352-0810	7
Landmark Opera Plaza Cinemas	601 Van Ness Ave	415-352-0810	6
Lowes Theater/IMAX at Metreon	150 4th St	415-369-6200	8
Marin Theater	101 Caledonia St	415-331-0255	110
Red Vic	1727 Haight St	415-668-3994	9
Roxie	3117 16th St	415-863-1087	11
UA Alexandria	5400 Geary Blvd	415-752-5100	20
UA Coronet	3575 Geary Blvd	415-752-4400	22
UA Galaxy 4	1285 Sutter St	415-474-8700	6
UA Metro	2055 Union St	415-931-1685	2
UA Stonestown Twin	501 Buckingham Way	415-221-8182	28
UA Vogue	3290 Sacramento St	415-221-8183	5

Arts and Entertainment · **Restaurants**

Map 1 · Marina / Cow Hollow (West)

Ace Wasabi's Rock and Roll Sushi	3339 Steiner St	567-4913	$$$$	Lively sushi bar. Bingo at 6:30.
Andale Taqueria	2150 Chestnut St		$$$	Good, quick Mexican.
Baker Street Bistro	2953 Baker St	931-1475	$$$	Truly French and not too expensive.
Bistro Aix	3340 Steiner St	202-0100	$$$$	Great food, great patio in the back.
Café Marimba	2317 Chestnut St	776-1506	$$$	Fun Oaxacan Mexican.
Cozmo's Corner Grill	2100 Chestnut St	351-0175	$$$$	Good food, but way too loud. What? What?!
Dragon Well	2142 Chestnut St	474-6888	$$$	Cheap modern Chinese.
Isa	3324 Steiner St	567-9588	$$$$	French tapas and beautiful people.
Izzy's Steak and Chops	3345 Steiner St		$$$$	Casual steakhouse. Don't miss the creamed spinach and Izzy's potatoes.
Liverpool Lil's	2942 Lyon St	921-6664	$$$	Quiet, comfy little pub tucked away by the Presidio.
Marinette	3352 Steiner St	614-2941	$$*	French bakery and cafe—don't miss the desserts.
Meze's	2372 Chestnut St		$$$	Popular Marina Greek.
Parma	3314 Steiner St	567-0500	$$$	Casual Italian. Try the carbonara.
Rose's Café	2298 Union St	775-2200	$$$	Charming and fantastic for wine and dinner al fresco. Don't miss the breakfast pizza.
The Grove	2250 Chestnut St		$$*	Cozy laptop friendly cafe. They have outlets and beer.
Three Seasons	3317 Steiner St	567-9989	$$$	Excellent Vietnamese.

Map 2 · Marina / Cow Hollow (East)

Amici's East Coast Pizzeria	2033 Union St	885-4500	$$	Predictable pie.
Betelnut Pejiu Wu	2030 Union St	929-8855	$$$$	Popular Asian fusion.
Brazen Head	3166 Buchanan St	921-7600	$$$$*	No sign. Pop in for a drink and dinner on the hush-hush.
Charlie's	1838 Union St	474-3773	$$$	A scene.
Greens	Ft Mason Ctr Bldg A	771-6222	$$$$	Killer vegetarian. Great brunch. Outstanding view.
La Canasta	3006 Buchanan St	474-2627	$*	Take-out Mexican.
Mas Sake	2030 Lombard St	440-1505	$$$	Hip Japanese.
Merenda	1809 Union St	346-7373	$$$$$	Great inventive Italian food & wine bar.
Pasta Pomodoro	1875 Union St	771-7900	$$	Fast, cheap pasta.
PlumpJack Café	3127 Fillmore St	563-4755	$$$$$	Top-drawer neighborhood spot.
Zao Noodle Bar	2031 Chestnut St	928-3088	$$	Fast, cheap noodles.

Map 3 · Russian Hill / Fisherman's Wharf

Antica Trattoria	2400 Pols St	928-5797	$$$$	Average Italian.
Baldoria	2162 Larkin St	447-0441	$$$	More good Italian.
Boulange de Polk	2310 Polk St	345-1107	$$*	Exceptional French bakery.
Frascati	1901 Hyde St	928-1406	$$$	Neighborhoody and friendly.
Gary Danko	800 North Point St	749-2060	$$$$$	The best of the big names. Truly astonishing.
Gaylord India	Ghiradelli Square	771-8822	$$$	Expensive Indian with a view.
I Fratelli	1896 Hyde St	474-8240	$$$	Homey Italian.
In-N-Out Burger	333 Jefferson St	800-786-1000	$*	Legendary fast food burgers. Double double with cheese, please.
La Folie	2316 Polk St	776-5577	$$$$$	One of the greats.
Le Petit Robert	2300 Polk St	922-8100	$$$	Excellent bistro fare.
Pesce	2227 Polk St	928-8025	$$$	Yet another attempt at tapas.
Rex Cafe	2323 Polk St	441-1244	$$	Russian Hill restaurant that's best for cocktails and appetizers.

Spoon	2209 Polk St	268-0140	$$$$	Modern comfort food.
Sushi Groove	1916 Hyde St	440-1905	$$$$	Hip.
Yabbie's Coastal Kitchen	2237 Polk St	474-4088	$$$$	Pricey seafood.
Za Pizza	1919 Hyde St	771-3100	$*	Great hole in the wall thin-crust pizza place. They deliver too.
Zarzuela	2000 Hyde St	346-0800	$$$	Authentic Spanish tapas.

Map 4 • North Beach (East) / Telegraph Hill

Café Jacqueline	1454 Grant Ave	981-5565	$$$$$	Romantic... and they only serve souffle.
Capp's Corner	1600 Powell St	989-2589	$$$	Bare-bones Italian.
Golden Boy Pizza	542 Green St	982-9738	$*	Great cheap pizza.
Houston's	1800 Montgomery St	392-9280	$$$	Nice American grill. Great greyhounds.
L'Osteria del Forno	519 Columbus Ave	982-1124	$$$*	Tiny and everything is cooked in the wood oven.
Mama's on Washington Square	1701 Stockton St	362-6421	$$*	Outstanding (literally) breakfast. Go early.
Mario's Bohemian Cigar Store Café	566 Columbus Ave	362-0536	$$*	Great focaccia sandwiches.
Michelangelo Restaurant Caffe	579 Columbus Ave	986-4058	$$$*	Good basic Italian.
Mo's Grill	1322 Grant Ave	788-3779	$$	Really good burgers.
Moose's	1652 Stockton St	989-7800	$$$$$	An institution. Herb Caen drank martinis here.
North Beach Pizza	1499 Grant Ave	433-2444	$$	Good local "chain" pizza.
North Beach Pizza	1310 Grant Ave	433-2444	$$	Good local "chain" pizza.
Pasta Pomodoro	655 Union St	399-0300	$$	Fast cheap pasta.
Pier 23 Café	Pier 23, The Embarcadero	362-5125	$$$	Live music by night and brunch on the deck on a nice, sunny day.
Pipperade	1015 Battery Street	391-2555	$$	Really good Basque.
Rose Pistola	532 Columbus Ave	399-0499	$$$$	Popular "family-style" Ligurian.
Trattoria Contadina	1800 Mason St	982-5728	$$$	More good basic Italian.
Washington Square Bar & Grill	1707 Powell St	982-8123	$$	The old Washbag is back again. The bar is better than the food.

Map 5 • Pacific Heights / Western Addition

Café Kati	1963 Sutter St	775-7313	$$$$$	Vertical food.
Chez Nous	1911 Fillmore St	441-8044	$$$	Mediterranean small plates. Worth the wait.
Dino's Pizzeria	2101 Fillmore St	922-4700	$	Tasty Pac Heights pizza joint.
Elite Café	2049 Fillmore St	346-8668	$$$	Closest we've got to Cajun.
Eliza's	2877 California St	621-4819	$$$	Healthy modern Chinese.
Ella's	500 Presisio Ave	441-5669	$$$	A weekend brunch institution.
Fillmore Grill	2298 Fillmore St	776-7600	$$	Nice, casual American grill with a full bar. New to Pac Heights and we hope it stays.
Florio	1915 Fillmore St	775-4300	$$$$	Cozy French/Italian. Great atmosphere.
Galette	2043 Fillmore St	928-1300	$$$	Affordable French, focusing on crepes, Brittany-style (buckwheat). Yum.
Garibaldi's on Presidio	347 Presidio Ave	563-8841	$$$$	California cuisine and upscale local crowd.
Godzilla	1800 Divisadero St	931-1773	$$	Great casual neighborhood sushi.
Jackson Fillmore Trattoria	2506 Fillmore St	346-5288	$$$$	A Pac Heights favorite for casual Italian.
Julia	2101 Sutter St	441-2101	$$$	Standard contemporary American.
La Mediterranee	2210 Fillmore St	921-2956	$$	Cozy Middle Eastern.
Pasta Pomodoro	1865 Post St	674-1826	$$	Fast cheap pasta.
Vivande Porta Via	2125 Fillmore St	346-4430	$$$	First-rate Italian with a great deli for take-out.
Zao Noodle Bar	2406 California St	345-8088	$$	Fast, cheap noodles.

Arts and Entertainment · **Restaurants**

Key: $: Under $10 / $$: $10–$20 / $$$: $20–$30 / $$$$: $30+; * : Does not accept credit cards. / † : Accepts only American Express. All area codes are 415 unless otherwise noted.

Map 6 · Pacific Heights / Japantown

Harris'	2100 Van Ness Ave	673-1888	$$$$$	Local beef serving real California cattle.
House of Prime Rib	1906 Van Ness Ave	885-4605	$$$$	Beef and martini fest.
Mifune	Japan Ctr, 1737 Post St	922-0337	$$	Casual noodles.
Stars	555 Golden Gate Ave	861-7827	$$$$$	Somewhat passe, but still good. A safe pre-symphony choice (if you must).

Map 7 · Nob Hill / Chinatown / SOMA

Acquerello	1722 Sacramento St	567-5432	$$$$$	Good swanky Italian.
Allegro	1701 Jones St	928-4002	$$$$	Simple, neighborhood, white table cloth Italian.
Crustacean	1475 Polk St	776-2722	$$$$	Vietnamese roasted crab and garlic noodles.
Farallon	450 Post St	956-6969	$$$$$	Shi-shi seafood and a cool aquatic decor.
Fleur De Lys	777 Sutter St	673-7779	$$$$$	One of the greats.
Hyde Street Bistro	1521 Hyde St	292-4415	$$$	Casual neighborhood French.
Millennium	580 Geary Ave	345-3900	$$$$	Fancy vegan and organic everything.
Nob Hill Café	1152 Taylor St	776-6500	$$$	Still good.
Pakwan	501 O'Farrell St	776-0160	$$	Indian. Bare bones, cheap, and good.
Sears Fine Food	439 Powell St	788-1004	$$*	A Union Square breakfast institution.
Shalimar	532 Jones St	928-0333	$$*	Excellent, cheap, bare bones Indian.
Swan Oyster Depot	1517 Polk St	673-1101	$$$*	An institution. Open for lunch only, and of course you can't not have the oysters.
The Bagelry	2139 Polk St	441-3003	$*	Local, fresh-baked bagels.
The Big Four	Huntington Hotel, 1075 California St	771-1140	$$$$$	Classy, clubby, elegant San Francisco.
Tu Lan	8 6th St	626-0927	$$	Good Vietnamese in the seedy Tenderloin.
Venticello	1257 Taylor St	922-2545	$$$	Italian. Oozing Nob Hill charm.
Victoria Pastry Co	1362 Stockton St	781-2015	$$	One of the city's oldest bakeries, try the cakes and tiramisu.

Map 8 · Union Square / Embarcadero / South Beach

B44	44 Belden Pl	986-6287	$$$	Catalan and great paella.
Bacar	448 Brannan St	904-4100	$$$$$	Amazing wine list (loads by the glass, too). Upscale and trendy.
Bix	56 Gold St	433-6300	$$$$	First-rate martinis. The food's OK.
Boulevard	1 Mission St	543-6084	$$$$$	Wonderful classic San Francisco institution.
Cafe Bastille	22 Beldon Pl	986-5673	$$$	Popular French bistro downtown with outdoor seating.
Caffe Centro	12 South Park St	882-1500	$$	Cool cafe in South Park for a quick lunch.
Caffe Macaroni	50 Columbus Ave	956-9737	$$$*	Casual friendly Italian.
Elisabeth Daniel	580 Washington St	397-6129	$$$$$	Snooty, but getting better.
Enrico's Sidewalk Café	504 Broadway	982-6223	$$$$	Broadway fixture. Great live music and people watching.
Fifth Floor	Hotel Palomar, 12 4th St	348-1555	$$$$$	Fancy and elegant.
Globe	290 Pacific Ave	391-4132	$$$$	Casual California cuisine. Open late.
Harbor Village	4 Embarcadero Ctr	781-8833	$$$	Classy dim sum.
House of Nanking	919 Kearny St	421-1429	$$	Legendary cheap Chinese.
Hunan	110 Natoma St	546-4999	$$	Great Chinese.
Hunan	674 Sacramento St	788-2234	$$	Great Chinese.
Hunan	622 Jackson St	982-2844	$$	Great Chinese.
Kokkari Estiatorio	200 Jackson St	981-0983	$$$$$	Comfortable glamorous Greek.
Kyo-Ya	Palace Hotel, 2 New Montgomery St	546-5090	$$$$$	Top-drawer Japanese.
Le Central Bistro	453 Bush St	391-2233	$$$$	Clubby lunch scene.
Maya	303 Second St	543-2928	$$$	High-end Mexican.

MoMo's	760 Second St	227-8660	$$$$	Fun spot across from Pac Bell Park.
North Beach Pizza	715 Harrison St	371-0930	$$	Good local "chain" pizza.
One Market	1 Market St	777-5577	$$$$$	Consistently good.
Pakwan	653 Clay St	834-9904	$$	Indian. Bare bones, cheap, and good.
Plouf	40 Belden Pl	986-6491	$$$$	Really good mussels.
Rubicon	558 Sacramento St	434-4100	$$$$$	Another one of the greats.
Slanted Door	100 Brannan St	861-8032	$$$	First-rate Vietnamese. Make a reservation.
South Park Café	108 South Park St	495-7275	$$$	Distinguished casual French.
Tadich Grill	240 California St	391-1849	$$$$	Legendary old-world seafood.
Tommaso's	1042 Kearny St	398-9696	$$$	Best pizza in North Beach since 1935.
Tommy Toy's Cuisine Chinoise	655 Montgomery St	397-4888	$$$$$	Fancy, expensive Chinese.
Yank Sing	Rincon Ctr, 101 Spear St	957-9300	$$$	Terrific dim sum.
Zare	568 Sacramento St	291-9145	$$$$$	Northern Italian and Southern French.

Map 9 · Haight Ashbury / Cole Valley

Boulange de Cole Valley	1000 Cole St	242-2442	$$*	Cafe with excellent baked goods.
Cha Cha Cha	1801 Haight St	386-5758	$$$	Popular Caribbean-style tapas. Be ready to wait.
Eos Restaurant & Wine Bar	901 Cole St	566-3063	$$$$$	Asian fusion, nice wines.
Kan Zaman	1793 Haight St	751-9656	$$$	Popular Middle Eastern with hookas.
North Beach Pizza	1649 Haight St	751-2300	$$	Good local "chain" pizza.
North Beach Pizza	800 Stanyan St	751-2300	$$	Good local "chain" pizza.
Pork Store Café	1451 Haight St	864-6981	$$	Greasy breakfast joint.
Zazie's	941 Cole St	564-5332	$$$	

Map 10 · Castro / Lower Haight

2223 Restaurant	2223 Market St	431-0692	$$$$	Popular American
Brother-in-Law's Bar-B-Que	705 Divisadero St	931-7427	$$	Texas-style take-out ribs.
Burger Joint	700 Haight St	864-3833	$$	Jetsons-like burger joint.
Café Flore	2298 Market St	621-8579	$$*	Great people watching.
Chow	215 Church St	552-2469	$$	Good, affordable home-cookin'.
Herbivore	983 Valencia St	826-5657	$$	Calm, clean, and reasonable vegetarian.
Home	2100 Market St	503-0333	$$$	Comfy home-cookin'! Great patio in the back.
Indian Oven	233 Fillmore St	626-1628	$$$	Above-average Indian.
Kate's Kitchen	471 Haight St	626-3984	$$*	Breakfast and lunch with a Southern edge.
La Mediterranee	288 Noe St	431-7210	$$	Cozy Middle Eastern.
Ma Tante Sumi	4243 18th St	626-7864	$$$$	Well-known neighborhood Asian fusion.
Mecca	2029 Market St	621-7000	$$$$$	Glam hipsters and good food.
Pasta Pomodoro	598 Haight St	436-9800	$$	Fast, cheap pasta.
Pasta Pomodoro	2304 Market St	558-8123	$$	Fast, cheap pasta.
RNM	598 Haight St	551-7900	$$	Hip and trendy in the Lower Haight (lock the car).
Rosamunde Sausage Grill	545 Haight St	437-6851	$$*	Gourmet sausage joint.
Thai House	2200 Market St	864-5006	$$	Above-average Thai.
Thai House	151 Noe St	863-0374	$$	Above-average Thai.
Thep Phanom Thai Cuisine	400 Waller St	431-2526	$$$	Thai food at its finest.
Tin-Pan Asian Bistro	2251 Market St	565-0733	$$	Cheap, clean Asian fusion.
Zao Noodle Bar	3583 16th St	864-2888	$$	Fast, cheap noodles.

Arts and Entertainment • **Restaurants**

Key: $: Under $10 / $$: $10–$20 / $$$: $20–$30 / $$$$: $30+; * : Does not accept credit cards. / † : Accepts only American Express.
All area codes are 415 unless otherwise noted.

Map 11 • Hayes Valley / The Mission

Absinthe	398 Hayes St	551-1590	$$$$	Standard bistro fare and good cocktails.
Andalu	3198 16th St	621-2211	$$$$	Yet another hip attempt at tapas.
Blowfish, Sushi To Die For	2170 Bryant St	285-3848	$$$$	Sushi deluxe.
Burger Joint	807 Valencia St	824-3494	$$*	Jetsons-like burger joint.
Caffe Delle Stelle	395 Hayes St	252-1110	$$$	Cozy, simple Italian.
Cha Cha Cha @ Original McCarthy's	2327 Mission St	648-0504	$$$	Caribbean-style tapas.
Chez Spencer	82 14th St	864-2191	$$$	Pricey French.
Citizen Cake	399 Grove St	861-2228	$$$	Bakery cafe turned restaurant.
Delfina	3621 18th St	552-4055	$$$$	Exceptional Italian. If we ever get in we'll like it.
El Toro Taqueria	588 Valencia St	431-3351	$$	Fantastic tacos and burritos.
Hayes Street Grill	320 Hayes	863-5545	$$$$	Good basic seafood—popular with the symphony crowd.
Jardiniere	300 Grove St	861-5555	$$$$$	Warm, romantic, yummy.
Limon	3316 17th St	252-0918	$$$	Hip Peruvian.
Manora's Thai Cuisine	1600 Folsom St	861-6224	$$$	Above-average Thai.
Midori Mushi	465 Grove St	503-1377	$$$	Tiny, edgy Japanese.
Pakwan	3180 16th St	255-2440	$$	Indian. Bare bones, cheap, and good.
Paul K	199 Gough St	552-7132	$$$$	Mediterranean, open late.
Suppenkuche	601 Hayes St	252-9289	$$$	Authentic German and tasty beers.
Sushi Groove	1516 Folsom St	503-1950	$$$$	Hip sushi.
Taqueria Pancho Villa	3071 16th St	864-8840	$$	Try the prawn quesadilla.
Tartine Bakery	600 Guerrero St	487-2600	$*	Great French cafe.
Ti Couz	3108 16th St	252-7373	$$	Good, cheap crepes.
Timo's	842 Valencia St	647-0558	$$$	Lively tapas.
Tokyo Go Go	3174 16th St	864-2288	$$$$	Excellent Mission sushi.
Universal Café	2814 19th St	821-4608	$$$$	A really nice little spot.
Vicolo	201 Ivy St	863-2382	$$	Pizza with cornmeal crust. By the slice or the whole pie, this is a good thing.
Zuni Café	1658 Market St	552-2522	$$$$	An institution... and there's so much more than the sublime roasted chicken.

Map 12 • SOMA / Potrero Hill (North)

Chez Papa	1401 18th St	824-8210	$$$	Small, popular Provençal French.
Eliza's	1457 18th St	648-9999	$$$	Healthy modern Chinese.
Goat Hill Pizza	300 Connecticut St	641-1440	$*	Well-known Potrero Hill pizza joint.
Hunan	1016 Bryant St	861-5808	$$	Great Chinese.

Map 13 • SOMA East

Acme Chop House	24 Willie Mays Plaza	644-0240	$$$	Refined steakhouse at the ballpark.
Aperto	1434 18th St	252-1625	$$$	Cute, unpretentious Italian.
Bizou	598 Fourth St	543-2222	$$$	Great flatbread and beef cheeks.
Chez Papa Bistrot	1401 18th St	824-8210	$$$	French bistro that's quickly becoming a city favorite.
Fringale	570 Fourth St	543-0573	$$$$$	Typical French.
Kelly's Mission Rock	817 China Basin	626-5355	$$	Maritime joint, fish and chips, beer. Very casual, good deck.
Thanya & Salee's	1469 18th St	647-6469	$$$	Thai with an island style bar next door.
The Ramp	855 Terry Francois Blvd	621-2378	$$	Simple food with a great deck. Go on a sunny day.

Map 14 · Noe Valley

Chloe's Café	1399 Church st	648-4116	$$*	Popular Noe Valley brunch spot.
Eric's	1500 Church st	282-0919	$$	Modern, clean Chinese.
Firefly	4288 24th St	821-7652	$$$$	Fantastic, warm and cozy home-style restaurant.
Lovejoy's Tea Room	1351 Church St	648-5895	$$	Homey high tea. Chicks dig it.
Miss Millie's	4123 24th St	285-5598	$$$	Great breakfast place.
Pasta Pomodoro	4000 24th St	920-9904	$$	Fast, cheap pasta.

Map 15 · Mission (Outer)

Bruno's	2389 Mission St	648-7701	$$$	Way cool supper club that's still got it.
Cha Cha Cha	2327 Mission St	648-0504	$$$	Carribean-style tapas.
Firecracker	1007 1/2 Valencia St	642-3470	$$$	Trendy Chinese.
Foreign Cinema	2534 Mission St	648-7600	$$$$	Cool outdoor (and indoor) dining where you can catch a talkie in the courtyard.
Jay's Cheese Steak	3285 21st St	285-5200	$*	Philly-style cheesesteak.
La Luna	3126 24th St	282-7110	$$$	Creative Latin fusion.
La Rondalla	901 Valencia St	647-7474	$$*	It's always a party.
La Taqueria	2889 Mission St	285-7117	$$*	Hands down best tacos in town.
Roosevelt Tamale Parlor	2817 24th St	550-9213	$$*	Bare bones, and of course great tamales.
Watergate	1152 Valencia St	648-6000	$$$$	Nice, relaxed, European inspired foods.

Map 16 · Potrero Hill (Southwest)

Klein's Delicatessen	501 Connecticut St	821-9149	$*	Popular corner deli on Potrero Hill.

Map 18 · Outer Richmond (West) / Ocean Beach

Beach Chalet Brewery	1000 Great Hwy	386-8439	$$$	Brewpub with a view.

Map 20 · Richmond

Aziza	5800 Geary Blvd	752-2222	$$$$	Belly dancers and everything.
Chapeau!	1408 Clement St	750-9787	$$$$$	Casual hearty French.
Hong Kong Flower Lounge	5322 Geary Blvd	668-8998		Great Chinese and dim sum.
Kabuto Sushi	5116 Geary Blvd	752-5652	$$$	Fresh, consistent sushi.
Khan Toke Thai House	5937 Geary Blvd	668-6654	$$$	Thai with a garden.
La Vie	5830 Geary Blvd	668-8080	$$$	Tasty Vietnamese.
Ton Kiang	5821 Geary Blvd	387-8273	$$$	Authentic Chinese and good dim sum.

Map 21 · Inner Richmond

Bella Trattoria	3854 Geary Blvd	221-0305	$$$	Hit or miss neighborhood Italian.
Brother's Korean Restaurant	4128 Geary Blvd	387-7991	$$$	Cook it at your table Korean.
Brother's Korean Restaurant	4014 Geary Blvd	668-2028	$$$	Cook it at your table Korean.
Café Riggio	4112 Geary Blvd	221-2114	$$$	Above-average Italian.
Clementine	126 Clement St	381-0408	$$$$	Understated, but nice, French.
Coriya Hot Pot City	852 Clement St	387-7888	$$	More cook it at your table Korean.
Katia's Russian Tea Room	600 Fifth Ave	668-9292	$$$	Traditional Russian food, and tea too.
Le Soleil	133 Clement St	668-4848	$$$	Casual, clean-tasting Vietnamese.
Royal Thai	951 Clement St	386-1795	$$$	Above-average Thai.

Map 22 · Presidio Heights / Laurel Heights

Mel's Drive-In	3355 Geary Blvd	387-2255	$$	Anybody see American Graffiti?
Sociale	3665 Sacramento St	921-3200	$$$$	Upscale, casual patio dining.
Straits Café	3300 Geary Blvd	668-1783	$$$	High-end Singaporean.

Map 23 · Outer Sunset

Thanh Long	4101 Judah St	665-1146	$$$$$	Vietnamese roasted crab and garlic noodles.

Map 24 · Sunset

Marnee Thai	2225 Irving St	665-9500	$$$	Above-average Thai.
Micado	2126 Irving St	564-1122		Good Sushi
Shangri La	2026 Irving St	731-2548		Vegetarian Chinese.

Key: *$: Under $10 / $$: $10–$20 / $$$: $20–$30 / $$$$: $30+; * : Does not accept credit cards. / † : Accepts only American Express.*
All area codes are 415 unless otherwise noted.

Map 25 · Inner Sunset / Golden Gate Heights

Desiree	Film Society Bldg, 29 Mesa St	561-2336	$$	Tiny and wonderful. Only open for lunch. They'll make you a nice picnic too.
Ebisu	1283 Ninth Ave	566-1770	$$$$	Sushi worth the wait, and there's one at SFO now too.
Park Chow	1240 9th Ave	665-9012	$$	Comfort food.
Pasta Pomodoro	816 Irving St	566-0900	$$	Fast, cheap pasta.
PJ's Oyster Bed	737 Irving St	566-7775	$$$$	Cajun/Creole.

Map 26 · Parkside (Outer)

North Beach Pizza	3054 Taraval St	242-9100	$$	Good local "chain" pizza.

Map 27 · Parkside (Inner)

Rick's	1940 Taraval St	731-8900	$$$	Hawaiian-style American.

Map 29 · Twin Peaks

Pomelo	92 Judah St	731-6175	$$	Small, cheap, Asian-style foods.

Map 30 · West Portal

El Toreador	50 West Portal Ave	566-2673		Standard Mexican, very friendly.
Fresca	24 West Portal Ave	759-8087		Tasty Peruvian.
Manor Coffee Shop	321A West Portal Ave	661-2468		Diner food, good for breakfast.

Map 32 · Diamond Heights / Glen Park

Chenery Park	683 Chenery St	337-8537	$$$$	Chic American food.
La Corneto Taqueria	2834 Diamond St	469-8757		Great tacos and burritos.
Pomelo	1793 Church St	285-2257	$$	Small, cheap, Asian-style foods.
Tyger's	2798 Diamond St	239-4060		Busy breakfast joint on the weekends..

Map 35 · Bernal Heights

Blue Plate	3218 Mission St	282-6777	$$$	Fantastic comfort food.
Cottage Bakery	410 Cortland Ave	695-8777	$$	Great little bakery and wine bar behind Liberty Cafe.
Emmy's Spaghetti Shack	18 Virginia Ave	206-2086	$$*	Cozy, wonderful comfort foods.
Liberty Café & Bakery	410 Cortland Ave	695-8777	$$$	This is a great neighborhood restaurant.
Little Nepal	925 Cortland Ave	643-3881	$$	Cozy and casual Nepalese.
Maggie Mudd	903 Cortland Ave	641-5291	$*	Ice cream parlor and internet cafe.
Moki's Sushi & Pacific Grill	830 Cortland Ave	970-9336	$$$	Sushi and Cal-Asian food with a tiki patio.
Palatino	803 Cortland Ave	641-8899	$$$	Charming Italian.
Rock Soup	3299 Mission St	641-7687	$$	Live music, comfort food, relaxed atmosphere.
Taqueria Can-Cun	2211 Mission St	550-1414	$*	Gigantic burritos.
Valentina	419 Cortland Ave	285-6000	$$$	Small neighborhood Italian.

Map 38 · Excelsior / Crocker Amazon

North Beach Pizza	4787 Mission St	586-1400	$$	Good local "chain" pizza.

Sausalito

Avatars	2656 Bridgeway	332-8083	$$	Interesting Indian-fusion cuisine, such as curry enchiladas and tostadas.
Feng-Nian	2650 Bridgeway	331-5300	$$	Excellent Chinese.
Fred's Place	1917 Bridgeway	332-4575	$*	Great breakfast; don't miss the deep-fried french toast.
Sartaj India Cafe	43 Caledonia St	332-7103	$*	Tiny take-out joint with a few tables, offering a few choice Indian dishes and 'Indian burritos'. Don't miss the spicy eggs and chapati for breakfast.
Sushi Ran	107 Caledonia St	332-3620	$$$$$	Crowded, excllent, top-rated sushi.

Arts and Entertainment · **Shopping**

All area codes are 415 unless otherwise noted.

Map 1 · Marina / Cow Hollow (West)

Benefit	2219 Chestnut St	567-1173	Cosmetics galore.
Body Options	2108 Chestnut St	567-1122	Women's sports and yoga wear.
Books Inc	2251 Chestnut St	931-3633	
Chadwick's of London	2068 Chestnut St	775-3423	Lingerie.
City Optix	2154 Chestnut St	921-1188	Cool eyewear.
Fiori	2314 Chestnut St	346-1100	Well done flowers.
Fleet Feet	2076 Chestnut St	921-7188	Running shoes and clothes.
House of Magic	2025 Chestnut St	346-2218	Magic supplies and fun plastic toys.
Lucca Delicatessen	2120 Chestnut St	921-7873	Good Italian deli and staples.
Lucky Brand	2301 Chestnut St	749-3750	Jeans and casual stuff for gals and guys.
Pure Beauty	2085 Chestnut St	922-2526	The 411 on beauty products.
Smash	2030 Chestnut St	673-4736	Hip shoes.

Map 2 · Marina / Cow Hollow (East)

Ambassador Toys	1981 Union St	345-8697	Great toys and books for junior.
Ambiance	1864 Union St	923-9797	All the hip local girls shop here.
Canyon Beachwear	1728 Union St	885-5070	All bikinis, all the time.
Jest Jewels	1869 Union St	563-8839	Super girly store. Chicks dig it. Guys, just sit on the bench outside and wait.
Kozo Arts	1969A Union St	351-2114	Fancy and beautiful paper. Handmade books.
Krimsa	2190 Union St	441-4321	Beautiful handmade rugs, from one of a kind oriental to modern.
MetroSport	2198 Filbert St	923-6453	Running, biking, and swimming gear.
Plumpjack Wines	3201 Fillmore St	346-9870	Great wine selelction with a really knowledgable staff and some reasonable prices.
Uko	2070 Union St	563-0330	Hip fashions for men and women—cool little store.

Map 3 · Russian Hill / Fisherman's Wharf

Andrew Rothstein Fine Foods	2238 Polk St	447-4094	Upscale deli, dinners to go.
Atelier des Modistes	1903 Hyde St	775-0545	Custom made evening and bridal gowns. By appointment only.
Brown Dirt Cowboy	2406 Polk St	922-9065	Eclectic home decor.
Focus Gallery	2423 Polk St	567-9067	Local photography with a darkroom available for hourly or monthly rental.
Nest	2340 Polk St	292-6198	French inspired gifts and things.
Prize	1415 Green St	771-7215	Vintage collectables
Smoke Signals	2223 Polk St	292-6025	International magazine stand.
Swallowtail	2217 Polk St	567-1555	Unique, eclectic, and quirky objects. Frequented by stylists and designers for shoots and props.
Tower Records	2525 Jones St	885-0500	Convenient record store when you've got to get that new release. Don't miss the Classical Annex across the street.
William Cross Wine Merchants	2253 Polk St	346-1314	Great little wine shop on Russian Hill and don't miss the tasting bar in the back.

Map 4 · North Beach (East) / Telegraph Hill

101 Music	1414 Grant Ave	392-6369	Vintage vinyl for serious collectors.
A Cavelli & Sons	1441 Stockton St	421-4219	All kinds of Italian goods.
AB Fits	1519 Grant Ave	982-5726	Jeans from all over the world
Biordi Arts	412 Columbus Ave	392-8096	Imported Italian handmade Majolica pottery.
Eastwind Books & Trading Co	1435 Stockton St	772-5888	Chinese & Asian culture & medicine books
Liguria	1700 Stockton St	421-3786	This is the best place to buy focaccia—go early, they will sell out.
Tilt	507 Columbus Ave	788-2211	Postcard mania for short attention span browsing

Map 5 • Pacific Heights / Western Addition

American Pie	3101 Sacramento St	929-8025	
Artisan Cheese	2413 California St	929-8610	Tiny shop with excellent cheeses.
Benefit	2117 Fillmore	567-0242	Cosmetic galore.
Betsy Johnson	2033 Fillmore St	567-2726	Fun(ky) women's clothing.
Boulangerie Bay Bread	2325 Pine St	440-0356	Sublime bakery and patisserie. Great breads and excellent little lemon tarts.
Button Down	3145 Sacramento St	563-1311	Very high-end, very pricey, and very nice men's and women's sportswear.
Crossroads	1901 Fillmore St	775-8885	Used clothes.
Departures from the Past	2028 Fillmore St	885-3377	Vintage clothing.
Fetish	344 Presidio Ave	409-7429	Ultra girly shop for unique beautiful women's shoes.
Forrest Jones	3274 Sacramento St	567-2483	Housewares.
Fresh Air Bicycles	1943 Divisadero St	563-4824	Racing frames, complete bikes, mountain bikes.
George	2411 California St	441-0564	Priveledged pet supplies.
Gimme Shoes	2358 Fillmore St	441-3040	Top-notch hip shoes.
Kiehl's	2360 Fillmore St	359-9260	Skin care.
Marcus Books	1712 Fillmore St	346-4222	African-American history, culture and thought.
Margartet O'Leary	2400 Fillmore St	771-9982	Really nice sweaters and sportswear made on Potrero Hill.
Mrs Dewson's Hats	2050 Fillmore St	346-1600	Stylish chapeaux for men and women.
Narumi	1902 Filmore St	346-8626	Decorards and gifts from Japan
Nest	2300 Fillmore St	292-6199	French-inspired gifts and things.
Paper Source	1925 Fillmore St	409-7710	All kinds of paper for all kinds of things.
Quatrine	3235 Sacramento St	345-8590	Nice, washable furniture. It's not cheesy, really.
Shabby Chic	2185 Fillmore St	771 3881	Big, comfy, casual, expensive furniture.
Sue Fisher King	3067 Sacramento St	888-911-7276	Top notch bath, bedroom, tabletop, & home furnishings.
The Bar	340 Presidio Ave	409-4901	Great selection of designers at this chic women's boutique.
Zinc Details	1905 Fillmore St	776-2100	Clean, contemporary, home furnishings.
Zonal	1942 Fillmore St	553-2220	Modern American and vintage furniture. Nice collections of '30s & '40s vintage steel furniture.

Map 6 • Pacific Heights / Japantown

American Rag	1305 Van Ness Ave	474-5214	Trendy new and vintage clothes.
Maruwa Food Co	1737 Post St	563-1901	Completely Japanese grocery. Cool packaging too.
Whole Foods Market	1765 California St	674-0500	Great produce, meats, fish, and cheese.

Map 7 • Nob Hill / Chinatown / SOMA

City Discount	1542 Polk St	771-4649	Great deals on cooking-related items run by the nicest woman ever.
European Book Co	925 Larkin St	474-0626	European language and travel.
General Bead	637 Minna St	255-2323	Beads, beads, beads. Best selection in town.
Ghiradelli	44 Stockton St	397-3615	Site of the West Coast chocolate empire's original factory
Imperial Tea Court	1411 Powell St	788-6080	Traditional Chinese teahouse with an absolutely amazing selection of teas.
Leonard's 2001	2001 Polk St	921-2001	Cheese and hard to find specialty gourmet foods.
Plants on Polk	1475 Polk St	921-1012	Unique and creative asian-inspired plant shop.
Rasputin's	69 Powell St	800-350-8700	Another excellent independent music store.
The Levi's Store	300 Post St	501-0100	Levi's flagship store where you can get a pair of custom jeans made just for you.
Zonal	2139 Polk St	553-2220	Modern American and vintage furniture. Nice collections of '30s and '40s vintage steel furniture.

Map 8 • Union Square / Embarcadero / South Beach

Adolph Gasser	181 2nd St	495-3852	One of the best camera stores in town.
AG Ferrari Fine Foods	688 Mission St	344-0644	Italian food and wine, and wonderful deli items.
Califia Books	20 Hawthorne St	284-0314	Fine press, letterpress and artists' books
City Lights	261 Columbus Ave	362-4921	Made famous by the Beats, this bookstore will always be cool. Check out the poetry room upstairs.
Discount Cameras	33 Kearny St	392-1103	One of the other best camera stores in town.
Don Sherwood's Golf & Tennis World	320 Grant Ave	989-5000	Local chain for duffers and pros.
Gump's	135 Post St	982-1616	Very upscale home décor.
Japonesque	824 Montgomery St	391-8860	Japanese gallery of the most beautiful rocks and wood you've ever seen.
John Walker & Co	175 Sutter St	986-2707	Liquor store with style, class, elegance, and great wines, too.
Margaret O'Leary	1 Claude Ln	381-1010	Really nice sweaters and sportswear made on Potrero Hill.
Marina Morrison Bridal Salon	30 Maiden Ln	984-9360	Quintessential bridal salon.
Scharffen Berger	Ferry Building, The Embarcadero	981-9150	Chocolate nirvana, made in Berkeley. The best ever.
Stacey's Bookstore	581 Market St	421-4687	General bookstore established in 1921.
Sur La Table	77 Maiden Ln	732-7900	Remarkable kitchen stuff.
Sur La Table	Ferry Building, The Embarcadero		Remarkable kitchen stuff.
William Stout Architectural Books	804 Montgomery St	391-6757	Architecture, art, furniture and landscaping books.
Wings America	262 Sutter St	989-9464	Aircraft models and other flight-related goods.

Map 9 • Haight Ashbury / Cole Valley

Ambiance	1458 Haight St	522-5095	All the hip local girls shop here.
Amoeba Music	1855 Haight St	831-1200	Huge music store, new and used.
Anubis Warpus	1525 Haight St	431-2218	Tattoo, body manipulation, and general oddness...
Backseat Betty	1590 Haight St	431-8393	Racy women's clothes, and some nice stuff, too.
Cal Surplus	1541 Haight St	861-0404	Patches with your name on it and army surplus kinds of things.
Crossroads	1519 Haight St	355-0555	Used clothes.
Discount Fabrics	1432 Haight St	621-5584	A little dingy, but fabric people go nuts for this place.
Haight Ashbury Music Center	1540 Haight St	863-7327	Guitars, drums, flutes, and all your music needs.
Kweejibo	1612 Haight St	552-3555	Locally designed and manufactured men's clothing. Pretty cool.
La Rosa Vintage	1711 Haight St	668-3744	Fine vintage clothing.
Luichiny	1529 Haight St	252-7065	Shoes as art. Beautiful Italian next to outlandish (and sometimes scary) boots.
Mendel's Art Supplies	1556 Haight St	621-1287	Art supplies and far out fabrics.
Occasions Boutique	858 Cole St	731-0153	Beauty products, candles and scents
Off the Wall	1669 Haight St	863-8170	Ready-to-hang posters and prints as well as custom framing
Piedmont Boutique	1452 Haight St	864-8075	The ultimate source for custom-made hats, feather boas, wigs, and other fancy frilly stuff.
Positively Haight	1400 Haight St	252-8747	All your Grateful Dead and psychedelic needs. Get your Steal Your Face for the back of your car here.
San Francisco Cyclery	494 Fredrick St	221-2413	General bikes and gear.
Say Cheese	856 Cole St	665-5020	One of the best specialty cheese shops in the city. Wine and other epicurean delights as well.
Shoe Biz	1446 Haight St	864-0990	Hard to find and alternative style shoes. Yes, there really are 3 on Haight.
Shoe Biz II	1553 Haight St	861-3933	See above.
Super Shoe Biz	1420 Haight St	861-0313	See above.
The Booksmith	1644 Haight St	863-8688	Good independent bookstore.
Villains	1672 Haight St	626-5939	Urban chic institution.
Villains Vault	1653 Haight St	864-7727	Upscale urban chic housed in an old bank.
Wasteland	1660 Haight St	863-3150	Super cool vintage clothes—another Haight Street institution.
X Generation	1401 Haight St	863-6040	Hip, trendy, sparkly t's and sexy little dresses.

Map 10 • Castro / Lower Haight

A Different Light	489 Castro St	431-0891	Gay, lesbian, and bisexual writing.
AG Ferrari Fine Foods	468 Castro St	255-6590	Italian foods and wine, and wonderful deli items.
Best in Show	300 Sanchez St	863-PETS	Best in pet shops. They even clean teeth.
Cookin'	339 Divisadero St	861-1854	Huge, disorganized selection of professional cookware.
Costumes on Haight	735 Haight St	621-1356	Huge and funky selection of costumes for all budgets all the time.
Crossroads	2231 Market St	626-8989	Used clothes.
Gamescape	333 Divisadero St	621-4263	All kinds of board and computer games.
Groove Merchant	687 Haight St	252-5766	Lots of vinyl.
H Starch	142 Filmore St	864-8343	Beautiful custom-designed lighting.
Harvest Market	2285 Market St	626-0805	Remarkable healthy soups and one of the best salad bars in town. Fancy groceries too.
Manasek	2344 Market St	621-3321	Traditional artist's supplies.
Only on Castro	518A Castro St	522-0122	Large variety of home furnishings.
Streetlight Records	2350 Market St	888-396-2350	New, used, and rare music.
The Bead Store	417 Castro St	861-7332	All your basic beading supplies plus exotics and handblown glass.
Tower Records	2280 Market St	255-5920	Convenient record store when you've got to get that new release.

Map 11 • Hayes Valley / The Mission

826 Valencia	826 Valencia St	642-5905	Writing center for students and pirate supply store. Need lard, flags, eye patches, mops, glass eyes, and the like? One of our favorite places.
AC Trading	2370 Mission St	337-9910	Trinkets and gag gifts—good browsing.
Alabaster	597 Hayes St	558-0482	High end, upscale alabaster everything. Great lamps, vessels, urns, and more.
Alternative Design Studio	3458 18th St	255-2787	Handmade and imported hats.
Anderson Harrison	552 Hayes St	554-0435	Out-of-print and uncommon books
Babies	235 Gough St	701-7387	Everything you need to pamper your pooch.
Bombay Ice Creamery	552 Valencia St	431-1103	Indian ice cream like Almond Saffron Pistachio, and Rose.
Borderlands	866 Valencia St	824-8203	Sci-fi, fantasy and horror.
Buu	506 Hayes St	626-1503	High-end clothing and housewares.
Champ de Mars	347 Hayes St	252-9434	Frenchy furniture and housewares.
Dark Garden	321 Linden St	431-7684	Custon made corsets, bridal gowns and bras.
Evelyn's	381 Hayes St	255-1815	Antique Chinese furniture.
Flax	1699 Market St	552-2355	Excellent art and craft supplies for all kinds of projects.
Flight 001	525 Hayes St	487-1001	Hip travel store with everything you need to carry everything you want everywhere you go.
Get Lost	1825 Market St	437-0529	Travel books, maps, globes, and travel accessories.
Gimme Shoes	416 Hayes St	864-0691	Top-notch hip shoes.
Good Vibrations	601B Valencia St	974-2504	Sex toys, books, videos. Friendly staff supplies straightforward information.
Howling Bull Syndicate	826 Valencia St	282-0339	Counterculture books, toys and music.
M&W	2352 Mission St	643-1224	Cheap, bizarre gifts and other stuff.
Paxton's Gate	824 Valencia St	824-1872	Taxidermy, fossils, and other things once living.
Pomp	516 Hayes St	864-1830	Moderm furniture.
Prop City	1645 Market St	621-4390	Home furnishings, movie props and sets.
Rainbow Grocery	1745 Folsom St	863-0620	Best natural, organic, vegetarian-focused, foods market in town—not just for hippies anymore.
Subterranean Shoe Room	877 Valencia St	401-9504	Eclectic selection of shoes ranging from classic sneaks to casual urban to classic boots. Totally cool.
Trout Farm Retrospect Fine Furniture	1649 Market St	863-7414	Fine vintage furniture.

Map 12 • SOMA / Potrero Hill (North)

Flower Mart	640 Brannan St	392-7944	THE wholesale flower market. Opens to the public at 10:00 am.
Joseph Schmidt Confections	1489 16th St	861-8682	Very high-quality chocolates and sweets.
Podesta Baldocci	410 Harriet St	346-1300	A San Francisco institution for elegant flowers.
Stormy Leather	1158 Howard St	626-1672	The city's best alternative leather.
The Ribbonerie	191 Potrero Ave	626-6184	Absolutely every kind of ribbon ever.

Map 13 • SOMA East

Arch	99 Missouri St	433-2724	All your drafting and graphic design needs. They sell cool quirky gifts too.

K & L Wine Merchants	638 4th St	896-1734	The best wine shop in town. Great selection, including old and rare wines. Great prices too.
Limn	290 Townsend St	543-5466	Modern furniture.
Sports Basment	1301 6th St		Warehouse sporting goods at outlet prices.

Map 14 • Noe Valley

Ambiance	3985 24th St	647-7144	All the hip local girls shop here.
Noe Valley Bread Co	4073 24th St	550-1405	Great bread & pasteries, supplies lots of restaurants.
Plumpjack Wines	4011 24th St	282-3841	Great wine selelction with a really knowledgable staff and some reasonable prices.
See Jane Run	3870 24th St	401-8338	Women's athletic gear.
Streetlight Records	3979 24th St	888-682-3550	New, used, and rare music.

Map 15 • Mission (Outer)

Aquarius Records	1055 Valencia St	647-2272	Independent record shop with all types of music.
Retro Fit	910 Valencia St	550-1530	Vintage used clothes and remakes of old t-shirts.
The Freewheel	980 Valencia St	643-9213	Bike parts, accessories, and clothing.
Valencia Cyclery	1077 Valencia St	550-6600	Great bike shop, and repairs are at 1065 Valencia.
X-21 Modern	896 Valencia St		Funky retro furniture and they rent props too. Need a giant cowboy boot?

Map 20 • Richmond

Hobby Company of San Francisco	5150 Geary Blvd	386-2802	Independent source for craft and hobby supplies.
Purple Skunk	5820 Geary Blvd	668-7905	Skate, surf and snowboard gear.
San Francisco Brewcraft	1555 Clement St	751-9338	Mmmm beer. Everything you need to make beer.

Map 21 • Inner Richmond

| Green Apple Books and Music | 506 Clement St | 387-2272 | Get lost for hours in here, literally. New and used books and music. |
| Sloat Garden Center | 327 3rd Ave | 752-1614 | All kinds of plants and gardening supplies. |

Map 22 • Presidio Heights / Laurel Heights

AG Ferrari Fine Foods	3490 California St	923-4470	Italian foods and wine, and wonderful deli items.
Bryan's Quality Meats	3445 California St	752-0179	Best place to buy meat, fish, and poultry in SF.
Kindersport	3566 Sacramento St	563-7778	Kids' ski and sport outfitters.
Mom's the Word	3385 Sacramento St	441-8261	Funky maternity clothes.
The Grocery Store	3625 Sacramento St	928-3615	High-end casual women's clothes.

Map 25 • Inner Sunset / Golden Gate Heights

Andronico's Market	1200 Irving St	661-3220	Another good spot for fancy groceries.
Oriental Art Gallery	1340 9th Ave	681-6448	Asian paper and brushes; doll and figurine accessories.
Wishbone	601 Irving St	242-5540	Unique shopping experience for individual tastes-personal and home items. You love Wishbone.

Map 26 • Parkside (Outer)

Free as a Bird	3620 Wawona St	665-4359	Wind powered stuff.
Occidental Power	3629 Taraval St	681-8861	
Sloat Garden Center	2700 Sloat Blvd	566-4415	All kinds of plants and gardening supplies.

Map 27 • Parkside (Inner)

| Tower Records | 3205 20th Ave | 681-2001 | When you've got to get that new release. |

Map 30 • West Portal

Ambassador Toys	186 West Portal Ave	759-8697	Great toys and books for junior.
Growing Up	240 West Portal Ave	661-6304	Books and toys for kids.
Hausen Home	80 West Portal Ave	731-6600	Stuff for the home.
Irish Delights	77 West Portal Ave	664-1250	Irish food and gifts.

Sausalito

Great Overland Book Co	215 Caledonia St	332-1532	Used bookshop; lots of nautical books.
Pinestreet Papery	42 1/2 Caledonia St	332-5458	High-quality paper goods.
Sausalito Ferry Company	688 Bridgeway	332-9590	Paul Frank merchandise and other hipster-wanna-be paraphenalia.

Arts and Entertainment • **Theaters**

Perhaps you prefer the "serious" stagecraft of thespians from the American Conservatory Theater or the Curran. Or maybe the pomp and hilarity of Beach Blanket Babylon is more to your liking. San Francisco has a solid array of both serious and whimsical theatrical venues, plus several smaller treasures like the "Word for Word" series at the Magic Theater in Fort Mason and the Brava! For Women in the Arts.

All area codes are 415 unless otherwise noted.

Theater	Address	Phone	Map
AP Gianni Auditorium	555 California St	777-3211	8
Actor's Theatre of San Francisco	533 Sutter St	296-9179	7
Alcazar Theatre	650 Geary St	441-6655	7
American Conservatory Theater	405 Geary St	749-2228	7
Audium	1616 Bush St	564-2324	6
Bannam Place Theater	50 Bannam Pl	986-2701	4
Bayfront Theater	Fort Mason Center, Building B	474-8935	2
Beach Blanket Babylon	678 Green St	421-4222	4
Bindlestiff Studio	185 6th St	974-1167	7
Brava! For Women in the Arts	2781 24th St	641-7657	15
Buriel Clay Theatre	762 Fulton St	292-1850	6
Cellspace	2050 Bryant St	648-7562	11
Center for Variety Arts	608 Taraval St	242-4433	30
Climate Theater	285 9th St	364-1411	12
Club Fugazi	687 Green St	421-4222	4
Curran Theater	445 Geary St	551-2000	7
Dance Mission	3316 24th St	826-4499	15
El Teatro de la Esperanza	2940 16th St	255-2320	11
Eureka Theater	215 Jackson St	788-1125	8
Exit on Taylor	277 Taylor St		7
Exit Theater	156 Eddy St	673-3847	7
Florence Gould Theatre	100 34th Ave	750-3638	19
Golden Gate Theatre	1 Taylor St	551-2000	7
Herbst Theatre	401 Van Ness Ave	621-6600	6
Il Teatro 450	449 Powell St	433-1172	7
Intersection for the Arts	446 Valencia St	626-2787	11
Jon Sims Center for the Performing Arts	1519 Mission St	554-0402	11
Le Palais Nostalgique	Piers 27-29	438-2668	4
Lorraine Hansberry Theatre	555 Sutter St	288-0336	7
Magic Theatre	Fort Mason Center, Building D	441-8822	2
Marines Memorial Theatre	609 Sutter St	771-6900	7
Mission Cultural Center for Latino Arts	2868 Mission St	821-1155	15
New Conservatory Theatre Center	25 S Van Ness Ave	861-8972	11
Next Stage Theater	1620 Gough St	248-9371	6
Noh Space	2840 Mariposa St	621-7978	11
ODC Theater	3153 17th St	863-9834	11
Orpheum Theatre	1192 Market St	551-2000	7
Palace of Fine Arts Theatre	3301 Lyon St	567-6642	1
Phoenix Theatre	414 Mason St	989-0023	7
Post Street Theatre	450 Post St	362-9065	7
Shelton Theatre	533 Sutter St	433-7875	7
Shotwell Studios	3252A 19th St		11
The Marsh	1062 Valencia St	826-5750	15
The Xenodrome	1320 Potrero Ave	285-9366	16
Theater Rhinoceros	2940 16th St	861-5079	11
Theatre Artaud	450 Florida St	621-7797	11
Theatre on the Square	450 Post St	433-9500	7
Thick House	1695 18th St		12
Venue 9	252 9th St	626-2169	12
Victoria Theatre	2961 16th St	863-7576	11
Yerba Buena Center for the Arts Theatre	700 Howard St	978-2787	8
Young Performers Theater	Fort Mason Center, Building C	346-5550	2

San Francisco Museum of Modern Art

OPEN LATE.
1/2 PRICE.

THURSDAY
NITES@SFMOMA

Kick off your Thursday nights with STYLE! Meet your friends at SFMOMA to enjoy the RELAXED ATMOSPHERE of the galleries after hours, GREAT SHOPPING at the MuseumStore, and TASTY FOOD at Caffè Museo. SFMOMA is open late EVERY THURSDAY NIGHT, from 6 to 9 p.m., for HALF-PRICE admission.

Thursday nights are sponsored by BANANA REPUBLIC
Media sponsors: San Francisco Bay Guardian and SFSTATION.COM

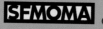 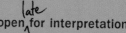 open late for interpretation

151 Third Street   415 357 4000   www.sfmoma.org

A retail experience
that recreates the
thrill of an international
airport with merchandise
that addresses every
travel need with style
and comfort.

 FLIGHT 001

NEW YORK	96 GREENWICH AVENUE
	212 691 1001
SAN FRANCISCO	525 HAYES STREET
	415 487 1001
LOS ANGELES	8235 WEST 3RD STREET
	323 966 0001
FLIGHT 001 SHUTTLE	HENRI BENDEL
	712 5TH AVENUE 2ND FLOOR
AUTOPILOT	FLIGHT001.COM

Street Index

Street	Page	Grid
1st St	8	A1/A2/B2
2nd Ave		
(2-798)	21	A2/B2
(1200-1298)	29	A1
2nd St	8	A1/B1/B2
3rd Ave		
(2-798)	21	A2/B2
(1200-1398)	29	A1
3rd St		
(1-650)	8	B1/B2
(651-2250)	13	A1/B1
(2251-3150)	17	A1/B1
(3151-5263)	36	A2/B2
(5265-6699)	40	A1/B1
4th Ave		
(100-798)	21	A2/B2
(1200-1398)	29	A1
4th St		
(1-599)	8	B1
(556-1599)	13	A1/A2
5th Ave		
(2-798)	21	A2/B2
(1200-1698)	29	A1
5th St		
(1-365)	7	B2
(366-405)	8	B1
(406-621)	12	A2
(622-899)	13	A1
6th Ave		
(-)	37	B2
(2-801)	21	A2/B2
(802-1598)	29	A1
6th St		
(1-253)	7	B2
(254-1250)	12	A2
(1251-1699)	13	A1/B1
7th Ave		
(2-749)	21	A1/B1
(750-1798)	25	A2/B2
(1-1150)	12	A2/A1/B2
7th St		
(16-115)	7	B1/B2
(1151-1599)	13	B1
8th Ave		
(2-801)	21	A1/B1
(802-1998)	25	A2/B2
8th St		
(1-75)	7	B1
(76-1299)	12	A1/A2/B2
9th Ave		
(2-1197)	21	A1/B1
(1198-2398)	25	A1/B1
9th St		
(1-95)	7	B1
(96-699)	12	A1/B1
10th Ave		
(2-801)	21	A1/B1
(802-2198)	25	A2/B2
10th St	11	A2
11th Ave		
(2-798)	21	A1/B1
(1200-1998)	25	A2/B2
11th St	11	A2
12th Ave		
(2-798)	21	A1/B1
(1200-2298)	25	A1/B1
(2300-2398)	30	A1
12th St	11	A1/A2
13th St	11	A1/A2
14th Ave		
(2-798)	20	A2/B2
(1200-2249)	25	A1/B1
(2250-2898)	30	A1
14th St		
(1-519)	11	B1/B2
(520-1099)	10	B1/B2/A2
15th Ave		
(2-798)	20	A2/B2
(1200-2249)	25	A1/B1
(2250-2898)	30	A1
15th St		
(1-750)	12	B1/B2
(751-1825)	11	B1/B2
(1826-2599)	10	B1/B2
16th Ave		
(2-798)	20	A2/B2
(1200-2249)	25	A1/B1
(2250-2698)	30	A1
16th St		
(101-1050)	13	B1
(1051-2099)	12	B2
(2101-3266)	11	B1/B2
(3267-3899)	10	B1/B2
17th Ave		
(2-798)	20	A2/B2
(1200-2249)	25	A1/B1
(2250-2698)	30	A1
17th St		
(401-1350)	13	B1/B2
(1351-2399)	12	B2
(2401-3516)	11	B2
(3517-4250)	10	B1/B2
(4251-4999)	9	B1/B2
18th Ave		
(2-798)	20	A2/B2
(1200-2249)	25	A1/B1
(2250-2698)	30	A1
18th St		
(501-4719)	29	A2
(551-1450)	13	B1
(1451-2499)	12	B2
(2501-3625)	11	B1/B2
(3626-4514)	10	B1/B2
19th Ave		
(2-798)	20	A1/B1
(1200-2249)	24	A2/B2
(2250-3349)	27	A2/B2
(3350-3874)	28	A2/B2
(3875-4198)	33	B1
19th St		
(501-4849)	29	A2
(551-1450)	13	B1
(1451-2499)	12	B2
(2501-3625)	11	B1/B2
(3626-4525)	10	B2/B1
20th Ave		
(2-7428)	20	A1/B1
(1200-2249)	24	A2/B2
(2250-3298)	27	A2/B2
20th St		
(301-1250)	17	A1
(1251-2650)	16	A2/A1
(2651-3750)	15	A1/A2
(3751-4599)	14	A1/A2
21st Ave		
(2-798)	20	A1/B1
(1200-2249)	24	A2/B2
(2250-3098)	27	A2/B2
21st St		
(2601-3412)	15	A1/A2
(3413-4399)	14	A1/A2
22nd Ave		
(2-798)	20	A1/B1
(1200-2249)	24	A2/B2
(2250-3098)	27	A2/B2
22nd St		
(401-1250)	17	A1
(251-2625)	16	A1/A2
(2626-3411)	15	A1/A2
(3412-4299)	14	A1/A2
23rd Ave		
(100-798)	20	A1/B1
(1200-2098)	24	A2/B2
(2400-3098)	27	A2/B2
23rd St		
(401-1399)	17	A1
(1501-2725)	16	B1/A2
(2726-3612)	15	A1/A2
(3613-4561)	14	A1/A2
(4562-4599)	29	B2
24th Ave		
(100-898)	19	A2/B2
(1200-2249)	24	A2/B2
(2250-3098)	27	A2/B2
24th St		
(301-999)	17	B1/A2
(2101-2725)	16	B1
(2726-3623)	15	B1/A2
(3624-4499)	14	B1/B2/A2
25th Ave		
(2-1197)	19	A2/B2
(1198-2249)	24	A2/B2
(2250-3098)	27	A2/B2
25th St		
(101-1450)	17	B1/B2
(1451-2825)	16	B2/B1
(2826-3725)	15	B1/B2
(3726-4899)	14	B1/B2
26th Ave		
(2-898)	19	A2/B2
(1200-2249)	24	A2/B2
(2250-3098)	27	A2/B2
26th St		
(801-1099)	17	B1
(1701-2499)	16	B1/B2
(2801-3725)	15	B1/B2
(3726-4899)	14	B1/B2
27th Ave		
(2-898)	19	A2/B2
(1200-2298)	24	A2/B2
(2300-2598)	27	A1/A2
27th St		
(1-150)	35	A1
(151-899)	14	B1/B2
28th Ave		
(100-898)	19	A2/B2
(1200-2249)	24	A1/B1
(2250-2698)	27	A1
28th St	14	B1/B2
29th Ave		
(100-898)	19	A2/B2
(1200-2249)	24	A1/B1
(2250-2598)	27	A1
29th St		
(1-150)	35	A1
(151-699)	32	A1/A2

Street	Page	Grid
30th Ave		
(100-901)	19	A2/B2
(902-951)	Golden Gate Park	
(952-2249)	24	A1/B1
(2250-2598)	27	A1
30th St	32	A1/A2
31st Ave		
(200-898)	19	A1/B1
(1200-2249)	24	A1/B1
(2250-2698)	27	A1
32nd Ave		
(100-898)	19	A1/B1
(1200-2249)	24	A1/B1
(2250-2598)	27	A1
33rd Ave		
(400-898)	19	B1
(1200-2249)	24	A1/B1
(2250-2698)	27	A1
34th Ave		
(2-898)	19	A1/B1
(1200-2249)	24	A1/B1
(2250-2898)	27	A1/B1
35th Ave		
(400-898)	19	B1
(1200-2249)	24	A1/B1
(2250-2898)	27	A1/B1
36th Ave		
(2-902)	19	A1/B1
(1200-2249)	24	A1/B1
(2250-2898)	27	A1/B1
37th Ave		
(400-898)	19	B1
(1200-2249)	23	A2/B2
(2250-2898)	26	A2/B2
38th Ave		
(400-898)	19	A1/B1
(1200-2249)	23	A2/B2
(2250-2798)	26	A2/B2
39th Ave		
(400-898)	18	A2/B2
(1200-2249)	23	A2/B2
(2250-2898)	26	A2/B2
40th Ave		
(400-898)	18	A2/B2
(1200-2249)	23	A2/B2
(2250-2798)	26	A2/B2
41st Ave		
(400-898)	18	A2/B2
(1200-2249)	23	A2/B2
(2250-2798)	26	A2/B2
42nd Ave		
(400-898)	18	A2/B2
(1200-2249)	23	A2/B2
(2250-2798)	26	A2/B2
43rd Ave		
(400-898)	18	A2/B2
(1200-2249)	23	A2/B2
(2250-2798)	26	A1/B1
44th Ave		
(400-898)	18	A2/B2
(1200-2249)	23	A2/B2
(2250-2798)	26	A1/B1
45th Ave		
(400-898)	18	A2/B2
(1200-2249)	23	A2/B2
(2250-2798)	26	A1/B1
46th Ave		
(400-898)	18	A2/B2
(1200-2249)	23	A1/A2/B2
(2250-2798)	26	A1/B1
47th Ave		
(400-901)	18	A1/B1
(902-2249)	23	A1/B1
(2250-2798)	26	A1/B1
48th Ave		
(400-898)	18	A1/B1
(1200-2249)	23	A1/B1
(2250-2498)	26	A1

A

Street	Page	Grid
Abbey St	10	B2
Acacia St	39	B1
Acadia St	32	B1
Access Rd 1	35	B1
(651-1099)	32	B2
Access Rd 3	39	B2
	40	B1
Acevedo Ave	28	B2
Acorn Aly	7	A1
Acton St	34	B1
Ada Ct	7	B1
Adair St	11	B1
Addison St	32	A1
Adele Ct	7	A2
Admiral Ave	32	B2
Adolph Sutro Ct	29	A1
Aerial Way	25	B1
Agnon Ave	32	B2
Agua Way	31	A1
Ahern Way	12	A2
Alabama St		
(101-750)	11	B2
(751-1550)	15	A2/B2
(1551-1873)	35	A2
Aladdin Ter	3	B2
Alameda St		
(201-399)	13	B2
(1701-2299)	12	B2/B1
(2301-2899)	11	B2
Albatross Ct	37	B2
Alberta St	39	B2
Albion St	11	B1
Alder St	39	B2
Aldrich Aly	8	B1
Alemany Blvd		
(1-499)	35	B2/B1
(1101-1574)	32	B1/B2
(1575-1923)	38	A1
(1924-3140)	34	B1/B2/A2
(3141-4099)	33	B1/B2
Alert Aly	10	B2
Alhambra St	1	A2
Allen St	3	B1
Allison St	34	B1
Allston Way	30	A2
Alma St	9	B1
Almaden Ct	22	B1
Aloha Ave	25	A1
Alpha St	39	B2
Alpine Ter	10	A1
Alta Mar Way	18	A2
Alta St	4	B1
Alta Vista Ter	4	B1
Alton Ave	25	B2
Alvarado St		
(1-99)	15	A1
(401-999)	14	A1/A2
Alviso St	33	A1
Amador St	37	A1
Amatista Ln	32	A2
Amatury Loop	Presidio	
Amazon Ave		
(1-150)	34	B2
(151-899)	38	B1
Amber Dr	31	B2
Ames St	14	A2
Amethyst Way	31	B2
Amherst St	39	A1
Anderson St	35	A1/B1
Andover St	35	A1/B1
Anglo Aly	25	B1
Ankeny St	39	B2
Annapolis Ter	22	B2
Annie St	8	B1
Anson Pl	7	A2
Anthony St	8	A1/B1
Antonio St	7	B1
Anza St		
(101-988)	22	B1/B2
(989-2225)	21	B1/B2
(2226-3250)	20	B1/B2
(3251-4750)	19	B1/B2
(4751-5699)	18	A1/A2
Anzavista Ave	5	B1
Apollo St		
(1-150)	36	B1
(151-199)	40	A1
Apparel Way	36	A1
Appleton Ave		
(36-150)	32	A2
(151-199)	35	B1
Aptos Ave	30	B2/B1
Aquavista Way	29	B2
Arago St	31	B1
Arballo Dr	28	A2/B2
Arbol Ln	5	B1
Arbor St	32	A1
Arch St	33	A1/B1
Arco Way	34	A2
Ardath Ct	37	A1
Ardenwood Way	30	A1
Arellano Ave	28	B2
Argent Aly	29	B2
Argonaut Ave	39	B1
Arguello Blvd		
(2-949)	21	A2/B2
(950-1099)	Golden Gate Park	
(1100-1348)	29	A1
Arkansas St		
(1-472)	12	B2
(473-899)	16	A2
Arkansas Way	12	B2
Arleta Ave	39	B2
Arlington St	32	B2/A2/B1
Armistead Rd	Presidio	
Armory Rd	92	GR
Armstrong Ave	40	A1/A2
Arnold Ave	35	B1
Arroyo Way	31	B2
Arthur Ave	36	A2
Ash St	6	B1/B2

Street Index

Street	Page	Grid
Ashbury St		
(2-98)	22	B2
(100-1198)	9	A1/A2/B2
Ashbury Ter	9	B2
Ashton Ave	33	A2
Ashwood Ln	29	B1
Aspen Ct	38	B2
Atalaya Ter	22	B2
Athens St	38	B1/A2/A1
Atoll Cir	37	B2
Attridge Aly	3	B1
Auburn St	7	A2
August Aly	4	B1
Augusta St	36	B1
Austin St		
(1-150)	7	A1
(151-499)	6	A2/A1
Auto Dr	25	A2
Automobile Pathway	30	A2
Avalon Ave	38	A1/A2
Avery St	5	A2
Avila St	1	A2
Avoca Aly	31	A1
Avon Way	30	A1
Aztec St	35	A1
B		
Bache St	35	B1
Bacon St	39	A1/A2
Baden St	32	B1
Badger St	32	B1
Baker Ct		Presidio
Baker St		
(1-550)	10	A1
(551-2450)	5	A1/B1
(2451-3699)	1	A1/B1
Balance St	8	A1
Balboa St		
(1-1225)	21	B1/B2
(1226-2250)	20	B1/B2
(2251-3750)	19	B1/B2
(3751-4899)	18	B1/B2
Balceta Ave	31	A1
Baldwin Ct	37	B1
Balhi Ct	34	A2
Balmy St	15	B2
Baltimore Way	38	B1
Banbury Dr	28	B2
Bancroft Ave	40	A1
Banks St	35	A2/B2
Bannam Pl	4	B1
Banneker Way	6	B1
Bannock St	34	A2
Barcelona Ave	5	B1
Barnard Ave		Presidio
Barneveld Ave		
(1-699)	36	A1/B1
(701-899)	39	A2
Bartlett St	15	A1/B1
Bartol St	8	A1
Bass Ct	37	A1
Battery Blaney Rd		Presidio
Battery Caulfield Rd		Presidio
Battery Dynamite Rd		Presidio
Battery East Rd		Presidio
Battery Safford Rd		Presidio
Battery St		
(1-850)	8	A1
(851-1399)	4	B2
Battery Wagner Rd		Presidio
Baxter Aly	30	A2
Bay Shore Blvd		
(1-2699)	40	A1/B1
(16-699)	35	A2/B2
(701-761)	39	A2
(762-1156)	36	B1
Bay St		
(1-450)	4	A1
(451-1050)	3	A1/A2
(1051-2150)	2	A1/A2
(2151-2499)	1	A1
Bayside Village Pl	8	B2
Bayview Cir	36	B2
Bayview Park Rd	40	B2
Bayview St	36	B2
Baywood Ct	34	A2
Beach St		
(1-350)	4	A1
(351-950)	3	A1/A2
(951-1725)	2	A1
(1726-2299)	1	A1/A2
Beachmont Dr	30	B1
Beacon St	32	A1/A2
Beale St	8	A2/B2
Beatrice Ln	37	B1
Beaumont Ave	22	B1
Beaver St	10	B1
Beckett St	8	A1
Bedford Pl	7	A2
Beeman Ln	39	B2
Behr Ave	29	A1
Beideman St	5	B1
Belcher St	10	A2
Belden Pl	8	A1
Belgrave Ave	29	A2/A1
Bell Ct	37	A1
Bella Vista Way	31	A1/B2/A2
Bellair Pl	4	A1/B1
Belle Ave	33	B1
Bellevue Ave	34	B2
Belmont Ave	29	A1
Belvedere St		
(2-649)	9	A1/B1
(650-698)	29	A2
Bemis St	32	A2/A1
Bengal Aly	30	A2
Bennington St	35	A1/B1
Benton Ave		
(1-247)	32	B2
(301-699)	35	B1
Bepler St	33	B2/B1
Bergen Pl	3	A1
Berkeley Way	32	A1
Berkshire Way	26	B2
Bernal Hts Blvd	35	A1/A2
Bernard St	7	A1
Bernice St	11	A2
Berry St		
(1-57)	8	B2
(58-417)	13	A1
(418-599)	12	B2/A2
Bertha Ln	37	A1
Bertie Minor Ln	6	B1
Bertita St	34	A2
Berwick Pl	12	A1
Bessie St	35	A1
Beulah St	9	B1
Beverly St	33	A1/B1
Birch St	6	B1
Birchwood Ct	38	B2
Bird St	11	B1
Birmingham Rd		Presidio
Bishop St	39	B2
Bitting Ave	40	A1
Black Pl	3	B2
Blackstone Ct	2	B2
Blair Ter	16	B2
Blairwood Ln	29	B1
Blake St	22	B2
Blanche St	14	A2
Blandy St	37	B2
Blanken Ave	40	B1
Bliss Rd		Presidio
Bluxome St		
(1-150)	13	A1
(151-199)	12	A1
Blythdale Ave	39	B1
Boardman Pl	12	A2
Bob Kaufman Aly	4	B1
Bocana St	35	A1/B1
Bonifacio St	8	B1
Bonita St	3	B1
Bonnie Brae Ln	26	B2
Bonview St	35	A1
Borica St	33	A1
Bosworth St		
(1-1350)	32	B1/B2
(1351-1399)	31	B1
Boutwell St	36	B1
Bowdoin St	39	A1/A2/B2
Bowley St		Presidio
Bowling Green Dr		Golden Gate Park
Bowman Ct	37	A1
Boylston St	39	A2
Boynton Ct	10	B2
Bradford St	35	A2/B2
Brady St	11	A1
Brannan St		
(1-480)	8	B2
(481-550)	13	A1
(551-1099)	12	A2/B1
Brant Aly	4	B2
Brazil Ave		
(1-1350)	38	A1/A2
(1351-1399)	39	B1
Breen Pl	7	B1
Brentwood Ave		
(1-179)	31	A2
(180-399)	30	B2
Bret Harte Ter	3	A2
Brewster St	35	A2
Briarcliff Ter	27	A2
Bridgeview Dr	36	B2/B1
Bright St	33	A2/B2
Brighton Ave	34	A1
Britton St	39	B1
Broad St		
(1-50)	34	B1
(51-299)	33	B2
Broadmoor Dr		
(1-150)	30	B1
(151-199)	28	A2
Broadway St		
(1-668)	8	A1
(669-1550)	7	A1/A2
(1551-2166)	6	A1/A2
(2167-2999)	5	A1/A2

Street	Page	Grid
Broderick St		
(1-650)	10	A1
(651-2550)	5	A1/B1
(2551-3799)	1	A1/B1
Bromley Pl	6	A1
Brompton Ave	32	B1
Bronte St	35	A2/B2
Brook St	32	A2
Brookdale Ave	39	B1
Brookhaven Ln	26	B2
Brooklyn Pl	8	A1
Brooks St		Presidio
Brosnan St	11	B1
Brotherhood Way		
(1-999)	28	B2
(23-677)	33	B1
Bruce Ave	34	A1
Brumiss Ter	34	B1
Brunswick St	34	B2/B1
Brush Pl	12	A1
Brussels St	39	A2/B2
Bryant Ln	8	B2
Bryant St		
(1-650)	8	B2/B1
(651-1199)	12	A1/A2
(1201-2150)	11	B2/A2
(2151-2999)	15	A2/B2
Bucareli Dr	28	B2
Buchanan St		
(1-825)	10	A2
(826-2750)	6	A1/B1
(2751-3799)	2	A1/B1
Buckingham Way		
(1-363)	28	A2
(364-3400)	27	B2
Buena Vista Ave		
(1-400)	10	A1
(401-999)	6	A2/B2
Buena Vista Ter	10	A1
Burgoyne St	7	A1
Burke Ave	37	A1
Burlwood Dr	31	A2
Burnett Ave	29	B2
Burns Pl	11	A2
Burnside Ave	32	B1
Burr Ave	39	B1
Burritt St	7	A2
Burrows St		
(1-1750)	39	A1/A2
(1751-2099)	38	A2
Bush St		
(1-555)	8	A1
(556-1450)	7	A1/A2
(1451-2050)	6	A1/A2
(2051-2999)	5	A1/A2
Butte Pl	12	A2
Byington St	5	B2
Byron Ct	34	B2
Byxbee St	33	A1/B1

C

Street	Page	Grid
C St	37	B2
Cable Car Turnaround	7	B2
Cabrillo St		
(1-1225)	21	B1/B2
(1226-2250)	20	B1/B2
(2251-3750)	19	B1/B2
(3751-4899)	18	B1/B2
Cadell Pl	4	B1
Caine Ave	34	B1
Caire Ter	16	B2
Caledonia St	11	B1
Calgary St	39	B1
Calhoun Ter	4	B2
California St		
(1-780)	8	A1/A2
(781-1650)	7	A1/A2
(1651-2250)	6	A1/A2
(2251-3250)	5	A1/A2
(3251-3875)	22	A1/A2
(3876-5125)	21	A1/A2
(5126-6150)	20	A1/A2
(6151-7099)	19	A1/A2
Cambon Dr	28	B2
Cambridge St	39	A1
Camellia Ave	32	B1
Cameo Way	31	B2
Cameron Way	40	B2/B1/A2
Camp St	11	B1
Campbell Ave	39	B2
Campton Pl	8	A1
Campus Cir	28	A2
Campus Ln	39	A1
Canby St		Presidio
Canyon Dr	38	B1
Capistrano Ave		
(1-233)	32	B1
(234-333)	38	A1
(334-499)	34	A2
Capitol Ave	33	A2/B2
Capp St		
(1-450)	11	B1
(451-1199)	15	A1/B1
Capra Way	1	A2
Card Aly	4	B1
Cardenas Ave	28	B2
Cargo Way	37	A1
Carl St		
(1-250)	9	B1
(251-499)	29	A1
Carmel St	29	A2
Carmelita St	10	A1
Carnelian Way	14	B1
Carolina St		
(101-650)	12	B2
(651-1299)	16	A2/B2
Carpenter Ct	37	A1
Carr St	40	B1
Carrie St	32	B1
Carrizal St	39	B1
Carroll Ave		
(1101-2050)	40	A1/B2
(2051-2199)	36	B1
Carson St	29	A2
Carter St	39	B1
Carver St	35	A2
Casa Way	1	A2
Cascade Walk	25	B1
Caselli Ave		
(1-23)	10	B1
(24-399)	29	A2
Cashmere St	37	A1
Casitas Ave	30	A2/B2
Cassandra Ct	34	B1
Castelo Ave	28	B2
Castenada Ave		
(1-224)	25	B2
(225-599)	30	A2
Castillo St	39	B1
Castle Manor Ave	32	B1
Castle St	4	B2
Castro St		
(1-650)	10	A1/B1
(651-2150)	14	A1/B1/B2
(2151-3199)	32	A1/B1
Cayuga Ave		
(1-650)	32	B1/B2
(651-890)	38	A1
(891-2299)	34	B1/B2/A2
Cecilia Ave		
(2100-2199)	25	B1
(2200-2398)	30	A1
Cedar St		
(2-150)	7	B1
(151-199)	6	B2
Cedro Ave	30	B1
Central Ave		
(1-650)	9	A2
(651-999)	5	B1
Central Fwy	11	A2/B2/A1
Century Pl	8	A1
Ceres St	40	A1
Cerritos Ave	33	A1
Cervantes Blvd		
(1-65)	2	A1
(66-299)	1	A2
Cesar Chavez St		
(1-3750)	15	B1/B2
(451-1626)	17	B1
(1627-2824)	16	B1/B2
(3751-4399)	14	B1/B2
Chabot Ter	22	B2
Chain of Lakes Dr		
(100-349)	18	B2
(350-598)	Golden Gate Park	
Chancery Ln	34	B2
Channel St		
(201-299)	13	A1
(373-399)	12	B2
Chapman St	35	A2
Charles St	32	A2
Charlton Ct	2	B1
Charter Oak Ave	36	B1
Chase Ct	11	A1
Chatham Pl	8	A1
Chattanooga St	14	A2/B2
Chaves Ave	31	A1
Chelsea Pl	7	A2
Chenery St	32	B1/B2/A2/A1
Cherry St	22	A1
Chersley St	12	A2
Chester Ave	33	B1
Chestnut St		
(1-660)	4	B1/A2/B2
(661-1250)	3	B1/A2/B2
(1251-2055)	2	B1/B2
(2057-2699)	1	B1/B2
Chicago Way	38	B1/B2
Child St	4	A1
Chilton Ave	32	B1
Chism Rd		Presidio
Christmas Tree Pt Rd	29	B2
Christopher Dr	29	B1
Chula Ln	10	B2
Chumasero Dr	28	B2

Street Index

Street	Page	Grid
Church St		
(1-775)	10	A2/B2
(776-1625)	14	A2/B2
(1626-1899)	32	A2
Cielito Dr	39	B1
Circular Ave		
(79-251)	32	B1
(252-650)	31	B1
(651-699)	34	A2
Cityview Way	29	B1/B2
Clairview Ct	29	B2
Clara St		
(101-250)	8	B1
(251-299)	12	A2
Claremont Blvd	30	A2
Clarence Pl	8	B2
Clarendon Ave	29	B1/A1/A2
Clarendon Woods Ave	29	B1
Clarion Aly	11	B1
Clark St		Presidio
Claude Ln	8	A1
Clay St		
(1-883)	8	A1/A2
(884-1750)	7	A1/A2
(1751-2350)	6	A1/A2
(2351-3350)	5	A1/A2
(3351-3999)	22	A1/A2
Clayton St		
(2-50)	22	B2
(51-1224)	9	A1/B1/B2
(1225-1498)	29	A2
Clearfield Dr	27	B1
Clearview Ct	36	B2
Cleary Ct	6	B1
Clement St		
(1-1225)	21	A1/A2
(1226-2250)	20	A1/A2
(2251-3750)	19	A1/A2
(3751-4399)	18	A2
Clementina St		
(1-399)	8	B2/B1
(401-450)	7	B2
(451-779)	12	A1
Cleo Rand Ln	37	B2
Cleveland St	12	A2
Clifford Ter	9	B2
Clinton Park		
(1-225)	11	B1
(226-299)	10	A2
Clipper St		
(1-880)	14	B1/B2
(881-999)	31	B2
Clipper Ter	14	B2
Clover Ln	29	A2
Clover St	29	A2
Clyde St	13	A1
Cochrane St	37	B2
Codman Pl	7	A2
Cohen Pl	7	B1
Colby St	39	A1/A2/B2
Cole St		
(2-50)	22	B2
(51-1462)	9	A1/B1
(1463-1598)	29	A2
Coleman St	37	B2
Coleridge St	35	A1
Colin P Kelly Jr St	8	B2
Colin Pl	7	B1
College Ave	32	B2
College Ter	32	B2
Collier St	7	A2
Collingwood St		
(1-250)	10	B1
(251-499)	14	A1
Collins St	22	A2/B2
Colon Ave	31	A2
Colonial Way	31	B1
Colton St	11	A1
Columbia Square St	12	A2
Columbus Ave		
(1-350)	8	A1
(351-950)	4	B1
(951-1399)	3	A1/A2
Colusa Pl	11	A1
Comerford St	14	B2
Commer Ct	37	A1
Commerce St	4	B2
Commercial St	8	A1/A2
Commonwealth Ave	22	A1/B1
Compton Rd		Presidio
Concord St	34	B2
Concourse Dr		Golden Gate Park
Congdon St	32	B2
Congo St		
(-)	28	B2
(1-899)	31	B1
Conkling St	36	B1
Connecticut St		
(1-450)	12	B2
(451-1299)	16	A2/B2
Conrad St	9	B2
Conservatory Dr		Golden Gate Park
Constanso Way	27	B1
Converse St	12	A1
Cook St	22	B2
Cooper Aly	8	A1
Copper Aly	29	B2
Cora St	39	B2
Coral Ct	37	B2
Coral Rd	16	B2
Coralino Ln	31	B2
Corbett Ave		
(1-50)	10	B1
(51-999)	29	A2/B2
Corbin Pl	9	B2
Cordelia St	7	A2
Cordova St	38	B1
Cornwall St	21	A2
Corona St	33	A1
Coronado St	40	B1
Cortes Ave	30	A2
Cortland Ave	35	A1/A2
Corwin St	14	A1
Cosmo Pl	7	A1/A2
Coso Ave	35	A1
Costa St	35	A2
Cottage Row	5	A2
Cotter St	32	B1
Country Club Dr	26	B2
Coventry Ct	31	A2
Cowell Pl	4	B2
Cowles St		Presidio
Cragmont Ave	25	B2
Crags Ct	32	A1
Crane St	40	B1
Cranleigh Dr	30	B1
Craut St	32	B2
Crescent Ave		
(1-165)	32	B2
(166-1199)	35	B1/B2
Crescio St	34	B2
Crespi Dr	28	B2
Cresta Vista Dr	31	A2
Crestlake Dr	27	B1/B2/A1
Crestline Dr	29	B2
Crestmont Dr	29	B1/A1
Crisp Rd		
(-)	37	B1
(201-299)	40	A1
Crissy Field Ave		Presidio
Crook St		Presidio
Cross St	34	B2
Crossover Dr		
(100-698)		Golden Gate Park
(900-998)	19	B2
Crown Ct	29	A2
Crown Ter	29	A2
Crystal St	33	B2
Culebra Ter	3	B1
Cumberland St	10	B2
Cunningham Pl	11	B1
Curtis St		
(1-225)	34	B2
(226-299)	38	B1
Cushman St	7	A2
Custer Ave	36	A2
Custom House Pl	8	A1
Cutler Ave	26	A1
Cuvier St	32	B2
Cypress St	15	B1
Cyril Magnin St	7	B2
Cyrus Pl	7	A1

D

D St	37	B2
Daggett St	13	B1
Dakota St	16	B2
Dale Pl	7	B1
Dalewood Way	31	A1
Daniel Burnham Ct	6	B2
Danton St	32	B1
Danvers St	29	A2
Darien Way	30	B1/B2
Darrell Pl	4	B2
Dartmouth St	39	A1/A2/B2
Dashiell Hammett St	7	A2
Davidson Ave	36	A2
Davis Ct	8	A1
Davis St		
(1-750)	8	A1
(751-899)	4	A1
Dawnview Way	29	B2
Dawson Pl	7	A2
Day St	32	A1/A2
De Boom St	8	B2
De Forest Way	10	B1
De Haro St		
(99-750)	12	B2
(751-1499)	16	A1/B1
De Long St	33	B1/B2
De Montfort Ave	33	A1
De Soto St	33	A1
De Wolf St	34	B1
Dearborn St	11	B1
Decatur St	12	A1
Dedman Ct	37	A1

Street	Page	Grid
Dehon St	10	B2
Del Monte St	34	B2
Del Sur Ave	31	A1
Del Vale Ave	31	B2
Delancey St	8	B2
Delancy St	8	B2
Delano Ave	34	B2/A2
Delaware St	17	B2
Delgado Pl	3	B1
Dellbrook Ave	29	B1/A1
Delmar St	9	A2/B2
Delta St	39	B2
Deming St	29	A2
Denslowe Dr	28	A2/B2
Derby St	7	B2
Desmond St	39	B2
Detroit St	31	B1
Devonshire Way	29	B1
Dewey Blvd	30	A2
Diamond Heights Blvd		
(5001-5152)	31	B2
(5153-5310)	14	B2
(5311-5899)	32	A1
Diamond St		
(1-250)	10	B2
(251-1650)	14	A1/B1
(1651-2999)	32	A1/B1
Diana St	40	A1
Diaz Ave	28	B2
Dichiera Ct	34	B2
Digby St	32	A1
Divisadero St		
(1-750)	10	A1
(751-2650)	5	A1/B1
(2651-3899)	1	A1/B1/B2
Division St		
(101-274)	12	B1/B2
(275-499)	11	B2
Dixie Aly	14	A1
Dodge Pl	7	B1
Dolores St		
(1-675)	10	A2/B2
(676-1525)	14	A2/B2
(1526-1799)	32	A2
Dolores Ter	10	B2
Dolphin Ct	37	B2
Donahue St	37	B2
Donner Ave	40	A1/B2
Dorado	30	B2
Dorado Ter	30	B2
Dorantes Ave	30	A2
Dorcas Way	31	B2/B1
Dorchester Way	30	A2
Dore St	12	A1
Doric Aly	7	A2
Dorland St	10	B2
Dorman Ave	36	A1
Dormitory Rd	37	B1
Doublerock St	40	B2
Douglass St		
(1-343)	10	B1
(344-1499)	14	A1/B1
Dow Pl	8	B2
Downey St	9	A1/B2
Doyle		Presidio
Dr Carlton B Goodlett Pl	7	B1
Drake St	38	B1
Drumm St	8	A2
Drummond Aly	36	B2
Dublin St	38	B2/A2
Duboce Ave		
(1-250)	11	A1
(251-999)	10	A1/A2
Dukes Ct	37	A1
Duncan St		
(1-150)	35	A1
(151-920)	14	B1/B2
(921-2099)	31	B2
Duncombe Aly	8	A1
Dunnes Aly	8	A1
Dunshee St	36	B2
Dunsmuir St	39	A1
Dwight St	39	A2/B2

E

Street	Page	Grid
E St	37	B2
Eagle St	29	A2
Earl St	37	B2
Eastman End	3	B1
Eastman Pl	3	B1
Eastwood Dr		
(1-67)	34	A1
(68-199)	31	A2
Eaton Pl	4	B1
Ecker Pl	8	A1
Ecker St	8	B2
Eddy St		
(51-750)	7	B1/B2
(751-1350)	6	B1/B2
(1351-2099)	5	B1/B2
Edgar Pl	34	A1
Edgardo Pl	4	B1
Edgehill Way	30	A2
Edgewood Ave	29	A1
Edie Rd		Presidio
Edinburgh St		
(1-150)	32	B2
(151-999)	38	A1/B1/A2
Edith St	4	B1
Edna St		
(1-50)	34	A2
(51-899)	31	B1
Edward St	22	B1
Egbert Ave	40	A1/A2
El Camino del Mar		
(101-1249)	19	A1/A2
(1232-2699)	18	A1/A2
El Mirasol Pl	27	B1
El Plazuela Way	30	B1
El Polin Loop		Presidio
El Sereno Ct	31	B2
El Verano Way	30	B2
Eldorado St	13	B2
Elgin Park	11	A1
Elizabeth St		
(1-99)	15	B1
(301-999)	14	A1/A2
Elk St	32	A1/B1
Elkhart St	8	B2
Ellert St	35	B1
Ellington Ave	34	B2/B1
Elliot St	39	B2
Ellis St		
(1-850)	7	B2/B1
(851-1450)	6	B1/B2
(1451-2199)	5	B1/B2
Ellsworth St	35	A1/B1
Elm St		
(1-399)	6	B2
(1101-1199)	5	B2
Elmhurst Dr	30	B1
Elmira St	36	B1
Elmwood Way	30	B2
Elsie St	35	A1/B1
Elwood St	7	B1
Embarcadero North St	4	A1
Embarcadero South St	8	A2/B2
Emerson St	22	B2
Emery Ln	4	B1
Emma St	8	A1
Emmett Ct	35	A1
Encanto Ave	5	B1
Encinal Walk	25	A1
Encline Ct	31	B2
English St	37	B2
Enterprise St	11	B2
Entrada Ct	33	A1
Erie St	11	B1/B2
Ervine St	39	B2
Escolta Way	27	A1
Escondido Ave	27	B1
Esmeralda Ave	35	A1/A2
Espanola St	37	B2
Esquina Dr	39	B1
Essex St	8	B2
Estero Ave	33	A1
Eucalyptus Dr		
(101-162)	30	B1
(163-1799)	27	B1/B2
Euclid Ave		
(1-850)	22	A2/A1
(851-899)	21	A2
Eugenia Ave	35	A1/A2
Eureka St		
(1-250)	10	B1
(251-599)	14	A1
Evans Ave		
(1001-1540)	37	A1
(1541-2130)	36	A2
(2131-2199)	16	B2
Evelyn Way	31	A1/B2
Everglade Dr	27	B1
Everson St	32	A2/A1
Ewer Pl	7	A2
Ewing Ter	22	B2
Excelsior Ave	38	A1/A2
Exchange St	8	A1
Executive Park Blvd	40	B1
Exeter St	40	B1

F

Street	Page	Grid
Fair Ave	35	A1
Fair Oaks St	14	A2/B2
Fairfax Ave		
(1201-1499)	37	A1
(1565-1599)	36	A2
Fairfield Way	30	B2
Fairmount St	32	A1
Faith St	35	A2
Fallon Pl	3	B2
Falmouth St	12	A2
Fanning Way	25	B1

Street Index

Street		
Farallones St		
(1-50)	34	B1
(51-299)	33	B2
Farnsworth Ln	29	A1
Farnum St	32	A1
Farragut Ave	34	B1
Farren St	5	B2
Farview Ct	29	B2
Faxon Ave		
(1-650)	33	A2/B2
(651-999)	30	B2
Federal St	8	B2
Felix Ave	28	B2
Fell St		
(1-550)	11	A1/A2
(551-1450)	10	A1/A2
(1451-2199)	9	A2/A1
Fella Pl	7	A2
Felton St		
(1-1650)	39	A1/A2
(1651-1899)	38	A2
Fern St		
(1-150)	7	A1
(151-399)	6	A2
Fernandez St		Presidio
Fernwood Dr	30	B2
Fielding St	4	B1
Filbert St		
(1-850)	4	B1/B2
(851-1450)	3	B1/B2
(1451-2250)	2	B1/B2
(2251-2899)	1	B1/B2
Filbert Steps	4	B2
Fillmore St		
(1-850)	10	A2
(851-2750)	5	A2/B2
(2751-3799)	2	A1/B1
Fischer Ave	37	B2
Fisher Aly	7	A2
Fisher Loop		Presidio
Fishermans Wharf	3	A2
Fitch St	40	A2/B2
Fitzgerald Ave	40	A1/B1/B2
Flint St	10	B1
Flood Ave	31	A2/B1
Flora St	36	B2
Florence St	3	B2
Florentine St	34	B2
Florida St		
(1-750)	11	A2
(751-1550)	15	A2/B2
(1551-1699)	35	A2
Flournoy St	33	B2
Flower St		
(1-75)	35	A2
(76-99)	36	A1
Foerster St	31	B1
Folger Aly	5	B2
Folsom St		
(1-850)	8	B1/B2/A2
(851-973)	7	B2
(974-1376)	12	A1/A2
(1377-2350)	11	A1/A2
(2351-3119)	15	A2/B2
(3120-4299)	35	
		A1/A2/B2/B1
Font Blvd	28	A2/B2
Fontinella Ter	16	B1

Street		
Foote Ave	34	B1/B2
Ford St	10	B2
Forest Knolls Dr	29	B1
Forest Side Ave	30	A1
Forest View Dr	27	B2
Fortuna Ave	5	B1
Fountain St	14	B1
Fowler Ave	31	A1
France Ave	38	A1/B1
Francis St	38	A1
Francisco St		
(51-550)	4	A1
(551-1150)	3	A1/A2
(1151-1599)	2	A2
(2201-2599)	1	A1/A2/B1
Franconia St	35	A2
Franklin St		
(28-450)	11	A1
(451-2350)	6	A2/B2
(2351-3199)	5	A2/B2
Fratessa Ct	39	B2
Frederick St		
(1-550)	9	B1/B2
(551-799)	29	A1
Fredson Ct	34	B2
Freelon St		
(1-99)	8	B1
(101-199)	13	A1
Freeman Ct	7	A2
Freeman St		Presidio
Fremont St	8	B2/A2
Fresno St	4	B1
Friedell St	37	B2
Friendship Ct	5	B2
Front St		
(1-850)	8	A1
(851-1199)	4	B2
Fuente Ave	28	B2
Fulton St		
(345-772)	6	B1/B2
(773-1750)	5	B1/B2
(1751-2509)	22	B1/B2
(2510-4034)	21	B1/B2
(4035-5003)	20	B1/B2
(5004-6293)	19	B1/B2
(6294-7399)	18	B1/B2
Funston Ave		
(2-798)	21	A1/B1
(1200-2198)	25	A1/B1
(2300-2498)	30	A2

G

Street		
Gabilan Way	27	B2
Gaiser Ct	11	B1
Galewood Cir	29	B1
Galilee Ln	6	B1
Galindo Ave	28	B2
Gallagher Ln	8	B1
Galvez Ave		
(1501-1617)	37	A1/B2
(1618-2099)	36	A2
Gambier St		
(1-150)	32	B2
(151-399)	38	A2
Garces Dr	28	B2
Garcia Ave	30	A2
Garden St	5	B1
Gardenside Dr	29	B1

Street		
Garfield St	33	A1/A2
Garlington Ct	37	A1
Garnett Ter	37	A1
Garrison Ave	39	B1
Gates St	35	A1/B1
Gateview Ct		
(2-1232)	25	B2
Gatun Aly	31	B2/B1
Gaven St	39	A2/A1
Gaviota Way	31	B2
Geary Blvd		
(1-8399)	18	A2/A1
(1101-1624)	6	B2/B1
(1625-2650)	5	B1/B2
(2651-3666)	22	B1/B2
(3667-4925)	21	B1/B2
(4926-5950)	20	B1/B2
(5951-7450)	19	B1/B2
Geary St		
(1-150)	8	B1
(151-1050)	7	B1/B2
(1051-1099)	6	B2
Gellert St	27	B1
Genebern Way	32	B2
Geneva Ave		
(1-1025)	34	A1/A2/B2
(1026-1700)	38	B1/B2
(1701-2249)	39	B1
Gennessee St	31	A2
Genoa Pl	4	B1
George Ct	37	B1
Gerke Aly	4	B1
Germania St	10	A2
Getz St	34	A1
Giants Dr	40	B2
Gibb St	8	A1
Gibson Rd		Presidio
Gilbert St	12	A2
Gillette Ave	40	B1
Gilman Ave	40	A1/B1/B2
Gilroy St	40	B1
Girard Rd		Presidio
Girard St	39	A2/B2
Gladeview Way	29	B2
Gladstone Dr		
(1-150)	39	A1
(151-300)	32	B2
Gladys St	32	A2
Glenbrook Ave	29	A2
Glendale St	29	B2
Glenhaven Ln	29	B1
Glenview Dr		
(-)	31	B2
(1-299)	29	B2
Globe Aly	31	A2
Gloria Ct	34	B2
Glover St	7	A1
Godeus St	35	A1
Goethe St	33	B2
Goettingen St	39	A2/B2
Gold Mine Dr	32	A1
Gold St	8	A1
Golden Ct	7	A1
Golden Gate Ave		
(44-550)	7	B1/B2
(551-1150)	6	B1/B2
(1151-2150)	5	B1/B2
(2151-2899)	22	B1/B2

Street	Page	Grid
Goleta Ave	27	B2
Gonzalez Dr	28	B2
Gordon St	12	A1
Gorgas Ave		Presidio
Gorham St	32	B1
Gough St		
(1-550)	11	A1
(551-2450)	6	A1/A2/B2
(2451-3299)	2	A2/B2
Gould St	40	A1
Grace St	12	A1
Grafton Ave		
(1-250)	34	A1
(251-905)	33	A2
Graham St		Presidio
Granada Ave		
(1-350)	33	A2
(351-399)	34	A1
Grand View Ave		
(1-62)	29	B2
(63-749)	14	A1/B1
Grand View Ter	29	A2
Grant Ave		
(1-1282)	8	A1/B1
(1283-2299)	4	A1/B1
Granville Way	30	A2
Grattan St	9	B1
Graystone Ter	29	A2/B2
Great Hwy		
(900-2249)	23	A1/B1
(925-948)		Golden Gate Park
(950-1024)	18	A1/B1
(2250-2898)	26	A1/B1
Green St		
(1-870)	4	B1/B2
(871-1450)	3	B1/B2
(1451-2250)	2	B1/B2
(2251-2899)	1	B1/B2
Greenough Ave		Presidio
Greenview Ct	29	B1
Greenwich St		
(1-875)	4	B1/B2
(876-1460)	3	B1/B2
(1461-2250)	2	B1/B2
(2251-2899)	1	B2/B1
Greenwich Ter		
(1101-1150)	3	B1
(1151-1199)	4	B1
Greenwood Ave	31	A2
Grenard Ter	3	B1
Griffith St		
(1201-1250)	37	B1
(1251-2999)	40	A2/B1/B2
Grijalva Dr	28	B2
Grote Pl	8	B2
Grove St		
(1-150)	7	B1
(151-650)	11	A1
(651-1550)	10	A1/A2
(1551-2199)	9	A1/A2
Guerrero St		
(1-775)	11	A1/B1
(776-1475)	15	A1/B1
(1476-1599)	35	A1
Guttenberg St	34	B2
Guy Pl	8	B2

H

Street	Page	Grid
H St	37	B2
Hahn St	39	B1
Haight St		
(1-250)	11	A1
(251-1148)	10	A1/A2
(1149-1899)	9	A1/A2
Hale St	39	A1
Hallam St	12	A1
Halleck St	8	A1
Hallidie Plz	7	B2
Hamerton Ave	32	B1
Hamilton St	39	B2
Hampshire St		
(101-750)	11	B2
(751-1550)	15	A2/B2
(1551-1599)	35	A2
Hampton Pl	8	B1
Hancock St	10	B2
Hangah St	8	A1
Hanover St	34	B2
Harbor Rd	37	A1
Hardie Ave		Presidio
Hardie Pl	8	A1
Harding Rd	28	A1
Hare St	37	A1
Harkness Ave	39	B2
Harlan Pl	8	A1
Harlem Aly	7	B1
Harlow St	10	B2
Harney Way	40	B1
Harold Ave	34	A1
Harper St	32	A2
Harriet St	12	A1
Harrington St	38	A1
Harris Pl	2	B1
Harrison Blvd		Presidio
Harrison St		
(1-1366)	12	A2/A1
(51-912)	8	B2/B1
(1367-2375)	11	A2/B2
(2376-3150)	15	A2/B2
(3151-3399)	35	A2
Harry St	32	A2
Hartford St	10	B1
Harvard St		
(1-150)	32	B2
(151-499)	39	A1
Hastings Ter	3	B1
Hattie St	29	A2
Havelock St	34	A2
Havens St	3	B1
Havenside Dr	27	B1
Hawes St		
(401-1250)	37	A1
(1251-2999)	40	A2/B1
Hawkins Ln	37	A1
Hawthorne St	8	B1
Hayes St		
(1-150)	7	B1
(151-650)	11	A1
(651-1550)	10	A1/A2
(1551-2299)	9	A1/A2
Hayward St	12	A1
Hazelwood Ave	31	A2
Head St	33	A2/B2/B1
Hearst Ave		
(1-150)	32	B1
(151-699)	31	A2/B1
Heather Ave	22	A1
Helen Pl	7	A1
Helena St		
(-)	36	B1
	7	A1
Hemlock St		
(5-150)	7	B1
(151-699)	6	B1
Hemway Ter	22	B2
Henry Adams St	12	B2
Henry St	10	B1/B2
Herbst Rd		Golden Gate Natl Rec Area
Hermann St	10	A2
Hernandez Ave		
(1-150)	31	A1
(151-299)	30	A1
Heron St	12	A1
Hester Ave	40	B1
Heyman St	35	A1
Hickory St		
(1-450)	11	A1
(451-599)	10	A2
Hicks Rd		Presidio
Hidalgo Ter	10	B2
High St		
(1-94)	14	B1
(95-99)	29	B2
Highland Ave		
(1-161)	32	A2
(162-399)	35	B1
Higuera Ave	28	B2
Hiliritas Ave	32	A1
Hill Dr	37	B2
Hill Point Ave	29	A1
Hill St		
(1-99)	15	A1
(301-599)	14	A2
Hillcrest Ct	31	A2
Hillview Ct	37	A1
Hillway Ave	29	A1
Hilton St	35	B2/A2
Himmelmann Pl	7	A2
Hitchcock St		Presidio
Hobart Aly	7	A2
Hodges Aly	4	B2
Hoff St	11	B1
Hoffman Ave	14	A1/B1
Holladay Ave	35	B2
Holland Ct	8	B1
Hollis St	6	B1
Hollister Ave	40	B1/A1
Holloway Ave		
(1-250)	34	A1
(251-1435)	33	A1/A2
(1436-1799)	28	B2/A2
Holly Park Cir	35	B1
Hollywood Ct	34	B2
Holyoke St	39	A2/B2
Homer St	12	A2
Homestead St	14	B1
Homewood Ct	30	B2
Hooper St	12	B2
Hopkins Ave	29	B2
Horace St	15	B2
Horn Ave	37	B2
Hotaling St	8	A1

Street Index

Street	Page	Grid
Houston St	3	A2
Howard Rd		Presidio
Howard St		
(1-861)	8	B1/A2/B2
(862-1030)	7	B2
(1031-1380)	12	A1
(1381-1699)	11	A2
Howe Rd		Presidio
Howth St	34	A1
Hubbell St		
(101-159)	13	B1
(160-199)	12	B2
Hudson Ave		
(901-1599)	37	A1/B2
(1603-1699)	36	A2
Hudson Ct	37	A1
Hugo St	29	A1
Humboldt St	17	A1
Hunt St	8	B1
Hunters Point Blvd	37	A1
Hunters Point Expy	40	B2
Huntington Dr	26	B2
Huron Ave	34	B1/B2
Hussey St	37	B2
Hyde St		
(1-1750)	7	A1/B1
(1751-2999)	3	A1/B1

I

Street	Page	Grid
I St	37	B2
	31	B1
	35	B1/B2
	12	B2/A2
	39	A2
(100-698)	13	B1
(200-1798)	36	B1/A1/A2
(850-1598)	17	A1/B1
(4400-5098)	32	B1/B2
I-280		
(5900-7449)	34	A2/B1/A1
(7450-8198)	33	B1/B2
I-80		
(200-5098)	12	A2/B2
(6980-6998)	8	B2/A1
Ice House Aly	4	B2
Idora Ave		
(1-102)	31	A1
(103-151)	30	A2
Ignacio Ave	40	B2
Illinois St		
(1-861)	13	A2/B2
(862-1499)	17	A1/B1
(1801-1899)	37	A1
Ils Ln	8	A1
Imperial Ave	2	B2
Ina Ct	38	A2
Inca Ln	6	B1
Indiana St		
(501-750)	13	B1
(751-1637)	17	A1/B1
(1638-1699)	36	A2
Industrial St	36	B1
Infantry Ter		Presidio
Ingalls St		
(1101-1550)	37	B1/A1
(1551-3299)	40	A1/A2/B1
Ingerson Ave	40	B1
Innes Ave		
(801-2099)	36	A1/B2/A2
(850-1533)	37	A1/B1/B2
Inverness Dr	27	B2
Iowa St		
(301-450)	13	B1
(451-1099)	17	A1/B1
Iris Ave	22	A2
Iron Aly	29	A2
Irving St		
(1-550)	29	A1
(551-1750)	25	A1/A2
(1751-3575)	24	A1/A2
(3576-4899)	23	A1/A2
Irwin St		
(401-459)	13	B1
(460-499)	12	B2
Isadora Duncan Ln	7	B2
Isis St	11	A2
Islais St	36	A2
Isola Way	31	A1
Issleib	40	A1
Italy Ave		
(1-50)	34	A2
(51-899)	38	A1/B1
Ivy St		
(1-50)	7	B1
(51-550)	11	A1
(551-699)	10	A2

J

Street	Page	Grid
J St	37	B2
Jack Kerouac Aly	8	A1
Jack London Aly	8	B2
Jackson St		
(1-779)	8	A1
(780-1650)	7	A1/A2
(1651-2250)	6	A1/A2
(2251-3250)	5	A1/A2
(3251-3899)	22	A1/A2
Jade Pl	31	B2
Jakey Ct	37	A1
James Lick Fwy		
(-)	8	B2
(400-498)	40	B1
(500-1098)	39	A2/B2
(4200-4598)	12	B2
James Pl	7	A2
Jamestown Ave	40	B1/B2
Jansen St	4	B1
Jarboe Ave	35	B1/B2
Jason Ct	8	A1
Jasper Pl	4	B1
Jauss St		Presidio
Java St	9	B2
Javowitz St		Presidio
Jean Way	22	B2
Jefferson St		
(1-150)	4	A1
(151-599)	3	A1/A2
(1401-1850)	2	A1
(1851-2199)	1	A1
Jennifer Ct	8	B1
Jennings Ct	40	B1
Jennings St		
(1-1550)	37	A1
(1551-3599)	40	B1/A1/A2
Jerome Aly	8	A1
Jerrold Ave		
(701-1550)	37	B2
(1551-2350)	36	A1/A2/B2
(2351-2399)	35	A2
Jersey St	14	B1/B2
(1-350)	8	B1/A1
(351-850)	7	B1/B2
Jessie St		
(851-1399)	11	A1/A2
Jewett St	13	A1
John F Kennedy Dr		Golden Gate Park
John F Shelley Dr	39	B1/B2
John Muir Dr	28	B2/B1
John St	7	A2
Johnstone Dr	29	A1
Joice St	7	A2
Jones St		
(98-1763)	7	A1/B1/B2
(1764-2999)	3	A2/B2
Joost Ave		
(1-250)	32	B1
(251-899)	31	A2/B1
Jordan Ave	22	A1/B1
Josepha Ave	28	B2
Josiah Ave	34	A1/B1
Joy St	35	A2
Juan Bautista Cir	28	B2
Juanita Way		
(1-252)	31	A1
(253-399)	30	A1
Judah St		
(23-150)	29	A1
(151-1350)	25	A1/A2
(1351-3175)	24	A1/A2
(3176-4499)	23	A1/A2
Judson Ave	31	A2/B1
Jules Ave	33	A2
Julia St	12	A1
Julian Ave	11	B1
Julius St	4	B1
Junior Ter	34	A2
Juniper St	11	A2
Junipero Serra Blvd		
(1-662)	30	B1
(663-1559)	33	A1/B1
Juri St	15	B1
Justin Dr	32	B2

K

Street	Page	Grid
Kalmanovitz	40	A1
Kansas St		
(201-750)	12	B2
(751-1650)	16	A1/B1
(1651-1699)	36	A2
Kaplan Ln	8	B1
Karen Ct	39	A2
Kate St	12	A2
Kearny St		
(1-1148)	8	A1/B1
(1149-2099)	4	A1/B1
Keith St		
(601-1550)	37	A1
(1551-3599)	40	B1/A1/A2
Kelloch Ave	39	B1
Kempton Ave	33	B1
Kendall Dr		Presidio
Kennedy Dr		Presidio
Kenny Aly	38	B1
Kensington Way	30	A2
Kent St	4	B1
Kenwood Way	30	B2
Kern St	32	A1
Key Ave	40	B1
Keyes Aly	7	A2

Street	Col	Grid
Keyes Ave		Presidio
Keystone Way	30	B2
Kezar Dr		
(2-249)	9	A1
(250-798)		Golden Gate Park
Kimball Pl	7	A1
King St		
(1-150)	8	B2
(151-299)	13	A1
(549-699)	12	A2
Kingston St		
(1-50)	32	A2
(51-299)	35	A1
Kinzey St		Presidio
Kirkham St		
(1-250)	29	A1
(251-1450)	25	A1/A2
(1451-3275)	24	A1/A2
(3276-4499)	23	A1/A2
Kirkwood Ave		
(198-1537)	37	A1/B2
(1538-2099)	36	A1/B2
Kiska Rd	37	B1
Kissling St	11	A2
Kittredge Ter	22	B2
Knockash Hill	30	A2
Knollview Way	29	B2
Knott Ct	34	B2
Kobbe Ave		Presidio
Kohler Pl	4	B2
Kramer Ct	4	B1
Krausgrill Pl	4	B1
Kronquist Ct	14	B1

L

Street	Col	Grid
La Avanzada St	29	B1/A1
La Ferrera Ter	4	B1
La Grande Ave	38	A2/B2
La Playa St		
(600-898)	18	B1
(1200-1498)	23	A1
La Salle Ave		
(601-1622)	37	A1/B1/B2
(1623-1799)	36	B2
Lafayette St	11	A2
Laguna Honda Blvd		
(101-437)	25	B2
(438-537)	30	A2
(538-999)	31	A1
Laguna St		
(1-716)	11	A1
(717-2650)	6	A1/B1
(2651-3599)	2	A1/B1/B2
Lagunitas Dr	30	B1
Laidley St	32	A2/B1
Lake Forest Ct	29	B1
Lake Merced Blvd		
(-)	26	B2
(200-698)	27	B1
(700-1298)	28	B2/B2
Lake Merced Hill No St	28	B2
Lake Merced Hill So St	28	B2
Lake St		
(1-1225)	21	A1/A2
(1226-2250)	20	A1/A2
(2251-2999)	19	A2/A1
Lakeshore Dr	26	B2
Lakeshore Plz	27	B1

Street	Col	Grid
Lakeview Ave		
(1-575)	34	A1/B1
(576-799)	33	A2
Lakewood Ave	30	B2
Lamartine St	32	B1
Lamson Ln	29	A2
Lancaster Ln	26	B2
Landers St	10	B2
Lane St		
(1101-1550)	37	A1
(1551-2399)	40	A1
Langdon Ct		Presidio
Langton St	12	A1/A2
Lansdale Ave		
(1-313)	30	A2
(314-799)	31	A2
Lansing St	8	B2
Lapham Way	38	B1/B2
Lapidge St	11	B1
Lapu St	8	B1
Larch St	6	B2/B1
Larkin St		
(1-2050)	7	A1/B1
(2051-3099)	3	A1/B1
Las Villas Ct	37	A1
Laskie St	7	B1
Lathrop Ave	40	B1
Latona St	36	B2
Laura St	34	B1
Laurel St	22	A2
Laussat St	10	A2
Lawrence Ave	34	B1
Lawton St		
(1-1250)	25	A1/A2
(1251-3075)	24	A1/A2
(3076-4299)	23	A1/A2
Le Conte Ave	40	B1
Leavenworth St		
(1-1766)	7	A1
(1767-2899)	3	A1/B2/A2
Ledyard St	36	B1
Lee Ave	34	A1
Leese St	32	A2/B2
Legion Ct	33	A2
Leidesdorff St	8	A1
Leland Ave	39	B1/B2
Lendrum Ct		Presidio
Lenox Way	30	A2
Leo St	38	A1
Leona Ter	5	B1
Leroy Pl	7	A1
Lessing St	33	B2
Letterman Dr		Presidio
Lettuce Ln	36	A1
Levant St	9	B2
Lexington St		
(1-250)	11	B1
(251-399)	15	A1
Liberty St		
(1-150)	15	A1
(151-599)	14	A2
Lick Pl	8	A1
Liebig St	33	B2
Liggett Ave		Presidio
Lilac St	15	B1
Lillian St	37	B1

Street	Col	Grid
Lily St		
(1-350)	11	A1
(351-499)	10	A2
Linares Ave	25	B2
Lincoln Blvd		Presidio
Lincoln Ct	34	B2
Lincoln Way		
(1-550)	29	A1
(551-1750)	25	A1/A2
(1751-3575)	24	A1/A2
(3576-4899)	23	A1/A2
Linda St	11	B1
Linda Vista Steps St	38	B1
Linden St		
(201-550)	11	A1
(551-687)	10	A2
Lindsay Cir	37	A1
Lippard Ave	32	B1
Lisbon St		
(1-56)	32	B2
(57-899)	38	A1/B1
Littlefield Ter	16	B2
Livingston St		Presidio
Lloyd St	10	A1
Lobos St		
(1-50)	34	B1
(51-299)	33	B2
Locksley Ave	29	A1
Lockwood St	37	B2
Locust St	22	A2
Loehr St	39	B1
Lois Ln	40	B1
Loma Vista Ter	9	B2
Lombard St		
(1-773)	4	B1/B2
(774-1350)	3	B1/B2
(1351-2150)	2	B1/B2
(2151-2799)	1	B1/B2
Lomita Ave	25	A1
London St		
(101-750)	38	A1
(751-899)	34	B2
Lone Mountain Ter	22	B1
Long Ave		Presidio
Longview Ct	29	B1
Loomis St	36	A1/B1
Lopez Ave	25	B2
Loraine Ct	22	B1
Lori Ln	29	B1
Los Palmos Dr	31	A2/B1
Lottie Bennett Ln	6	B1
Louisburg St	34	A1
Lowell St	34	B2
Lower Ter	9	B2
Loyola Ter	22	B2
Lucerne St	12	A2
Lucky St	15	B2
Lucy St	40	A1
Ludlow Aly	30	A2
Lulu Aly	31	A2
Lunado Ct	33	A1
Lunado Way	33	A1
Lundeen St		Presidio
Lundys Ln	35	A1
Lupine Ave	22	A2
Lurline St	25	A1
Lurmont Ter	3	B1

Lusk St	13	A1
Lydia Ave	40	A1
Lyell St	32	B1
Lynch St	7	A1
Lyndhurst Dr		
(1-18)	33	A1
(19-99)	28	A2
Lyon St		
(1-550)	9	A2
(551-2450)	5	A1/B1
(2451-3699)	1	A1/B1

M

Mabini St	8	B1
Mabrey Ct	37	A1
Macarthur Ave		
(42-803)	2	A2
(804-899)		Presidio
Macedonia St	35	B2
Macondray Ln	3	B2
Maddux Ave	36	B1
Madera St	16	A2
Madison St		
(1-75)	32	B2
(76-399)	38	A2
Madrid St		
(1-150)	32	A1
(151-1099)	38	B1/A1/A2
Madrone Ave	30	A2/A1
Magellan Ave		
(1-250)	25	B2
(251-599)	30	A2
Magnolia St	2	A1
Mahan St	37	B2
Maiden Ln	8	A2
Main St	8	B2
Majestic Ave	34	B1/A1
Malden Aly	8	B1
Mallorca Way	1	A1
Malta Dr	31	B1
Malvina Pl	7	A2
Manchester St	35	A1
Mandalay Ln	25	B1
Mangels Ave		
(1-174)	32	A1
(175-999)	31	A2/B1
Manor Dr	30	B2
Manseau St	37	B2
Mansell St	39	B1/B2
Mansfield St	38	A2
Manzanita Ave	22	A1
Maple St	22	A1
Marcela Ave	25	B2
Marcy Pl	7	A2
Marengo St	35	B2
Margaret Ave	34	B1/A1
Margrave Pl	4	A1
Marietta Dr	31	A1/B2
Marin St		
(801-1069)	37	A1
(1070-2550)	36	A1/A2
(2551-2599)	35	A2
Marina Blvd		
(1-350)	2	A1
(351-899)	1	A1/A2
Marion Pl	3	B2

Mariposa St		
(401-1350)	13	B1
(1351-2399)	12	B2
(2401-2999)	11	B2
Marist St	37	A1
Mark Ln	8	A1
Market St		
(1-816)	8	B1/A1/A2
(817-1399)	7	B2/B1
(1401-1948)	11	A1/A2
(1451-3563)	29	A2/B2
(1949-2850)	10	B1/B2/A2
(3564-3999)	14	A1
Marlin Ct	37	B2
Marne Ave	30	A2
Mars St	29	A2
Marshall St		Presidio
Marsilly St	32	B2
Marston Ave	31	B1
Martha Ave	32	B1
Martinez St		Presidio
Marvel Ct	19	A1
Marview Way	29	B2
Marx Meadow Dr		Golden Gate Park
Mary St	7	B2
Maryland St	17	B2
Mason Ct		
(1101-1150)	7	A2
Mason St		
(49-1527)	7	A2/B2
(1528-2699)	4	A1/B1
Masonic Ave		
(2-649)	22	B2/A2
(650-1699)	9	A2
Massasoit St	35	A2
Masset Pl	8	B1
Mateo St	32	A2/B2
Matthew Ct	37	B1
Mauldin St		Presidio
Mayfair Dr	22	A1/A2
Mayflower St	35	A2
Maynard St	32	B2
Maywood Dr	30	B2/A2
McAllister St		
(1-450)	7	B1/B2
(451-1050)	6	B1/B2
(1051-2050)	5	B1/B2
(2051-2799)	22	B1
McCann St	37	B2
McCarthy Ave	39	B1
McCoppin St	11	A1
McCormick St	7	A1
McDonald St		Presidio
McDowell Ave	2	A1/A2
McKinnon Ave		
(199-1617)	37	A1/B1
(1618-2299)	36	A1/B2
McLaren Ave	19	A2
McLea Ct	12	A1
McRae St		Presidio
Meacham Pl	7	B1
Meade Ave	40	B1
Meadowbrook Dr	27	B1
Meda Ave	34	A2
Medau Pl	4	B1
Melba Ave	27	B2
Melra Ct	39	B2
Melrose Ave	31	A2/B1

Mendell St		
(1-1450)	37	A1
(1451-2599)	40	A1
Mendosa Ave	25	B2
Mercato Ct	31	B1
Merced Ave	30	A2
Mercedes Way		
(1-33)	33	A1
(34-99)	30	B1
Merchant Rd		Presidio
Merchant St	8	A1/A2
Mercury St		
(1-150)	36	B1
(151-199)	40	A1
Merlin St	12	A2
Merrie Way	18	A1
Merrill St	39	A2
Merrimac St	13	A2
Merritt St	29	A2
Mersey St	14	A2
Mesa Ave	25	B2
Mesa St		Presidio
Metson Rd		Golden Gate Park
Michigan St		
(1-299)	13	A2/B2
(801-1675)	17	A1/B1
(1676-1799)	37	A1
Midcrest Way	29	B2
Middle Dr		Golden Gate Park
Middle Point Rd	37	B1
Middlefield Dr	27	B1
Midway St	4	A1
Miguel St	32	A2
Milan Ter	34	B1
Miles Ct	7	A2
Miley St	1	B1
Mill St	39	B2
Miller Pl	7	A2
Miller Rd		Presidio
Mills Pl	8	A1
Milton I Ross Ln	36	A1
Milton St	32	B1
Minerva St		
(1-50)	34	B1
(51-299)	33	B2
Minna St		
(1-358)	8	B1/A1
(359-575)	7	B2
(576-799)	12	A1
(901-1399)	11	A2/B1
Minnesota St		
(501-750)	13	B1
(751-1599)	17	A1/B1
Mint St	7	B2
Mirabel Ave	35	A1
Miraloma Dr	30	A2
Miramar Ave		
(1-350)	33	A2
(351-999)	30	B2
Mirando Way	32	B2
Mission Rock St	13	A2
Mission St		
(1-850)	8	B1/A1/A2
(851-1133)	7	B2
(1134-1380)	12	A1
(1381-2350)	11	A2/A1/B1
(2351-3125)	15	A1/B1
(3126-3467)	35	A1

Mission St		
(3468-4425)	32	A2/B2/B1
(4426-4963)	38	A1
(4964-5999)	34	B1/B2/A2
Mississippi St		
(1-450)	13	B1
(451-1299)	16	A2/B2
Missouri St		
(1-450)	13	B1
(451-1299)	16	A2/B2
Mistral St	11	B2
Mitchell St		Presidio
Mizpah St	32	A1
Modoc Ave	34	B1
Moffitt St	32	A1
Mojave St	35	B2
Molimo Dr	31	
	A2/B1/A1/B2	
Moncada Way		
(1-150)	33	A1
(151-399)	30	B1
Moneta Ct	34	B1
Moneta Way	34	B1
Mono St	29	A2
Montague Pl	4	B2
Montalvo Ave	30	A2
Montana St		
(1-50)	34	B1
(51-299)	33	B2
Montcalm St	35	A2
Montclair Ter	3	B1
Montecito Ave	31	A2
Monterey Blvd		
(1-250)	32	B1
(251-958)	31	A2/B1
(959-2199)	30	B1/B2
Montezuma St	35	A1
Montgomery St		
(1-1075)	8	A1
(1076-1899)	4	A2/B2
Monticello St	33	A1/B1
Moore Pl	3	B1
Moraga Ave		Presidio
Moraga St		
(101-1250)	25	A1/A2
(1251-3075)	24	A1/A2
(3076-4299)	23	A1/A2
Moreland St	32	A1
Morgan Aly	14	A1
Morningside Dr	27	B1
Morrell St	7	A1
Morris St	12	A2
Morse St		
(1-121)	38	B1
(122-799)	34	B2
Morton St		Presidio
Moscow St	38	A2/B1
Moss St	12	A2
Moulton St		
(1-250)	2	B1
(251-299)	1	B2
Moultrie St	35	A1/B1
Mount Ln	25	B1
Mount Vernon Ave	34	A1/B2/A2
Mountain Spring Ave	29	A2
Mountview Ct	29	B2
Muir Loop		Presidio
Mullen Ave	35	A2
Munich St	38	B1/A2
Murray St		
(1-299)	32	B2
(401-499)	35	B1
Museum Way	10	B1
Myra Way	31	A2/A1
Myrtle St		
(99-150)	6	B2
(151-201)	7	B1

N

N Burnett Ave	29	B2
N Willard St	22	B1
Nadell Ct	34	B2
Naglee Ave	34	B1/B2
Nahua Ave	34	B2/A2/A1
Nantucket Ave	31	B1
Napier Ln	4	B2
Naples St		
(1-50)	32	B2
(51-1299)	38	B1/A1/A2
Napoleon St	36	A2/A1
Natick St	32	B1
Natoma St		
(1-199)	8	B1/A2
(401-573)	7	B2
(574-799)	12	A1
(901-1399)	11	A2/B1
Nautilus Ct	37	B1
Navajo Ave	34	A2
Navy Cir	37	B1
Navy Rd	37	B1/B2
Naylor St	38	B1
Nebraska St	35	A2
Nellie St	14	A2
Neptune St		
(1-100)	36	B1
(101-199)	40	A1
Nevada St	35	A2/B2
New Montgomery St	8	B1
Newburg St	14	B1
Newcomb Ave		
(1401-1618)	37	A1
(1619-2499)	36	A1/B2
Newell St	4	B1
Newhall St		
(1-800)	37	A1
(801-1899)	36	B2
(2501-2799)	40	A1
Newman St	35	B1
Newton St	38	B2
Ney St	32	B2
Niagara Ave	34	A1/A2/B2
Niantic Ave	33	B1
Nibbi Ct	40	B1
Nichols Way	40	B2
Nido Ave	5	B1
Nimitz Ave	37	B2
Nob Hill Cir	7	A2
Nob Hill Pl	7	A2
Nobles Aly	4	B1
Noe St		
(1-675)	10	A1/B1/B2
(676-1525)	14	A2/B2
(1526-1799)	32	A2
Nordhoff St	32	B1
Norfolk St	11	A1
Noriega St		
(1-1150)	25	B1/A1/B2
(1151-2975)	24	B1/B2
(2976-4999)	23	B1/B2
Normandie Ter	1	B2
North Point St		
(1-450)	4	A1
(451-1050)	3	A1/A2
(1051-2150)	2	A1
(2151-2399)	1	A1
North View Ct	3	A1
Northgate Dr	30	B2
Northridge Rd	37	B1
Northwood Dr		
(1-50)	31	A2
(51-299)	30	B2
Norton St	38	A1
Norwich St	35	A2
Nottingham Pl	8	A1
Nueva Ave	40	B1

O

O'Farrell St	22	B2
(1-75)	8	B1
(76-950)	7	B1/B2
(951-1550)	6	B2
(1551-2550)	5	B1/B2
O'Shaughnessy Blvd	31	A1/B1/B2
Oak Grove St	12	A2
Oak Park Dr	29	B1
Oak St		
(1-450)	11	A1
(451-1350)	10	A1/A2
(1351-2099)	9	A1/A2
Oakdale Ave		
(1001-1610)	37	A1/B1
(1611-2823)	36	A1/B2/B1
(2824-2899)	35	A2
Oakwood St	10	B2
Ocean Ave		
(1-91)	38	A1
(92-1250)	34	A1/A2
(1251-2184)	33	A1/A2
(2185-2666)	30	B1
(2667-4699)	27	B1/B2
(4701-2999)	26	B2
Octavia St		
(21-625)	11	A1
(626-2550)	6	A1/B1/B2
(2551-3399)	2	A2/B2
Ogden Ave	35	A2
Old Chinatown Ln	8	A1
Old Mason St		Presidio
Olive St		
(1-150)	7	B1
(151-1099)	6	B2
Oliver St	34	B1
Olmstead St	39	B2/A2
Olympia Way	29	B1
Omar Way	31	B2/A1
Oneida Ave	34	A2
Onique Ln	32	A1
Onondaga Ave		
(1-61)	38	A1
(62-299)	34	A2
Opera Aly	8	B1

Street	Page	Grid
Ophir Aly	7	A1
Ora Way	32	A1
Orange Aly	15	B1
Orben Pl	5	A2
Ord Ct	9	B2
Ord St		
(1-105)	9	B2
(106-199)	29	A2
Ordway St	39	B2
Oreilly Ave		Presidio
Orian Ln	4	B1
Oriole Way	25	B2
Orizaba Ave	33	A2/B2
Orsi Cir	40	A1
Ortega St		
(1-1150)	25	B1/B2
(1151-2970)	24	B1/B2
(2971-4199)	23	B1/B2
Ortega Way	25	B1
Osage St	15	B1
Oscar Aly	8	B1
Osceola Ln	37	A1
Osgood Pl	8	A1
Otega Ave	34	B2
Otis St	11	A1
Otsego Ave	34	A2
Ottawa Ave	34	B2
Overlook Dr		Golden Gate Park
Owens St	13	B1
Oxford St	39	A1

P

Street	Page	Grid
Pacheco St		
(1-225)	30	A2
(226-1450)	25	B1/B2
(1451-3275)	24	B1/B2
(3276-4499)	23	B1/B2
Pacific Ave		
(1-782)	8	A1
(783-1650)	7	A1/A2
(1651-2250)	6	A1/A2
(2251-3250)	5	A1/A2
(3251-3900)	22	A1/A2
(3301-4399)	21	A1/A2
Page St		
(98-350)	11	A1
(351-1250)	10	A1/A2
(1251-1999)	9	A1/A2
Palm Ave	22	A1/B1
Palmetto Ave	33	B1
Palo Alto Ave	29	B2
Paloma Ave	30	B1
Palos Pl	27	B1
Palou Ave		
(898-950)	40	A2
(951-1528)	37	A1/B1
(1529-2299)	36	A1/B1/B2
Panama St	33	B1
Panorama Dr	29	B1/B2
Panton Aly	12	A2
Paradise Ave	32	B1
Paraiso Pl	27	B2
Paramount Ter	22	B1
Pardee Aly	4	B1
Paris St		
(101-799)	38	A1/B1
(801-999)	34	B2
Park Blvd		Presidio
Park Hill Ave	10	B1
Park Presidio Blvd		
(50-949)	20	A2/B2
(950-1098)		Golden Gate Park
Park St		
(1-150)	32	A1
(151-399)	35	B1
Parker Ave	22	A1/B1
Parkhurst Aly	7	A2
Parkridge Dr	29	B2
Parnassus Ave		
(1-225)	9	B1
(226-499)	29	A1
Parque Dr	39	B1
Parsons St	22	B1
Pasadena St	39	B1
Path St	30	Presidio
Patten Rd		Presidio
Patterson St	35	A2
Patton St	32	A2
Paul Ave		
(1-612)	40	A1
(613-699)	39	A2
Paulding St	31	B1
Payson St	33	B1
Peabody St	39	B2
Pearce St		Presidio
Pearl St	11	A1
Pelton Pl	8	A1
Pemberton Pl	29	A2
Pena St		Presidio
Peninsula Ave	40	B1
Pennington		Presidio
Pennsylvania Ave		
(1-450)	13	B1
(451-1299)	17	A1/B1
Peralta Ave	35	A2/B2
Perego Ter	29	B2
Perine Pl	5	A2
Perry St	8	B2
Pershing Dr		Presidio
Persia Ave		
(1-1250)	38	A1/A2
(1251-1499)	39	B1
Peru Ave		
(101-250)	32	B2
(251-899)	38	A2
Peter Yorke Way	6	B2
Peters Ave	35	A1
Petrarch Pl	8	A1
Pfeiffer St	4	A1
Phelan Ave		
(1-100)	34	A1
(101-399)	31	A2
Phelps St		
(301-1499)	36	A2/B2
(2401-2799)	40	A1
Phoenix Ter	7	A1
Pico Ave	33	A2
Piedmont St	9	B2
Pier 48	13	B2
Pierce St		
(1-599)	10	A1/A2
(801-2650)	5	A2/B2
(2651-3599)	1	A2/B2
Pilgram Ave	32	B1
Pine St		
(1-650)	8	A1
(651-1550)	7	A1/A2
(1551-2150)	6	A1/A2
(2151-3099)	5	A1/A2
Pinehurst Way	30	B2
Pink Aly	11	A1
Pino Aly	24	A1
Pinto Ave	28	B2
Pioche St		
(101-250)	39	A1
(251-450)	32	B2
(451-499)	38	A2
Pixley St		
(1-250)	2	B1
(251-299)	1	B2
Pizarro Way	30	B2
Plaza St	25	B2
Pleasant St	7	A1
Plymouth Ave		
(1-1250)	33	A2/B2
(1251-1350)	34	A1
(1351-1675)	31	A2
(1676-1699)	30	B2
Point Lobos Ave	18	A1/A2
Polaris Way	38	B1
Polk St		
(-)	11	A2
(1-3199)	3	A1/B1
(51-2150)	7	A1/B1
Pollard Pl	4	B1
Pomona St	36	B2
Pompei Cir		Golden Gate Park
Pond St	10	B2
Pope Rd	2	A2
Pope St		
(1-1338)	34	B2
(1339-1341)		Presidio
Poplar St	15	B1
Poppy Ln	32	B2
Porter St	35	B1
Portola Dr		
(67-198)	29	B2
(199-1075)	31	B2
(1076-1699)	30	A1/A2
Portola Ave		
(738-776)		Presidio
(745-750)	31	A1
Post St		
(1-250)	8	A1
(251-1132)	7	A1
(1133-1750)	6	B1/B2
(1751-2699)	5	B1/B2
Potomac St	10	A2
Potrero Ave		
(1-746)	12	B1
(747-1599)	16	A1/B1
Powell St		
(1-1450)	7	A2/B2
(1451-2599)	4	A1/B1
Powers Ave	35	A1
Powhattan Ave	35	A1/A2
Prado St	1	A2
Prague St	38	B1/A2/B2
Precita Ave	35	A1/A2
Prentiss St	35	A2/B2
Prescott Ct	4	B2
Presidio Ave	5	A1/B1

Street Index

Street	Page	Grid
Presidio Blvd		Presidio
Presidio Ter	21	A2
Pretor Way	34	B2
Priest St	7	A1
Princeton St	39	A1
Progress St	37	A1
Prospect Ave	35	A1
Prosper St	10	B2
Pueblo St	39	B1
Putnam St	35	A2/B2

Q

Street	Page	Grid
Quane St	14	A2
Quarry Rd		Presidio
Quartz Way	31	B2
Quesada Ave		
(1001-1650)	40	A1/A2
(1651-2299)	36	B1/B2
Quickstep Ln	6	B1
Quincy St	8	A1
Quint St	36	B1/B2/A2
Quintara St		
(1-950)	25	B1/B2
(951-2775)	24	B1/B2
(2776-3999)	23	B1/B2

R

Street	Page	Grid
Raccoon Dr	29	A2
Racine Ln	39	B2
Radio Ter	25	B1
Rae Ave	34	B1
Raleigh St	31	B1
Ralston Ave	33	B1
Ralston St	33	A1/B1
Ramona Ave	10	A2/B2
Ramsel Ct		Presidio
Ramsell St	33	A1/B1
Randall St	32	A2
Randolph St	33	B1/B2
Rankin St	36	A2/B1
Rausch St	12	A1
Ravenswood Dr	30	B2
Rayburn St	14	A2
Raycliff Ter	5	A1
Raymond Ave	39	B1/B2
Reardon Rd	37	B1
Rebecca Ln	37	A1
Red Leaf Ct	38	B2
Red Rock Way	31	B2
Reddy St	40	A1
Redfield Aly	3	A1
Redondo St	40	B1
Redwood St	6	B1/B2
Reed St	7	A1
Regent St	33	B2
Reno Pl	4	B2
Reposa Way	31	B2/A1
Reservoir St	10	B2
Restani Way	34	A2
Retiro Way		
(1-150)	1	A2
(151-199)	2	A1
Reuel St	37	A1
Revere Ave		
(1098-1650)	40	A1/A2
(1651-2299)	36	B1/B2
Rex Ave	31	A1
Rey St	39	B2/B1

Street	Page	Grid
Rhine St	33	B2
Rhode Island St		
(1-750)	12	B2
(751-1499)	16	A1/B1
Rice St	33	B2
Richards Cir	37	A1
Richardson Ave	1	B1/A1
Richland Ave		
(1-250)	32	B2/A2
(251-399)	35	B1
Rickard St	39	A2
Rico Way	1	A2
Ridge Ct		
(-)	39	B1
(1398-1214)	38	B2
Ridge Ln	34	A1
Ridgewood Ave	31	A2
Riley Ave		Presidio
Rincon St	8	B2
Ringold St	12	A1
Rio Ct	31	B2
Rio Verde St	39	B1
Ripley St	35	A1/A2
Ritch St		
(201-250)	13	A1
(251-399)	8	B2
Rivas Ave	28	B2
Rivera St		
(201-850)	25	B1
(851-2675)	24	B1/B2
(2676-3899)	23	B1/B2
Riverton Dr	27	B1
Rivoli St	9	B1
Rizal St	8	B1
Roach St	3	B2
Roanoke St	32	A2/B2
Robblee Ave	36	B1
Robert Kirk Ln	8	A1
Robinhood Dr	31	A1
Robinson Dr	38	B2
Robinson St	37	B2
Rockaway Ave	31	A1
Rockdale Dr	31	A1
Rockland St	3	B1
Rockridge Dr	25	B1
Rockwood Ct	31	A1
Rodgers St	12	A1
Rodriguez St		Presidio
Roemer Way	34	B2
Rolph St		
(1-175)	34	B2
(176-999)	38	B1/B2
Romain St		
(1-250)	14	A1
(251-299)	29	B2
Rome St	34	B2
Romolo St	4	B2
Rondel Pl	11	B1
Roosevelt Way		
(1-250)	10	B1
(251-599)	9	B1
Roscoe St	35	B1
Rose St		
(98-299)	11	A1
(498-499)	10	A2
Rosella Ct	34	A2
Roselyn Ter	22	B2
Rosemary Ct	27	A2

Street	Page	Grid
Rosemont Pl	10	A2
Rosenkranz St	35	A2
Rosewood Dr	30	B2
Rosie Lee Ln	37	A1/B1
Ross Aly	8	A1
Rossi Ave	22	B1
Rossmoor Dr	30	B1
Rotteck St	32	B2
Rousseau St	32	B2
Rowland St	8	A1
Royal Ln	38	B1
Ruckman Ave		Presidio
Rudden Ave	34	A2
Russ St		
(1-67)	7	B2
(68-199)	12	A2/A1
Russell St	3	B1
Russia Ave	38	A1/B2
Russian Hill St	3	B2
Ruth St	38	A1
Rutland St	39	B1
Rutledge St	35	A2

S

Street	Page	Grid
S Hill Blvd	38	B1
S Park Ave	8	B1
S Tea Garden Dr		Golden Gate Park
S Van Ness Ave		
(1-850)	11	A1/A2/B2/B1
(851-1599)	15	A1/B1
Sabin St	8	A1
Sacramento St		
(1-880)	8	A1/A2
(881-1750)	7	A1/A2
(1751-2350)	6	A1/A2
(2351-3350)	5	A1/A2
(3351-3999)	22	A1/A2
Saddleback Dr	38	B2
Sadowa St		
(1-50)	34	B1
(51-299)	33	B2
Safira Ln	14	B1
Sagamore St	33	B2
Saint Francis Pl	8	B1
Saint Louis Aly	8	A1
Sal St		Presidio
Sala Ter	34	B2
Salinas Ave	40	A1/B1
Salmon St	7	A2
Samoset St	35	A2
San Aleso Ave	30	B2
San Andreas Way	30	B2
San Anselmo Ave	30	A1/A2/B2
San Antonio Pl	4	B1
San Benito Way	30	A1/B1
San Bruno Ave		
(-)	35	B2
(1-750)	12	B2
(751-999)	16	A1/B1
(2201-4154)	39	A2/B2
(4155-4199)	40	A2/B2
San Buenaventura Way	30	A2/B2
San Carlos St		
(1-250)	11	B1
(251-399)	15	A1
San Diego Ave	33	B1

Street Index

Street	Page	Grid
San Felipe Ave	30	B2
San Fernando Way	30	A1/B1
San Gabriel Ave	32	B1
San Jacinto Way	30	B2
(1-399)	15	A1/B1
(551-725)	35	A1
(726-1862)	32	B2/A2/B1
(1863-1888)	31	B1
San Jose Ave		
(1889-2925)	34	B1/A2/A1
(2926-3299)	33	B2
San Juan Ave		
(1-250)	38	A1
(251-599)	34	A2
San Leandro Way	30	A1/B1
San Lorenzo Way	30	A2
San Luis Ave	33	B1
San Marcos Ave		
(1-149)	30	A2
(151-499)	25	B1/B2
San Mateo Ave	33	B1
San Miguel St	34	A1
San Pablo Ave	30	A2
San Rafael Way	30	B1
San Ramon Way	34	A1
Sanches St		Presidio
Sanchez St		
(1-675)	10	B2
(676-1525)	14	A2/B2
(1526-1799)	32	A2
Sansome St		
(1-950)	8	A1
(951-1699)	4	A2/B2
Santa Ana Ave	30	A1/B1
Santa Barbara Ave	33	B1
Santa Clara Ave	30	A2/B2
Santa Cruz Ave	33	B1
Santa Fe Ave	36	B1
Santa Marina St		
(1-72)	32	A2
(73-199)	35	A1
Santa Monica Way	30	A2
Santa Paula Ave	30	A2
Santa Rita Ave	25	B2
Santa Rosa Ave		
(1-170)	38	A1
(171-399)	32	B1
Santa Ynez Ave		
(1-37)	38	A1
(38-299)	34	A2
Santa Ysabel Ave		
(1-99)	38	A1
(101-299)	32	B1
Santiago St		
(301-750)	30	A1
(751-2575)	27	A1/A2
(2576-3799)	26	A1/A2
Santos St	39	B1
Sargent St	33	B1/B2
Saturn St	9	B2
Savings Union Pl	8	B1
Sawyer St	39	B1
Scenic Way	19	A2
Schofield Rd	2	A2
School Aly	4	B2
Schwerin St	39	B2/B1
Scotia Ave	36	B1
Scotland St	4	B1
Scott Aly	8	B1
Scott St		
(1-750)	10	A1
(751-2650)	5	A1/B2
(2651-3999)	1	A2/B2
Sea Cliff Ave	19	A2
Sea View Ter	19	A1/A2
Seal Rock Dr	18	A2/A1
Sears St	34	B1
Selby St	36	B1/A1/A2
Selma Way	25	B1
Seminole Ave	34	A2
Seneca Ave	34	B2/B2
Sequoia Way	31	B2
Serrano Dr	28	B2
Service St	1	B2
Severn St	14	A2
Seville St	38	B1
Seward St		
(1-27)	14	A1
(28-99)	29	A2
Seymour St	5	B2
Sgt John V Young Ln	34	A2
Shafter Ave		
(1001-1650)	40	A1/A2
(1651-2299)	36	B1
Shafter Rd		Presidio
Shakespeare St	33	B2
Shannon St	7	B2
Sharon St	10	B2
Sharp Pl	3	B1
Shaw Aly	8	A1
Shawnee Ave	34	A2
Sheldon Ter	25	B1
Shephard Pl	7	A2
Sheridan Ave		Presidio
Sheridan St	12	A1
Sherman Rd		Presidio
Sherman St	12	A2
Sherwood Ct	31	A2
Shields St	33	A1/A2
Shipley St		
(101-199)	8	B1
(201-225)	7	B2
(226-299)	12	A2
Shore View Ave	19	B1
Short St	29	A2
Shotwell St		
(1-550)	11	B2
(551-1350)	15	A1/B2
(1351-1599)	35	A1
Shrader St		
(2-50)	22	B1
(51-1524)	9	A1/B1
(1525-1698)	29	A2
Sibley Rd		Presidio
Sickles Ave	34	B1
Sierra St	16	A2
Silliman St		
(1-1650)	39	A1/A2
(1651-1899)	38	A2
Silver Ave		
(201-723)	32	B1/B2
(724-1631)	39	A1/A2
(1632-2399)	36	B1
Silverview Dr	36	B1
Simonds Loop		Presidio
Skyline Blvd		
(2-195)	26	B2
(196-682)	28	A1
(684-1098)	92	GR
Skyview Way	29	B2
Sloan Aly	8	B2
Sloat Blvd		
(-)	23	B1
30	B1	
(341-1891)	27	B1/B2
(1892-2323)	26	B1/B2
Sola Ave	25	B2
Somerset St	39	A2/B2
Sonoma St	4	B1
Sonora Ln	5	B1
Sotelo Ave	25	B2
South Dr		Golden Gate Park
Southard Pl	3	B1
Southern Heights Ave	16	A1/A2
Southwood Dr		
(1-75)	34	A1
(76-199)	30	B1
Sparrow St	11	B1
Sparta St	39	B2
Spear Ave	37	B2
Spear St		
(1-)	8	A2/B2
Spencer St	11	B1
Spofford St	8	A1
Spreckels Lake Dr	19	B1
Spring St	8	A1
Springfield Dr	27	B1
Sproule Ln	7	A2
Spruce St	22	A1/B1
St Charles Ave	33	B1
St Croix Dr	30	B1
St Elmo Way	30	B1/B2
St Francis Blvd	30	B1
St George Aly	8	A1
St Germain Ave	29	A2
St Josephs Ave	5	B1
St Marys Ave	32	B2
Stanford Heights Ave	31	A2/B1
Stanford St	8	B2
Stanley St	33	B2
Stanton St	29	A2
Stanyan St		
(2-435)	22	B1
(436-1349)	9	A1/B1
(1350-1398)	29	A2
Staples Ave	31	A2/B1
Stark St	7	A2
Starr King Way	6	B2
Starview Way	29	B1
State Dr	28	A2
State Highway 1		Presidio
States St		
(1-250)	10	B1
(251-299)	9	B2
Steiner St		
(1-850)	10	A2
(851-2750)	5	A2/B2
(2751-3399)	1	B2
Sterling St	8	B2
Steuart St	8	A2
Steveloe Pl	7	B2
Stevens Aly	8	A1
Stevenson St		
(1-299)	8	B1/A1
(401-850)	7	B1/B2
(851-1499)	11	A1/B1
Still St	32	B1/B2
Stillings Ave	31	B1
Stillman St	8	B1/B2
Stillwell Rd		Presidio

Street Index

Stockton St
| (1-1375) | 7 | A2/B2 |
| (1376-2499) | 4 | A1/B1 |
Stone St 7 A2
Stonecrest Dr
(-)	33	A1
(1-275)	30	B1
(276-399)	28	A2
Stoneman St 35 A1
Stoneridge Ln 38 B2
Stoneybrook Ave 32 B2
Stoneyford Ave 39 A1
Storey Ave Presidio
Storrie St 29 A2
Stow Lake Dr Golden Gate Park
Stratford Dr
(1-265)	28	A2/B2
(267-399)	33	A1
Summit St 34 B1/A1
Sumner St 12 A1
Sunbeam Ln 34 A2
Sunglow Ln 39 A1
Sunnydale Ave
(201-338)	40	B1
(339-2699)	39	B1/B2
Sunrise Way 39 B1
Sunset Blvd
(1197-3099)	27	B1/A1
(1199-2250)	24	A1/B1
Sunview Dr 31 B2
Surrey St 32 A1/B1
Sussex St 32 A1
Sutro Heights Ave 18 B1
Sutter St
(1-350)	8	A1
(351-1250)	7	A1/A2
(1251-1850)	6	B1/A2
(1851-2799)	5	A1/A2
Sweeny St 39 A1/A2
Swiss Ave 32 A1
Sycamore St 11 B1
Sydney Way 31 A1
Sylvan Dr 27 B1

T
Taber Aly 8 B2
Tacoma St 20 A2
Talbert Ct 39 B2
Talbert St 39 B2
Tamalpais Ter 22 B2
Tandang Sora St 8 B1
Tapia Dr 28 A2/B2
Tara St 34 A1
Taraval St
(1-850)	30	A1/A2
(851-2675)	27	A1/A2
(2676-3899)	26	A1/A2
Taylor Rd Presidio
Taylor St
(1-1625)	7	A1/A2/B2
(1626-2800)	3	A2/B2
Teddy Ave 39 B2
Tehama St
(1-350)	8	B1
(351-499)	7	B2
(783-715)	12	A1
Telegraph Hill Blvd 4 B2/B1
Telegraph Pl 4 B1
Temescal Ter 22 B2

Temple St 9 B2
Tennessee St
(601-850)	13	B1
(851-1750)	17	A1/B1
(1751-1799)	36	A2
Tenny Pl 8 B2
Teresita Blvd 31 A1/B2/B1
Terra Vista Ave 8 A1
Terrace Dr 30 A2
Terrace Walk 30 A2
Terry Francois St 13 B2/A2
Texas St
(101-450)	13	B1
(451-1099)	16	A2/B2
The Embarcadero
(1-550)	8	A2
(551-1701)	4	A1/A2/B2
Theresa St 32 B1
Thomas Ave
(1001-1650)	40	A1/A2
(1651-2199)	36	B1
Thomas Mellon Dr 40 B1
Thomas Moore Way 28 B2
Thor Ave 32 B1
Thornburg Rd Presidio
Thornton Ave 36 B1/B2
Thorp Ln 29 A2
Thrift St
(1-50)	34	A1
(51-323)	33	B2
Tiffany Ave 35 A1
Tillman Pl 8 A1
Tingley St 32 B1
Tioga Ave 39 B2
Tocoloma Ave 40 B1
Todd St Presidio
Toland St 36 A2/A1
Toledo Way 1 A2
Tomaso Ct 39 B2
Tompkins Ave 35 B1/B2
Topaz Way 32 A1
Topeka Ave 36 B1/B2
Torney Ave Presidio
Torrens Ct 7 A1
Touchard St 7 A1
Townsend St
(1-190)	8	B2
(191-450)	13	A1
(451-709)	12	A2/B2
Toyon Ln 38 B1
Tracy Pl
(1-60)	8	A1
(61-99)	4	B1
Trader Vic Aly 7 A2
Trainor St 11 B2
Transverse Dr Golden Gate Park
Treasury Pl 8 A1
Treat Ave
(3-675)	11	B2
(676-1299)	15	A2/B2
(1501-1699)	35	A2
Trenton St 7 A2
Trinity Pl 8 A1
Troy Aly 7 A1
Truby St Presidio
Truett St 7 A2
Trumbull St 32 B2
Tubbs St 17 A1
Tucker Ave 39 B2

Tulane St 39 A1
Tulare St 36 A2
Tunnel Ave 40 B1/A1
Turk Blvd
(901-1250)	6	B1/B2
(1251-2275)	5	B1/B2
(2276-3199)	22	B1/B2
Turk Murphy Ln 7 A2
Turk St
(1-650)	7	B1/B2
(651-899)	6	B2
Turner Ter 16 A2
Turquoise Way 31 B2
Tuscany Aly 4 B1
Twin Peaks Blvd 29 A2/B2

U
Ulloa St
(1-400)	31	A1
(401-1750)	30	A1/A2
(1751-3575)	27	A1/A2
(3576-4699)	26	A1/A2
Uncle Wish Mem Rd 18 A1
Underwood Ave 40 A1/A2
Union St
(1-850)	4	B1/B2
(851-1450)	3	B1/B2
(1451-2250)	2	B1/B2
(2251-2899)	1	B1/B2
(400-2328)	39	A2
(450-4098)		Presidio
(1471-2624)	11	A1
(2345-3449)	35	A2/B2
United States Highway 101
(3450-3949)	16	A1/B1
University St 39 A1/B2
Upland Dr 30 B2
Upper Great Hwy
(2-1499)	18	B1
(1500-1698)	23	A1
(2800-2998)	92	GR
(3500-3598)	28	A1
Upper Service Road 29 A1
Upper Ter 9 B2
Upton Ave Presidio
Upton St 36 A1
Uranus Ter 29 A2
Urbano Dr 33 A1/A2
Utah St
(1-599)	12	B2
(1201-1499)	16	B1

V
Valdez Ave 31 A2
Vale Ave 27 B2
Valencia St
(50-875)	11	A1/B1
(876-1625)	15	A1/B1
(1626-1699)	35	A1
Valerton St 34 A1
Vallejo St
(1-958)	4	B1/B2
(959-1550)	3	B1/B2
(1551-2350)	2	B1/B2
(2351-2999)	1	B1/B2
Valletta Ct 31 B1
Valley St 32 A1/A2

Street Index

Street	Page	Grid
Valmar Ter	38	A2
Valparaiso St		
(1-50)	4	B1
(51-199)	3	B2
Van Buren St	32	A1
Van Dyke Ave	40	A1/A2
Van Keuran Ave	37	B2
Van Ness Ave		
(1-400)	11	A1
(401-2250)	6	A2/B2
(2251-3299)	2	A2/B2
Vandewater St	4	A1
Varela Ave	28	B2
Varennes St	4	B1
Varney Pl	8	B2
Vasquez Ave		
(1-54)	31	A1
(55-299)	30	A2
Vassar Pl	8	B2
Vega St	5	B1
Velasco Ave	39	A1
Venard Aly	4	B1
Ventura Ave	25	B2
Venus St		
(1-99)	36	B1
(101-199)	40	A1
Verdi Pl	8	A1
Verdun Way	30	A2
Vermehr Pl	8	A1
Vermont St		
(1-750)	12	B2
(751-1599)	16	A1/B1
Verna St	31	B1
Vernon St	33	A1/B1
Vesta St	40	A1
Via Buffano	4	B1
Via Ferlinghetti	4	B1
Vicente St		
(1-750)	30	A1/A2
(751-2575)	27	A1/A2
(2576-3699)	26	A1/A2
Vicksburg St	14	A2/B2
Victoria St	33	A2/A1/B1
Vidal Dr	28	B2/A2
Vienna St	38	B1/A2/A1
Villa Ter	29	A2
Vine Ter	7	A2
Vinton Ct	8	A1
Virgil St	15	B1
Virginia Ave	35	A1
Visitacion Ave		
(401-550)	40	B1
(551-2499)	39	B1/B2
Vista Ct		Presidio
Vista Verde Ct	31	B1
Vistaview Ct	36	B2
Vulcan Stairway	9	B2

W

Street	Page	Grid
Wabash Ter	39	B2
Wagner Aly	7	B1
Waithman Way	31	A1
Walbridge St	39	B1
Waldo Aly	7	A1
Wall Pl	7	A1
Wallace Ave	40	A1/A2
Wallen Ct		Presidio
Wallen St		Presidio
Waller St		
(1-99)	11	A1
(201-899)	10	A1/A2
(1201-1850)	9	A1/A2
(1851-1899)	Golden Gate Park	
Walnut St	22	A2
Walter St	10	A2
Walter U Lum Pl	8	A1
Waltham St	35	A2
Wanda St	34	A2
Ward St	39	B2
Warner Pl	3	B1
Warren Dr	29	A1/B1
Washburn St	12	A1
Washington Blvd		Presidio
Washington St		
(1-885)	8	A1/A2
(886-1750)	7	A1/A2
(1751-2350)	6	A1/A2
(2351-3350)	5	A1/A2
(3351-3999)	22	A1/A2
Watchman Way	16	A2
Water St	4	B1
Waterloo St		
(1-34)	36	B1
(35-99)	35	A2
Waterville St	36	B1
Watson Rd	38	A1
Watt Ave	34	B2
Waverly Pl	8	A1
Wawona St		
(1-750)	30	A1/A2
(751-2575)	27	A1/A2
(2576-3699)	26	B1/B2
Wayland St	39	A1/A2
Wayne Pl	7	A2
Webb Pl	4	B1
Webster St		
(1-750)	10	A2
(751-2650)	5	A2/B2
(2651-3899)	2	A1/B1
Weldon St	39	A2
Welsh St		
(1-150)	8	A1
(151-299)	12	A2
Wentworth Pl	8	A1
West Clay St	8	A2
West Point Rd	37	A1
West Portal Ave	30	A2/A1
Westbrook Ct	37	A1
Western Shore Ln	6	B1
Westgate Dr	30	B2
Westmoorland Dr	27	B1
Westview Ave	39	A1
Westwood Dr	30	B2
Wetmore St	7	A2
Wheat St	40	A1
Wheeler Ave	40	B1
Whipple Ave	34	B1/B2
White St	3	B1
Whitecliff Way	36	B2
Whitfield Ct	37	B1
Whiting St	4	B1
Whitney St	32	A2
Whitney Young Cir	37	A1
Whittier St	34	B1/B2
Wiese St	11	B1
Wilde Ave	39	B2
Wilder St	32	B1
Wildwood Way		
(1-250)	31	A2
(251-599)	30	B2
Willard St	29	A1
Williams Ave	40	A1
Williar Ave	34	A1
Willow St		
(1-150)	7	B1
(151-699)	6	B1/B2
Wills St	37	A1
Wilmot St	5	A2
Wilson St	33	B2
Winding Way	38	B1
Windsor Pl	4	B2
Winfield St	35	A1
Winston Dr		
(1-50)	33	A1
(51-183)	30	B1
(184-699)	27	B1
Winter Pl	4	B1
Winthrop St	4	B2
Wisconsin St		
(1-550)	12	B2
(551-1299)	16	A2/B2
Wood St	22	A2/B2
Woodacre Dr	30	B1
Woodhaven Ct	29	B1
Woodland Ave	29	A1
Woodside Ave	31	A1
Woodward St	11	B1
Wool Ct		Presidio
Wool St	35	A1
Woolsey St	39	A2
Worcester Ave	33	B1
Worden St	4	A1
Worth St	14	A1
Wright Loop		Presidio
Wright St	35	A2
Wyman Ave		Presidio
Wyton Ln	28	A2

Y

Street	Page	Grid
Yacht Road 1	1	A1
Yale St	39	A1
Yerba Buena Ave	30	A2/B2
Yorba Ln	26	B2
Yorba St		
(2201-2575)	27	B1
(2576-2999)	26	B2
York St		
(101-750)	11	B2
(751-1550)	15	A2/B2
(1551-1699)	35	A2
Yosemite Ave	40	A1/A2
Young St		Presidio
Youngs Ct	37	A1
Yukon St	29	A2

Z

Street	Page	Grid
Zampa Ln	6	B1
Zeno Pl	8	B2
Zircon Pl	32	A1
Zoe St	8	B1/B2
Zoo Rd	Golden Gate Natl Rec Area	